D1446639

SERMONS
❧ *on the* ❧
LAST DAYS

Other Sermon Collections
by Charles H. Spurgeon

SERMONS
✥ on the ✥
LAST DAYS

CHARLES H. SPURGEON

HENDRICKSON
PUBLISHERS

Sermons on the Last Days

Hendrickson Publishers Marketing, LLC
P. O. Box 3473
Peabody, Massachusetts 01961-3473

ISBN 978-1-59856-354-2

Printed in the United States of America

First Printing — May 2009

Cover Art: Julis Schnorr von Carolsfeld's (1794-1872) "Four Horsemen and
Throne Room," an engraving from "Die Bibel in Bildern" published in 1853.
Courtesy of the Pitts Theology Library, Candler School of Theology, Emory
University.

Table of Contents

The Second Coming of Christ

Delivered at the Metropolitan Tabernacle, Newington. No. 594.
Verily I say unto you, There be some standing here, which shall not taste of death, till they see the Son of man coming in his kingdom. —MATTHEW 16:28

Delivered on Sunday morning, January 21, 1866, at the Metropolitan Tabernacle, Newington. No. 671.
When the Son of man shall come in his glory, and all the holy angels with him, then shall he sit upon the throne of his glory: and before him shall be gathered all nations: and he shall separate them one from another, as a shepherd divideth his sheep from the goats: and he shall set the sheep on his right hand, but the goats on the left. Then shall the King say unto them on his right hand, "Come, ye blessed of my Father, inherit the kingdom prepared for you from the foundation of the world: for I was an hungered, and ye gave me meat: I was thirsty, and ye gave me drink: I was a stranger, and ye took me in: naked, and ye clothed me: I was sick, and ye visited me: I was in prison, and ye came unto me." —MATTHEW 25:31–36

Delivered on Sunday evening, August 12, 1866, at the Metropolitan Tabernacle, Newington. No. 710.
And I saw a great white throne, and him that sat on it, from whose face the earth and the heaven fled away; and there was found no place for them. —REVELATION 20:11

Delivered on Lord's Day evening, August 25, 1872, at the Metropolitan Tabernacle, Newington. No. 1076.
For we must all appear before the judgment seat of Christ; that everyone may receive the things done in his body, according to that he hath done, whether it be good or bad. —2 CORINTHIANS 5:10

Sermons on Heaven and Hell

Publisher's Preface

Charles Haddon Spurgeon
1834–1892

Ask most people today who Charles Haddon Spurgeon was, and you might be surprised at the answers. Most know he was a preacher, others remember that he was Baptist, and others go so far as to remember that he lived in England during the nineteenth century. All of this is true. Yet Charles Haddon Spurgeon was so much more.

Born into a family of Congregationalists in 1834, Spurgeon's father and grandfather were both Independent preachers. This designation seems benign today, but in the mid-nineteenth century, it describes a family committed to a Nonconformist path—meaning they did not conform to the established Church of England. Spurgeon grew up in a rural village, a village virtually cut off from the Industrial Revolution rolling over most of England.

Spurgeon was born again at a Primitive Methodist meeting in 1850, at age sixteen. He soon became a Baptist (to the sorrow of his mother) and almost immediately began to preach. Considered a preaching prodigy—"a boy wonder of the fens"—Spurgeon attracted huge audiences and garnered a reputation that reached throughout the countryside and into London. As a result of his great success, Spurgeon was invited to preach at the New Park Street Chapel in London in 1854, when he was just nineteen. When he first preached at the church, they were unable to fill even two hundred seats. Within the year, Spurgeon filled the twelve-hundred-seat church to overflowing; he soon began preaching in larger and larger venues, outgrowing each, until finally in 1861, the Metropolitan Tabernacle was completed, which seated six thousand persons. This would be Spurgeon's home base for the rest of his career, until his death in 1892, at age fifty-seven.

Spurgeon married Susannah Thompson in 1856 and soon they had twin sons, Charles and Thomas, who would later follow him in his work. Spurgeon opened Pastors' College, a training school for preachers, that trained more than nine hundred preachers during his lifetime. He also opened orphanages for underprivileged boys and girls, providing educations to each of the orphans. And with Susannah, he developed a program to publish and distribute Christian literature. He is said to have preached to more than ten million people in his forty years of ministry. His sermons sold more than twenty-five thousand copies each week, and were translated into twenty languages. He was utterly committed to spreading the Gospel, through preaching and through the written word.

During Spurgeon's lifetime, the Industrial Revolution transformed England from a rural, agricultural society, to an urban, industrial society, with all the attendant difficulties and horrors of a society in major transition. The people displaced by these sweeping changes, the factory workers, the shopkeepers, these became Spurgeon's congregation. From a small village himself and transplanted to a large and inhospitable city, he was a common man, and he understood innately the spiritual needs of the common people. He was a communicator who made the Gospel so relevant, who spoke so brilliantly to people's deepest needs, that listeners welcomed his message.

Keep in mind that Spurgeon preached in the days before microphones or speakers; in other words, he preached without benefit of amplifier systems. Once he preached to a crowd of over twenty-three thousand people without mechanical amplification of any sort. He himself was the electrifying presence on the platform: he did not stand and simply read a stilted sermon. Spurgeon used an outline, developing his themes extemporaneously, and speaking "in common language to common people." His sermons were filled with stories and poetry, drama and emotion. He was larger than life, always in motion, striding back and forth across the stage. He gestured broadly, acted out stories, used humor, and painted word pictures. For Spurgeon, preaching was about communicating the truth of God, and he would use any gift at his disposal to accomplish this.

Spurgeon's preaching was anchored in his spiritual life, a life rich in prayer and the study of Scripture. He was not tempted by fashion, be it theological, social, or political. Scripture was the cornerstone of Spurgeon's life and his preaching. He was an expositional preacher mostly, exploring a passage of Scripture for its meanings both within the text as well as in the lives of each member of his congregation. To Spurgeon, Scripture was alive and specifically relevant to people's lives, whatever their social status, economic situation, or time in which they live.

One has a sense that Spurgeon embraced God's revelation completely: God's revelation through Jesus Christ, through Scripture, and through his own prayer and study. For him, revelation was not a finished act: God still reveals Himself, if one makes oneself available. Some recognize Spurgeon for the mystic he was, one who was willing and eager to explore the mysteries of God, able to live with those bits of truth that do not conform to a particular system of theology, perfectly comfortable with saying, "This I know, and this I don't know—yet will I trust."

This collection of sermons includes Spurgeon's thoughts on matters of eternity: on Christ's promised return and on the rewards that await each of us. What manner of reward is of course the great question. But for those uncertain readers who have lingering reservations, Spurgeon leaves no doubts, no gray areas of ambiguity, no wiggle room. He offers clear answers, gleaned from Scripture, that instruct, encourage, and motivate.

Each of these sermons was preached at different times of Spurgeon's career, and each has distinct characteristics. They have not been homogenized or edited to sound as though they are all of a kind. Instead, they reflect the preacher himself, allowing the voice of this remarkable man to ring clearly as he guides the reader into a particular account, a particular event—to experience, with Spurgeon, God's particular revelation.

As you read, *listen.* These words are meant to be heard, not merely read. Listen carefully and you will hear the cadences of this remarkable preaching, the echoes of God's timeless truth traveling across the years. And above all, enjoy Spurgeon's enthusiasm, his fire, his devotion, his zeal to recognize and respond to God's timeless invitation to engage the Creator himself.

The Second Coming of Christ

An Awful Premonition

Delivered at the Metropolitan Tabernacle, Newington. No. 594.

Verily I say unto you, There be some standing here, which shall not taste
of death, till they see the Son of man coming in his kingdom.
—MATTHEW 16:28

I must confess that I have frequently read this verse with but a vague sense of its profound impressiveness, and I have passed it over rapidly because I did not understand it clearly. Though well acquainted with the usual interpretations, none of them had ever satisfied my mind. It seemed to me as if the text had awakened surprise without suggesting a simple obvious meaning, and therefore the good commentators had invented explanations and offered suggestions, widely different one from another, but all equally obscure and improbable. Lately, however, in reading a volume of sermons by Bishop Horsley, I have met with altogether a new view of the passage, which I firmly believe to be the correct one. Though I do not suppose I shall carry the judgment of all of you with me, yet I shall do my best to bring out of it that terrible denunciation which I believe the Savior has here left on record. With his own cross and passion in view, he was admonishing his disciples to steadfastness, appealing to them at any sacrifice to take up their cross and follow him; then portraying the inestimable value of the soul and reflecting on the horror of the soul being lost—a doom, the full force of which, it would be impossible to comprehend until he should come in the glory of his Father, with all his holy angels—he stopped short, looked upon some of the company, and said in words like these, "There are certain persons standing here who shall never taste of death, till they see the Son of man coming in his kingdom."

Now what did he mean by this? Obviously it is either a marvelous promise to some who were his disciples indeed, or else it is a portent of woe to others who should die in their sins. How do the popular interpretations of our learned expositors look at it?

Some say it refers to the transfiguration, and it certainly is remarkable that the account of the transfiguration immediately follows this verse, both in Mark and in Luke, as well as in this record of Matthew. But can you for a moment bring your minds to believe that Christ was describing his transfiguration when he spoke of "the Son of man coming in his kingdom," and whether you can see any connection between the transfiguration and the preceding verse, which says, "For the Son of man shall come in the glory of his Father with his angels; and then he shall reward every man according to his works"? We grant you that Christ was in his glory upon Mount Tabor, but he did not there "reward every man according to his works," nor is it fair to call that a "coming" of the Son of man at all. He did not "come" on Mount Tabor, for he was on the earth already; and it is a misuse of language to construe that into an advent. Besides, where would be the occasion for such a solemn prefix, "Verily I say unto you"? Does it not raise expectation merely to cause disappointment, if he intended no more than this, "There be some standing here who shall see me transfigured"? That scene took place six days afterward. The next verse tells you so, "And after six days Jesus takes Peter, James, and John his brother, and brings them up into a high mountain apart." Why, the majesty of the prediction which carries our thoughts forward to "the last things" in the world's history makes us shrink from accepting an immediate fulfillment of it all. I cannot imagine, therefore, that the transfiguration is in the slightest degree referred to here; and I do not think that anyone would have thought of such a thing unless he had been perplexed and utterly nonplussed for an explanation.

And again—though it seems almost incredible—Dr. Gill endorses this view, and moreover says, that it also refers to the descent of the Holy Ghost. At this I am staggered. How any man can find an analogy with Pentecost in the connection here I cannot think. Pentecost took place six months after this event, and why Jesus Christ should say, "Verily I say unto you, there be some standing here who will live six months," I really cannot comprehend. It seems to me that my Master did not waste people's time by talking such platitudes. Who that reads this passage can think it has any reference to the descent of the Holy Ghost, "For the Son of man shall come in the glory of his Father with his angels; and then shall he reward every man according to his works"? Did Christ come at Pentecost in the glory of his Father? Was there then any company of angels? Did he then reward every man according to his works? Scarcely can the descent of the Holy Spirit, or the appearance of cloven tongues, like as of fire, be called the "coming of the Son of man in the glory of his Father with his angels, to give every man according to his works," without a gross misuse of our mother tongue, or a strange violation of symbolic imagery.

Both these constructions, however, which I now mention, have now been given up as unsatisfactory by those modern students who have thought most carefully upon the subject. The third still holds its ground and is currently received, though I believe it to be quite as far from the truth as the others. Will you carefully read the chapter through at your leisure, and see if you can find anything about the siege of Jerusalem in it? Yet this is the interpretation that finds favor at the present time. Some persons were standing there who would be alive when Jerusalem should be destroyed by the Romans! Nothing surely could be more foreign to the entire scope of our Lord's discourse, or the narrative of the evangelists. There is not the slightest shadow of a reference to the siege of Jerusalem. It is the coming of the Son of man which is here spoken of, "in the glory of his Father with his angels, to reward men according to their works." Whenever Jesus spoke of the siege of Jerusalem and of its coming, he was inclined to say, "Verily I say unto you, this generation shall not pass till all these things be fulfilled"; but he never singled out some few persons and said to them, "Verily I say unto you, there be some standing here, which shall not taste of death, till the city of Jerusalem is besieged and destroyed."

If a child were to read this passage, I know what he would think it meant: he would suppose Jesus Christ was to come, and there were some standing there who should not taste of death until really and literally he did come. This, I believe, is the plain meaning.

"Well," says one, "I am surprised; do you think, then, that this refers to the apostle John?" No; by no means. The fable passed current, you know, that John was to live till Christ came again. But John himself repudiated it. For at the end of his gospel, he says, "Then went this saying abroad among the brethren, that that disciple should not die: yet Jesus said not unto him, 'He shall not die'; but, 'If I will that he tarry till I come, what is that to thee?'" This, you see, was putting a supposititious case, and in no sense the language of prediction.

Now, dear brethren, if you are so far convinced of the unreasonableness of each of these efforts to solve the difficulty by feigning a sense, I shall hope to have your minds in readiness for that explanation which appears to me to harmonize with every requirement. I believe the "coming" here spoken of is the coming of the Son of God to judgment at the last great and terrible assize, when he shall judge the righteous and separate the wicked from among them.

The next question is, "Of whom were the words spoken?" Are we warranted in supposing that our Lord intended this sentence as a gracious promise, or a kindly expectation that he would kindle in the breast of his disciples? I think not. To me it appears to have no reference whatever to any man who ever had grace in his soul: such language is far more applicable to the ungodly than the wicked. It may well have been aimed directly at those followers who should apostatize from the faith, grasp at the world, shrink at the cross, endeavor to save their lives, but really lose them, and barter their souls. At the glorious appearing of Christ there are some who will taste death, but will they be the righteous? Surely, my dear friends, when Christ comes, the righteous will not die; they will be caught up with the Lord in the air. His coming will be the signal for the resurrection of all his saints. But mark you, at the time of his coming, the men who have been without God, and without Christ, will begin for the first time to "taste of death." They passed the first stage of dissolution when the soul quit the body, but they have never known the "taste of death." Till then, they will not have known its tremendous bitterness and its awful horror. They will never drink of the wormwood and the gall, so as really to "taste of death," till the Lord shall come. This tasting of death here may be explained, and I believe it is to be explained, by a reference to the second death, which men will not taste of till the Lord comes. And what a dreadful sentence that was, when the Savior said—perhaps singling out Judas as he spoke, "Verily I say unto you, there be some standing here, who shall never know what that dreadful word 'death' means, till the Lord shall come. You think that if you save your lives, you escape from death. Ah! you do not know what death means. The demise of the body is but a prelude to the perdition of the soul. The grave is but the porch of death; you will never understand the meaning of that terrible word till the Lord comes." This can have no reference to the saints, because in the eighth chapter of John, and the fifty-first verse, you find this passage, "Verily, verily, I say unto you, 'If a man keep my saying, he shall never see death.' Then said the Jews unto him, 'Now we know that thou hast a devil. Abraham is dead, and the prophets; and thou sayest, "If a man keep my saying, he shall never taste of death."'" No righteous man, therefore, can ever "taste of death." He will fall into that deep oblivious sleep in which the body sees corruption; but that is another and a very different thing from the bitter cup referred to as tasting of death. When the Holy Ghost wanted an expression to set forth that which was the equivalent for the divine wrath, what expression was used? "Christ, by the grace of God, tasted death for every man." The expression "to taste of death" means the reception of that true and essential death, which kills both the body and the soul in hell forever. The Savior said then, as he might say, I fear, if he stood in this pulpit tonight, "Verily I say unto you, There be some standing here, which shall not taste of death, till they see the Son of man coming in his kingdom."

If this be the meaning, and I hold that it is in keeping with the context, it explains the verse, sets forth the reason why Christ bespoke breathless attention with the word "verily," answers both the grammar and the rhetoric, and is not by any argument that I have ever heard of to be moved—if this be so, what thrilling denunciations are contained in my text. Oh, may the Holy Spirit deeply affect our hearts and cause our souls to thrill with its solemnity!

What thoughts it stirs up! Compared with the doom which will be inflicted upon the ungodly at the coming of Christ, the death of nature is nothing. We go farther: compared with the doom of the wicked at the coming of Christ, even the torments of souls in a separate state are scarcely anything. The startling question then comes up. Are there any sitting or standing here who will have to taste of death when the Lord comes?

1. *The sinner's death is but a faint presage of the sinner's doom at the coming of the Son of man in his glory.*

Let me endeavor to show the contrast. We can make but little comparison between the two *in point of time.* Many men meet with their death so suddenly that it can scarcely involve any pain to them. They are crushed, perhaps, by machinery; a shot sends them to find a grave upon the battlefield; or they may be speedily poisoned. If they be for hours, or days, or weeks, or months, upon the bed of sickness, yet the real work of dying is but short. It is rather a weary sort of living than an actual sense of dying while hope lingers though even in fitful dreams. Dying is but the work of a moment: if it shall be said to last for hours, yet the hours are brief. Misery may count them long, but oh! with what swift wings do they fly! To die, to fall asleep, to suffer, it may be but a pin's prick, and then to have passed away from the land of the living to the realm of shades! But oh! the doom which is to be brought upon the wicked when Christ comes! This is a death which never dies. Here is a heart palpitating with eternal misery. Here is an eye never filmed by the kind finger of generous forgetfulness. Here will be a body never to be stiffened in apathy; never to be laid quietly in the grave, rid of keen pangs, wearing disease, and lingering wretchedness. To die, you say, is nature's kind release: it brings ease. It comes to a man, for this world at least, a farewell to his woes and griefs; but there shall be no ease, no rest, no pause in the destination of impenitent souls. "Depart, ye cursed," shall ever ring along the endless aisles of eternity. The thunderbolt of that tremendous word shall follow the sinner in his perpetual flight from the presence of God; from its baleful influence he shall never be able to escape; no, never. A million years shall make not so much difference to the duration of his agony as a cup of water taken from the sea would to the volume of the ocean. No, when millions of years told a million times shall have rolled their fiery orbits over his poor tormented head, he shall be no nearer to the end than he was at first. Talk of *death*! I might even paint him as an angel when once I think of the terrors of the wrath to come. Soon come, soon gone is death. That sharp scythe gives but one cut, and down falls the flower and withers in the heat of the sun; but eternity, eternity, eternity, who shall measure its wounds, who shall fathom the depths of the gashes? When eternity wields the whip, how dreadfully will it fall! When eternity grasps the sword, how deep shall be the woundings, how terrible its killing!

> To linger in eternal pain,
> Yet death forever fly.

You are afraid of death, sinner; you are afraid of death; but were you wise, you would be ten thousand times ten thousand times more afraid of the coming and the judgment of the Son of man.

In point of loss there is no comparison. When the sinner dies it is not tasting of death in its true sense, for what does he lose? He loses wife, and children, and friends; he loses all his dainty bits and his sweet drafts. Where now his viol and his lute? Where now the merry dance and the joyful company? For him no more the pleasant landscape nor the gliding stream. For him no more the light of the sun by day, nor the light of moon and stars by night. He has lost at one stroke every comfort and every hope. But then the loss, as far as death is concerned, is but a loss of earthly things, the loss of temporal and temporary comforts, and he might put up with that. It is wretched enough to lose these, but let your imagination follow me, faint as is my power to describe the everlasting and infinite loss of the man who is found impenitent at the last great judgment day. What loses he then? The harps of heaven and the songs thereof; the joys of God's presence and the light thereof; the jasper sea and the gates of pearl. He has lost peace and immortality and the crown of life; no, he has lost all hope, and when a man has lost that, what remains to him? His spirit sinks with a terrible depression, more frightful than maniac ever knew in his wildest moods of grief. His soul sinks never to recover itself into the depths of dark despair, where not a ray of hope can ever reach him. Lost to God; lost to heaven; lost to time; lost to the preaching of the gospel; lost to the invitation of mercy; lost to the prayers of the gracious; lost to the mercy seat; lost to the blood of sprinkling; lost to all hope of every sort; lost, lost, forever! Compared with this loss, the losses of death are nothing, and well might the Savior say, that lost spirits shall not even "taste of death" until he shall come, and they shall receive their sentence.

Neither does death bear any comparison with the last judgment *in point of terror*. I do not like to paint the terrors of the deathbed of unawakened men. Some, you know, glide gently into their graves. It is, in fact, the mark of the wicked that they have no bands in their death: but their strength is firm; they are not troubled like other men are. Like the sheep they are laid in the grave. A peaceful death is no sign of grace. Some of the worst of men have died with a smile upon their countenance to have it changed for one eternal weeping. But there are more men of other exquisite sensibility, instructed men, who cannot die like brutes, and they have alarms and fears and terrors when they are on their deathbeds. Many an atheist has cried to God under dying pangs, and many an infidel who heretofore could brag and speak high things against God has found his cheek turn pale and his throat grow hoarse when he has come there. Like the mariner, the boldest man in that great storm reels to and fro and staggers like a drunken man and is at his wits' ends; for he finds that it is no child's play to die. I try sometimes to picture that hour, when we shall perhaps be propped up in the bed or lying down with pillows round about us, be diligently watched; and as they hush their footfalls and gaze anxiously on, there is a whisper that the solemn time has come, and then there is a grappling of the strong man with the stronger than he. Oh! what must it be to die without a Savior, to die in the dark without a light except the lurid glare of the wrath to come! Horrors there are, indeed, around the deathbed of the wicked, but these are hardly anything compared with the terrors of the day of judgment. When the sinner wakes from his bed of dust, the first object he will see will be the great white throne and the Judge seated upon it: the first sound that will greet his ears will be the trumpet sounding—

> Come to judgment, come to judgment,
> Come to judgment, sinner, come.

He will look up, and there will be the Son of man on his judgment throne, the King's officers arranged on either side, the saints on his right hand, and angels round about; then the books will be opened. What creeping horror will come upon the flesh of the wicked man! He knows his turn will arrive in a moment; he stands expecting it; fear takes hold upon him, while the eyes of the Judge look him through and through, and he cries to the rocks to hide him, and the mountains to fall upon him. Happy would he be now to find a friendly shelter in the grave, but the grave has burst its doors, and can never be closed upon him again. He would even be glad to rush back to his former state in hell, but he must not. The judgment has come, the assize is set; again the trumpet rings—

Come to judgment, come to judgment,
Come to judgment, come away.

And then the book is opened, and the dread sentence is pronounced; and, to use the words of Scripture, "Death and hell are cast into the lake of fire. This is the second death. And whosoever was not found written in the book of life was cast into the lake of fire." The man never knew what death was before. The first death was but a flea bite; this is death indeed. The first death he might have looked back upon as a dream, compared with this tasting of death now that the Lord has come.

From what we can glean darkly from hints of Scripture, *the pains of death* are not at all comparable to the pains of the judgment at the second advent. Who will speak in a depreciating manner of the pains of death? If we should attempt to do so, we know that our hearts would contradict us. In the shades of night, when deep sleep falls upon men, you sometimes suddenly awake. You are alarmed. The terror by night has come upon you. You expect—you hardly know what it is, but you are half afraid that you are about to die. You know how the cold sweat comes upon the brow. You may have a good hope through grace, but the very thought of death brings a peculiar pang. Or when death has really come in view, some of us have marked with terrible grief the sufferings of our dearest friends. We have heard the eye-strings break; we have seen the face all pallid, and the cheek all hollow and sunken. We have some-times seen how every nerve has become a road for the hot feet of pain to travel on, and how every vein has been a canal of grief. We have marked the pains and moans and groans and dying strife that fright the soul away. These, however, are common to man. Not so the pangs which are to be inflicted both on body and on soul at the coming of the Son of God; they are such that I cast a veil over them, fearful of the very thought. Let the Master's words suffice, "Fear him who is able to cast both body and soul into hell; yea, I say unto you, fear him." Then the body in all the parts shall suffer; the members which were once instruments of unrighteousness shall now be instruments of suffering. And the mind, the major sinner, shall be also the greater sufferer. The mem-ory, the judgment, the understanding, the will, the imagination, and every power and passion of the soul become a deep lake of anguish. But I spare you these things; oh! spare yourselves! God alone knows with what pain I dis-course upon these horrors. Were it not that they must be spoken of, or else I must give my account at the day of judgment as a faithless servant; were it not that I speak of them in mercy to your souls, poor sinners, I would fain forget them altogether, seeing that my own soul has a hope in him who saves from the wrath to come. But as long as you will not have mercy upon yourselves, we must lay this ax at your root; so long as you will make a mock of sin and set at naught the terrors of the world to come, we must warn you of hell. If it be hard to *talk* of these things, what must it be to *endure* them? If a dream makes you quiver from head to foot, what must it be to endure really, and in person, the wrath to come? O souls, were I to speak as I ought, my knees would knock together with trembling now; were you to feel as you should, there would not be an unconverted man among you who would not cry, "Sirs, what must I do to be saved?" I do conjure you to remember that death, with all its pangs, is but a drop of a bucket compared with the deep, mysterious, fathomless, shoreless sea of grief you must endure forever at the coming of the Lord Jesus except you repent.

Death makes great discoveries. The man thought himself wise, but death draws the curtain, and he sees written up in large letters, "Thou fool!" He said he was prudent, for he hoarded up his gold and silver and kept the wages of the laborer; but now he finds that he has made a bad bargain, while the question is propounded to him, "What doth it profit thee, to have gained the world, and to have lost thy soul?" Death is a great revealer of secrets. Many men are not believers at all until they die; but death comes, and makes short work with their skepticism. It gives but one blow upon the head of doubt, and all is done; the man believes then, only he believes too late. Death gives to the sinner the discovery that there is a God, an angry God, and punishment is wrapped up in the wrath to come. But how much greater the discoveries that await the day of judgment! What will the sinner see then? He will see the man who was crucified sitting upon the throne. He will hear how Satan has been defeated in all his craftiest undertakings. Read from those mysterious books, the secrets of all hearts shall then be revealed. Then men shall understand how the Lord reigned supremely even when Satan roared most loudly; how the mischief and the folly of man did but after all bring forth the great purposes of God. All this shall be in the books, and the sinner shall stand there defeated, terribly defeated, worsted at every point, baffled, foiled, stultified in every act and every purpose by which he thought to do well for himself; yes, and utterly confounded in all the hostility and all the negligence of his heart toward the living and true God who would and who did rule over him. Too late, he will discover the preciousness of the blood he despised, the value of the Savior he rejected, the glory of the heaven which he lost, the terror of the hell to which he is sentenced. How wise, how dreadfully wise will he be when fully aware of his terrible and eternal destruction! Thus sinners shall not taste of death in the real meaning of the term, until the Lord shall come.

2. Still further—*in the state of separate spirits they have not fully tasted of death, nor will they do so until Christ comes.*

The moment that a man dies, his spirit goes before God. If without Christ, that spirit then begins to feel the anger and the wrath of God. It is as when a man is taken before a magistrate. He is known to be guilty, and therefore he is remanded and put in prison till his trial shall come. Such is the state of souls apart from the body: they are spirits in prison, waiting for the time of their trial. There is not, in the sense in which the Romanist teaches it, any purgatory; yet there is a place of waiting for lost spirits which is in Scripture called "hell," because it is one room in that awful prison house in which must dwell forever spirits that die finally impenitent and without faith in Christ. But those of our departed countrymen and fellow citizens of earth who die without Christ have not yet fully tasted of death, nor can they until the advent of the Lord.

Just consider why not. *Their bodies do not suffer.* The bodies of the wicked are still the prey of the worm; still the atoms are the sport of the winds and are traversing their boundless cycles, and must do so until they are gathered up into the body again, at the trump of the archangel—at the voice of God.

The ungodly know that their present state is to have an end at the judgment, but after the judgment their state will have no end; it is then to go on, and on, and on, forever and forever, unchanged and unchangeable. Now there may be half a hope, an anticipation of some change, for change brings some relief; but to the finally damned, upon whom the sentence has been pronounced, there is no hope even of a change. Forever and forever shall there be the same ceaseless wheel of misery.

The ungodly, too, in their present state, have not as yet been put to the shame of a public sentence. They have, as it were, merely been cast into prison, the facts being too clear to admit of any doubt as to the sentence, and they are their own tormentors, vexing and paining themselves with the fear of what is yet to come. They have never yet heard that dreadful sentence, " Depart, ye cursed, into everlasting fire, prepared for the devil and his angels."

I was struck while studying this subject, to find how little is said about the pains of the lost while they are merely souls, and how much is said concerning this when the Lord comes. You have that one parable of the rich man and Lazarus, and there it speaks of the soul being already tormented in the flame; but if you turn to the thirteenth chapter of Matthew, and read the parable of the tares, you will find it is at the end of the world that the tares are to be cast into the fire. Then comes the parable of the dragnet. It is when the dispensation comes to an end that the net is to be dragged to shore, and then the good are to be put in vessels, and the bad cast away; and then the Lord says, "The Son of man shall send forth his angels, and they shall gather out of his kingdom all things that offend, and them which do iniquity; and shall cast them into a furnace of fire: there shall be wailing and gnashing of teeth." That memorable description in Matthew of those of whom he said, "I was an hungered, and ye gave me no meat; I was thirsty, and ye gave me no drink," is described as happening when the "Son of man shall come in his glory, and all his holy angels with him." The apostle Paul, too, tells us plainly in the Epistle to the Thessalonians, that the wicked are to be destroyed at his coming by the brightness of his power. The recompense of the ungodly, like the reward of the righteous, is anticipated now: but the full reward of the righteous is to be at his coming; they are to reign with Christ; their fullness of bliss is to be given them when the King himself in his glory shall sit upon his throne. So, too, the wicked have the beginning of their heritage at death, but the dread fullness of it is to be hereafter.

At the present moment, death and hell are not yet cast into the lake of fire. Death is still abroad in the world slaying men; hell is yet loose; the devil is not yet chained, but still does he go about the "dry places, seeking rest, and finding none." At the last day, at the coming of Christ, "death and hell shall be cast into the lake of fire." We do not understand the symbol; but if it means anything, one would think it must mean this, that at that day the scattered powers of evil, which are to be the tormentors of the wicked, but which have thus far been wandering up and down throughout the world, shall all be collected together, and then, indeed, shall it be that the wicked shall begin to "taste of death" as they have never tasted of it before!

My soul is bowed down with terror while I speak these words to you. I scarcely know how to find suitable words to express the weight of thought which is upon me. My dear hearers, instead of speculating upon these matters, let us try to shun the wrath to come; and what can help us to do that better than to weigh the warning words of a dear and loving Savior, when he tells us that at his coming such a doom shall pass upon impenitent souls, that compared with it, even death itself shall be as nothing? Christians, by the faith of their risen Lord, swallow death in victory; but if you die impenitent, you swallow death in ignorance. You do not feel its bitterness now. But oh! that bitter pill has yet to work its way, and that fierce draft has yet to be drained even to the dregs, unless you repent.

And now, does not the meditation of these terrors prompt *a question?* Jesus said, "Verily I say unto you, there be some standing here, which shall not taste of death, till they see the Son of man coming in his kingdom." *Are there any standing or sitting here who shall not taste of death till then?*

In that little group addressed by the Savior stood Judas. He had been trusted by his Master, and he was an apostle, but after all he was a thief and a hypocrite. He, the son of perdition, would not taste of death till Christ should come in his kingdom. Is there a Judas here? I look into your faces, and many of you are members of this church, and others of you I doubt not are members of other Christian churches, but are you sure that you have made sound work of it? Is your religion genuine? Do you wear a mask, or are you an honest man? O sirs, try your own hearts, and since you may fail in the trial, ask the Lord to search you; for as the Lord my God lives, unless you thus search yourselves and find that you are in the right, you may come presumptuously to sit at the Lord's table. Though with a name to live, you may be among his people here, you will have to taste of death when the Lord comes. You may deceive *us,* but you cannot deceive *him.* The preacher reflects that he himself may be mistaken, that he himself may be self-deceived. If it be so, may the Lord open his eyes to know the worst of his own state. Will you put up this prayer for yourselves, professors? Do not be too bold, you who say you are Christ's; never be satisfied till you are quite sure of it; and the best way to be sure is to go again just as you went at first, and lay hold on eternal life through the power of the blessed Spirit, and not by any strength of your own.

No doubt, however, there stood in that little throng around the Savior some who were careless sinners. He knew that they had been so during the whole of his teaching, and that they would be so still, and therefore they would taste of death at his coming. Are there not some careless persons come in here tonight? I mean you who never think about religion, who generally look upon the Sunday as a day of pleasure, or who loll about in your shirt-sleeves nearly all the day; you who look upon the very name of religion as a bugbear to frighten children with; who mock at God's servants, and contemn the very thought of earnestly seeking after the most High. Oh! will you, will you be among the number of those who taste of death when the Son of man shall come in his kingdom? Oh! must I ring your death knell tonight? Must my warning voice be lost upon you? I beseech you to recollect that you must either *turn* or *burn.* I beseech you to remember this, "Let the wicked forsake his way and the unrighteous man his thoughts; and let him turn unto the Lord, and he will have mercy upon him; and to our God, for he will abundantly pardon." By the wounds of Jesus, sinner, stop and think. If God's dear Son was slain for human sin, how terrible must that sin be! And if Jesus died, how base are you if you are disobedient to the doctrine of faith! I pray you if you think of your body, give some thought to your soul. "Wherefore do ye spend money for that which is not bread? and your labor for that which satisfieth not?" Hearken diligently unto Jehovah's Word, and eat of that which is good, real, and substantial food. Come to Jesus, and your soul shall live.

And there are some here of another class, Bethsaida sinners, Capernaum sinners. I mean some of you who constantly occupy these pews and stand in yonder area and sit in yonder gallery Sunday after Sunday. The same eyes look down on me week after week; the same faces salute me often with a smile when the Sabbath comes, and I pass you journeying to this the tabernacle of your worship, and yet how many of you are still without God and without Christ! Have I been unfaithful to you? If I have, forgive me, and pray to God both for me and for yourselves that we may mend our ways. But if I have warned you of the wrath to come, why will you choose to walk in the path which leads to it? If I have preached to you Christ Jesus, how is it that his charms move you not, and that the story of his great love does not bring you to repentance? Oh, that the Spirit of God would come and deal with you, for I cannot. My hammer breaks not your flinty hearts, but God's arm can do it, and oh, may he turn you yet. Of all sinners over whom a minister ought to weep, you are the worst; for while the careless perish, you perish doubly. You know your Master's will, and yet you do it not. You see heaven's gate set open, and yet you will not enter. Your vicious free will ruins you; your base and wicked love of self and sin destroys you. "Ye will not come unto me that ye might have life," said Christ. You are so vile that you will not turn even though Jesus should woo you. I do pray you let the menace of judgment to come contained in my text, stir you now if you have never been stirred before. May God have pity on you even if you will have no pity upon yourselves.

Peradventure among that company there were some who held the truth, but who held it in licentiousness—and there may be such here present. You believe in the doctrine of election, so do I; but then you make it a cloak for your sin. You hold the doctrine of the perseverance of the saints, but you still persevere in your iniquity. Oh! there is no way of perishing that I know of worse than perishing by making the doctrines of grace an excuse for one's sins. The apostle has well said of such that their damnation is just: it is just to any man, but to a sevenfold degree is it just to such as you are. I would not have you forget the doctrine, nor neglect it, nor despise it, but I do beseech you do not prostitute it, do not turn it to the vile purposes of making it pander to your own carnal ease. Remember, you have no evidence of election except you are holy, and that you have no right to expect you will be saved at the last unless you are saved now. A present faith in a present Savior is the test.

Oh, that my Master would bring some of you to trust him tonight. The plan of salvation is simple. Trust Christ, and you are saved; rely upon him, and you shall live. This faith is the *gift of God,* but remember that though God gives it, he works in you to will and to do of his own good pleasure. God does not believe for you; the Holy Spirit does not believe for you; you must believe, or else you will be lost: and it is quite consistent with the fact that it is the gift of God, to say that it is also the act of man. You must, poor soul, be led to trust the Savior, or into heaven you can never enter. Is there one here who says, "I would find the Savior tonight"? Go not to your bed until you have sought him, and seek you him with sighs and with tears.

I think this is a night of grace. I have preached the law and the terrors of the Lord to you, but it will be a night of grace to the souls of some of you. My Master does but kill you that he may make you alive; he does but wound you that he may make you whole. I feel a sort of inward whisper in my heart that there are some of you who even now have begun your flight from the wrath to come. Whither do you flee? Fly to Jesus. Haste, sinner, haste. I trust you will find him before you retire to your beds, or if you lie tossing there in doubt and fear, then may he manifest himself unto you before the morning light. I think I would freely give my eyes if you might but see Christ, and that I would willingly give my hands if you might but lay hold on him. Do, I conjure you, put not from you this warning, but let it have its proper work upon you and lead you to repentance. May God save you, and may the prayer we have already offered this evening be answered, that the company of you may be found among his elect at his right hand. To that end, let us pray.

Our Father, save us with your great salvation. We will say unto God, do not condemn us; deliver us from going down to the pit, for you have found the ransom; may we not be among the company that shall taste of death when the Son of man shall come. Hear us, Jesus, through your blood. God be merciful to us sinners. Amen.

The Reward of the Righteous

~∞~

Delivered on Sunday morning, January 21, 1866, at the Metropolitan Tabernacle, Newington. No. 671.

*When the Son of man shall come in his glory, and all the holy angels with him, then shall he sit upon the throne of his glory: and before him shall be gathered all nations: and he shall separate them one from another, as a shepherd divideth his sheep from the goats: and he shall set the sheep on his right hand, but the goats on the left. Then shall the King say unto them on his right hand, "Come, ye blessed of my Father, inherit the kingdom prepared for you from the foundation of the world: for I was an hungered, and ye gave me meat: I was thirsty, and ye gave me drink: I was a stranger, and ye took me in: naked, and ye clothed me: I was sick, and ye visited me: I was in prison, and ye came unto me." —*MATTHEW 25:31–36

It is exceedingly beneficial to our souls to mount above this present evil world to something nobler and better. The cares of this world and the deceitfulness of riches are apt to choke everything good within us, and we grow fretful, desponding, perhaps proud, carnal. It is well for us to cut down these thorns and briars, for heavenly seed sown among them is not likely to yield a harvest, and I do not know a better sickle with which to cut them down than thoughts of the kingdom to come. In the valleys in Switzerland, many of the inhabitants are deformed and dwarfish, and the whole of them wear a sickly appearance, for the atmosphere is charged with miasma, and is close and stagnant; you traverse them as rapidly as you can, and are glad to escape from them. Up yonder on the mountain, you will find a hardy race, who breathe the clear fresh air as it blows from the virgin snows of the Alpine summits. It would be well for their frames if the dwellers in the valley could frequently leave their abodes among the marshes and the fever mists and get themselves up into the clear atmosphere above. It is to such an exploit of climbing that I invite you this morning. May the Spirit of God bear us as upon eagles' wings, that we may leave the mists of fear and the fevers of anxiety, and all the ills which gather in this valley of earth, and get ourselves up to the mountains of future joy and blessedness where it is to be our delight to dwell world without end! Oh, may God disentangle us now for a little while, cut the cords that keep us here below, and permit us to mount! We sit, some of us, like chained eagles fastened to the rock, only that, unlike the eagle, we begin to love our chain and would, perhaps, if it came really to the test, be loath to have it snapped. May God now grant us grace if we cannot at once escape from the chain of mortal life as to our bodies, yet to do so as to our spirits; and leaving the body like a servant at the foot of the hill, may our soul, like Abraham, go to the top of the mountain, and there may we have communion with the most High.

While expounding my text, I shall ask your attention this morning, first, *to the circumstances which surround the rewarding of the righteous;* second, *to their portion;* and third, *to the persons themselves.*

1. There is *much of teaching in the surrounding circumstances.*

We read, "When the King shall come in his glory." It appears, then, that we must not expect to receive our reward till by and by. Like the hireling we must fulfill our day, and then at evening we shall have our penny. Too many Christians look for a present reward for their labors, and if they meet with success, they begin doting upon it as though they had received their recompense. Like the disciples who returned saying, "Lord, even the devils are subject unto us," they rejoice too exclusively in present prosperity; whereas the Master bade them not to look upon miraculous success as being their reward, since that might not always be the case. "Nevertheless," said he, "rejoice not in this, but rather rejoice because your names are written in heaven." Success in the ministry is not the Christian minister's true reward: it is an earnest, but the wages still wait. The approbation of your fellowmen you must not look upon as being the reward of excellence, for often you will meet with the reverse; you will find your best actions misconstrued, and your motives ill interpreted. If you are looking for your reward *here,* I may warn you of the apostle's words, "If in this life only we have hope, we are of all men most miserable," because other men get their reward; even the Pharisee gets his: "Verily, I say unto you, they have their reward"; but we have none here. To be despised and rejected of men is the Christian's lot. Among his fellow Christians he will not always stand in good repute. It is not unmitigated kindness nor unmingled love that we receive even from the saints. I tell you, if you look for your reward to Christ's bride herself, you will miss it; if you expect to receive your crown from the hand even of your brethren in the ministry who know your labors, and who ought to sympathize with your trials, you will be mistaken. "When the King shall come in his glory," then is your time of recompense; but not today nor tomorrow nor at any time in this world. Reckon nothing which you acquire, no honor which you gain, to be the reward of your service to your Master; that is reserved to the time "when the King shall come in his glory."

Observe with delight the august person by whose hand the reward is given. It is written, "When the King shall come." Brethren, we love the King's courtiers; we delight to be numbered with them ourselves. It is no mean thing to do service to him whose head, "Though once 'twas crowned with thorns, is crowned with glory now." But it is a delightful thought that the service of rewarding us will not be left to the courtiers. The angels will be there, and the brethren of the King will be there; but heaven was not prepared by them, nor can it be given by them. Their hands shall not yield us a coronation; we shall join their songs, but their songs would be no reward for us; we shall bow with them and they with us, but it will not be possible for them to give us the recompense of the reward—that starry crown is all too weighty for an angel's hand to bring, and the benediction all too sweet to be pronounced, even by seraphic lips. The King himself must say, "Well done, good and faithful servant." What say you to this, my dear brother? You have felt a temptation to look to God's servants, to the approbation of the minister, to the kindly look of parents, to the word of commendation from your fellow worker; all these you value, and I do not blame you; but these may fail you, and therefore never consider them as being the reward. You must wait till the time when the King comes, and then it will neither be your brethren, your pastors, your parents, nor your helpers, but the King himself who shall say to you, "Come, you blessed." How this sweetens heaven! It will be Christ's own gift. How this makes the benediction doubly blessed! It shall come from his lips, which drop like myrrh and flow with honey. Beloved, it is Christ who became a curse for us, who shall give the blessing to us. Roll you this as a sweet morsel under your tongues.

The character in which our Lord Jesus shall appear is significant. Jesus will then be revealed as truly "the King." "When the King shall come." It was to him as King that the service was rendered, and it is from him as King that the reward must therefore come; and so upon the very threshold a question of self-examination arises: "The King will not reward the servants of another prince—am I therefore his servant? Is it my joy to wait at the threshold of his gates, and sit like Mordecai at the courts of Ahasuerus—at the entrance of his door? Say, soul, do you serve the King?" I mean not the kings and queens of earth; let them have loyal servants for their subjects; but saints are servants of the Lord Jesus Christ, the King of kings—are you so? If you be not so, when the King comes in his glory, there can be no reward for you. I long in my own heart to recognize Christ's kingly office more than ever I have done. It has been my delight to preach to you Christ dying on the cross, and "God forbid that I should glory, save in the cross"; but I want for my own self to realize him on his throne, reigning in my heart, having a right to do as he wills with me, that I may get to the condition of Abraham, who, when God spoke, though it was to tell him to offer up his own Isaac, never asked a question, but simply said, "Here am I." Beloved, seek to know and feel the controlling power of the King, for else when he comes, since you have not known him as King, he cannot know you as servant; and it is only to the servant that the King can give the reward which is spoken of in the text, "When the King shall come."

Now pass on. "When the King shall come in his *glory*." The fullness of that it is impossible to conceive.

> *Imagination's utmost stretch,*
> *In wonder dies away.*

But this we know—and it is the sweetest thing we can know—that if we have been partakers with Jesus in his shame, we also shall be sharers with him in the luster which shall surround him. Are you, beloved, one with Christ Jesus? Are you of his flesh and of his bones? Does a vital union knit you to him? Then you are today with him in his shame; you have taken up his cross, and gone with him without the camp bearing his reproach; you will doubtless be with him when the cross is exchanged for the crown. But judge yourself this morning; if you are not with him in the regeneration, neither will you be with him when he shall come in his glory. If you start back from the black side of communion, you shall not understand its bright, its happy period, when the King shall come in his glory and all his holy angels with him. What, are angels with him? And yet he took not up angels, he took up the seed of Abraham. Are the holy angels with him? Come, my soul, then you cannot not be far from him. If his friends and his neighbors are called together to see his glory, what do you think if you are married to him? Shall you be distant? Though it be a day of judgment, yet you cannot be far from that heart which having admitted angels into intimacy has admitted you into union. Has he not said to you, O my soul, "I have betrothed thee unto me in faithfulness, and in judgment, and in righteousness"? Have not his own lips said it, "I am married unto thee, and my delight is in thee"? Then if the angels, who are but the friends and the neighbors, shall be with him, it is abundantly certain that his own beloved Hephzibah, in whom is all his delight, shall be near to him and shall be a partaker of his splendor. It is when he comes in his glory, and when his communion with angels shall be distinctly recognized, it is then that his unity with his church shall become apparent. *"Then shall he sit upon the throne of his glory."* Here is a repetition of the same reason why it should be your time and my time to receive the reward from Christ if we be found among his faithful servants. When *he* sits upon his throne it were not fit that his own beloved ones should be in the mire. When he was in the place of shame, they were with him, and now he is on the throne of gold they must be with him too. There were no oneness, union with Christ were a mere matter of talk, if it were not certain that when he is on the throne they shall be upon the throne too.

But I want you to notice one particular circumstance with regard to the time of the reward. It is *when he shall have divided the sheep from the goats.* My reward, if I be a child of God, cannot come to me while I am in union with the wicked. Even on earth you will have the most enjoyment of Christ when you are most separated from this world: rest assured, although the separated path does not seem an easy one, and it will certainly entail upon you persecution and the loss of many friends, yet it is the happiest walking in the world. You conforming Christians, who can enter into the world's mirth to a certain degree, you cannot, you never can know as you now are, the inward joys of those who live in lonely but lovely fellowship with Jesus. The nearer you get to the world, the further you must be from Christ, and I believe the more thoroughly a bill of divorce is given by your spirit to every earthly object upon which your soul can set itself, the more close will be your communion with your Lord. "Forget also thine own country and thy Father's house; so shall the King greatly desire thy beauty, for he is thy Lord, and worship thou him." It is significant that not until the King has separated the sheep from the goats does he say, "Come, ye blessed"; and though the righteous will have enjoyed a felicity as disembodied spirits, yet as risen from the grave in their bodies, their felicity is not fully accomplished till the great Shepherd shall have appeared to separate them once for all, by a great gulf which cannot be passed, from all association with the nations that forget God. Now then, beloved, these circumstances all but together come to this, that the reward of following Christ is not today, is not among the sons of men, is not from men, is not even from the excellent of the earth, is not even bestowed by Jesus while we are here, but the glorious crown of life which the Lord's grace shall give to his people is reserved for the second advent, "when the King shall come in his glory, and all his holy angels with him." Wait with patience, wait with joyful expectation, for he shall come, and blessed be the day of his appearing.

2. We have now to turn to the second point—*the portion itself.*

Every word is suggestive. I shall not attempt to exhaust, but merely to glance at all. The reward of the righteous is set forth by the loving benediction pronounced to them by the Master, but *their very position* gives some foreshadowing of it. He put the sheep on his right hand. Heaven is a position of the most elevated dignity authoritatively conferred, and of divine complacency manifestly enjoyed. God's saints are always at his right hand according to the judgment of faith, but hereafter it shall be more clearly manifested. God is pleased to be close to his people, and to place them near to himself in a place of protection. Sometimes it seems as if they were at the left hand; they certainly have, some of them, less comfort than the worldlings. "I have seen the wicked in great power, and spreading himself like a green bay tree; their eyes stand out with fatness, they have more than heart could wish"; whereas his people are often made to drink waters of less than a full cup, and their meat and their drink are bittered with wormwood and gall. The world is upside down now; the gospel has begun to turn it the right way uppermost, but when the day of grace is over, and the day of glory comes, then shall it be righted indeed; then those that wandered about in sheepskins and goatskins shall be clothed in glittering apparel, being transfigured like the Savior upon Tabor; then those of whom the world was not worthy shall come to a world that shall be worthy of them; then those who were hurried to the stake and to the flames shall triumph with chariots of fire and horses of fire, and swell the splendor of the Master's pompous appearing. Yes, beloved, you shall eternally be the object of divine complacency, not in secret and unmanifested communion, but your state and glory shall be revealed before the sons of men. Your persecutors shall gnash their teeth when they see you occupying places of honor at his right hand, and themselves, though greater far than you on earth, condemned to take the lowest room. How shall Dives bite his fire-tormented tongue in vain as he sees Lazarus, the beggar on the dunghill, made to sit at the right hand of the King eternal and immortal! Heaven is a place of dignity. "There we shall be as the angels," says one, but I know that we shall be even superior than they. Is it not written of him who in all things is our representative, "Thou hast put all things under his feet"! Even the very seraphs themselves so richly blessed, what are they but "ministering spirits sent forth to minister to the heirs of salvation"?

But now turning to the welcome uttered by the Judge: the first word is "come." It is the gospel symbol. The law said "go"; the gospel says "come." The Spirit says it in invitation; the bride says it in intercession; "let him that hears" say it by constantly, laboriously endeavoring to spread abroad the good news. Since Jesus says, "Come," we learn that the very essence of heaven is communion. "Come!" You came near enough to say, "Lord, we believe, help thou our unbelief!" On the cross you looked to me and were lightened. You had fellowship with me in bearing my cross. You filled up that which was behind of the sufferings of Christ for his body's sake, which is the church. Still come! Ever, come! Forever, come! Come up from your graves, you risen ones! Come up from among the ungodly, you consecrated ones! Come up from where you cast yourselves down in your humiliation before the great white throne! Come up to wear my crown and sit with me upon my throne! Oh, that word has heaven lurking within it. It shall be to you your joy forever to hear the Savior say to you, "Come." I protest before you my soul has sometimes been so full of joy that I could hold no more when my beloved Lord has said "Come" to my soul; for he has taken me into his banqueting house, and his love-banner has waved over my head, and he has taken me away from the world, and its cares and its fears, and its trials and its joys, up to "the top of Amana, from the top of Shenir and Hermon," where he manifested himself to me. When this "Come" shall come into your ear from the Master's lips, there shall not be the flesh to drag you back, there shall be no sluggishness of spirit, no heaviness of heart; you shall come eternally then; you shall not mount to descend again, but mount on and on in one blessed excelsior forever and forever. The first word indicates that heaven is a state of communion— "come."

Then it is *"Come, ye blessed,"* which is a clear declaration that this is a state of happiness. They cannot be more blessed than they are. They have their hearts' desire, and though their hearts have been enlarged and their desires have been expanded by entering into the Infinite, and getting rid of the cramping influences of corruption and of time, yet even when their desire shall know no bound, they shall have all the happiness that the utmost stretch of their souls can by any possibility conceive. This much, and this is all we know—they are supremely blessed. Their blessedness you perceive does not come from any secondary joy, but from the great primary Source of all good. "Come, ye blessed of my Father." They drink the unadulterated wine at the winepress itself, where it joyously leaps from the bursting clusters; they pluck celestial fruits from the unwithering boughs of the immortal tree; they shall sit at the wellhead and drink the waters as they spring with unrivaled freshness from the depths of the heart of Deity; they shall not be basking in the beams of the sun, but they shall be like Uriel, the angel in the sun; they shall dwell in God, and so their souls shall be satisfied with favor and full and more than full with his presence and benediction.

Notice, once again, that according to the words used it is a state where they shall recognize their right to be there; a state therefore of perfect freedom, and ease and fearlessness. It is *"inherit the kingdom."* A man does not fear to lose that which he wins by descent from his parent. If heaven had been the subject of earning, we might have feared that our merits had not really deserved it, and therefore suspect that one day a writ of error would be issued and that we should be ejected; but we do know whose sons we are; we know whose love it is that makes glad our spirits, and when we "inherit" the kingdom we shall enter it not as strangers or as foreigners, but as sons coming to their birthright. Looking over all its streets of gold and surveying all its walls of pearl we shall feel that we are at home in our own house and have an actual right, not through merit but through grace, to everything that is there. It will be a state of heavenly bliss; the Christian shall feel that law and justice are on his side, and that those stern attributes have brought him there as well as mercy and loving-kindness. But the word "inherit" here imports full possession and enjoyment. They have inherited in a certain sense before, but now as an heir, when he has arrived at full maturity, begins to spend his own money, and to farm his own acres, so do they enter into their heritage. We are not full grown as yet, and therefore are not admitted to full possession. But wait awhile; those gray hairs show, my brethren, that you are getting ripe. These, these, these my still youthful locks show me, alas, that I may have to tarry for a little longer, and yet I know not, the Lord may soon permit me to sleep with my fathers; but later or earlier, be it as he wills, we shall one day come into possession of the good land. Now if it is sweet to be an heir while you are in nonage, what is it to be an heir when arrived at perfect manhood? Was it not delightful to sing that hymn just now, and to behold the land of pure delight, whose everlasting spring and never-withering flowers are just across the narrow stream of death. O you sweet fields! You saints immortal who lie down therein! When shall we be with you and be satisfied? If the mere thinking of heaven ravishes the soul, what must it be to be there, to plunge deep into the stream of blessedness, to dive and find no bottom, to swim and find no shore? To sip of the wine of heaven as we sometimes do makes our hearts so glad that we know not how to express our joy; but what will it be to drink deep and drink again, and sit forever at the table and know that the feast will never be over and the cups will never be empty, and that there will be no worse wine to be brought out at the last, but if possible better still and better still in infinite progression?

The word "kingdom," which stands next, indicates the richness of the heritage of saints. It is no petty estate, no alms rooms, no happy corner in obscurity. I heard a good man say he should be content to win a corner behind the door. I shall not be. The Lord says we shall inherit a *kingdom*. We would not be satisfied to inherit less, because less than that would not suit our character. "He hath made us kings and priests unto God," and we must reign forever and ever, or be as wretched as deposed monarchs. A king without a king-dom were an unhappy man. If I were a poor servant, an alms room would be a boon, for it would consort with my condition and degree; but if I am made by grace a king, I must have a kingdom, or I shall not have attained to a posi-tion equal to my nature. He who makes us kings will give us a kingdom to fit the nature which he has bestowed upon us. Beloved, do strive after, more and more, that which the Spirit of God will give you, a kingly heart; do not be among those who are satisfied and contented with the miserable nature of ordinary humanity. A child's glass bead is all the world is to a truly royal spirit; these glittering diadems are only nursery toys to God's kings; the true jewels are up there; the true treasury wealth looks down upon the stars. Do not stint your soul; be not straitened! Get a kingly heart—ask the King of kings to give it to you, and beg of him a royal spirit. Act royally on earth toward your Lord, and for his sake toward all men. Go about the world not as mean men in spirit and act, but as kings and princes of a race superior to the dirt-scrapers who are on their knees, crawling in the mud after yellow earth. Then, when your soul is royal, remember with joy that your future inheri-tance shall be all that your kingly soul pants after in its most royal moments. It will be a state of unutterable richness and wealth of soul.

According to the word "prepared," we may conceive it to be a condition of surpassing excellence. It is a *kingdom prepared,* and it has been so long a time prepared, and he who prepares it is so wondrously rich in resources, that we cannot possibly conceive how excellent it must be. If I might so speak, God's common gifts, which he throws away as though they were but nothing, are priceless; but what will be these gifts upon which the infinite mind of God has been set for ages of ages in order that they may reach the highest degree of excellence? Long before Christmas chimes were ringing, mother was so glad to think her boy was coming home, after the first quarter he had been out at school, and straightway she began preparing and planning all sorts of joys for him. Well might the holidays be happy when mother had been contriving to make them so. Now in an infinitely nobler manner, the great God has pre-pared a kingdom for his people; he has thought, "that will please them, and that will bless them, and this other will make them superlatively happy." He prepared the kingdom to perfection; and then, as if that were not enough, the glorious man Christ Jesus went up from earth to heaven; and you know what he said when he departed, "I go to prepare a place for you." We know that the infinite God can prepare a place fitting for a finite creature, but the words smile so sweetly at us as we read that Jesus himself, who is a man, and there-fore knows our hearts' desires, has had a finger in it; he has prepared it too. It is a kingdom prepared for *you,* upon which the thoughts of God have been set to make it excellent "from before the foundation of the world."

But we must not pause: it is a "kingdom prepared for *you.*" Mark that! I must confess I do not like certain expressions which I hear sometimes, which imply that heaven is prepared for some who will never reach it; prepared for those who will be driven as accursed ones into the place of torment. I know there is a sacred expression which says, "let no man take thy crown"; but that refers to the crown of ministerial success, rather than of eternal glory. An expression which grated on my ear the other evening, from the lips of a certain good man, ran something in this fashion: "There is a heaven prepared for all of you, but if you are not faithful you will not win it. There is a crown in heaven laid up for you, but if you are not faithful it will be without wearer." I do not believe it, I cannot believe it. That the crown of eternal life, which is laid up for the blessed of the Father, will ever be given to anybody else or left without possessor, I do not believe. I dare not conceive of crowns in heaven and nobody to wear them. Think you that in heaven, when the whole number of saints is complete, you will find a number of unused crowns? "Ah! what are these for? Where are the heads for these?" "They are in hell!" Then, brother, I have no particular desire to be in heaven, for if all the family of Christ are not there, my soul will be wretched and forlorn because of their sad loss, because I am in union with them all. If one soul that believed in Jesus does not get there, I shall lose respect for the promise and respect for the Master too; he must keep his word to every soul that rests on him. If your God has gone the length of actually preparing a place for his people and has made provision for them and been disappointed, he is no God to me, for I could not adore a disappointed God. I do not believe in such a God. Such a being would not be God at all. The notion of disappointment in his eternal preparations is not consistent with Deity. Talk thus of Jupiter and Venus if you please, but the infinite Jehovah is, as far as human speech can dishonor him, dishonored by being mentioned in such a connection. He has prepared a place for you. Here is personal election. He has made a distinct ordinance for every one of his people that where he is there shall they be.

"Prepared from before the foundation of the world." Here is eternal election appearing before men were created, preparing a crown before heads were made to wear it. And so God had before the starry skies began to gleam carried out the decree of election in a measure which when Christ shall come shall be perfected to the praise of the glory of his grace, "who worketh all things after the counsel of his will." Our portion then is one prepared from all eternity for us according to the election of God's grace, one suitable to the loftiest character to which we can ever attain, which will consist in nearness to Christ, communion with God, and standing forever in a place of dignity and happiness.

3. And now I have very little time to speak, as I hoped to have spoken this morning about *the persons who shall come there*.

They are recognizable by a secret and by a public character. Their *name* is "blessed of the Father"—the Father chose them, gave his Son for them, justified them through Christ, preserved them in Christ Jesus, adopted them into the family, and now accepted them into his own house. Their nature you have described in the word "inherit." None can inherit but sons; they have been born again, and have received the nature of God; having escaped the corruption which is in the world through lust, they have become partakers of the Divine nature: they are sons. Their appointment is mentioned; "inherit the kingdom prepared for you, from before the foundation of the world." Their name is "blessed," their nature is that of a child, their appointment is that of God's decree.

Their doings, their outward doings, these we want to speak a minute upon. They appear to have been distinguished among men for deeds of charity, and these were not in any way associated with ceremonies or outward observances. It is not said that they preached—they did so, some of them; it is not said that they prayed—they must have done so, or they would not have been spiritually alive. The actions which are selected as their type are actions of charity to the indigent and forlorn. Why these? I think, because *the general audience assembled around the throne would know how to appreciate this evidence of their newborn nature.* The King might think more of their prayers than of their alms, but the multitude would not. He speaks so as to gain the verdict of all assembled. Even their enemies could not object to his calling those blessed who had performed these actions; for if there be an action which wins for men the universal consent to their goodness, it is an action by which men would be served. Against this there is no law. I have never heard of a state in which there was a law against clothing the naked and feeding the hungry. Humanity at once, when its conscience is so seared that it cannot see its own sinfulness, yet detects the virtuousness of feeding the poor. Doubtless this is one reason why these actions were selected. And again, they may have been chosen as evidences of grace, because, *as actions, they are a wonderful means of separating between the hypocrite and the true Christian.* Dr. Gill has an idea, and perhaps he is right, that this is not a picture of the general judgment, but of the judgment of the professing church, and if so, it is all the more reasonable to conclude that these works of mercy are selected as the appropriate discerner between the hypocrite and the sincere. I fear that there are some of you high professors who could not stand the test. "Good praying people" they call you, but what do you give to the Lord? Your religion has not touched your pockets. This does not apply to some of you, for there are many here of whom I would venture to speak before the bar of God, that I know their substance to be consecrated to the Lord and his poor, and I have sometimes thought that beyond their means they have given both to the poor and to God's cause. But there are others of a very different disposition.

Now here I shall give you a little plain English talk which none can fail to understand. You may talk about your religion till you have worn your tongue out, and you may get others to believe you; and you may remain in the church twenty years, and nobody ever detect you in anything like an inconsistency; but, if it be in your power, and you do nothing to relieve the necessities of the poor members of Christ's body, you will be damned as surely as if you were drunkards or whoremongers. If you have no care for God's church this text applies to you, and will as surely sink you to the lowest hell as if you had been common blasphemers. That is very plain English, but it is the plain meaning of my text, and it is at my peril that I flinch from telling you of it. "I was an hungered, and you gave me"—what? Good advice; yes, but no meat. "I was thirsty, and you gave me"—what? A tract, and no drink. "I was naked, and you gave me"—what? Your good wishes, but no clothes. I was a stranger and—you pitied me, but—you took me not in. I was sick, you said you could recommend me a doctor, but you did not visit me. I was in prison, I, God's servant, a persecuted one, put in prison for Christ's sake, and you said I should be more cautious; but you did not stand by my side and take a share of the blame, and bear with me reproach for the truth's sake. You see this is a very terrible winnowing fan to some of you tightfisted ones whose main object is to get all you can and hold it fast, but it is a fan which frequently must be used. Whoever deceives you or spares you, by the grace of God, I will not, but will labor to be more bold than ever in denouncing sin. "Well," says one, "what are those to do who are so poor that they have nothing to give away?" My dear brother, do you notice how beautifully the text takes care of you? It hints that there are some who cannot give bread to the hungry, and clothes to the naked, but what about them? Why you see they are the persons spoken of as "my brethren," who receive the boon of kindness, so that this passage comforts the poor and by no means condemns them. Certain of us honestly give to the poor all we can spare, and then of course everybody comes to such; and when we say, "Really, I cannot give any more," somebody snarls and says, "Call yourself a Christian?" "Yes, I do, I should not call myself a Christian if I gave away other people's money; I should not call myself a Christian if I gave away what I have not got; I should call myself a thief, pretending to be charitable when I could not pay my debts." I have a very great pity indeed for those people who get into the bankruptcy court. I do not mean the debtors; I have seldom much sympathy with them. I have a good deal for the creditors who lose by having trusted dishonest people. If any man should say, "I will live beyond my means in order to get a good character," my dear brother, you begin wrong, that action is in itself wrong. What you have to give must be that which is your own. "But I shall have to pinch myself," says one, "if I do it." Well, pinch yourself! I do not think there is half the pleasure in doing good till you get to the pinching point. This remark of course applies only to those of us of moderate means, who can soon distribute our alms and get down to the pinch point. When you begin to feel, "Now, I must go without that; now I must curtail these in order to do more good." Oh! you cannot tell; it is then when you really can feel, "Now I have not given God merely the cheese parings and candle ends that I could not use, but I have really cut out for my Master a good piece of the loaf; I have not given him the old crusts that were getting moldy, but I have given him a piece of my own daily bread, and I am glad to do it, if I can show my love to Jesus Christ by denying myself." If you are doing this, if you are thus out of love to Jesus feeding the hungry, clothing the naked, I believe that these are put down as tests, because they are such blessed detectives between the hypocrites and the really godly people. When you read "for" here, you must not understand it to be that their reward is *because* of this, but that they are proved to be God's servants by this; and so, while they do not merit it because of these actions, yet these actions show that they were saved by grace, which is evidenced by the fact that Jesus Christ worked such and such works in them. If Christ does not work such things in you, you have no part in him; if you have not produced such works as these, you have not believed in Jesus. Now somebody says, "Then I intend to give to the poor in the future in order that I may have this reward." Ah, but you are very much mistaken if you do that.

The duke of Burgundy was waited upon by a poor man, a very loyal subject, who brought him a very large root which he had grown. He was a very poor man indeed, and every root he grew in his garden was of consequence to him; but merely as a loyal offering he brought to his prince the largest his little garden produced. The prince was so pleased with the man's evident loyalty and affection that he gave him a very large sum. The steward thought, "Well, I see this pays; this man has got fifty pounds for his large root, I think *I* shall make the duke a present." So he bought a horse and he reckoned that he should have in return ten times as much for it as it was worth, and he presented it with that view: the duke, like a wise man, quietly accepted the horse, and gave the greedy steward nothing. That was all. So you say, "Well, here is a Christian man, and he gets rewarded. He has been giving to the poor, helping the Lord's church, and see he is saved; the thing pays, I shall make a little investment." Yes, but you see the steward did not give the horse out of any idea of loyalty and kindness and love to the duke, but out of very great love to himself, and therefore had no return; and if you perform deeds of charity out of the idea of getting to heaven by them, why it is yourself that you are feeding, it is yourself that you are clothing; all your virtue is not virtue, it is rank selfishness, it smells strong of selfhood, and Christ will never accept it; you will never hear him say "thank you" for it. You served yourself, and no reward is due. You must first come to the Lord Jesus Christ, and look to him to save you; you will forever abjure all idea of doing anything to save yourself, and being saved, you will be able to give to the poor and so on without selfishness mixing with your motive, and you will get a reward of grace for the love token which you have given. It is necessary to believe in Christ in order to be capable of true virtue of the highest order. It is necessary to trust Jesus, and to be yourself fully saved, before there is any value in your feeding the hungry or clothing the naked. God give you grace to go to my Master wounded yonder, and to rest in the precious atonement which he has made for human sin; and when you have done that, being loved at such a rate, show that you love in return; being purchased so dearly, live for him that bought you; and among the actions by which you prove it, let these gleam and glisten like God-given jewels—the visiting of the sick, the comforting of the needy, the relieving of the distressed, and the helping of the weak. God accept these offerings as they come from gracious souls, and to him be praise evermore. Amen.

The Great White Throne

ༀ

Delivered on Sunday evening, August 12, 1866, at the Metropolitan Tabernacle, Newington. No. 710.

> *And I saw a great white throne, and him that sat on it, from whose face the earth and the heaven fled away; and there was found no place for them.*
> —REVELATION 20:11

Many of the visions which John saw are very obscure, and although a man who is assured of his own salvation may possibly be justified in spending his days in endeavoring to interpret them, yet I am sure of this, that it will not be a profitable task for unconverted persons. *They* have no time to spare for speculations, for they have not yet made sure of positive certainties. *They* need not dive into difficulties, for they have not yet laid a foundation of simplicities by faith in Christ Jesus. Better far to meditate upon the atonement than to be guessing at the little horn, and better far to know the Lord Jesus in his power to save than to fabricate an ingenious theory upon the number of the beast. But *this* particular vision is so instructive, so unattended by serious difficulties, that I may invite all here present to consider it, and the more so because it has to do with matters which concern our own eternal prospects. It may be, if God the Holy Spirit shall illuminate the eyes of our faith to look and see that "great white throne and him that sat upon it," that we may reap so much benefit from the sight as forever to make the arches of heaven ring with gratitude that we were brought in this world to look at the "great white throne," for by so doing we shall not be afraid to look upon it in the day when the Judge shall sit, and the quick and dead shall stand before him.

I shall, first, endeavor to explain what John saw; and then, in the second place, I shall try to set forth the effect which I think would be produced by this sight if the eyes of our faith should now be fixed thereon.

1. First, then, I have to call your very earnest attention to *what John saw.*

It was a scene of the last day, that wondrous day whose coming none can tell.

For, as a thief unheard, unseen, it steals
Through night's dark shade.

When the eagle-eyed seer of Patmos, being in the Spirit, looked aloft into the heavens, *he saw a throne,* from which I gather that there is a throne of moral government over the sons of men, and that he who sits upon it presides over all the inhabitants of this world. There is a throne whose dominion reaches from Adam in paradise down to "the last man," whoever he may be. We are not without a governor, lawgiver, and judge. This world is not left so that men may do in it as they will, without a legislator, without an avenger, without One to give reward or to inflict punishment. The sinner, in his blindness, looks, but he sees no throne; and therefore he cries, "I will live as I list, for there is none to call me to account"; but John, with illuminated eye, distinctly saw a throne, and a personal ruler upon it, who sat there to call his subjects to account. When our faith looks through the glass of revelation it sees a throne too. It were well for us if we felt more fully the influence of that everpresent throne. That "the Lord reigns" is true, believer, tonight, and true at all times. There is a throne whereon sits the King eternal, immortal, invisible; the world is governed by laws made and kept in force by an intelligent lawgiver. There is a moral governor. Men are accountable and will be brought to account at the last great day, when they shall all be either rewarded or punished. "I saw a great white throne." How this invests the actions of men with solemnity!

If we were left to do exactly as we willed without being called to account for it, it were wise even then to be virtuous, for rest assured it is best for ourselves that we should be good, and it is in itself malady enough to be evil. But we are not so left. There is a law laid down, to break which involves a penalty. There is a lawgiver who looks down and spies every action of man and who does not suffer one single word or deed to be omitted from his notebook. That governor is armed with power; he is soon coming to hold his assize, and every responsible agent upon the face of the earth must appear at his bar and receive, as we are told, "according to the deeds done in the body, whether they be good or whether they be evil." Let it, then, be gathered from the text that there is in very deed a personal and real moral governor of the world, an efficient and suitable ruler, not a mere name, not a myth, not an empty office, but a person who sits on the throne, who judges right, and who will carry out that judgment before long. Now, brethren and sisters, we know that this moral governor is God himself, who has an undisputed *right* to reign and rule. Some thrones have no right to be, and to revolt from them is patriotism; but the best lover of his race delights the most in the monarchy of heaven. Doubtless there are dynasties which are tyrannies, and governors who are despots; but none may dispute the right of God to sit upon the throne, or wish that another hand held the scepter. He created all, and shall he not judge all? He had a right, as Creator, to lay down his laws, and, as those laws are the very pattern of everything that is good and true, he had, therefore, because of this an eternal right to govern, in addition to the right which belonged to him as Creator. He is the Judge of all, who must do right from a necessity of his nature. Who else, then, should sit upon the throne, and who shall dare to claim to do so? He may cast down the gauntlet to all his creatures, and say, "I am God, and beside me there is none else;" if he reveals the thunder of his power, his creatures must silently own that he is Lord alone. None can venture to say that this throne is not founded upon right.

Moreover, there are some thrones on which the kings, however right, are deficient in *might,* but this is not the case with the King of kings. We constantly see little princes whose crowns fit their heads so ill that they cannot keep them on their brows; but our God has might invincible as well as right infallible. Who shall meet him in the battle? Shall the stubble defy the fire, or shall the wax make war with the flame? Jehovah can easily swallow up his enemies when they set themselves in battle array against him. "Behold he toucheth the hills, and they smoke; he looketh upon the mountains, and they tremble; he breaketh Leviathan in pieces in the depths of the sea. The winds are his chariots, and the tempests are his messengers. At his bidding there is day, and at his will night covereth the earth. Who shall stay his hand, or say unto him, 'What doest thou?'" His throne is founded in right and supported by might. You have justice and truth to settle it, but you have omnipotence and wisdom to be its guards, so that it cannot be moved.

In addition to this, his throne is one *from the power of which none can escape.* The sapphire throne of God, at this moment, is revealed in heaven, where adoring angels cast their crowns before it; and its power is felt on earth, where the works of creation praise the Lord. Even those who acknowledge not the divine government are compelled to feel it, for he does as he wills, not only among the angels in heaven, but among the inhabitants of this lower world. Hell feels the terror of that throne. Those chains of fire, those pangs unutterable, are the awful shadow of the throne of Deity; as God looks down upon the lost, the torment that flashes through their souls darts from his holiness, which cannot endure their sins. The influence of that throne, then, is found in every world where spirits dwell, and in the realms of inanimate nature it bears rule. Every leaf that fades in the trackless forest trembles at the Almighty's bidding, and every coral insect that dwells in the unfathomable depths of the sea feels and acknowledges the presence of the all-present King.

So, then, my brethren, if such is the throne which John saw, see how impossible it will be for you to escape from its judgment when the great day of assize shall be proclaimed, and the Judge shall issue his summons, bidding you appear. Where can the enemies of God flee? If up to heaven their high-flown impudence could carry them, his right hand of holiness would hurl them thence, or, if under hell's profoundest wave they dive, to seek a sheltering grave, his left hand would pluck them out of the fire, to expose them to the fiercer light of his countenance. Nowhere is there a refuge from the most High. The morning beams cannot convey the fugitive so swiftly as the almighty Pursuer could follow him; neither can the mysterious lightning flash, which annihilates time and space, journey so rapidly as to escape his far-reaching hand. "If I mount up to heaven, thou art there; if I make my bed in hell, thou art there." It was said of the Roman Empire under the Caesars that the whole world was only one great prison for Caesar, for if any man offended the emperor it was impossible for him to escape. If he crossed the Alps, could not Caesar find him out in Gaul? If he sought to hide himself in the Indies, even the swarthy monarchs there knew the power of the Roman arms, so that they would give no shelter to a man who had incurred imperial vengeance. And yet, perhaps, a fugitive from Rome might have prolonged his miserable life by hiding in the dens and caves of the earth. But O sinner, there is no hiding from God! The mountains cannot cover you from him, even if they would, neither can the rocks conceal you. See, then, at the very outset how this throne should awe our minds with terror. Founded in right, sustained by might, and universal in its dominion, look you and see the throne which John of old beheld.

This, however, is but the beginning of the vision. The text tells us that it was a "white throne," and I would call your attention to that. "I saw a great white throne." Why white? Does not this indicate its immaculate purity? There is no other white throne, I fear, to be found. The throne of our own happy land I believe to be as white and as pure as any throne might well be on earth, but there have been years, even in the annals of that throne, when it was stained with blood, and not many reigns back it was black with debauchery. Not always was it the throne of excellence and purity, and even now, though our throne possesses a lustrous purity, rare enough among earthly thrones, yet in the sight of God there must be in everything that is earthly something that is impure, and therefore the throne is not white to him. As for many other thrones that are still existing, we know that with them all is not white; this is neither the day nor the hour for us to call the princes to the bar of God, but there are some of them who will have much to answer for, because in their schemes of aggrandizement they took no account of the blood which would be shed, or of the rights which would be violated. Principle seldom moves the royal mind, but the knavish law of policy is the basis of kingcraft; a policy worthy of highwaymen and burglars, and some kings are little. On the continent of Europe, there are not a few thrones which I might describe as either black or crimson, as I think of the turpitude of the conduct of the monarch, or of the blood through which he has waded his way to dominion. But this is a great white throne, a throne of hallowed monarchy that is not stained with blood nor defiled with injustice.

Why, then, is it white for purity? Is it not because the King who sits on it is pure? Hark to the thrice-sacred hymn of the cherubic band and the seraphic choir, "Holy, holy, holy, Lord God of Sabaoth." Creatures who are perfectly spotless themselves unceasingly reverence and adore the yet superior holiness of the great King. He is too great to need to be unjust, and he is too good to be unkind. This King has done no wrong, and can do no wrong, but he is the only King of whom this can be said without fiction. He who sits on this white throne is himself the essence of holiness, justice, truth, and love. O fairest of all thrones! who would not be a willing subject of your peerless government?

Moreover, the throne is pure, because *the law the Judge dispenses is perfect.* There is no fault in the statute book of God. When the Lord shall come to judge the earth, there will be found no decree that bears too hardly upon any one of his creatures. "The statutes of the Lord are right"; they are true and righteous altogether. That book of the ten commands in which you find a summary of the divine will, who can improve it? Who can find anything in excess in it, or point out anything that is wanting? "The law of the Lord is perfect, converting the soul," and well may that be a white throne from which there emanates such a law. But you know that with a good law and a good lawgiver, yet sometimes the throne may make mistakes, and it may be stained by ignorance, if not by willful injustice. But the sentence which shall go forth from this great white throne, shall be so consistent with justice that even the condemned culprit himself must give his unwilling assent to it. "They stood speechless," it is said; speechless because they could neither bear the sentence nor in any way impugn it. It is a white throne, since never was a verdict delivered from it of which the culprit had a right to complain. Perhaps there are some here who view this as a matter of hope, but to ungodly persons it will be the very reverse. O sinner, if you had to be judged before an impure tribunal, you might, perhaps, escape; if the King were not holy, unholiness might, perhaps, go unpunished; if the law were not perfect, offenses might be condoned; or if the sentence were not just you might, through partiality, escape. But where everything is so pure and white,

> Careless sinner,
> What will there become of thee?

I have thought, too, that perhaps this throne is said to be a white throne to indicate that *it will be eminently conspicuous*. You will have noticed that a white object can be seen from a very great distance. You may have observed, perhaps, on the Welsh mountains, a white cottage far away, standing out conspicuously, for the Welsh like to make their cottages intensely white, so that though you would not have perceived it, had it been left of a stone color, you see it at once, for the bright whitewashed walls catch your eye. I suppose that a marksman would prefer a white object to aim at before almost any other color. And this great white throne will be so conspicuous that all the millions who were dead, but who shall rise at the sound of the last trumpet, shall all see it, nor shall it be possible for a single eye to close itself against the sight. We must see it; it shall be so striking a sight that none of us will be able to prevent its coming before us; "every eye *shall* see him."

Possibly it is called a white throne because of its being such a *convincing contrast to all the colors of this sinful human life*. There stand the crowd, and there is the great white throne. What can make them see their blackness more thoroughly than to stand there in contrast with the perfections of the law, and the Judge before whom they are standing? Perhaps that throne, all glistening, will reflect each man's character. As each unforgiven man shall look at that white throne, its dazzling whiteness will overcome him, and cover him with confusion and with terror when he sees his own defilement in contrast with it. "O God!" says he, "how can I bear to be judged by such a one as you are? I could face the judgment seat of my fellows, for I could see imperfections in my judges, but I cannot face you, you dread Supreme, for the awful whiteness of your throne, and the terrible splendor of your holiness utterly overcome me. Who am I, sinner as I am, that I should dare to stand before that great white throne?"

The next word that is used by way of adjective is "great." It was a "*great* white throne." You scarcely need me to tell you that it is called a great white throne because of the *greatness of him who sits upon it*. Speak of the greatness of Solomon? He was but a petty prince. Speak of the throne of the mogul or his celestial majesty of China, or of the thrones of Rome and Greece before which multitudes of beings assembled? They are nothing, mere representatives of associations of the grasshoppers of the world, who are as nothing in the sight of the Lord Jehovah. A throne filled by a mortal is but a shadow of dominion. This will be a great throne because on it will sit the great God of earth and heaven and hell, the King eternal, immortal, invisible, who shall judge the world in righteousness, and his people with equity. Brethren, you will see that this will be a "great white throne" when we remember *the culprits who will be brought before it*; not a handful of criminals, but millions upon millions, "multitudes, multitudes, in the Valley of Decision"; and these not all of the lesser sort, not serfs and slaves alone whose miserable bodies rested from their oppressors in the silent grave; but the great ones of the earth shall be there; not alone the downtrodden serf who toiled for nothing, and felt it sweet to die, but his tyrant master who fattened on his unrewarded toils shall be there; not alone the multitudes who marched to battle at their master's bidding, and who fell beneath the shot and the shell, but the emperors and kings who planned the conflict shall be there; crowned heads no greater than heads uncrowned. Men who were demigods among their fellows shall mix with their slaves, and be made as vile as they! What a marvelous procession! With what awe the imagination of it strikes the heart! What a pompous appearing! Aha! aha! you downtrodden multitudes, the great leveler has put you all upon a footing now! Death laid you in one equal grave, and now judgment finds you standing at one equal bar, to receive the sentence of one who fears no king, and dreads no tyrant, who has no respect of persons, but who deals justice alike to all. Can you picture the sight? Land and sea are covered with the living who once were dead. Hell is empty, and the grave has lost its victims! What a sight will that be! Xerxes on his throne with a million marching before him must have beheld a grand spectacle, but what will this be? No flaunting banner, but the ensigns of eternal majesty. No gaudy courtiers, but assembled angels! No sound of drum nor roar of culverin [cannon], but the blast of the archangel's trumpet, and the harping of ten thousand times ten thousand holy ones. There will be unrivaled splendor it is true, but not that of heraldry and war; mere tinsel and bauble shall have all departed, and in their place there shall be the splendor of the flashing lightning, and the deep bass of the thunder. Jesus the Man of sorrows, with all his angels with him shall descend, the pomp of heaven being revealed among the sons of men.

It will be a *great* white throne, because of *the matters that will be tried there.*
It will be no mere quarrel about a suit in chancery or an estate in jeopardy.
Our souls will have to be tried there; our future, not for an age, not for one
single century, but forever and forever. Upon those balances shall hang heaven
and hell; to the right shall be distributed triumph without end, to the left
destruction and confusion without a pause, and the destiny of every man and
woman shall be positively declared from that tremendous throne! Can you
perceive the greatness of it? You must measure heaven; you must fathom hell,
you must compass eternity, but until you can do this you cannot know the
greatness of this *great* white throne; great, last of all, because throughout
eternity there shall always be a looking back to the transactions of that day.
That day shall be unto you, you saints, "the beginning of days," when he shall
say, "Come, ye blessed of my Father." And that day shall be to you who perish the beginning of days too; just as that famous night of old in Egypt, when
the firstborn were spared in every house where the lamb had shed its blood,
was the first of days to Israel, but to Egypt the night when the firstborn felt
the avenging angel's sword was a dread beginning of nights forever. Many a
mother reckoned from that night when the destroyer came, and so shall you
reckon throughout a dread eternity from the day when you see this great
white throne.

Turn not away your eyes from the magnificent spectacle till you have seen
the glorious Person mentioned in the words, "And him that sat on it." I wonder whether anything I have said has made you solemnly to think of the great
day. I am afraid I cannot speak so as to get at your hearts, and if not I had better be silent; but do now for a moment think upon him who sat upon the great
white throne. The most fitting one in all the world will sit upon that throne.
It will be God, but hearken, it will also be man. "He shall judge the world by
this man. Christ Jesus, according to my gospel," says the apostle. The Judge
must needs be God. Who but God were fit to judge so many, and to judge so
exactly? The throne is too great for any but for him of whom it is written,
"Thy throne, O God, is forever and ever; a scepter of righteousness is thy
scepter." Christ Jesus, the Son of God, will judge, and he will judge as man as
well as God; and how fitting it is that it should be so! As man he knows our
infirmities, he understands our hearts, and we cannot object to this, that our
Judge should be himself like unto us. Who better could judge righteous judgment than one who is "bone of our bone and flesh of our flesh"? And then,
there is this fitness about it; he is not only God and man, but he is *the* man, the
man of men, of all men the most manly, the type and pattern of manhood.

He will be the test in his own person, for if a man be like Christ, that man is right, but if a man be otherwise than Christlike, that man deserves to be condemned. That wondrous Judge needs only look upon his own character to read the law, and to review his own actions to discern whether other men's actions be right or wrong. The thoughts of many hearts were revealed by Christ on earth, and that same Christ shall make an open exhibition of men at the last great day. He shall judge them, he shall discern their spirits, he shall find out the joints and the marrow of their being; the thoughts and intents of the heart he shall lay bare. Even you, believer, will pass the test before him; let no man deceive you with the delusion that you will not be judged: the sheep appeared before the great dividing Shepherd as well as the goats, those who used their talents were called to account as well as he who buried his pound, and the disciples themselves were warned that their idle words would bring them into judgment. Nor need you fear a public trial. Innocence courts the light. You are not saved by being allowed to be smuggled into heaven untested and unproved, but you will in the righteousness of Jesus pass the solemn test with joy. It may not be at the same moment as the wicked that the righteous shall be judged (I shall not contend for particulars), but I am clear that they will be judged, and that the blood and righteousness of Jesus are provided for this very cause, that they may find mercy of the Lord in *that* day. O sinner! It is far otherwise with you, for your ruin is sure when the testing time comes. There will be no witnesses needed to convict you, for the Judge knows all. The Christ whom you despised will judge you, the Savior whose mercy you trampled on, in the fountain of whose blood you would not wash, the despised and rejected of men—it is he who shall judge righteous judgment to you, and what will he say but this, "As for these mine enemies, who would not that I should reign over them, cut them in pieces before my eyes!"

2. I want a few minutes—and I have but too few left—*to draw the inferences which flow from such a sight as this,* and so turn the vision to practical account.

Believer in Christ, a word in your ear. Can you see the great white throne, and him that sits upon it? I think I see it now. Then, *let me search myself.* Whatever profession I may make, I shall have to face that great white throne. I have passed the elders; I have been approved by the pastor; I stand accepted by the church; but that great white throne is not passed yet. I have borne a reputable character among my fellow Christians; I have been asked to pray in public, and my prayers have been much admired, but I have not yet been weighed in the last balances, and what if I should be found wanting? Brother Christian, what about your private prayers? Can you live in neglect of the closet, and yet remember that your prayers will be tried before the great white throne? Is your Bible left unread in private? Is your religion nothing but a public show and sham? Remember the great white throne, for mere pretense will not pass there. Brother Christian, what about your heart and your treasure? Are you a mere money hunter? Do you live as others live? Is your delight in the fleeting present? Do you have dealings with the throne of heaven? Have you a stony heart toward divine things? Have you little love to Christ? Do you make an empty profession, and nothing more? Oh, think of that great white throne, that great white throne! Why, there are some of you, who, when I preach a stirring sermon, feel afraid to come again to hear me. Ah! but if you are afraid of my voice, how will you bear *his* voice who shall speak in tones of thunder? Do searching sermons seem to go through you like a blast of the north wind, chilling your very marrow and curdling your blood? Oh! but what must it be to stand before that dread tribunal? Are you doubting now? What will you be then? Can you not bear a little self-examination? How will you bear that God-examination? If the scales of earth tell you that you are wanting, what message will the scales of heaven give you? I do conjure you, fellow professors, speaking to you as I desire to speak now to my own heart, "Examine yourselves, whether you be in the faith; prove your own selves. Know you not your own selves, how that Jesus Christ is in you, except you be reprobates?"

Having spoken a word to the Christian, I should like to say to every one of you, in remembrance of this great white throne shun hypocrisy. Are you tempted to be baptized though you are not a believer, in order to please parents and friends? Beware of that great white throne, and consider how your insult to God will look at that great day! Are you persuaded to put on the cloak of religion because it will help your business, or make you seem respectable? Beware, you hypocrite, beware of that great white throne; for of all the terrors that shall come forth from it, there shall be none more severe than those which shall scathe the mere professor, who made a profession of religion for gain. If you must be damned, be damned anyhow sooner than as a hypocrite; for they deserve the deepest hell who for gain make a profession of godliness. The ruin of By-Ends and Hypocrisy will be just indeed. O you high-flying professors, whose wings are fastened on with wax, beware of the sun which will surely pour its heat upon you, for fearful will be your fall from so great a height!

But there are some of you who say, "I do not make any profession of religion." Still my text has a word to you. Still I want you to judge your actions by that last great day. O sir, how about that night of sin? "No," say you, "never mind it; bring it not to my remembrance." It shall be brought to your remembrance, and that deed of sin shall be published far wider than upon the housetops, gazetted to all the multitudes who have ever lived since the first man, and your infamy shall become a byword and a proverb among all created beings. What think you of this, you secret sinners? You lovers of wantonness and chambering? Ah! young man, you have commenced by filching, but you will go on to be a downright thief. It is known, sir, and "be sure your sin will find you out." Young woman, you have begun to dally with sin, and you think none has seen you, but the most mighty One has seen your acts and heard your words; there is no curtain between him and your sin. He sees you clearly, and what will you do with these sins of yours that you think have been concealed? "It was many years ago," you tell me. Yes, but though buried these many years to you, they are all alive to him, for everything is present to the all-seeing God; and your forgotten deeds shall one day stand out present to you also. My hearers, I conjure you do nothing which you would not do if you thought God saw you, for he does see you. Oh! look at your actions in the light of the judgment. Oh! that secret tippling of yours, how will that look when God reveals it? That private lust of yours which nobody knows of—how would you dare to do it if you recollected that God knows it? Young man, it is a secret, a fearful secret, and you would not whisper it in anyone's ear; but it shall be whispered, no, it shall be thundered out before the world! I pray you, friend, think of this. There is an observer who takes notes of all that we do, and will publish all to an assembled universe.

And as for us all, *are we ready to meet that last great day?* I had many things to say unto you, but I cannot keep you to say them now, lest you grow weary; but if tonight the trumpet should be sounded, what would be your state of mind? Suppose that now every ear in this place should be startled with a blast most loud and dread, and a voice were heard,

> *Come to judgment,*
> *Come to judgment, come away.*

Supposing some of you could hide in the vaults and in the foundations, would not many of you rush to the concealment? How few of us might go down these aisles walking steadily into the open air and saying, "I am not afraid of judgment, for 'there is therefore now no condemnation to them that are in Christ Jesus.'" Brethren and sisters, I hope there are some of us who could go gladly to that judgment seat, even if we had to traverse the jaws of death to reach it. I hope there are some of us who can sing in our hearts—

> *Bold shall I stand in that great day;*
> *For who aught to my charge shall lay?*
> *While, through thy blood, absolved I am*
> *From sin's tremendous curse and blame.*

It might put many of us much about to say that. It is easy to speak of full assurance, but, believe me, it is not quite so easy to have it in right down earnest in trying times. If some of you get the finger ache, your confidence oozes out at your joints, and if you have but a little sickness, you think, "Ah! it may be cholera, what shall I do?" Can you not bear to die, how then will you bear to live forever? Could you not look death in the face without a shudder, then how will you endure the judgment? Could you gaze upon death and feel that he is your friend and not your foe? Could you put a skull upon your dressing table and commune with it as your *memento mori*? Oh! it may well take the bravest of you to do this, and the only sure way is to come as we are to Jesus, with no righteousness of our own to trust to, but finding all in him. When William Carey was about to die, he ordered to have put upon his tombstone this verse—

> *A guilty, weak, and helpless worm,*
> *On Christ's kind arms I fall,*
> *He is my strength, my righteousness,*
> *My Jesus, and my all.*

I would like to wake up in eternity with such a verse as that in my mind, as I wish to go to sleep in this world with such a hope as that in my heart—

> *Nothing in my hand I bring,*
> *Simply to the cross I cling.*

Ah! I am talking about what some of us will know more of, perhaps, before this week is over. I am speaking now upon themes which you think are a long way off, but a moment may bring them near. A thousand years is a long time, but how soon it flies! One almost seems, in reading English history, to go back and shake hands with William the Conqueror; a few lives soon bring us even to the flood. You who are getting on to be forty years old, and especially you who are sixty or seventy, must feel how fast time flies. I only seem to preach a sermon one Sunday in time to get ready for the next. Time flies with such a whirl that no express train can overtake it, and even the lightning flash seems to lag behind it. We shall soon be at the great white throne; we shall soon be at the judgment bar of God. Oh! let us be making ready for it. Let us not live so much in this present, which is but a dream, an empty show, but let us live in the real, substantial future. Oh, that I could reach some heart here tonight! I have a notion that I am speaking to someone here who will not have another warning. I am sure that with such throngs as crowd here Sabbath after Sabbath, I never preach to the same congregation twice. There are always some here who are dead between one Sunday and another. Out of such masses as these it must be so according to the ordinary computation. Who among you will it be who will die this week? Oh! ponder the question well! Who among you will dwell with the devouring flames? Who among you will abide with everlasting burnings? If I knew you I would fain bedew you with tears. If I knew you who are to die this week, I would fain come and kneel down at your side, and conjure you to think of eternal things. But I do not know you, and therefore by the living God I do implore you all to fly to Jesus by faith. These are no trifles, sirs, are they? If they be, I am but a sorry trifler, and you may go your ways and laugh at me; but if they be true and real, it becomes me to be in earnest, and much more does it become you to be in earnest. "Prepare to meet your God!" He comes! Prepare now! "Now is the accepted time; now is the day of salvation!" The gates of mercy are not closed. Your sin is not unpardonable. You may yet find mercy. Christ invites you. His blood drops cry to you—

> Come and welcome,
> Come and welcome, sinner come.

Oh! may the Holy Spirit put life into these poor words of mine, and may the Lord help you to come now. The way to come, you know, is just to trust in Christ. It is all done when you trust in Christ, throw yourselves right on him, having nothing else to trust to. See now, my whole weight leans on the front of this platform. Should this rail give way, I fall. Lean on Christ just in that way.

> Venture on him, venture wholly,
> Let no other trust intrude.

If you can get a grip of the cross, and stand there beneath the crimson canopy of the atonement, God himself cannot smite you, and the last tremendous day shall dawn upon you with splendor and delight, and not with gloom and terror.

I must send you away, but not until all believers present have given you an invitation to return to the Lord Jesus. To do this we will sing the following verses—

> Return, O wanderer, to thy home.
> Thy Father calls for thee;
> No longer now an exile roam
> In guilt and misery;
> Return, return.

> Return, O wanderer, to thy home,
> 'Tis Jesus calls for thee:
> The Spirit and the bride say, Come;
> Oh, now for refuge flee;
> Return, return.

> Return, O wanderer, to thy home,
> 'Tis madness to delay;
> There are no pardons in the tomb,
> And brief is mercy's day.
> Return, return.

The Great Assize

Delivered on Lord's Day evening, August 25, 1872, at the Metropolitan Tabernacle, Newington. No. 1076.

For we must all appear before the judgment seat of Christ; that everyone may receive the things done in his body, according to that he hath done, whether it be good or bad. —2 CORINTHIANS 5:10

This morning we preached concerning the resurrection of the dead, and it seems consistent with order to carry forward our thoughts this evening, to that which follows immediately after the resurrection, namely, the general judgment; for the dead rise on purpose that they may be judged in their bodies. The resurrection is the immediate prelude to the judgment. There is no need that I try to prove to you from Scripture that there will be a general judgment, for the Word of God abounds with proof passages. You have them in the Old Testament. You find David anticipating that great assize in the Psalms (especially in such as the forty-ninth and fiftieth, the ninety-sixth Psalm, and the three that follow it), for most assuredly the Lord comes: he comes to judge the earth in righteousness. Very solemnly and very tenderly does Solomon in the Ecclesiastes warn the young man, that, let him rejoice as he may and cheer his heart in the days of his youth, for all these things God will bring him into judgment; for God will judge every secret thing. Daniel in the night visions beholds the Son of man coming with the clouds of heaven and drawing near to the Ancient of Days; then he sits upon the throne of judgment and the nations are gathered before him. It was no new doctrine to the Jews; it was received and accepted by them as a most certain fact that there would be a day in which God would judge the earth in righteousness. The New Testament is very express. The twenty-fifth of Matthew, which we read to you just now, contains language, which could not possibly be more clear and definite, from the lips of the Savior himself. He is the faithful Witness and cannot lie. You are told that before him will be gathered all nations, and he shall divide them the one from the other, as the shepherd divides the sheep from the goats. Other passages there are in abundance, as, for instance, the one that is now before us, which is plain enough. Another we might quote is in the Second Epistle to the Thessalonians, the first chapter, from the seventh to the tenth verse. Let us read it, "And to you who are troubled rest with us, when the Lord Jesus shall be revealed from heaven with his mighty angels, in flaming fire taking vengeance on them that know not God, and that obey not the gospel of our Lord Jesus Christ: who shall be punished with everlasting destruction from the presence of the Lord, and from the glory of his power; when he shall come to be glorified in his saints, and to be admired in all them that believe (because our testimony among you was believed) in that day."

The book of the Revelation is very graphic in its depicting that last general judgment. Turn to the twentieth chapter, at the eleventh and twelfth verses. The seer of Patmos says, "And I saw a great white throne, and him that sat on it, from whose face the earth and the heaven fled away; and there was found no place for them. And I saw the dead, small and great, stand before God; and the books were opened: and another book was opened, which is the book of life: and the dead were judged out of those things which were written in the books, according to their works." Time would fail me to refer you to all the Scriptures. It is asserted over and over again by the Holy Spirit, whose word is truth, that there will be a judgment of the quick and of the dead.

Beside that direct testimony, it should be remembered there is a cogent argument that so it must needs be, from the very fact that God is just as the ruler over men. In all human governments there must be an assize held. Government cannot be conducted without its days of session and of trial, and, inasmuch as there is evidently sin and evil in this world, it might fairly be anticipated that there would be a time when God will go on circuit, and when he will call the prisoners before him, and the guilty shall receive their condemnation. Judge for yourselves: is this present state the conclusion of all things? If so, what evidence would you adduce of the divine justice, in the teeth of the fact that the best of men are often in this world the poorest and the most afflicted, while the worst of men acquire wealth, practice oppression, and receive homage from the crowd? Who are they that ride in the high places of the earth? Are they not those, great transgressors, who "wade through slaughter to a throne and shut the gates of mercy on mankind"? Where are the servants of God? They are in obscurity and suffering full often. Do they not sit like Job among the ashes, subjects of little pity, objects of much upbraiding? And where are the enemies of God? Do not many of them wear purple and fine linen and fare sumptuously every day? If there be no hereafter, then Dives has the best of it; and the selfish man who fears not God is, after all, the wisest of men and more to be commended than his fellows. But it cannot be so. Our common sense revolts against the thought. There must be another state in which these anomalies will all be rectified. "If in this life only we have hope in Christ, we are of all men the most miserable," says the apostle. The best of men were driven to the worst of straits in those persecuting times for being God's servants. How say you then, *Finis coronat opus*, the end crowns the work? That cannot be the final issue of life, or justice itself were frustrated. There must be a restitution for those who suffer unjustly: there must be a punishment for the wicked and the oppressor.

Not only may this be affirmed from a general sense of justice, but there is in the conscience of most men, if not of all, an assent to this fact. As an old Puritan says, "God holds a petty session in every man's conscience, which is the earnest of the assize which he will hold by and by; for almost all men judge themselves, and their conscience knows this to be wrong and that to be right. I say 'almost all,' for there seems to be in this generation a race of men who have so stultified their conscience that the spark appears to have gone out, and they put bitter for sweet and sweet for bitter. The lie they seem to approve, but the truth they do not recognize. But let conscience alone and do not stupify her, and you shall find her bearing witness that there is a Judge of all the earth who must do right." Now this is peculiarly the case when conscience is allowed full play. Men who are busy about their work or entertained with their pleasures often keep their consciences quiet. As John Bunyan puts it, they shut up Mr. Conscience; they blind his windows; they barricade his doors; and as for the great bell on the top of the house, which the old gentleman was inclined to ring, they cut the rope of it, so that he cannot get at it, for they do not wish him to disturb the town of Mansoul. But when death comes, it often happens that Mr. Conscience escapes from his prison house, and then, I warrant you, he will make such a din that there is not a sleeping head in all Mansoul. He will cry out and avenge himself for his constrained silence, and make the man know that there is a something within him not quite dead, which cries out still for justice, and that sin cannot go unchastised. There must be a judgment, then. Scripture asserts it, that would be enough: but by way of collateral evidence the natural order of things requires it; and conscience attests it.

Now we come to consider what our text says about the judgment. I pray you, brethren, if I should speak coldly tonight on this momentous truth, or fail to excite your attention and stir your deepest emotions, forgive me, sirs; and may God forgive me, for I shall have good reason to ask God's forgiveness, seeing that if ever a topic should arouse the preacher to a zeal for the honor of his Lord and for the welfare of his fellow creatures, and so make him doubly in earnest, it is this. But, then, permit me to say, that, if ever there was a theme quite independent of the speaker, which on its own account alone should command your thoughtfulness, it is that which I now bring before you. I feel no need of oratory or of speech well selected: the bare mention of the fact that such a judgment is impending, and will before long occur, might well hold you in breathless silence, still the very throbbings of your pulse, and choke the utterance of my lips. The certainty of it, the reality of it, the terrors that accompany it, the impossibility of escaping from it, all appeal to us now and demand our vigilance.

1. Ask now, *who is it,* or *who are they that will have to appear before the throne of judgment?*

The answer is plain; it admits of no exemption: "We must *all* appear before the judgment seat of Christ." This is very decisive, if there were no other text. We must all appear; that is to say, every one of the human race. We must all appear. And that the godly will not be exempted from this appearance is very clear, for the apostle here is speaking to Christians. He says, "We walk by faith, not by sight. We are confident. We labor," and so on; and then he puts it, "We must all appear." So that, beyond all others, it is certain that all Christians must appear there. The text is quite conclusive upon that point. And if we had not that text, we have the passage in Matthew, which we have read, in which the sheep are summoned there as certainly as are the goats; and the passage in the Revelation, where all the dead are judged according to the things which are written in the books. They are all there. And if the objection should be raised, "We thought that the sins of the righteous being pardoned, and forever blotted out, they could never come into judgment," we have only to remind you, beloved, that if they are so pardoned and blotted out, as they undoubtedly are, the righteous have no reason to fear coming into judgment. They are the persons who covet the judgment, and will be able to stand there to receive a public acquittal from the mouth of the great Judge. Who among us wishes, as it were, to be smuggled into heaven unlawfully? Who desires to have it said by the damned in hell, "You were never tried, or else you might have been condemned as we were." No, brethren, we have a hope that we can stand the trial. The way of righteousness by Christ Jesus enables us to submit ourselves to the most tremendous tests which even that burning day can bring forth. We are not afraid to be put into the balances. We even desire that day when our faith in Jesus Christ is strong and firm; for we say, "Who is he that condemns?" We can challenge the day of judgment. Who is he that shall lay anything to our charge in that day, or at any other, since Christ has died and has risen again? It is needful that the righteous should be there that there may not be any partiality in the matter whatever; that the thing may be all clear and straight, and that the rewards of the righteous may be seen to be, though of grace, yet without any violation of the most rigorous justice. Dear brethren, what a day it will be for the righteous! For some of them were—perhaps some here present are—lying under some very terrible accusation of which they are perfectly guiltless. All will be cleared up then, and that will be one great blessing of that day. There will be a resurrection of reputations as well as of bodies. Men call the righteous, fools: then shall they shine forth as the sun in the kingdom of their Father. They hounded them to death, as not being fit to live. In early ages they laid to the Christians charges of the most terrible character, which I should count it shame to mention. But then they will all be clear; and those of whom the world was not worthy, who were driven and hunted about and made to dwell in the caves of the earth, they shall come forth as worthy ones, and the world shall know her true aristocracy, earth shall own her true nobility. The men whose names she cast out as evil shall then be held in great repute, for they shall stand out clear and transparent without spot or blemish. It is well that there should be a trial for the righteous, for the clearing of them, the vindication of them, and that it should be public, defying the cavil and criticism of all mankind.

"We must *all* appear." What a vast assembly, what a prodigious gathering, that of the entire human race! It struck me as I was meditating upon this subject, what would be the thoughts of Father Adam, as he stood there with Mother Eve and looked upon his offspring. It will be the first time in which he has ever had the opportunity of seeing all his children met together. What a sight will he then behold—far stretching, covering all the globe which they inhabit, enough not only to people all earth's plains, but crown her hilltops, and cover even the waves of the sea, so numberless must the human race have been, if all the generations that have ever lived, or shall ever live, shall at once rise from the dead! Oh, what a sight will that be! Is it too marvelous for our imagination to picture? Yet it is quite certain that the assemblage will be mustered, and the spectacle will be beheld. Everyone from before the flood, from the days of the patriarchs, from the times of David, from the Babylonian kingdom, all the legions of Assyria, all the hosts of Persia, all the phalanx of the Greeks, all the vast armies and legions of Rome, the barbarian, the Scythian, the bond, the free, men of every color and of every tongue—they shall all stand in that great day before the judgment seat of Christ. There come the kings—no greater than the men they call their slaves. There come the princes—but they have doffed their coronets, for they must stand like common flesh and blood. Here come the judges, to be judged themselves, and the advocates and barristers, needing an advocate on their own account. Here come those that thought themselves too good, and kept the street to themselves. There are the Pharisees, hustled by the publicans on either side and sunk down to the natural level with them. Mark the peasants rising from the soil; see the teeming myriads from outside the great cities streaming in, countless hosts such as no Alexander or Napoleon ever beheld! See how the servant is as great as his master! "Liberty, Equality, Fraternity" are now proclaimed. No kings, no princes, no nobles, can shelter themselves behind their order, assert a privilege or claim an immunity. Alike on one common level they stand together, to be tried before the last tremendous tribunal. There shall come the wicked of every sort. Proud Pharaoh shall be there; Sennacherib, the haughty; Herod, that would have slain the young child; Judas, that betrayed his Master; Demas, that sold him for gold; and Pilate, who would fain have washed his hands in innocence. There shall come the long list of infallibles, the whole line of popes, to receive their damnation at the Almighty's hands, and the priests that trod upon the necks of nations, and the tyrants that used the priests as their tools—they shall come to receive the thunderbolts of God which they so richly deserve. Oh, what a scene will it be! These little companies, which look to us so large when they are gathered together beneath this roof, how do they shrink into the drop of a bucket as compared with the ocean of life that shall swell around the throne at the last great judgment day. They shall all be there.

Now, the most important thought connected with this to me is that I shall be there; to you young men, that you will be there; to you, you aged of every sort, that you, *in propria persona*—each one shall be there. Are you rich? Your dainty dress shall be put off. Are you poor? Your rags shall not exempt you from attendance at that court. None shall say, "I am too obscure." You must come up from that hiding place. None shall say, "I am too public." You must come down from that pedestal. Everyone must be there. Note the word "we." "*We* must all appear."

And still further note the word "appear." "We must all *appear*." No disguise will be possible. You cannot come there dressed in masquerade of profession or attired in robes of state, but we must *appear*; we must be seen through, must be displayed, must be revealed; off will come your garments, and your spirit will be judged of God, not after appearance, but according to the inward heart. Oh, what a day that will be when every man shall see himself, and every man shall see his fellow, and the eyes of angels and the eyes of devils, and the eyes of God upon the throne, shall see us through and through. Let these thoughts dwell upon your minds, while you take this for the answer to our first inquiry, who is to be judged?

2. Our second question is, *who will be the Judge?*

"We must all appear before the judgment seat of Christ." That Christ should be appointed judge of all mankind is most proper and fitting. Our British law ordains that a man shall be tried by his peers, and there is justice in the statute. Now the Lord God will judge men, but at the same time it will be in the person of Jesus Christ the man. Men shall be judged by a man. He that was once judged by men shall judge men. Jesus knows what man should be; he has been under the law himself in deep humility, who is ordained to administer the law in high authority. He can hold the scales of justice evenly, for he has stood in man's place and borne and braved man's temptations; he therefore is the most fit judge that could be selected. I have sometimes heard and read sermons in which the preacher said that a Christian ought to rejoice that his Judge is his friend. There may be no impropriety intended, still it seems to me rather a questionable suggestion. I should not like to put it in that way myself; because any judge that was partial to his friends when he sat on the judgment seat would deserve to come off the seat immediately. As a judge I expect no favoritism from Christ. I expect when he sits there he will deal out evenhanded justice to all. I cannot see how it is right for any minister to hold it forth that we should find encouragement in the Judge being our friend. Friend or no friend, we shall go in for a fair trial every one of us, and Christ will not be a respecter of persons. Of him whom God has appointed to judge the world, it shall not be said when the assize is over that he winked at the crimes of some and extenuated them, while he searched out the faults of others and convicted them. He will be fair and upright throughout. He is our friend, I grant you, and he will be our friend and Savior forever; but, as a judge, we must keep to the thought, and believe and maintain it that he will be impartial to all the sons of men. You will have a fair trial, man. He that will judge you will not take sides against you. We have sometimes thought that men have been shielded from the punishment they deserved, because they were of a certain clerical profession, or because they occupied a certain official position. A poor laborer who kills his wife shall be hanged, but when another man of superior station does the like deed of violence, and stains his hands with the blood of her whom he had vowed to love and cherish, the capital sentence shall not be executed upon him. Everywhere we see in the world that with the best intentions justice somehow or other does squint a little. Even in this country there is just the slightest possible turning of the scale, and God grant that may be cured before long. I do not think it is intentional, and I hope the nation will not long have to complain about it. There ought to be the same

justice for the poorest beggar that crawls into a casual ward, as for his lordship
that owns the broadest acres in all England. Before the law, at least, all men
ought to stand equal. So shall it be with the Judge of all the earth. *Fiat justitia,
ruat caelum.* Christ will by all means hold the scales even. You shall have a fair
trial and a full trial too. There shall be no concealment of anything in your
favor, and no keeping back of anything against you. No witnesses shall be
borne across the sea to keep them out of the way. They shall all be there, and
all testimony shall be there, and all that is wanted to condemn or to acquit
shall be produced in full court at that trial, and hence it will be a final trial.
From that court there will be no appeal. If Christ says, "Cursed!" cursed must
they be forever. If Christ says, "Blessed!" blessed shall they be forever. Well,
this is what we have to expect then, to stand before the throne of the man
Christ Jesus the Son of God, and there to be judged.

3. Now the third point is, *what will be the rule of judgment?*

The text says "that everyone may receive the things done in his body
according to that he hath done, whether it be good or bad." Then it would
appear that our *actions* will be taken in evidence at the last. Not our profession,
not our boastings, but our actions will be taken in evidence at the last, and
every man shall receive according to what he has done in the body. That implies
that everything done by us in this body will be known. It is all recorded; it will
be all brought to light. Hence, in that day every secret sin will be published.
What was done in the chamber, what was hidden by the darkness, shall be
published as upon the housetop—every secret thing. With great care you have
concealed it, most dexterously you have covered it up; but it shall be brought
out to your own astonishment to form a part of your judgment. There, hypocritical actions as well as secret sins will be laid bare. The Pharisee who
devoured the widow's house and made a long prayer will find that widow's
house brought against him and the long prayer too, for the long prayer will
then be understood as having been a long lie against God from beginning to
end. Oh, how fine we can make some things look with the aid of paint and
varnish and gilt; but at the last day off will come the varnish and veneer, and
the true metal, the real substance, will then be seen.

When it is said that everything that is done in the body will be brought up
as evidence against us or for us, remember this includes every omission as well
as every commission; for that which is not done that ought to have been done
is as greatly sinful as the doing of that which ought not to be done. Did not
you notice when we were reading that twenty-fifth chapter of Matthew, how
those on the left hand were condemned, not for what they did, but for what

they did not do: "I was an hungered, and you gave me no meat: I was thirsty, and you gave me no drink." Where would some of you stand, according to this rule, who have lived in neglect of holiness, and neglect of faith, and neglect of repentance, before all your days? Consider yourselves, I pray you.

Recollect, too, that all our words will be brought up. For every idle word that man shall speak he will have to give an account. And all our thoughts too, for these lie at the bottom of our actions and give the true color to them good or bad. Our motives, our heart sins, especially, our hatred of Christ, our neglect of the gospel, our unbelief—all of these shall be read aloud and published unreservedly. "Well," says one, "who then can be saved?" Ah! indeed, who then can be saved! Let me tell you who. There will come forward those who have believed in Jesus, and albeit they have many sins to which they might well plead guilty, they will be able to say, "Great God, you did provide for us a substitute, and you did say that if we would accept him he should be a substitute for us and take our sins upon himself, and we did accept him and our sins were laid on him, and we have now no sins; they have been transferred from us to the great Savior, substitute and sacrifice." And in that day there will be none who can put in a demurrer to that plea: it will hold good; for God has said, "Whosoever believeth on Christ Jesus shall never be condemned." Then will the actions of the righteous, the gracious actions, be brought forth to prove that they had faith. For that faith which never evidences itself by good works is a dead faith and a faith that will never save a soul. Now, if the dying thief were brought up, he would say, "My sins were laid on Jesus." "Yes, but how about your good works? You must have some evidence of your faith," Satan might reply. Then would the recording angel say, "The dying thief said to his fellow thief who was dying with him, 'Wherefore are you railing?' In his last moments he did what he could: he rebuked the thief that was dying with him and made a good confession of his Lord. There was the evidence of the sincerity of his faith." Dear hearer, will there be any evidence of the sincerity of your faith? If your faith has no evidence before the Lord, what will you do? Suppose you thought you had a faith and went on drinking. Suppose you did as I know some have done here, go straight from this place into the public house? Or suppose you joined the Christian church and remained a drunkard? Yes, and women have done that also as well as men. Suppose you professed to have faith in Christ and yet cheated in your weights and measures and common dealings? Do you think that God will never require these things at your hands? O sirs, if you be no better than other men in your conduct, you *are* no better than other men in your character, and you will stand no better than other men in the judgment day. If your actions are not superior to theirs, you may profess what you will about your faith, but you are deceived, and, as deceivers, you will be discovered at the last great day. If grace does not make us differ from other men, it is not the grace which God gives his elect. We are not perfect, but all God's saints keep their eyes on the great standard of perfection, and, with strong desire, aim to walk worthy of their high calling of God and to bring forth works which prove that they love God; and if we have not these signs following faith, or if they are not put in as evidence for us, at the last great day we shall not be able to prove our faith. O you who have no faith in Christ, no faith in Jesus the substitute; that terrible negative, that treacherous unbelief of yours, will be a condemning sin against you! It will be proof positive that you hated God; for a man must hate God indeed who will spurn his counsels, give no heed to his reproof, scorn his grace, and dare the vengeance of him who points out the way of escape and the path that leads to life. He that will not be saved by God's mercy proves that he hates the God of mercy. If God gives his own Son to die and men will not trust in his Son, will not have him as their Savior, that one sin, if they had no other, would at once prove that they were enemies of God and black at heart. But if your faith be in Jesus, if you love Jesus, if your heart goes out to Jesus, if your life be influenced by Jesus, if you make him your example as well as your Savior, there will be evidence—you cannot see it, but there will be evidence—in your favor. For notice those gracious things, when the evidence was brought, and Christ said, "I was an hungered, and ye gave me meat—thirsty, and ye gave me drink," they said, "O Lord, we never knew this." Should any man stand up here and say, "I have plenty of evidence to prove my faith," I should reply, "Hold your tongue, sir! Hold your tongue! I am afraid you have no faith at all, or you would not be talking about your evidence." But if you are saying, "Oh, I am afraid I have not the evidence that will stand me in good stead at the last," yet if all the while you have been feeding the hungry, and clothing the naked, and doing all you can for Christ, I would tell you not to be afraid. The Master will find witnesses to say, "That man relieved me when I was in poverty. He knew I was one of Christ's and he came and helped me." And another will come and say (perhaps it will be an angel), "I saw him when he was alone in his chamber and heard him pray for his enemies." And the Lord will say, "I read his heart when I saw how he put up with rebuke, and slander, and persecution, and would not make any answer for my sake. He did it all as evidence that my grace was in his heart." You will not have to fetch up the witnesses: the Judge will call them, for he knows all about your case; and as he calls up the witnesses, you will be surprised to find how even the ungodly will be obliged to consent to the just salvation of the righteous. Oh, how the secret deeds and the true heart sincerity of the righteous, when thus unveiled, will make devils bite their tongues in wrath to think that there was so much of grace given to the sons of men, with which to defeat persecution, to overcome temptation, and to follow on in obedience to the Lord. Oh yes, the deeds, the deeds, the deeds of men—not their prating, not their profession, not their talk, but their deeds (though nobody shall be saved by the merits of his deeds)—their deeds shall be the evidence of their grace, or their deeds shall be the evidence of their unbelief; and so, by their works shall they stand before the Lord, or by their works shall they be condemned as evidence and nothing more.

4. Now the last point is this: *What is the object of this judgment?*

Will sentence of acquittal and condemnation be given, and then the whole thing be over? Far from it. The judgment is with a view to the thereafter—"That every man may receive the things done in his body." The Lord will grant unto his people an abundant reward for all that they have done. Not that they deserve any reward, but that God first gave them grace to do good works, then took their good works as evidence of a renewed heart, and then gave them a reward for what they had done. Oh, what a bliss it will be to hear it said, "Well done, good and faithful servant"—to you that have worked for Christ when nobody knew it, to find that Christ took stock of it all—to you that served the Lord under misrepresentation, to find that the Lord Jesus cleared the chaff away from the wheat, and knew that you were one of his precious ones. For him, then, to say, "Enter into the joy of thy Lord," oh, what a bliss will it be to you.

But to the ungodly how terrible. They are to receive the things that they have done; that is to say, the punishment due—not every man alike, but the greater sinner the greater doom; to the man who sinned against light a greater damnation than to the man who had not the same light—Sodom and Gomorrah their place, Tyre and Sidon their place, and then to Capernaum and Bethsaida their place of more intolerable torment, because they had the gospel and rejected it—so the Lord himself tells us. And the punishment will not only be meted out in proportion to the transgression, but it will be a development of the evil actions done in the evil consequences to be endured, as every man shall eat the fruit of his own ways. Sin, after the natural order, ripens into sorrow. This is not a blind fate, but it is the operation of a divine law, wise and invariable. Oh, how dreadful it will be for the malicious man to have forever to gnaw his own envious heart, to find his malice come home to him, as birds come home to roost, to hoot for forever in his own soul; for the lustful man to feel lust burning in every vein, which he can never gratify; for the drunkard to have a thirst, which not even a drop of water can allay; for the glutton who has fared sumptuously every day to be in hunger perpetually; and the soul that has been wrathful to be forever wrathful, with the fire of wrath forever burning like a volcano in his soul; and the rebel against God forever a rebel, cursing God whom he cannot touch, and finding his curses come back upon himself. There is no punishment worse than for a man who is sinfully disposed to gratify his lusts, to satiate his bad propensities, and to multiply and fatten his vices. Only let men grow into what they would be, and then see what they would be like! Take away the policemen in some parts of London, and give the people plenty of money, and let them do just as they like. Last Saturday, it may be, there were half a dozen broken heads, and wives and children were in one general skirmish. Keep those people together: let their vigor continue unimpaired by age or decay, while they keep on developing their characters. Why, they would be worse than a herd of tigers. Let them give way to their rage and anger, with nothing to check their passions; let miserly, greedy people forever go on with their greed. It makes them miserable here, but let these things be indulged in forever, and what worse hell do you want? Oh, sin is hell and holiness is heaven. Men will receive the things done in their body. If God has made them love him, they shall go on to love him; if God has made them trust him, they shall go on to trust in him; if God has made them to be like Christ, they shall go on to be like Christ, and they shall receive the things done in their body as a reward; but if a man has lived in sin, "he that is filthy shall be filthy still"; he that has been unbelieving shall be unbelieving still. This, then, shall be the worm that never dies, and the fire which never shall be quenched, to which shall be added the wrath of God forever and forever. Oh, that we may have grace every one of us to flee to Christ! There is our only safety. Simple faith in Jesus is the basis for the character which will evidence at last that you are chosen of God. A simple belief in the merit of the Lord Jesus, worked in us by the Holy Ghost, is the rocky foundation upon which shall be built up, by the same divine hands, the character which shall evidence that the kingdom was prepared for us from before the foundations of the world. God work in us such a character, for Christ's sake. Amen.

Jesus Admired in Them That Believe

Delivered on Lord's Day morning, June 1, 1879, at the Metropolitan Tabernacle, Newington. No. 1477.

> *When he shall come to be glorified in his saints, and to be admired in all them that believe (because our testimony among you was believed) in that day.*
> —2 THESSALONIANS 1:10

What a difference between the first and second comings of our Lord! When he shall come a second time it will be to be glorified and admired, but when he came the first time it was to be despised and rejected of men. He comes a second time to reign with unexampled splendor, but the first time he came to die in circumstances of shame and sorrow. Lift up your eyes, you sons of light, and anticipate the change, which will be as great for you as for your Lord; for now you are hidden even as he was hidden, and misunderstood even as he was misunderstood when he walked among the sons of men. "We know that, when he shall appear, we shall be like him; for we shall see him as he is." His manifestation will be our manifestation, and in the day in which he is revealed in glory then shall his saints be glorified with him.

Observe that our Lord is spoken of as coming in his glory, and as at the same time taking vengeance in flaming fire on them that know not God, and that obey not the gospel. This is a note of great terror to all those who are ignorant of God, and wickedly unbelieving concerning his Christ. Let them take heed, for the Lord will gain glory by the overthrow of his enemies, and those who would not bow before him cheerfully shall be compelled to bow before him abjectly: they shall crouch at his feet, they should lick the dust in terror, and at the glance of his eyes they shall utterly wither away, as it is written, they "shall be punished with everlasting destruction from the presence of the Lord, and from the glory of his power." But this is not the main object for which Christ will come, nor is this the matter in which he finds his chief glory, for, observe, he does this as it were by the way, when he comes for another purpose. To destroy the wicked is a matter of necessity in which his spirit takes no delight, for he does this, according to the text, not so much when he comes to do it as when he shall come with another object, namely, "to be glorified in his saints, and to be admired in them that believe."

The crowning honor of Christ will be seen in his people, and this is the design with which he will return to this earth in the latter days, that he may be illustrious in his saints and exceedingly magnified in them. Even now his saints glorify him. When they walk in holiness they do, as it were, reflect his light; their holy deeds are beams from him who is the Sun of righteousness. When they believe in him they also glorify him, for there is no grace which pays lowlier homage at the throne of Jesus than the grace of faith whereby we trust him, and so confess him to be our all in all. We do glorify our gracious Lord, but, beloved brethren, we must all confess that we do not this as we could desire, for, alas, too often we dishonor him, and grieve his Holy Spirit. By our want of zeal and by our many sins we are guilty of discrediting his gospel and dishonoring his name. Happy, happy, happy day when this shall no more be possible, when we shall be rid of the inward corruption which now works itself into outward sin, and shall never dishonor Christ again, but shall shine with a clear, pure radiance, like the moon on the Passover night, when it looks the sun full in the face, and then shines upon the earth at her best. Today we are like vessels on the wheel, but half fashioned, yet even now somewhat of his divine skill is seen in us as his handiwork. Still the unformed clay is in part seen, and much remains to be done; how much more of the great Potter's creating wisdom and sanctifying power will be displayed when we shall be the perfect products of his hand! In the bud and germ our new nature brings honor to its Author; it will do far more when its perfection manifests the Finisher. Then shall Jesus be glorified and admired in every one of us when the days of the new creation are ended and God shall usher in the eternal Sabbath by pronouncing his grace work to be very good.

This morning, as God shall help me, I shall speak first of *the special glorification of Christ here intended*: and, second, I shall conclude the sermon by calling your attention to *the special considerations which this grand truth suggests*.

1. Let us consider carefully *the special glorification here intended.*

And the first point to note is *the time*. The text says, "When he shall come to be glorified in his saints." The full glorification of Christ in his saints will be when he shall come a second time, according to the sure word of prophecy. He is glorified in them now, for he says, "All mine are thine, and thine are mine; and I am glorified in them"; but as yet that glory is perceptible to himself rather than to the outer world. The lamps are being trimmed, they will shine before long. These are the days of preparation before that Sabbath which is in an infinite sense a high day. As it was said of Esther, that for so many months she prepared herself with myrrh and sweet odors before she entered the king's palace, to be espoused of him, even so are we now being purified and made ready for that august day when the perfected church shall be presented unto Christ as a bride unto her husband. John says of her that she shall be "prepared as a bride adorned for her husband." This is our night, wherein we must watch, but behold the morning comes, a morning without clouds, and then shall we walk in a sevenfold light because our well beloved has come. That second advent of his will be his revelation: he was under a cloud here, and men perceived him not, save only a few who beheld his glory; but when he comes a second time all veils will be removed and every eye shall see the glory of his countenance. For this he waits and his church waits with him. We know not when the set time shall arrive, but every hour is bringing it nearer to us, therefore let us stand with loins girded, awaiting it.

Note, second, *in whom* this glorification of Christ is to be found. The text does not say he will be glorified "by" his saints, but "*in* his saints." There is a shade of difference, yes, more than a shade, between the two terms. We endeavor to glorify him now by our actions, but then he will be glorified in our own persons, and character, and condition. He is glorified *by* what we do, but he is at the last to be glorified in what we are. Who are these in whom Jesus is to be glorified and admired? They are spoken of under two descriptions: "in his saints," and "in all them that believe."

In "his saints" first. All those in whom Christ will be glorified are described as holy ones or saints: men and women who have been sanctified, and made pure, whose gracious lives show that they have been under the teaching of the Holy Spirit, whose obedient actions prove that they are disciples of a holy master, even of him who was "holy, harmless, undefiled, and separate from sinners." But, inasmuch as these saints are also said to be believers, I gather that the holiness which will honor Christ at last is a holiness based on faith in him, a holiness of which this was the root, that they first trusted in Christ, and then, being saved, they loved their Lord and obeyed him. Their faith worked by love and purified their souls, and so cleansed their lives. It is an inner as well as an outer purity, arising out of the living and operative principle of faith. If any think that they can attain to holiness apart from faith in Christ, they are as much mistaken as he who should hope to reap a harvest without casting seed into the furrows. Faith is the bulb, and saintship is the delightfully fragrant flower which comes of it when planted in the soil of a renewed heart. Beware, I pray you, of any pretense to a holiness arising out of yourselves, and maintained by the energy of your own unaided wills; as well look to gather grapes of thorns or figs of thistles. True saintship must spring from confidence in the Savior of sinners, and if it does not it is lacking in the first elements of truth. How can that be a perfect character which finds its basis in self-esteem? How could Christ be glorified by saints who refuse to trust in him?

I would call your attention once again to the second description, "All them that believe." This is enlarged by the hint that they are believers in a certain testimony, according to the bracketed sentence—"because our testimony among you was believed." Now, the testimony of the apostles was concerning Christ. They saw him in the body, and they bore witness that he was "God manifest in the flesh"; they saw his holy life, and they bore witness to it; they saw his death of grief, and they witnessed that "God was in Christ reconciling the world unto himself"; they saw him risen from the dead, and they said, "We are witnesses of his resurrection"; they saw him rise into heaven, and they bore witness that God had taken him up to his right hand. Now, all that believe this witness are saved. "If thou shalt confess with thy mouth the Lord Jesus, and shalt believe in thine heart that God hath raised him from the dead, thou shalt be saved." All who with a simple faith come and cast themselves upon the incarnate God, living and dying for men, and ever sitting at the right hand of God to make intercession for them, these are the people in whom Christ will be glorified and admired at the last great day. But inasmuch as they are first said to be saints, be it never forgotten that this faith must be a living faith, a faith which produces a hatred of sin, a faith which renews the character and shapes the life after the noble model of Christ, thus turning sinners into saints. The two descriptions must not be violently rent asunder; you must not say that the favored people are sanctified without remembering that they are justified by faith, nor may you say that they are justified by faith without remembering that without holiness no man shall see the Lord, and that at the last the people in whom Christ will be admired will be those holy ones who were saved by faith in him.

So far, then, we see our way, but now a question arises: by whom will Christ be thus glorified and admired? He shines in his people, but who will see the glory? I answer first, that his people will see it. Every saint will glorify Christ in himself, and admire Christ in himself. He will say, "What a wonder that such a poor creature as I am should be thus perfected! How glorious is my Lord, who has worked this miracle upon me!" Surely our consciousness of having been cleansed and made holy will cause us to fulfill those words of John Berridge which we sang just now—

He cheers them with eternal smile,
They sing hosannas all the while;

Or, overwhelm'd with rapture sweet,
Sink down adoring at his feet.

This I know, that when I personally enter heaven I shall forever admire and adore the everlasting love which brought me there. Yes, we will all glorify and admire our Savior for what he has worked in us by his infinite grace.

The saints will also admire Christ in one another. As I shall see you and you shall see your brethren and sisters in Christ all perfect, you will be filled with wonderment and gratitude and delight. You will be free from all envy there, and therefore you will rejoice in all the beauty of your fellow saints: their heaven will be a heaven to you, and what a multitude of heavens you will have as you will joy in the joy of all the redeemed! We shall as much admire the Lord's handiwork in others as in ourselves, and shall each one praise him for saving all the rest. You will see your Lord in all your brethren, and this will make you praise and adore him world without end with a perpetual amazement of ever-growing delight.

But that will not be all. Besides the blood bought and ransomed of Christ there will be on that great day of his coming all the holy angels to stand by and look on and wonder. They marveled much when first he stooped from heaven to earth, and they desired to look into those things, which then were a mystery to them. But when they shall see their beloved Prince come back with ten thousand times ten thousand of the ransomed at his feet, all of them made perfect by having washed their robes and made them white in his blood, how the principalities and powers will admire him in every one of his redeemed! How they will praise that conquering arm which has brought home all these spoils from the war! How will the hosts of heaven shout his praises as they see him lead all these captives captive with a new captivity, in chains of love, joyfully gracing his triumph and showing forth the completeness of his victory!

We do not know what other races of innocent creatures there may be but I think it is no stretch of imagination to believe that, as this world is only one speck in the creation of God, there may be millions of other races in the countless worlds around us, and all these may be invited to behold the wonders of redeeming love as manifested in the saints in the day of the Lord. I seem to see these unfallen intelligences encompassing the saints as a cloud of witnesses, and in rapt vision beholding in them the love and grace of the redeeming Lord. What songs! What shouts shall rise from all these to the praise of the ever-blessed God! What an orchestra of praise will the universe become! From star to star the holy hymn shall roll, till all space shall ring out the hosannas of wondering spirits. "The Wonderful, the Counselor, the mighty God, the everlasting Father, the Prince of peace" shall have brought home all the men wondered at, and they with himself shall be the wonder of eternity.

Then shall Satan and his defeated legions, and the lost spirits of ungodly men, bite their lips with envy and rage, and tremble at the majesty of Jesus in that day. By their confessed defeat and manifest despair, they shall glorify him in his people, in whom they have been utterly overthrown. They shall see that there is not one lost whom he redeemed by blood, not one snatched away of all the sheep his Father gave him, not one warrior enlisted beneath his banner fallen in the day of battle, but all more than conquerors through him that loved them. What despair shall seize upon diabolic spirits as they discover their entire defeat! Defeated in men who were once their slaves! Poor dupes whom they could so easily beguile by their craftiness, defeated even in these! Jesus, triumphant by taking the lambs from between the lion's jaws, and rescuing his feeble sheep from their power, will utterly put them to shame in his redeemed. With what anguish will they sink into the hell prepared for them, because now they hear with anger all earth and heaven and every star ringing with the shout, "Hallelujah, Hallelujah, Hallelujah, for the Lord God omnipotent reigns, and the Lamb hath conquered by his blood."

You see then that there are enough spectators to magnify Christ in his saints; and so, fourthly, let us inquire *in what degree* will the Lord Jesus be glorified? Our answer is, it will be to the very highest degree. He shall come to be glorified in his saints to the utmost, for this is clear from the words, "to be admired." When our translation was made, the word "admired" had to ordinary Englishmen a stronger flavor of wonder than it has to us now. We often speak of admiring a thing in the softer sense of loving it, but the real meaning of the English word, and of the Greek also, is *wonder*: our Lord will be wondered at in all them that believe. Those who look upon the saints will feel a sudden wonderment of sacred delight; they will be startled with the surprising glory of the Lord's work in them; "We thought he would do great things, but this! This surpasses conception!" Every saint will be a wonder to himself. "I thought my bliss would be great, but not like this!" All his brethren will be a wonder to the perfected believer. He will say, "I thought the saints would be perfect, but I never imagined such a transfiguration of excessive glory would be put upon each of them. I could not have imagined my Lord to be so good and gracious." The angels in heaven will say that they never anticipated such deeds of grace: they did know that he had undertaken a great work, but they did not know that he would do so much for his people and in his people. The firstborn sons of light, used to great marvels from of old, will be entranced with a new wonder as they see the handiwork of Emmanuel's free grace and dying love. The men who once despised the saints, who called them canting hypocrites and trampled on them, and perhaps slew them, the kings and princes of the earth who sold the righteous for a pair of shoes, what will they say when they see the least of the Savior's followers become a prince of more illustrious rank than the great ones of the earth, and Christ shining out in every one of these favored beings? For their uplifting Jesus will be wondered at by those who once despised both him and them.

My next point leads us into the very bowels of the subject; *in what respects* will Christ be glorified and wondered at? I cannot expect to tell you one tenth part of it. I am only going to give you a little sample of what this must mean; exhaustive expositions were quite impossible to me. I think with regard to his saints that Jesus will be glorified and wondered at on account of their number—"a number that no man can number." John was a great arithmetician, and he managed to count up to 144,000 of all the tribes of the children of Israel; but that was only a representative number for the Jewish church: as for the church of God, comprehending the Gentile nations, he gave up all idea of computation, and confessed that it is "a number which no man can number." When he heard them sing he says, "I heard a voice like the voice of many waters and like great thunder." There were so many of them that their song was like the Mediterranean sea lashed to fury by a tempest, no, not one great sea in uproar, but ocean upon ocean, the Atlantic and the Pacific piled upon each other, and the Arctic upon these, and other oceans upon these, layers of oceans, all thundering out their mightiest roar: and such will be the song of the redeemed, for the crowds which swell the matchless hymn will be beyond all reckoning. Behold, and see, you who laughed at his kingdom, see how the little one has become a thousand: Now look you, you foes of Christ, who saw the handful of corn on the top of the mountains; see how the fruit thereof does shake like Lebanon, and they of the city do flourish like grass of the earth. Who can reckon the drops of the dew or the sands on the seashore? When they have counted these then shall they not have guessed at the multitude of the redeemed that Christ shall bring to glory. And all this harvest from one grain of wheat, which except it had fallen into the ground and died would have remained alone! What said the Word? "If it die, it shall bring forth much fruit." Is not the prophecy fulfilled? O beloved, what a harvest from the lone Man of Nazareth! What fruit from that glorious man—the branch! Men esteemed him stricken, smitten of God, and afflicted; and they made nothing of him, and yet there sprang of him (and he as good as dead) these multitudes which are many as the stars of heaven. Is he not glorified and wondered at in them? The day shall declare it without fail.

But there is quality as well as quantity. He is admired in his saints because they are every one of them proofs of his power to save from evil. My eye can hardly bear, even though it be but in imagination, to gaze upon the glittering ranks of the white-robed ones, where each one outshines the sun, and they are all as if a sevenfold midday had clothed them. Yet all these, as I look at them, tell me, "We have washed our robes, for they were once defiled. We have made them white, but this whiteness is caused by the blood of the Lamb." These were heirs of wrath even as others, these were dead in trespasses and sins; all these like sheep had gone astray and turned every one to his own way; but look at them and see how he has saved them, washed them, cleansed them, perfected them! His power and grace are seen in all of them. If your eye will pause here and there, you will discover some that were supremely stubborn, whose neck was as an iron sinew, and yet he conquered them by love. Some were densely ignorant, but he opened their blind eyes; some grossly infected with the leprosy of lust, but he healed them; some under Satan's most terrible power, but he cast the devil out of them. Oh, how he will be glorified in special cases! In you drunkard made into a saint, in you blasphemer turned into a loving disciple, in you persecutor who breathed out threatening taught to sing everlastingly a hymn of praise! He will be exceedingly glorified in such. Brethren, beloved in the Lord, in each one of us there was some special difficulty as to our salvation, some impossibility which was possible with God, though it would have been forever impossible with us.

Remember, also, that all those saints made perfect would have been in hell had it not been for the Son's atoning sacrifice. This they will remember the more vividly, because they will see other men condemned for the sins with which they also were once polluted. The crash of vengeance upon the ungodly will make the saints magnify the Lord the more as they see themselves delivered. They will each feel—

> Oh, were it not for grace divine,
> That fate so dreadful had been mine.

In each one the memory of the horrible pit from which they were drawn and the miry clay out of which they were uplifted shall make their Savior more glorified and wondered at.

Perhaps the chief point in which Christ will be glorified will be—the absolute perfection of all the saints. They shall then be "without spot or wrinkle or any such thing." We have not experienced what perfection is, and therefore we can hardly conceive it; our thoughts themselves are too sinful for us to get a full idea of what absolute perfection must be; but, dear brethren, we shall have no sin left in us, for they are "without fault before the throne of God," and we shall have no remaining propensity to sin. There shall be no bias in the will toward that which is evil, but it shall be fixed forever upon that which is good. The affections will never be wanton again, they will be chaste for Christ. The understanding will never make mistakes. You shall never put bitter for sweet, nor sweet for bitter; you shall be "perfect, even as your Father which is in heaven is perfect": and truly, brethren, he who works this in us will be a wonder. Christ will be admired and adored because of this grand result. O mighty Master, with what strange moral alchemy did you work to turn that morose dispositioned man into a mass of love! How did you work to lift that selfish mammonite up from his hoarded gains to make him find his gain in you? How did you overcome that proud spirit, that fickle spirit, that lazy spirit, that lustful spirit—how did you contrive to take all these away? How did you extirpate the very roots of sin, and every little rootlet of sin, out of your redeemed, so that not a tiny fiber can be found? "The sins of Jacob shall be sought for and they shall not be found, yea, they shall not be, saith the Lord." Neither the guilt of sin nor the propensity to sin—both shall be gone, and Christ shall have done it, and he will be "glorified in his saints, and admired in them that believe."

This is but the beginning, however. There will be seen in every saint, in that last wondrous day, the wisdom and power and love of Christ in having brought them through all the trials of the way. He kept their faith alive when else it would have died out; he sustained them under trials when else they would have fainted; he held them fast in their integrity when temptation solicited them, and they had almost slipped with their feet. Yes, he sustained some of them in prison, and on the rack, and at the stake, and held them faithful still! One might hardly wish to be a martyr, but I reckon that the martyrs will be the admiration of us all, or rather Christ will be admired in them. However they could bear such pain as some of them did endure for Christ's sake none of us can guess, except that we know that Christ was in them suffering in his members. Eternally will Jesus be wondered at in them as all intelligent spirits shall see how he upheld them, so that neither tribulation nor distress nor nakedness nor famine nor sword could separate them from his love. These are the men that wandered about in sheepskins and goatskins, destitute, afflicted, tormented, of whom the world was not worthy, but now they stand arrayed as kings and priests in surpassing glory forever. Verily, their Lord shall be admired in them. Say you not so?

Recollect, dear friends, that we shall see in that day how the blessed Christ, as "Head over all things to his church," has ruled every providence to the sanctification of his people—how the dark days begat showers which made the plants of the Lord to grow, how the fierce sun which threatened to scorch them to the root, filled them with warmth of love divine and ripened their choice fruit. What a tale the saints will have to tell of how that which threatened to damp the fire of grace made it burn more mightily, how the stone which threatened to kill their faith was turned into bread for them, how the rod and staff of the good Shepherd was ever with them to bring them safely home. I have sometimes thought that if I get into heaven by the skin of my teeth I will sit down on the glory shore and bless forever him who, on a board, or on a broken piece of the ship, brought my soul safe to land; and surely they who obtain an abundant entrance, coming into the fair havens, like a ship in full sail, without danger of shipwreck, will have to praise the Lord that they thus came into the blessed port of peace: in each case the Lord will be specially glorified and admired.

I cannot stop over this, but I must beg you to notice that as a king is glorious in his regalia, so will Christ put on his saints as his personal splendor in that day when he shall make up his jewels. It is with Christ as it was with that noble Roman matron, who when she called at her friends' houses and saw their trinkets, asked them to come next day to her house, and she would exhibit her jewels. They expected to see ruby, and pearl, and diamond, but she called in her two boys, and said, "These are my jewels." Even so will Jesus, instead of emerald and amethyst and onyx and topaz, exhibit his saints. "These are my choice treasures," says he, "in whom I will be glorified." Solomon surely was never more full of glory than when he had finished the temple, when all the tribes came together to see the noble structure, and confessed it to be "beautiful for situation, the joy of the whole earth." But what will be the glory of Christ when all the living stones shall be put into their places and his church shall have her windows of agates and her gates of carbuncle, and all her borders of precious stones. Then, indeed, will he be glorified, when the twelve foundations of his new Jerusalem shall be courses of stones most precious, the like of which was never seen.

Now, inasmuch as my text lays special stress upon *believing*, I invite you just for a minute to consider how as believers as well as saints the saved ones will glorify their Lord.

First, it will be wonderful that there should be so many brought to faith in him: men with no God, and men with many gods, men steeped in ignorance, and men puffed up with carnal wisdom, great men and poor men, all brought to believe in the one Redeemer and praise him for his great salvation. Will he not be glorified in their common faith? It will magnify him that these will all be saved by faith, and not by their own merits. Not one among them will boast that he was saved by his own good works, but all of them will rejoice to have been saved by that blessedly simple way of "believe and live," saved by sovereign grace through the atoning blood, looked to by the tearful eye of simple faith. This, too, shall make Jesus glorious, that all of them, weak as they were, were made strong by faith; all of them personally unfit for battle were yet made triumphant in conflict because by faith they overcame through the blood of the Lamb. All of them shall be there to show that their faith was honored, that Christ was faithful to his promise, and never allowed them to believe in vain. All of them standing in heavenly places, saved by faith, will ascribe every particle of the glory to the Lord Jesus only—

> *I ask them whence their victory came?*
> *They, with united breath,*
> *Ascribe their conquest to the Lamb,*
> *Their triumph to his death.*

They believed and were saved, but faith takes no credit to itself; it is a self-denying grace, and puts the crown upon the head of Christ, and therefore is it written that he will be glorified in his saints, and he will also be admired in all them that believe.

I have scarcely skirted the subject even now, and time is failing me. I want you to reflect that Jesus will be glorified in the risen bodies of all his saints. Now, in heaven, they are pure spirits, but when he shall come they shall be clothed again. Poor body, you must sleep awhile, but what you shall be at your awaking does not yet appear. You are now the shriveled seed, but there is a flower to come of you which shall be lovely beyond all thought. Though sown in weakness, this body shall be raised in power; though sown in corruption, it shall be raised in incorruption. Weakness, weariness, pain, and death will be banished forever; infirmity and deformity will be all unknown. The Lord will raise up our bodies to be like unto his glorious body. Oh, what a prospect lies before us! Let us remember that this blessed resurrection will come to us because he rose, for there must be a resurrection to the members because the Head has risen. Oh, the charm of being a risen man perfect in body, soul, and spirit! All that charm will be due to Christ, and therefore he will be admired in us.

Then let us think of the absolute perfection of the church as to numbers: all who have believed in him will be with him in glory. The text says, he will be "admired in *all* them that believe." Now, if some of those who believe perished he would not be admired in them, but they will all be there, the little ones as well as the great ones. You will be there, you poor feeble folk who when you say, "Lord, I believe," are obliged to add, "help you mine unbelief." He shall be admired in all believers without a single exception, and peradventure there shall be more wonder at the going to heaven of the weak believers than at the stronger ones. Mr. Greatheart, when he comes there, will owe his victories to his Master and lay his laurels at his feet; but fainting Feeble-Mind, and limping Ready-to-Halt with his crutches, and trembling Little-Faith, when they enter into rest will make heaven ring with notes of even greater admiration that such poor creeping worms of the earth should win the day by mighty grace. Suppose that one of them should be missing at last! Stop the harps! Silence the songs! No beginning to be merry while one child is shut out! I am quite certain if as a family we were going to sing our evening hymn of joy and thankfulness, if mother said, "Where is the little mite? Where is the last one of the family?" there would be a pause. If we had to say—she is lost, there would be no singing and no resting till she was found. It is the glory of Jesus that as a shepherd he has lost none of his flock, as the Captain of salvation he has brought many sons to glory, and has lost none, and hence he is admired, not in some that believe, nor yet in all but one, but he is "admired in *all* them that believe."

Does not this delight you, you who are weak and trembling, that he will be admired in you? There is little to admire in you at present, as you penitently confess; but since Christ is in you now, and will be more fully manifested in you, there will before long be much to admire. May you partake in the excellence of our divine Lord and be conformed to his likeness that he may be seen in you and glorified in you.

Another point of admiration will be the eternal safety of all his believing people. There they are safe from fear of harm. You dogs of hell, you howled at their heels and hoped to devour them; but, lo, they are clean escaped from you! What must it be to be lifted above gunshot of the enemy, where no more watch shall need to be kept, for even the roar of the satanic artillery cannot be heard? O glorious Christ, to bring them all to such a state of safety, you are indeed to be wondered at forever.

Moreover, all the saints will be so honored, so happy, and so like their Lord that themselves and everything about them will be themes for never-ending admiration. You may have seen a room hung round with mirrors, and when you stood in the midst you were reflected from every point: you were seen here, and seen there, and there again, and there again, and so every part of you was reflected; just such is heaven, Jesus is the center, and all his saints like mirrors reflect his glory. Is he human? So are they! Is he the Son of God? So are they sons of God! Is he perfect? So are they! Is he exalted? So are they! Is he a prophet? So are they, making known unto principalities and powers the manifold wisdom of God. Is he a priest? So are they! Is he a King? So are they, for he has made us priests and kings unto God, and we shall reign forever and ever. Look where you will along the ranks of the redeemed, this one thing shall be seen, the glory of Christ Jesus, even to surprise and wonder.

2. I have no time to make those *suggestions* with which I intended to have finished, and so I will just tell you what they would have been.

First, the text suggests that the principal subject for self-examination with us all should be—Am I a saint? Am I holy? Am I a believer in Christ? Yes or no, for on that yes or no must hang your glorification of Christ, or your banishment from his presence.

The next thing is—observe the small value of human opinion. When Christ was here, the world reckoned him to be a nobody, and while his people are here they must expect to be judged in the same way. What do worldlings know about it? How soon will their judgment be reversed! When our Lord shall appear even those who sneered will be compelled to admire. When they shall see the glory of Christ in every one of his people, awestricken, they will have nothing to say against us; no, not even the false tongue of malicious slander shall dare to hiss out a serpent word in that day. Never mind them, then; put up with reproach which shall so soon be silenced.

The next suggestion is a great encouragement to inquirers who are seeking Christ; for I put it to you, you great sinners, if Jesus is to be glorified in saved sinners, would he not be glorified indeed if he saved you? If he were ever to save such a rebel as you have been, would it not be the astonishment of eternity? I mean you who are known in the village as Wicked Jack or known as a common swearer—what if my Master were to make a saint of you? Bad raw material! Yet suppose he transformed you into a precious jewel and made you to be as holy as God is holy, what would you say of him? "Say of him," say you, "I would praise him world without end." Yes, and you shall do so if you will come and trust him. Put your trust in him. The Lord help you to do so at once, and he shall be admired even in you forever and ever.

Our text gives an exhortation to believers also. Will Jesus Christ be honored and glorified in all the saints? Then let us think well of them all and love them all. Some dear children of God have uncomely bodies, or they are blind or deformed or maimed; and many of these have scanty purses, and it may be the church knows most of them as coming for alms: moreover, they have little knowledge, little power to please, and they are uncouth in manners and belong to what are called the lowest ranks of society: do not, therefore, despise them, for one day our Lord will be glorified in them. How he will be admired in yonder poor bedridden woman when she rises from the workhouse to sing hallelujah to God and the Lamb among the brightest of the shining ones. Why, I think the pain, the poverty, the weakness, and the sorrow of saints below will greatly glorify the Captain of their salvation as they tell how grace helped them to bear their burdens and to rejoice under their afflictions.

Lastly, brethren, this text ought to encourage all of you who love Jesus to go on talking about him to others and bearing your testimony for his name. You see how the apostle Paul has inserted a few words by way of parenthesis. Draw the words out of the brackets, and take them home, "because our testimony among you was believed." Do you see those crowds of idolatrous heathen, and do you see those hosts of saved ones before the throne? What is the medium which linked the two characters? By what visible means did the sinners become saints? Do you see that insignificant-looking man with weak eyes? That man whose bodily presence is weak and whose speech is contemptible? Do you not see his bodkin and needle case? He has been making and mending tents, for he is only a tentmaker. Now, those bright spirits which shine like suns, flashing forth Christ's glory, were made thus bright through the addresses and prayers of that tentmaker. The Thessalonians were heathens plunged in sin, and this poor tentmaker came in among them and told them of Jesus Christ and his gospel; his testimony was believed; that belief changed the lives of his hearers and made them holy, and they being renewed came at length to be perfectly holy, and there they are, and Jesus Christ is glorified in them. Beloved, will it not be a delightful thing throughout eternity to contemplate that you went into your Sunday school class this afternoon, and you were afraid you could not say much, but you talked about Jesus Christ with a tear in your eye, and you brought a dear girl to believe in his saving name through your testimony. In years to come that girl will be among those that shine out to the glory of Christ forever. Or you will get away this evening, perhaps, to talk in a lodging house to some of those poor, despised tramps; you will go and tell one of those poor vagrants, or one of the fallen women, the story of your Lord's love and blood, and the poor broken heart will catch at the gracious word, and come to Jesus, and then a heavenly character will be begun, and another jewel secured for the Redeemer's diadem. I think you will admire his crown all the more because, as you see certain stones sparkling in it, you will say, "Blessed be his name forever: he helped me to dive into the sea and find that pearl for him," and now it adorns his sacred brow. Now, get at it, all of you! You that are doing nothing for Jesus, be ashamed of yourselves, and ask him to work in you that you may begin to work for him, and unto God shall be the glory, forever and ever. Amen and amen.

The Ascension and the Second Advent Practically Considered

⊷⊱⊰⊶

Delivered on Lord's Day morning, December 28, 1884, at the Metropolitan Tabernacle, Newington. No. 1817.

> *And while they looked steadfastly toward heaven as he went up, behold, two men stood by them in white apparel; which also said, "Ye men of Galilee, why stand ye gazing up into heaven? this same Jesus, which is taken up from you into heaven, shall so come in like manner as ye have seen him go into heaven."*
> —ACTS 1:10–11

Four great events shine out brightly in our Savior's story. All Christian minds delight to dwell upon his birth, his death, his resurrection, and his ascension. These make four rounds in that ladder of light, the foot of which is upon the earth, but the top whereof reaches to heaven. We could not afford to dispense with any one of those four events, nor would it be profitable for us to forget, or to underestimate the value of any one of them. That the Son of God was born of a woman creates in us the intense delight of a brotherhood springing out of a common humanity. That Jesus once suffered unto the death for our sins, and thereby made a full atonement for us, is the rest and life of our spirits. The manger and the cross together are divine seals of love. That the Lord Jesus rose again from the dead is the warrant of our justification, and also a transcendently delightful assurance of the resurrection of all his people, and of their eternal life in him. Has he not said, "Because I live ye shall live also"? The resurrection of Christ is the morning star of our future glory. Equally delightful is the remembrance of his ascension. No song is sweeter than this—"Thou hast ascended on high; thou hast led captivity captive, thou hast received gifts for men, yea, for the rebellious also, that the Lord God might dwell among them."

Each one of those four events points to another, and they all lead up to it: the fifth link in the golden chain is our Lord's second and most glorious advent. Nothing is mentioned between his ascent and his descent. True, a rich history comes between; but it lies in a valley between two stupendous mountains: we step from alp to alp as we journey in meditation from the ascension to the second advent. I say that each of the previous four events points to it. Had he not come a first time in humiliation, born under the law, he could not have come a second time in amazing glory "without a sin offering unto salvation." Because he died once we rejoice that he died no more, death has no more dominion over him, and therefore he comes to destroy that last enemy whom he has already conquered. It is our joy, as we think of our Redeemer as risen, to feel that in consequence of his rising the trump of the archangel shall assuredly sound for the awaking of all his slumbering people, when the Lord himself shall descend from heaven with a shout. As for his ascension, he could not a second time descend if he had not first ascended; but having perfumed heaven with his presence, and prepared a place for his people, we may fitly expect that he will come again and receive us unto himself, that where he is there we may be also. I want you, therefore, as in contemplation you pass with joyful footsteps over these four grand events, as your faith leaps from his birth to his death, and from his resurrection to his ascension, to be looking forward, and even hastening unto this crowning fact of our Lord's history; for before long he shall so come in like manner as he was seen go up into heaven.

This morning, in our meditation, we will start from the ascension; and if I had sufficient imagination I should like to picture our Lord and the eleven walking up the side of Olivet, communing as they went, a happy company, with a solemn awe upon them, but with an intense joy in having fellowship with each other. Each disciple was glad to think that his dear Lord and Master who had been crucified was now among them, not only alive but surrounded with a mysterious safety and glory which none could disturb. The enemy was as still as a stone; not a dog moved his tongue; his bitterest foes made no sign during the days of our Lord's afterlife below. The company moved onward peacefully toward Bethany—Bethany which they all knew and loved. The Savior seemed drawn there at the time of his ascension, even as men's minds return to old and well-loved scenes when they are about to depart out of this world. His happiest moments on earth had been spent beneath the roof where lived Mary and Martha and their brother Lazarus. Perhaps it was best for the disciples that he should leave them at that place where he had been most hospitably entertained, to show that he departed in peace and not in anger. There they had seen Lazarus raised from the dead by him who was now to be taken up from them: the memory of the triumphant past would help the tried faith of the present. There they had heard the voice saying, "Loose him, and let him go," and there they might fitly see their Lord loosed from all bonds of earthly gravitation that he might go to his Father and their Father. The memories of the place might help to calm their minds and arouse their spirits to that fullness of joy which ought to attend the glorifying of their Lord.

But they have come to a standstill, having reached the brow of the hill. The Savior stands conspicuously in the center of the group, and, following upon most instructive discourse, he pronounces a blessing upon them. He lifts his pierced hands, and while he is lifting them and is pronouncing words of love, he begins to rise from the earth. He has risen above them all to their astonishment! In a moment he has passed beyond the olives, which seem with their silvery sheen to be lit up by his milder radiance. While the disciples are looking, the Lord has ascended into midair, and speedily he has risen to the regions of the clouds. They stand spellbound with astonishment, and suddenly a bright cloud, like a chariot of God, bears him away. That cloud conceals him from mortal gaze. Though we have known Christ after the flesh, now after the flesh know we him no more. They are riveted to the spot, very naturally so: they linger long in the place, they stand with streaming eyes, wonder struck, still looking upward.

It is not the Lord's will that they should long remain inactive; their reverie is interrupted. They might have stood there till wonder saddened into fear. As it was, they remained long enough; for the angel's words may be accurately rendered, "Why have you stood, gazing up into heaven?"

Their lengthened gaze needed to be interrupted, and, therefore, two shining ones, such as aforetime met the women at the sepulcher, are sent to them. These messengers of God appear in human form that they may not alarm them, and in white raiment as if to remind them that all was bright and joyous; and these white-robed ministers stood with them as if they would willingly join their company. As no one of the eleven would break silence, the men in white raiment commenced the discourse. Addressing them in the usual celestial style, they asked a question which contained its own answer, and then went on to tell their message. As they had once said to the women, "Why seek ye the living among the dead? He is not here, but is risen"; so did they now say, "Ye men of Galilee, why stand ye gazing up into heaven? this same Jesus, which is taken up from you into heaven, shall so come in like manner as ye have seen him go into heaven." The angels showed their knowledge of them by calling them "men of Galilee," and reminded them that they were yet upon earth by recalling their place of birth. Brought back to their senses, their reverie over, the apostles at once gird up their loins for active service; they do not need twice telling, but hasten to Jerusalem. The vision of angels has singularly enough brought them back into the world of actual life again, and they obey the command, "Tarry ye at Jerusalem." They seem to say, the taking up of our Master is not a thing to weep about: he has gone to his throne and to his glory, and he said it was expedient for us that he should go away. He will now send us the promise of the Father; we scarcely know what it will be like, but let us, in obedience to his will, make the best of our way to the place where he bade us await the gift of power. Do you not see them going down the side of Olivet, taking that Sabbath-day's journey into the cruel and wicked city without a thought of fear; having no dread of the bloodthirsty crew who slew their Lord, but happy in the memory of their Lord's exaltation and in the expectation of a wonderful display of his power? They held fellowship of the most delightful kind with one another, and anon entered into the upper room, where in protracted prayer and communion they waited for the promise of the Father. You see I have no imagination: I have barely mentioned the incidents in the simplest language. Yet try and realize the scene, for it will be helpful so to do, since our Lord Jesus is to come in like manner as the disciples saw him go up into heaven.

My first business this morning will be to consider *the gentle chiding* administered by the shining ones: "Ye men of Galilee, why stand ye gazing up unto heaven?" Second, *the cheering description* of our Lord which the white-robed messengers used, "This same Jesus"; and then, third, *the practical truth* which they taught, "This same Jesus, which is taken up from you into heaven, shall so come in like manner as ye have seen him go into heaven."

1. First, then, here is *a gentle chiding*.

It is not sharply uttered by men dressed in black who use harsh speech, and upbraid the servants of God severely for what was rather a mistake than a fault. No; the language is strengthening, yet tender: the fashion of a question allows them rather to reprove themselves than to be reproved; and the tone is that of brotherly love and affectionate concern.

Notice, that *what these saintly men were doing seems at first sight to be very right*. I think, if Jesus were among us now we would fix our eyes upon him, and never withdraw them. He is altogether lovely, and it would seem wicked to yield our eyesight to any inferior object so long as he was to be seen. When he ascended up into heaven, it was the duty of his friends to look upon him. It can never be wrong to look up; we are often bidden to do so, and it is even a holy saying of the psalmist, "I will direct my prayer unto thee, and will look up"; and, again, "I will lift up mine eyes unto the hills, from whence cometh my help." If it be right to look up into heaven, it must be still more right to look up while Jesus rises to the place of his glory. Surely it had been wrong if they had looked anywhere else; it was due to the Lamb of God that they should behold him as long as eyes could follow him. He is the Sun: where should eyes be turned but to his light? He is the King; and where should courtiers within the palace gate turn their eyes but to their King as he ascends to his throne? The truth is, there was nothing wrong in their looking up into heaven; but they went a little further than looking; they stood "gazing." A little excess in right may be faulty. It may be wise to look, but foolish to gaze. There is a very thin partition sometimes between that which is commendable and that which is censurable. There is a golden mean which it is not easy to keep. The exact path of right is often as narrow as a razor's edge, and he must be wise that does not err either on the right hand or on the left. "Look" is ever the right word. Why, it is "Look unto me, and be saved." Look, yes, look steadfastly and intently: be your posture that of one "looking unto Jesus," always throughout life. But there is a gazing which is not commendable, when the look becomes not that of reverent worship, but of an overweening curiosity, when there mingles with the desire to know what should be known, a prying into that which it is for God's glory to conceal. Brethren, it is of little use to look up into an empty heaven. If Christ himself be not visible in heaven, then in vain do we gaze, since there is nothing for a saintly eye to see. When the person of Jesus was gone out of the azure vault above them, and the cloud had effectually concealed him, why should they continue to gaze when God himself had drawn the curtain? If infinite wisdom had withdrawn the object upon which they desired to gaze, what would their gazing be but a sort of reflection upon the wisdom which had removed their Lord? Yet it did seem very right. Thus certain things that you and I may do may appear right, and yet we may need to be scolded out of them into something better: they may be right in themselves, but not appropriate for the occasion, not seasonable, nor expedient. They may be right up to a point, and then may touch the boundary of excess. A steadfast gaze into heaven may be to a devout soul a high order of worship, but if this filled up much of our working time, it might become the idlest form of folly.

Yet I cannot help adding that *it was very natural.* I do not wonder that the whole eleven stood gazing up, for if I had been there I am sure I should have done the same. How struck they must have been with the ascent of the Master out of their midst! You would be amazed if someone from among our own number now began to ascend into heaven! Would you not? Our Lord did not gradually melt away from sight as a phantom, or dissolve into thin air as a mere apparition: the Savior did not disappear in that way at all, but he rose, and they saw that it was his very self that was so rising. His own body, the materialism in which he had veiled himself, actually, distinctly, and literally, rose to heaven before their eyes. I repeat, the Lord did not dissolve, and disappear like a vision of the night, but he evidently rose till the cloud intervened so that they could see him no more. I think I should have stood looking to the very place where his cloudy chariot had been. I know it would be idle to continue so to do, but our hearts often urge us on to acts which we could not justify logically. Hearts are not to be argued with. Sometimes you stand by a grave where one is buried whom you dearly loved: you go there often to weep. You cannot help it, the place is precious to you; yet you could not prove that you do any good by your visits, perhaps you even injure yourself thereby, and deserve to be gently scolded with the question "why?" It may be the most natural thing in the world, and yet it may not be a wise thing. The Lord allows us to do that which is innocently natural, but he will not have us carry it too far; for then it might foster an evil nature. Hence he sends an interrupting messenger: not an angel with a sword, or even a rod; but he sends some man in white raiment—I mean one who is both cheerful and holy, and he, by his conduct or his words, suggests to us the question, "Why stand you here gazing?" *Cui bono?* What will be the benefit? What will it avail? Thus our understanding being called into action, and we being men of thought, we answer to ourselves, "This will not do. We must not stand gazing here forever," and therefore we arouse ourselves to get back to the Jerusalem of practical life, where in the power of God we hope to do service for our Master.

Notice, then, that the disciples were doing that which seemed to be right and what was evidently very natural, but that it is very easy to carry the apparently right and the absolutely natural too far. Let us take heed to ourselves, and often ask our hearts "why?"

For, third, notice that what they *did was not after all justifiable upon strict reason.* While Christ was going up it was proper that they should adoringly look at him. He might almost have said, "If you see me when I am taken up, a double portion of my spirit shall rest upon you." They did well to look where he led the way. But when he was gone, still to remain gazing was an act which they could not exactly explain to themselves and could not justify to others. Put the question thus: "What purpose will be fulfilled by your continuing to gaze into the sky? He is gone, it is absolutely certain that he is gone. He is taken up, and God himself has manifestly concealed all trace of him by bidding yonder cloud sail in between him and you. Why gaze you still? He told you, 'I go unto my Father.' Why stand and gaze?" We may under the influence of great love act unwisely. I remember well seeing the action of a woman whose only son was emigrating to a distant colony. I stood in the station, and I noticed her many tears and her frequent embraces of her boy; but the train came up and he entered the carriage. After the train had passed beyond the station, she was foolish enough to break away from friends who sought to detain her; she ran along the platform, leaped down upon the railroad and pursued the flying train. It was natural, but it had been better left undone. What was the use of it? We had better abstain from acts which serve no practical purpose; for in this life we have neither time nor strength to waste in fruitless action. The disciples would be wise to cease gazing, for nobody would be benefited by it, and they would not themselves be blessed. What is the use of gazing when there is nothing to see? Well, then, did the angels ask, "Why stand ye gazing up into heaven?"

Again, put another question: what precept were they obeying when they stood gazing up into heaven? If you have a command from God to do a certain thing, you need not inquire into the reason of the command, it is disobedient to begin to canvass God's will; but when there is no precept whatever, why persevere in an act which evidently does not promise to bring any blessing? Who bade them stand gazing up into heaven? If Christ had done so, then in Christ's name let them stand like statues and never turn their heads: but as he had not bidden them, why did they do what he had not commanded and leave undone what he had commanded? For he had strictly charged them that they should tarry at Jerusalem till they were "endued with power from on high." So what they did was not justifiable.

Here is the practical point for us: *what they did we are very apt to imitate.* "Oh," say you, "I shall never stand gazing up into heaven." I am not sure of that. Some Christians are very curious, but not obedient. Plain precepts are neglected, but difficult problems they seek to solve. I remember one who used always to be dwelling upon the vials and seals and trumpets. He was great at apocalyptic symbols; but he had seven children, and he had no family prayer. If he had left the vials and trumpets and minded his boys and girls, it would have been a deal better. I have known men marvelously great upon Daniel, and specially instructed in Ezekiel, but singularly forgetful of the twentieth of Exodus, and not very clear upon Romans the eighth. I do not speak with any blame of such folks for studying Daniel and Ezekiel, but quite the reverse; yet I wish they had been more zealous for the conversion of the sinners in their neighborhoods, and more careful to assist the poor saints. I admit the value of the study of the feet of the image in Nebuchadnezzar's vision, and the importance of knowing the kingdoms which make up the ten toes, but I do not see the propriety of allowing such studies to overlay the commonplaces of practical godliness. If the time spent over obscure theological propositions were given to a mission in the dim alley near the good man's house, more benefit would come to man and more glory to God. I would have you understand all mysteries, brethren, if you could; but do not forget that our chief business here below is to cry, "Behold the Lamb!" By all manner of means read and search till you know all that the Lord has revealed concerning things to come; but first of all see to it that your children are brought to the Savior's feet, and that you are workers together with God in the upbuilding of his church. The dense mass of misery and ignorance and sin which is round about us on every side demands all our powers; and if you do not respond to the call, though I am not a man in white apparel, I shall venture to say to you, "You men of Christendom, why stand you gazing up into the mysteries when so much is to be done for Jesus, and you are leaving it undone?" O you who are curious but not obedient, I fear I speak to you in vain, but I have spoken. May the Holy Spirit also speak.

Others are contemplative but not active, much given to the study of Scripture and to meditation thereon, but not zealous for good works. Contemplation is so scarce in these days that I could wish there were a thousand times as much of it; but in the case to which I refer everything runs in the one channel of thought, all time is spent in reading, in enjoyment, in rapture, in pious leisure. Religion never ought to become the subject of selfishness, and yet I fear some treat it as if its chief end was spiritual gratification. When a man's religion all lies in his saving his own self, and in enjoying holy things for his own self, there is a disease upon him. When his judgment of a sermon is based upon the one question, "Did it feed *me*?" it is a swinish judgment. There is such a thing as getting a swinish religion in which you are yourself first, yourself second, yourself third, yourself to the utmost end. Did Jesus ever think or speak in that fashion? Contemplation of Christ himself may be so carried out as to lead you away from Christ: the recluse meditates on Jesus, but he is as unlike the busy self-denying Jesus as well can be. Meditation unattended with active service in the spreading of the gospel among men, well deserves the rebuke of the angel, "Ye men of Galilee, why stand ye gazing up into heaven?"

Moreover, some are careful and anxious and deliriously impatient for some marvelous interposition. We get at times into a sad state of mind, because we do not see the kingdom of Christ advancing as we desire. I suppose it is with you as it is with me—I begin to fret, and I am deeply troubled, and I feel that there is good reason that I should be, for truth is fallen in the streets, and the days of blasphemy and rebuke are upon us. Then we pine; for the Master is away, and we cry, "When will he be back again? Oh, why are his chariots so long in coming? Why tarries he through the ages?" Our desires sour into impatience, and we commence gazing up into heaven, looking for his coming with a restlessness which does not allow us to discharge our duty as we should. Whenever anybody gets into that state, this is the word, "Ye men of Galilee, why stand ye gazing up into heaven?"

In certain cases this uneasiness has drawn to itself a wrong expectation of immediate wonders, and an intense desire for sign seeing. Ah me, what fanaticisms come of this! In America years ago, one came forward who declared that on such a day the Lord would come, and he led a great company to believe his crazy predictions. Many took their horses and fodder for two or three days and went out into the woods, expecting to be all the more likely to see all that was to be seen when once away from the crowded city. All over the States there were people who had made ascension dresses in which to soar into the air in proper costume. They waited, and they waited, and I am sure that no text could have been more appropriate for them than this, "You men of America, why stand you here gazing up into heaven?" Nothing came of it; and yet there are thousands in England and America who only need a fanatical leader, and they would run into the like folly. The desire to know the times and seasons is a craze with many poor bodies whose insanity runs in that particular groove. Every occurrence is a "sign of the times": a sign, I may add, which they do not understand. An earthquake is a special favorite with them. "Now," they cry, "the Lord is coming"; as if there had not been earthquakes of the sort we have heard of lately hundreds of times since our Lord went up into heaven. When the prophetic earthquakes occur in diverse places, we shall know of it without the warnings of these brethren. What a number of persons have been infatuated by the number of the beast and have been ready to leap for joy because they have found the number 666 in some great one's name. Why, everybody's name will yield that number if you treat it judiciously, and use the numerals of Greece, Rome, Egypt, China, or Timbuktu. I feel weary with the silly way in which some people make toys out of Scripture and play with texts as with a pack of cards. Whenever you meet with a man who sets up to be a prophet, keep out of his way in the future; and when you hear of signs and wonders, turn you to your Lord, and in patience possess your souls. "The just shall live by his faith." There is no other way of living among wild enthusiasts. Believe in God, and ask not for miracles and marvels, or the knowledge of times and seasons. To know when the Lord will restore the kingdom is not in your power. Remember that verse which I read just now in your hearing, "It is not for you to know the times or the seasons." If I were introduced into a room where a large number of parcels were stored up, and I was told that there was something good for me, I should begin to look for that which had my name upon it, and when I came upon a parcel and I saw in pretty big letters, *"It is not for you,"* I should leave it alone. Here, then, is a casket of knowledge marked, *"It is not for you* to know the times or the seasons, which the Father hath put in his own power." Cease to meddle with matters which are concealed and be satisfied to know the things which are clearly revealed.

2. Second, I want you to notice *the cheering description* which these bright spirits give concerning our Lord. They describe him thus, "this same Jesus."

I appreciate the description the more because *it came from those who knew him.* "He was seen of angels"; they had watched him all his life long, and they knew him, and when they, having just seen him rise to his Father and his God, said of him, "This same Jesus," then I know by an infallible testimony that he was the same, and that he is the same.

Jesus is gone, but he still exists. He has left us, but he is not dead; he has not dissolved into nothing like the mist of the morning. "This same Jesus" is gone up unto his Father's throne, and he is there today as certainly as he once stood at Pilate's bar. As surely as he did hang upon the cross, so surely does he, the selfsame man, sit upon the throne of God and reign over creation. I like to think of the positive identity of the Christ in the seventh heaven with the Christ in the lowest depths of agony. The Christ they spat upon is now the Christ whose name the cherubim and seraphim are hymning day without night. The Christ they scourged is he before whom principalities and powers delight to cast their crowns. Think of it and be glad this morning; and do not stand gazing up into heaven after a myth or a dream. Jesus lives; mind that you live also. Do not loiter as if you had nothing at all to do, or as if the kingdom of God had come to an end because Jesus is gone from the earth, as to his bodily presence. It is not all over; he still lives, and he has given you a work to do till he comes. Therefore, go and do it.

"This same Jesus"—I love that word, for "Jesus" means *a Savior.* O you anxious sinners here present, the name of him who has gone up into his glory is full of irritation to you! Will you not come to "this same Jesus"? This is he who opened the eyes of the blind and brought forth the prisoners out of the prison house. He is doing the same thing today. Oh, that your eyes may see his light! He that touched the lepers, and that raised the dead, is the same Jesus still, able to save to the uttermost. Oh, that you may look and live! You have only to come to him by faith, as she did who touched the hem of his garment; you have but to cry to him as the blind man did whose sight he restored; for he is the same Jesus, bearing about with him the same tender love for guilty men, and the same readiness to receive and cleanse all that come to him by faith.

"This same Jesus." Why, that must have meant that he who is in heaven is the same Christ who was on earth, but it must also mean that *he who is to come will be the same Jesus that went up into heaven.* There is no change in our blessed Master's nature, nor will there ever be. There is a great change in his condition:

> The Lord shall come, but not the same
> As once in lowliness he came,
> A humble man before his foes,
> A weary man, and full of woes.

He will be "the same Jesus" in nature though not in condition: he will possess the same tenderness when he comes to judge, the same gentleness of heart when all the glories of heaven and earth shall gird his brow. Our eye shall see him in that day, and we shall recognize him not only by the nail prints, but by the very look of his countenance, by the character that gleams from that marvelous face; and we shall say, "'Tis he! 'Tis he! the selfsame Christ that went up from the top of Olivet from the midst of his disciples." Go to him with your troubles, as you would have done when he was here. Look forward to his second coming without dread. Look for him with that joyous expectancy with which you would welcome Jesus of Bethany, who loved Mary, and Martha, and Lazarus.

On the back of that sweet title came this question, "Why stand ye here gazing into heaven?" They might have said, "We stay here because we do not know where to go. Our Master is gone." But oh, it is the same Jesus, and he is coming again, so go down to Jerusalem and get to work directly. Do not worry yourselves; no grave accident has occurred; it is not a disaster that Christ has gone, but an advance in his work. Despisers tell us nowadays, "Your cause is done for! Christianity is spun out! Your divine Christ is gone; we have not seen a trace of his miracle-working hand, nor of that voice which no man could rival." Here is our answer: we are not standing gazing up into heaven; we are not paralyzed because Jesus is away. He lives, the great Redeemer lives; and though it is our delight to lift up our eyes because we expect his coming, it is equally our delight to turn our heavenly gazing into an earthward watching, and to go down into the city, and there to tell that Jesus is risen, that men are to be saved by faith in him, and that whosoever believes in him shall have everlasting life. We are not defeated, far from it: his ascension is not a retreat, but an advance. His tarrying is not for want of power, but because of the abundance of his longsuffering. The victory is not questionable. All things work for it; all the hosts of God are mustering for the final charge. This same Jesus is mounting his white horse to lead forth the armies of heaven, conquering and to conquer.

3. Our third point is this, *the great practical truth.*

This truth is not one that is to keep us gazing into heaven, but one that is to make each of us go to his house to render earnest service. What is it?

Why, first, that *Jesus in gone into heaven*. Jesus is gone! Jesus is gone! It sounds like a knell. Jesus is taken up from you into heaven!—that sounds like a marriage peal. He is gone, but he is gone up to the hills, from which he can survey the battle; up to the throne, from which he can send us succor. The reserve forces of the Omnipotent stood waiting till their Captain came, and now that he is come into the center of the universe, he can send legions of angels, or he can raise up hosts of men for the help of his cause. I see every reason for going down into the world and getting to work, for he is gone up into heaven and "all power is given unto him in heaven and in earth." Is not that a good argument—"Go ye *therefore* and teach all nations, baptizing them in the name of the Father, and of the Son, and of the Holy Ghost"?

Jesus will come again. That is another reason for girding our loins, because it is clear that he has not quitted the fight, nor deserted the field of battle. Our great Captain is still heading the conflict; he has ridden into another part of the field, but he will be back again, perhaps in the twinkling of an eye. You do not say that a commander has given up the campaign because it is expedient that he should withdraw from your part of the field. Our Lord is doing the best thing for his kingdom in going away. It was in the highest degree expedient that he should go, and that we should each one receive the Spirit. There is a blessed unity between Christ the King and the commonest soldier in the ranks. He has not taken his heart from us, nor his care from us, nor his interest from us: he is bound up heart and soul with his people, and their holy warfare, and this is the evidence of it, "Behold, I come quickly; and my reward is with me, to give every man according as his work shall be."

Then, moreover, we are told in the text—and this is a reason why we should get to our work—*that he is coming in like manner as he departed.* Certain of the commentators do not seem to understand English at all. "He which is taken up from you into heaven shall so come in like manner as you have seen him go into heaven"; this, they say, relates to his spiritual coming at Pentecost. Give anybody a grain of sense, and do they not see that a spiritual coming is not a coming in the same manner in which he went up into heaven? There is an analogy, but certainly not a likeness between the two things. Our Lord was taken up; they could see him rise: he will come again, and "every eye shall see him." He went up not in spirit, but in person: he will come down in person. "This same Jesus shall so come in like manner." He went up as a matter of fact: not in poetic figure and spiritual symbol, but as a matter of fact, "this same Jesus" literally went up. "This same Jesus" will literally come again. He will descend in clouds even as he went up in clouds; and "he shall stand at the latter day upon the earth" even as he stood aforetime. He went up to heaven unopposed; no high priests nor scribes nor Pharisees nor even one of the rabble opposed his ascension; it were ridiculous to suppose that they could; and when he comes a second time none will stand against him. His adversaries shall perish; as the fat of rams shall they melt away in his presence. When he comes he shall break rebellious nations with a rod of iron, for his force shall be irresistible in that day.

Brethren, do not let anybody spiritualize away all this from you. Jesus is coming as a matter of fact, therefore go down to your sphere of service as a matter of fact. Get to work and teach the ignorant, win the wayward, instruct the children, and everywhere tell out the sweet name of Jesus. As a matter of fact, give of your substance and don't talk about it. As a matter of fact, consecrate your daily life to the glory of God. As a matter of fact, live wholly for your Redeemer. Jesus is not coming in a sort of mythical, misty, hazy way; he is literally and actually coming, and he will literally and actually call upon you to give an account of your stewardship. Therefore, now, today, literally not symbolically, personally and not by deputy, go out through that portion of the world which you can reach, and preach the gospel to every creature according as you have opportunity.

For this is what the men in white apparel meant—*be ready to meet your coming Lord.* What is the way to be ready to meet Jesus? If it is the same Jesus that went away from us who is coming, then let us be doing what he was doing before he went away. If it is the same Jesus that is coming, we cannot possibly put ourselves into a posture of which he will better approve than by going about doing good. If you would meet him with joy, serve him with earnestness. If the Lord Jesus Christ were to come today, I should like him to find me at my studying, praying, or preaching. Would you not like him to find you in your Sunday school, in your class, or out there at the corner of the street preaching, or doing whatever you have the privilege of doing in his name? Would you meet your Lord in idleness? Do not think of it. I called one day on one of our members, and she was whitening the front steps. She got up all in confusion; she said, "Oh dear, sir, I did not know you were coming today, or I would have been ready." I replied, "Dear friend, you could not be in better trim than you are: you are doing your duty like a good housewife, and may God bless you." She had no money to spare for a servant, and she was doing her duty by keeping the home tidy: I thought she looked more beautiful with her pail beside her than if she had been dressed according to the latest fashion. I said to her, "When the Lord Jesus Christ comes suddenly, I hope he will find me doing as you were doing, namely, fulfilling the duty of the hour." I want you all to get to your pails without being ashamed of them. Serve the Lord in some way or other; serve him always; serve him intensely; serve him more and more. Go tomorrow and serve the Lord at the counter, or in the workshop, or in the field. Go and serve the Lord by helping the poor and the needy, the widow and the fatherless; serve him by teaching the children, especially by endeavoring to train your own children. Go and hold a temperance meeting, and show the drunkard that there is hope for him in Christ, or go to the midnight meeting and let the fallen woman know that Jesus can restore her. Do what Jesus has given you the power to do, and then, you men of Britain, you will not stand gazing up into heaven, but you will wait upon the Lord in prayer, and you will receive the Spirit of God, and you will publish to all around the doctrine of "believe and live." Then when he comes, he will say to you, "Well done, good and faithful servant, enter thou into the joy of thy Lord." So may his grace enable us to do. Amen.

Coming Judgment of the Secrets of Men

⚜

Delivered on Lord's Day morning, June 12, 1885, at the Metropolitan Tabernacle, Newington. No. 1849.

The day when God shall judge the secrets of men by Jesus Christ according to my gospel. —ROMANS 2:16

It is impossible for any of us to tell what it cost the apostle Paul to write the first chapter of the Epistle to the Romans. It is a shame even to speak of the things which are done of the vicious in secret places; but Paul felt that it was necessary to break through his shame, and to speak out concerning the hideous vices of the heathen. He has left on record an exposure of the sins of his day which crimsons the cheek of the modest when they read it, and makes both the ears of him that hears it to tingle. Paul knew that this chapter would be read, not in his age alone, but in all ages, and that it would go into the households of the most pure and godly as long as the world should stand; and yet he deliberately wrote it, and wrote it under the guidance of the Holy Spirit. He knew that it must be written to put to shame the abominations of an age which was almost past shame. Monsters that revel in darkness must be dragged into the open, that they may be withered up by the light. After Paul has thus written in anguish he reminded himself of his chief comfort. While his pen was black with the words he had written in the first chapter, he was driven to write of his great delight. He clings to the gospel with a greater tenacity than ever. As in the verse before us he needed to mention the gospel, he did not speak of it as "the gospel," but as "*my gospel.*" "God shall judge the secrets of men by Jesus Christ, according to *my gospel.*" He felt that he could not live in the midst of so depraved a people without holding the gospel with both hands, and grasping it as his very own. "*My gospel,*" says he. Not that Paul was the author of it, not that Paul had an exclusive monopoly of its blessings, but that he had so received it from Christ himself, and regarded himself as so responsibly put in trust with it, that he could not disown it even for an instant. So fully had he taken it into himself that he could not do less than call it "my gospel." In another place he speaks of "our gospel"; thus using a possessive pronoun, to show how believers identify themselves with the truth which they preach. He had a gospel, a definite form of truth, and he believed in it beyond all doubt; and therefore he spoke of it as "my gospel." Herein we hear the voice of faith, which seems to say, "Though others reject it, I am sure of it, and allow no shade of mistrust to darken my mind. To me it is glad tidings of great joy: I hail it as 'my gospel.' If I be called a fool for holding it, I am content to be a fool, and to find all my wisdom in my Lord."

> Should all the forms that men devise
> Assault my faith with treacherous art,
> I'd call them vanity and lies,
> And bind the gospel to my heart.

Is not this word "my gospel" the voice of love? Does he not by this word embrace the gospel as the only love of his soul—for the sake of which he had suffered the loss of all things, and did count them but dung—for the sake of which he was willing to stand before Nero, and proclaim, even in Caesar's palace, the message from heaven? Though each word should cost him a life, he was willing to die a thousand deaths for the holy cause. "My gospel," says he, with a rapture of delight, as he presses to his bosom the sacred deposit of truth.

"My gospel." Does not this show his courage? As much as to say, "I am not ashamed of the gospel of Christ: for it is the power of God unto salvation to every one that believeth." He says, "my gospel," as a soldier speaks of "my colors" or of "my king." He resolves to bear this banner to victory, and to serve this royal truth even to the death.

"My gospel." There is a touch of discrimination about the expression. Paul perceives that there are other gospels, and he makes short work with them, for he says, "Though we, or an angel from heaven, preach any other gospel unto you than that which we have preached unto you, let him be accursed." The apostle was of a gentle spirit; he prayed heartily for the Jews who persecuted him, and yielded his life for the conversion of the Gentiles who maltreated him; but he had no tolerance for false preachers. He exhibited great breadth of mind, and to save souls he became all things to all men; but when he contemplated any alteration or adulteration of the gospel of Christ, he thundered and lightened without measure. When he feared that something else might spring up among the philosophers, or among the Judaizers, that should hide a single beam of the glorious Sun of righteousness, he used no measured language; but cried concerning the author of such a darkening influence, "Let him be accursed." Every heart that would see men blessed whispers an "amen" to the apostolic malediction. No greater curse can come upon mankind than the obscuration of the gospel of Jesus Christ. Paul says of himself and his true brethren, "We are not as many, which corrupt the word of God"; and he cries to those who turned aside from the one and only gospel, "O foolish Galatians, who hath bewitched you?" Of all new doctrines, he speaks as of "another gospel, which is not another; but there be some that trouble you."

As for myself, looking at the matter afresh, amid all the filthiness which I see in the world at this day, I lay hold upon the pure and blessed Word of God, and call it all the more earnestly, my gospel, mine in life and mine in death, mine against all comers, mine forever, God helping me: with emphasis—"my gospel."

Now let us notice what it was that brought up this expression, "my gospel." What was Paul preaching about? Certainly not upon any of the gentle and tender themes, which we are told nowadays ought to occupy all our time; but he is speaking of the terrors of the law, and in that connection he speaks of "my gospel."

Let us come at once to our text. It will need no dividing, for it divides itself. First, let us consider that *on a certain day God shall judge mankind;* second, on that day *God will judge the secrets of men;* third, when he judges the secrets of men, *it will be by Jesus Christ;* and fourth, *this is according to the gospel.*

1. We begin with the solemn truth, that *on a certain day God will judge men.*

A judgment is going on daily. God is continually holding court, and considering the doings of the sons of men. Every evil deed that they do is recorded in the register of doom, and each good action is remembered and laid up in store by God. That judgment is reflected in a measure in the consciences of men. Those who know the gospel, and those who know it not, alike, have a certain measure of light, by which they know right from wrong; their consciences all the while accusing or else excusing them. This session of the heavenly court continues from day to day, like that of our local magistrates; but this does not prevent but rather necessitates the holding of an ultimate great assize.

As each man passes into another world, there is an immediate judgment passed upon him; but this is only the foreshadowing of that which will take place in the end of the world.

There is a judgment also passing upon nations, for as nations will not exist as nations in another world, they have to be judged and punished in this present state. The thoughtful reader of history will not fail to observe, how sternly this justice has dealt with empire after empire, when they have become corrupt. Colossal dominions have withered to the ground, when sentenced by the King of kings. Go you and ask today, "Where is the empire of Assyria? Where are the mighty cities of Babylon? Where are the glories of the Medes and Persians? What has become of the Macedonian power? Where are the Caesars and their palaces?" These empires were forces established by cruelty and used for oppression; they fostered luxury and licentiousness, and when they were no longer tolerable, the earth was purged from their polluting existence. Ah me! what horrors of war, bloodshed, and devastation, have come upon men as the result of their iniquities! The world is full of the monuments, both of the mercy and the justice of God: in fact, the monuments of his justice, if rightly viewed, are proofs of his goodness; for it is mercy on the part of God to put an end to evil systems when, like a nightmare, they weigh heavily upon the bosom of mankind. The omnipotent Judge has not ceased from his sovereign rule over kingdoms, and our own country may yet have to feel his chastisements. We have often laughed among ourselves at the ridiculous idea of the New Zealander sitting on the broken arch of London Bridge amid the ruins of this metropolis. But is it quite so ridiculous as it looks? It is more than possible it will be realized if our iniquities continue to abound. What is there about London that it should be more enduring than Rome? Why should the palaces of *our* monarchs be eternal if the palaces of Koyunjik [in Assyria] have fallen? The almost boundless power of the pharaohs has passed away, and Egypt has become the meanest of nations; why should not England come under like condemnation? What are we? What is there about our boastful race, whether on this side of the Atlantic or the other, that we should monopolize the favor of God? If we rebel, and sin against him, he will not hold us guiltless, but will deal out impartial justice to an ungrateful race.

Still, though such judgments proceed every day, yet there is to be a day, a period of time, in which, in a more distinct, formal, public, and final manner, God will judge the sons of men. We might have guessed this by the light of nature and of reason. Even heathen peoples have had a dim notion of a day of doom; but we are not left to guess it, we are solemnly assured of it in Holy Scripture. Accepting this Book as the revelation of God, we know beyond all doubt that a day is appointed in which the Lord will judge the secrets of men.

By judging is here meant all that concerns the proceedings of trial and award. God will judge the race of men; that is to say, first, there will be a session of majesty, and the appearing of a great white throne, surrounded with pomp of angels and glorified beings. Then a summons will be issued, bidding all men come to judgment, to give in their final account. The heralds will fly through the realms of death, and summon those who sleep in the dust: for the quick and the dead shall all appear before that judgment seat. John says, "I saw the dead, small and great, stand before God"; and he adds, "The sea gave up the dead which were in it; and death and hell delivered up the dead which were in them." Those that have been so long buried that their dust is mingled with the soil, and has undergone a thousand transmutations, shall nevertheless be made to put in a personal appearance before the judgment seat of Christ. What an assize will that be! You and I and all the myriad myriads of our race shall be gathered before the throne of the Son of God. Then, when all are gathered, the indictment will be read, and each one will be examined concerning things done in the body, according to that he has done. Then the books shall be opened, and everything recorded there shall be read before the face of heaven. Every sinner shall then hear the story of his life published to his everlasting shame. The good shall ask no concealment, and the evil shall find none. Angels and men shall then see the truth of things, and the saints shall judge the world. Then the great Judge himself shall give the decision: he shall pronounce sentence upon the wicked, and execute their punishment. No partiality shall there be seen; there shall be no private conferences to secure immunity for nobles, no hushing up of matters, that great men may escape contempt for their crimes. All men shall stand before the one great judgment bar; evidence shall be given concerning them all, and a righteous sentence shall go forth from his mouth who knows not how to flatter the great.

This will be so, and it ought to be so: God should judge the world, because he is the universal ruler and sovereign. There has been a day for sinning, there ought to be a day for punishing; a long age of rebellion has been endured, and there must be a time when justice shall assert her supremacy. We have seen an age in which reformation has been commanded, in which mercy has been presented, in which expostulation and entreaty have been used, and there ought at last to come a day in which God shall judge both the quick and the dead, and measure out to each the final result of life. It ought to be so for the sake of the righteous. They have been slandered; they have been despised and ridiculed; worse than that, they have been imprisoned and beaten, and put to death times without number: the best have had the worst of it, and there ought to be a judgment to set these things right. Besides, the festering iniquities of each age cry out to God that he should deal with them. Shall such sin go unpunished? To what end is there a moral government at all, and how is its continuance to be secured, if there be not rewards and punishments and a day of account? For the display of his holiness, for the overwhelming of his adversaries, for the rewarding of those who have faithfully served him, there must be and shall be a day in which God will judge the world.

Why does it not come at once? And when will it come? The precise date we cannot tell. Man nor angel knows that day, and it is idle and profane to guess at it, since even the Son of man, as such, knows not the time. It is sufficient for us that the judgment day will surely come; sufficient also to believe that it is postponed on purpose to give breathing time for mercy, and space for repentance. Why should the ungodly want to know when that day will come? What is that day to you? To you it shall be darkness and not light. It shall be the day of your consuming as stubble fully dry: therefore bless the Lord that he delays his coming and reckon that his longsuffering is for your salvation.

Moreover, the Lord keeps the scaffold standing till he has built up the fabric of his church. Not yet are the elect all called out from among the guilty sons of men; not yet are all the redeemed with blood redeemed with power and brought forth out of the corruption of the age into the holiness in which they walk with God. Therefore the Lord waits for a while. But do not deceive yourselves. The great day of his wrath comes on apace, and your days of reprieve are numbered. One day is with the Lord as a thousand years, and a thousand years as one day. You shall die, perhaps, before the appearing of the Son of man; but you shall see his judgment seat for all that, for you shall rise again as surely as he rose. When the apostle addressed the Grecian sages at Athens he said, "God now commandeth all men everywhere to repent, because he has appointed a day, in the which he will judge the world in righteousness by that man whom he has ordained; whereof he has given assurance unto all men, in that he has raised him from the dead." See you not, O you impenitent ones, that a risen Savior is the sign of your doom. As God has raised Jesus from the dead, so shall he raise your bodies, that in these you may come to judgment. Before the judgment seat shall every man and woman in this house give an account of the things done in the body, whether they be good or whether they be evil. Thus says the Lord.

2. Now I call your attention to the fact that *"God will judge the secrets of men."*

This will happen to all men, of every nation, of every age, of every rank, and of every character. The Judge will, of course, judge their outward acts, but these may be said to have gone before them to judgment: their secret acts are specially mentioned, because these will make judgment to be the more searching.

By "the secrets of men," the Scripture means those secret crimes which hide themselves away by their own infamy, which are too vile to be spoken of, which cause a shudder to go through a nation if they be but dragged, as they ought to be, into the daylight. Secret offenses shall be brought into judgment; the deeds of the night and of the closed room, the acts which require the finger to be laid upon the lip, and a conspiracy of silence to be sworn. Revolting and shameless sins which must never be mentioned lest the man who committed them should be excluded from his fellows as an outcast, abhorred even of other sinners—all these shall be revealed. All that you have done, any one of you, or are doing, if you are bearing the Christian name and yet practicing secret sin, shall be laid bare before the universal gaze. If you sit here among the people of God, and yet where no eye sees you, if you are living in dishonesty, untruthfulness, or uncleanness, it shall all be known, and shame and confusion of face shall eternally cover you. Contempt shall be the inheritance to which you shall awake, when hypocrisy shall be no more possible. Be not deceived, God is not mocked; but he will bring the secrets of men into judgment.

Specially our text refers to the hidden motives of every action; for a man may do that which is right from a wrong motive, and so the deed may be evil in the sight of God, though it seem right in the sight of men. Oh, think what it will be to have your motives all brought to light, to have it proven that you were godly for the sake of gain, that you were generous out of ostentation, or zealous for love of praise, that you were careful in public to maintain a religious reputation, but that all the while everything was done for self, and self only! What a strong light will that be which God shall turn upon our lives, when the darkest chambers of human desire and motive shall be as manifest as public acts! What a revelation will that be which makes manifest all thoughts and imaginings and lustings and desires! All angers and envies and prides and rebellions of the heart—what a disclosure will these make!

All the sensual desires and imaginings of even the best regulated, what a foulness will these appear! What a day will it be, when the secrets of men shall be set in the full blaze of noon!

God will also reveal secrets that were secrets even to the sinners themselves, for there is sin in us which we have never seen and iniquity in us which we have never yet discovered.

We have managed for our own comfort's sake to blind our eyes somewhat, and we take care to avert our gaze from things which it is inconvenient to see; but we shall be compelled to see all these evils in that day, when the Lord shall judge the secrets of men. I do not wonder that when a certain rabbi read in the book of Ecclesiastes that God shall bring every work into judgment, with every secret thing, whether it be good, or whether it be evil, he wept. It is enough to make this best man tremble. Were it not for you, O Jesus, whose precious blood has cleansed us from all sin, where should we be! Were it not for your righteousness, which shall cover those who believe in you, who among us could endure the thought of that tremendous day? In you, O Jesus, we are made righteous, and therefore we fear not the trial hour, but were it not for you our hearts would fail us for fear!

Now if you ask me why God should judge, especially the secrets of men—since this is not done in human courts, and cannot be, for secret things of this kind come not under cognizance of our shortsighted tribunals—I answer it is because there is really nothing secret from God. We make a difference between secret and public sins, but he does not; for all things are naked and open to the eyes of him with whom we have to do. All deeds are done in the immediate presence of God, who is personally present everywhere. He knows and sees all things as one upon the spot, and every secret sin is but conceived to be secret through the deluded fantasy of our ignorance. God sees more of a secret sin than a man can see of that which is done before his face. "'Can any hide himself in secret places that I shall not see him?' saith the Lord."

The secrets of men will be judged because often the greatest of moral acts are done in secret. The brightest deeds that God delights in are those that are done by his servants when they have shut the door and are alone with him—when they have no motive but to please him; when they studiously avoid publicity, lest they should be turned aside by the praise of men; when the right hand knows not what the left hand does, and the loving, generous heart devises liberal things, and does it behind the screen, so that it should never be discovered how the deed was done. It were a pity that such deeds should be left out at the great audit. Thus, too, secret vices are also of the very blackest kind, and to exempt them were to let the worst of sinners go unpunished. Shall it be that these polluted beings shall escape because they have purchased silence with their wealth? I say solemnly, "God forbid." He does forbid it: what they have done in secret, shall be proclaimed upon the housetops.

Besides, the secret things of men enter into the very essence of their actions. An action is, after all, good or bad very much according to its motive. It may seem good, but the motive may taint it; and so, if God did not judge the secret part of the action, he would not judge righteously. He will weigh our actions, and detect the design which led to them, and the spirit which prompted them.

Is it not certainly true that the secret thing is the best evidence of the man's condition? Many a man will not do in public that which would bring him shame; not because he is not black-hearted enough for it, but because he is too much of a coward. That which a man does when he thinks that he is entirely by himself is the best revelation of the man. That which you will not do because it would be told of you if you did ill, is a poor index of your real character. That which you will do because you will be praised for doing well is an equally faint test of your heart. Such virtue is mere self-seeking or mean-spirited subservience to your fellowman; but that which you do out of respect to no authority but your own conscience and your God; that which you do unobserved, without regard to what man will say concerning it—that it is which reveals you, and discovers your real soul. Hence God lays a special stress and emphasis here upon the fact that he will in that day judge "the secrets" of men by Jesus Christ.

O friends, if it does not make you tremble to think of these things, it ought to do so. I feel the deep responsibility of preaching upon such matters, and I pray God of his infinite mercy to apply these truths to our hearts, that they may be forceful upon our lives. These truths ought to startle us, but I am afraid we hear them with small result; we have grown familiar with them, and they do not penetrate us as they should. We have to deal, brethren, with an omniscient God; with One who once knowing never forgets; with One to whom all things are always present; with One who will conceal nothing out of fear or favor of any man's person; with One who will shortly bring the splendor of his omniscience and the impartiality of his justice to bear upon all human lives. God help us, wherever we rove and wherever we rest, to remember that each thought, word, and act of each moment lies in that fierce light which beats upon all things from the throng of God.

3. Another solemn revelation of our text lies in this fact, that "God will judge the secrets of men by Jesus Christ."

He that will sit upon the throne as the vicegerent of God, and as a judge, acting for God, will be Jesus Christ. What a name for a judge! The Savior-Anointed—Jesus Christ: he is to be the Judge of all mankind. Our Redeemer will be the umpire of our destiny.

This will be, I doubt not, first for the display of his glory. What a difference there will be then between the babe of Bethlehem's manger, hunted by Herod, carried down by night into Egypt for shelter, and the King of kings and Lord of lords, before whom every knee must bow! What a difference between the weary man and full of woes, and he that shall then be girded with glory, sitting on a throne encircled with a rainbow! From the derision of men to the throne of universal judgment, what an ascent! I am unable to convey to you my own heart's sense of the contrast between the "despised and rejected of men," and the universally acknowledged Lord, before whom Caesar and pontiffs shall bow into the dust. He who was judged at Pilate's bar shall summon all to his bar. What a change from the shame and spitting, from the nails and the wounds, the mockery and the thirst, and the dying anguish, to the glory in which he shall come whose eyes are as a flame of fire, and out of whose mouth there goes a two-edged sword! He shall judge the nations, even he whom the nations abhorred. He shall break them in pieces like a potter's vessel, even those who cast him out as unworthy to live among them. Oh, how we ought to bow before him now as he reveals himself in his tender sympathy and in his generous humiliation! Let us kiss the Son lest he be angry; let us yield to his grace, that we may not be crushed by his wrath. You sinners, bow before those pierced feet, which else will tread you like clusters in the winepress. Look you up to him with weeping, and confess your forgetfulness of him, and put your trust in him; lest he look down on you in indignation. Oh, remember that he will one day say, "But those mine enemies, which would not that I should reign over them, bring hither, and slay them before me." The holding of the judgment by the Lord Jesus will greatly enhance his glory. It will finally settle one controversy which is still upheld by certain erroneous spirits: there will be no doubt about our Lord's deity in that day: there will be no question that this same Jesus who was crucified is both Lord and God. God himself shall judge, but he shall perform the judgment in the person of his Son Jesus Christ, truly man, but nevertheless most truly God. Being God he is divinely qualified to judge the world in righteousness, and the people with his truth.

If you ask again, "Why is the Son of God chosen to be the final Judge?" I could give as a further answer that he receives this high office not only as a reward for all his pains, and as a manifestation of his glory, but also because men have been under his mediatorial sway, and he is their Governor and King. At the present moment we are all under the sway of the Prince Emmanuel, God with us: we have been placed by an act of divine clemency, not under the immediate government of an offended God, but under the reconciling rule of the Prince of peace. "All power is given unto him in heaven and in earth." "The Father judgeth no man, but hath committed all judgment unto the Son: that all men should honor the Son, even as they honor the Father." We are commanded to preach unto the people, and "to testify that it is he which was ordained of God to be the Judge of quick and dead" (Acts 10:42). Jesus is our Lord and King, and it is meet that he should conclude his mediatorial sovereignty by rewarding his subjects according to their deeds.

But I have somewhat to say unto you which ought to reach your hearts, even if other thoughts have not done so. I think that God has chosen Christ, the man Christ Jesus, to judge the world that there may never be a cavil raised concerning that judgment. Men shall not be able to say—we were judged by a superior being who did not know our weaknesses and temptations, and therefore he judged us harshly, and without a generous consideration of our condition. No, God shall judge the secrets of men by Jesus Christ, who was tempted in all points like as we are, yet without sin. He is our brother, bone of our bone and flesh of our flesh, partaker of our humanity, and therefore understands and knows what is in men. He has shown himself to be skillful in all the surgery of mercy throughout the ages, and at last he will be found equally skillful in dissecting motives and revealing the thoughts and intents of the heart. Nobody shall ever be able to look back on that august tribunal and say that he who sat upon it was too stern, because he knew nothing of human weakness. It will be the loving Christ, whose tears and bloody sweat and gaping wounds attest his brotherhood with mankind; and it will be clear to all intelligences that however dread his sentences, he could not be unmerciful. God shall judge us by Jesus Christ, that the judgment may be indisputable.

But hearken well—for I speak with a great weight upon my soul—this judgment by Christ Jesus puts beyond possibility all hope of any after-interposition. If the Savior condemns, and such a Savior, who can plead for us? The owner of the vineyard was about to cut down the barren tree, when the dresser of the vineyard pleaded, "Let it alone this year also"; but what can come of that tree when the vinedresser himself shall say to the master, "It must fall; I myself must cut it down"! If your Savior shall become your Judge, you will be judged indeed. If he shall say, "Depart, you cursed," who can call you back? If he that bled to save men at last comes to this conclusion, that there is no more to be done, but they must be driven from his presence, then farewell hope. To the guilty the judgment will indeed be a "great day of dread, decision, and despair."

An infinite horror shall seize upon their spirits as the words of the loving Christ shall freeze their very marrow, and fix them in the ice of eternal despair. There is, to my mind, a climax of solemnity in the fact that God shall judge the secrets of men by Jesus Christ.

Does not this also show how certain the sentence will be? for this Christ of God is too much in earnest to play with men. If he says, "Come, you blessed," he will not fail to bring them to their inheritance. If he be driven to say, "Depart, you cursed," he will see it done, and into the everlasting punishment they must go. Even when it cost him his life, he did not draw back from doing the will of his Father, nor will he shrink in that day when he shall pronounce the sentence of doom. Oh, how evil must sin be since it constrains the tender Savior to pronounce sentence of eternal woe! I am sure that many of us have been driven of late to an increased hatred of sin; our souls have recoiled within us because of the wickedness among which we dwell; it has made us feel as if we would fain borrow the Almighty's thunderbolts with which to smite iniquity. Such haste on our part may not be seemly, since it implies a complaint against divine longsuffering; but Christ's dealing with evil will be calm and dispassionate, and all the more crushing. Jesus, with his pierced hand, that bears the attestation of his supreme love to men, shall wave the impenitent away; and those lips which bade the weary rest in him shall solemnly say to the wicked, "Depart, you cursed, into everlasting fire prepared for the devil and his angels." To be trampled beneath the foot which was nailed to the cross will be to be crushed indeed: yet so it is, God shall judge the secrets of men by Jesus Christ.

It seems to me as if God in this intended to give a display of the unity of all his perfections. In this same man, Christ Jesus, the Son of God, you behold justice and love, mercy and righteousness, combined in equal measure. He turns to the right, and says, "Come, you blessed," with infinite suavity; and with the same lip, as he glances to the left, he says, "Depart, you cursed." Men will then see at one glance how love and righteousness are one, and how they meet in equal splendor in the person of the well beloved, whom God has therefore chosen to be Judge of quick and dead.

4. I have done when you have borne with me a minute or two upon my next point, which is this: and *all this is according to the gospel.*

That is to say, there is nothing in the gospel contrary to this solemn teaching. Men gather to us, to hear us preach of infinite mercy, and tell of the love that blots out sin; and our task is joyful when we are called to deliver such a message; but O sirs, remember that nothing in our message makes light of sin. The gospel offers you no opportunity of going on in sin, and escaping without punishment. Its own cry is, "Except ye repent, ye shall all likewise perish." Jesus has not come into the world to make sin less terrible. Nothing in the gospel excuses sin; nothing in it affords toleration for lust or anger or dishonesty or falsehood. The gospel is as truly a two-edged sword against sin, as ever the law can be. There is grace for the man who quits his sin, but there is tribulation and wrath upon every man that does evil. "If ye turn not he will whet his sword; he hath bent his bow, and made it ready." The gospel is all tenderness to the repenting, but all terror to the obstinate offender. It has pardon for the very chief of sinners, and mercy for the vilest of the vile, if they will forsake their sins; but it is according to our gospel that he that goes on in his iniquity, shall be cast into hell, and he that believes not shall be damned. With deep love to the souls of men, I bear witness to the truth that he who turns not with repentance and faith to Christ shall go away into punishment as everlasting as the life of the righteous. This is according to our gospel: indeed, we had not needed such a gospel, if there had not been such a judgment. The background of the cross is the judgment seat of Christ. We had not needed so great an atonement, so vast a sacrifice, if there had not been an exceeding sinfulness in sin, an exceeding justice in the judgment, and an exceeding terror in the sure rewards of transgression.

"According to my gospel," says Paul; and he meant that the judgment is an essential part of the gospel creed. If I had to sum up the gospel, I should have to tell you certain facts: Jesus, the Son of God, became man; he was born of the Virgin Mary; lived a perfect life; was falsely accused of men, was crucified, dead, and buried; the third day he rose again from the dead; he ascended into heaven and sits on the right hand of God; from whence he shall also come to judge the quick and the dead. This is one of the elementary truths of our gospel; we believe in the resurrection of the dead, the final judgment, and the life everlasting.

The judgment is according to our gospel, and in times of righteous indignation its terrible significance seems a very gospel to the pure in heart. I mean this. I have read this and that concerning oppression, slavery, the treading down of the poor, and the shedding of blood, and I have rejoiced that there is a righteous judge. I have read of secret wickedness among the rich men of this city, and I have said within myself, "Thank God, there will be a judgment day." Thousands of men have been hanged for much less crimes than those which now disgrace gentlemen whose names are on the lips of rank and beauty. Ah me, how heavy is our heart as we think of it! It has come like a gospel to us that the Lord will be revealed in flaming fire, taking vengeance on them that know not God, and that obey not the gospel of our Lord Jesus Christ (2 Thess. 1:8). The secret wickedness of London cannot go on forever. Even they that love men best, and most desire salvation for them, cannot but cry to God, "How long! How long! Great God, will you forever endure this?" God has appointed a day in which he will judge the world, and we sigh and cry until it shall end the reign of wickedness, and give rest to the oppressed. Brethren, we must preach the coming of the Lord, and preach it somewhat more than we have done; because it is the driving power of the gospel. Too many have kept back these truths, and thus the bone has been taken out of the arm of the gospel. Its point has been broken; its edge has been blunted. The doctrine of judgment to come is the power by which men are to be aroused. There is another life; the Lord will come a second time; judgment will arrive; the wrath of God will be revealed. Where this is not preached, I am bold to say the gospel is not preached. It is absolutely necessary to the preaching of the gospel of Christ that men be warned as to what will happen if they continue in their sins. Ho, ho, sir surgeon, you are too delicate to tell the man that he is ill! You hope to heal the sick without their knowing it. You therefore flatter them; and what happens? They laugh at you; they dance upon their own graves. At last they die! Your delicacy is cruelty; your flatteries are poisons; you are a murderer. Shall we keep men in a fool's paradise? Shall we lull them into soft slumbers from which they will awake in hell? Are we to become helpers of their damnation by our smooth speeches? In the name of God, we will not. It becomes every true minister of Christ to cry aloud and spare not, for God has set a day in which he will "judge the secrets of men by Jesus Christ according to my gospel." As surely as Paul's gospel was true, the judgment will come. Wherefore flee to Jesus this day, O sinners. O you saints, come hide yourselves again beneath the crimson canopy of the atoning sacrifice, that you may be now ready to welcome your descending Lord and escort him to his judgment seat. O my hearers, may God bless you, for Jesus' sake. Amen.

The Two Appearings and the Discipline of Grace

—❦—

Delivered on Lord's Day morning, April 4, 1886, at the Metropolitan Tabernacle, Newington. No. 1894.

For the grace of God that bringeth salvation hath appeared to all men, teaching us that, denying ungodliness and worldly lusts, we should live soberly, righteously, and godly, in this present world; looking for that blessed hope, and the glorious appearing of the great God and our Savior Jesus Christ; who gave himself for us, that he might redeem us from all iniquity, and purify unto himself a peculiar people, zealous of good works. —TITUS 2:11–14

Upon reading this text one sees at a glance that Paul believed in a divine Savior. He did not preach a Savior who was a mere man. He believed the Lord Jesus Christ to be truly man, but he also believed him to be God over all, and he therefore uses the striking words, "the glorious appearing of the great God and our Savior Jesus Christ." There is no appearing of God the Father; there is no such expression in Scripture; the appearing is the appearing of that second person of the blessed Trinity in unity who has already once appeared, and who will appear a second time without a sin offering unto salvation in the latter days. Paul believed in Jesus as "the great God and our Savior." It was his high delight to extol the Lord who once was crucified in weakness. He calls him here, "the great God," thus specially dwelling upon his power, dominion, and glory; and this is the more remarkable because he immediately goes on to say, "who gave himself for us, that he might redeem us from all iniquity." He that gave himself, he that surrendered life itself upon the accursed tree, he that was stripped of all honor and glory and entered into the utmost depths of humiliation, was assuredly the great God notwithstanding all. O brothers, if you take away the deity of Christ what in the gospel is left that is worth the preaching? None but the great God is equal to the work of being our Savior.

We learn also at first sight that Paul believed in a great redemption. "Who gave himself for us that he might redeem us from all iniquity." That word "redemption" sounds in my ears like a silver bell. We are ransomed, purchased back from slavery, and this at an immeasurable price; not merely by the obedience of Christ, nor the suffering of Christ, nor even the death of Christ, but by Christ's giving himself for us. All that there is in the great God and Savior was paid down that he might "redeem us from all iniquity." The splendor of the gospel lies in the redeeming sacrifice of the Son of God, and we shall never fail to put this to the front in our preaching. It is the gem of all the gospel gems. As the moon is among the stars, so is this great doctrine among all the lesser lights which God has kindled to make glad the night of fallen man. Paul never hesitates; he has a divine Savior and a divine redemption, and he preaches these with unwavering confidence. Oh, that all preachers were like him!

It is also clear that Paul looked upon the appearing of the Savior as a Redeemer from all iniquity as a display of the grace of God. He says, "The grace of God that bringeth salvation hath appeared to all men." In the person of Christ the grace of God is revealed, as when the sun arises and makes glad all lands. It is not a private vision of God to a favored prophet on the lone mountain's brow; but it is an open declaration of the grace of God to every creature under heaven—a display of the grace of God to all eyes that are open to behold it. When the Lord Jesus Christ came to Bethlehem, and when he closed a perfect life by death upon Calvary, he manifested the grace of God more gloriously than has been done by creation or providence. This is the clearest revelation of the everlasting mercy of the living God. In the Redeemer we behold the unveiling of the Father's face. What if I say the laying bare of the divine heart? To repeat the figure of the text, this is the Dayspring from on high which has visited us: the Sun which has arisen with healing in his wings. The grace of God has shone forth conspicuously, and made itself visible to men of every rank in the person and work of the Lord Jesus. This was not given us because of any deserving on our part; it is a manifestation of free, rich, undeserved grace, and of that grace in its fullness. The grace of God has been made manifest to the entire universe in the appearing of Jesus Christ our Lord.

The grand object of the manifestation of divine grace in Christ Jesus is to deliver men from the dominion of evil. The world in Paul's day was sunk in immorality, debauchery, ungodliness, bloodshed, and cruelty of every kind. I have not time this morning to give you even an outline sketch of the Roman world when Paul wrote this letter to Titus. We are bad enough now; but the outward manners and customs of that period were simply horrible. The spread of the gospel has worked a change for the better. In the apostle's days the favorite spectacles for holiday entertainment were the butcheries of men; and such was the general depravity that vices which we hardly dare to mention were defended and gloried in. In the midnight of the world's history, our Lord appeared to put away sin. The Lord Jesus Christ, who is the manifestation of the divine grace to men, came into the world to put an end to the unutterable tyranny of evil. His work and teaching are meant to uplift mankind at large and also to redeem his people from all iniquity, and to sanctify them to himself as his peculiar heritage.

Paul looks upon recovery from sin as being a wonderful proof of divine grace. He does not talk about a kind of grace that would leave men in sin, and yet save them from its punishment. No, his salvation is salvation from sin. He does not talk about a free grace which winks at iniquity, and makes nothing of transgression; but of a greater grace by far, which denounces the iniquity and condemns the transgression, and then delivers the victim of it from the habit which has brought him into bondage. He declares that the grace of God has shone upon the world in the work of Jesus, in order that the darkness of its sin and ignorance may disappear, and the brightness of holiness and righteousness and peace, may rule the day. God send us to see these blessed results in every part of the world! God make us to see them in ourselves! May we ourselves feel that the grace of God has appeared to us individually! Our apostle would have Titus know that this grace was intended for all ranks of men, for the Cretans who were "always liars, evil beasts, slow bellies"; and even for the most despised bond slaves, who under the Roman Empire were treated worse than dogs. To each one of us, whether rich or poor, prominent or obscure, the gospel has come, and its design is that we may be delivered by it from all ungodliness and worldly lusts.

This being the run of the text, I ask you to come closer to it, while I try to show how the apostle stimulates us to holiness and urges us to overcome all evil. First, he describes *our position*; second, he describes *our instruction*; and, third, he mentions *our encouragements*. May the good Spirit bless our meditations at this hour!

1. First of all, the apostle in this text describes *our position*.

The people of God stand between two appearances. In the eleventh verse he tells us that "the grace of God that bringeth salvation hath appeared to all men"; and then he says, in the thirteenth verse, "Looking for that blessed hope, and the glorious appearing of the great God and our Savior Jesus Christ." We live in an age which is an interval between two appearings of the Lord from heaven. Believers in Jesus are shut off from the old economy by the first coming of our Lord. The times of man's ignorance God winked at, but now commands all men everywhere to repent. We are divided from the past by a wall of light, upon whose forefront we read the words "Bethlehem, Geth-semane, Calvary." We date from the birth of the Virgin's Son: we begin with *Anno Domini*. All the rest of time is before Christ, and is marked off from the Christian era. Bethlehem's manger is our beginning. The chief landmark in all time to us is the wondrous life of him who is the Light of the world. We look to the appearing of the grace of God in the form of the lowly One of Nazareth, for our trust is there. We confide in him who was made flesh and dwelt among us, so that men beheld his glory, the glory as of the only begot-ten of the Father, full of grace and truth. The dense darkness of the heathen ages begins to be broken when we reach the first appearing, and the dawn of a glorious day begins.

Brethren, we look forward to a second appearing. Our outlook for the close of this present era is another appearing—an appearing of glory rather than of grace. After our Master rose from the brow of Olivet, his disciples remained for a while in mute astonishment; but soon an angelic messenger reminded them of prophecy and promise by saying, "Ye men of Galilee, why stand ye gazing up into heaven? this same Jesus, which is taken up from you into heaven, shall so come in like manner as ye have seen him go into heaven." We believe that our Lord in the fullness of time will descend from heaven with a shout, with the trump of the archangel, and the voice of God.

> *The Lord shall come! the earth shall quake;*
> *The mountains to their center shake;*
> *And, withering from the vault of night,*
> *The stars shall pale their feeble light.*

This is the terminus of the present age. We look from *Anno Domini,* in which he came the first time, to that greater *Anno Domini,* or year of our Lord, in which he shall come a second time, in all the splendor of his power, to reign in righteousness, and break the evil powers as with a rod of iron.

See, then, where we are: we are compassed about, behind and before, with the appearings of our Lord. Behind us is our trust; before us is our hope. Behind us is the Son of God in humiliation; before us is the great God our Sav-ior in his glory. To use an ecclesiastical term, we stand between two epiphanies: the first is the manifestation of the Son of God in human flesh in dishonor and weakness; the second is the manifestation of the same Son of God in all his power and glory. In what a position, then, do the saints stand! They have an era all to themselves which begins and ends with the Lord's appearing.

Our position is further described in the text, if you look at it, as being *in this present world,* or age. We are living in the age which lies between the two blazing beacons of the divine appearings; and we are called to hasten from one to the other. The sacramental host of God's elect is marching on from the one appearing to the other with hasty foot. We have everything to hope for in the last appearing, as we have everything to trust to in the first appearing; and we have now to wait with patient hope throughout that weary interval which intervenes. Paul calls it "this present world." This marks its fleeting nature. It is present, but it is scarcely future; for the Lord may come so soon, and thus end it all. It is present now, but it will not be present long. It is but a little time, and he that will come shall come and will not tarry. Now it is this "present world"; oh, how present it is! How sadly it surrounds us! Yet by faith we count these present things to be unsubstantial as a dream; and we look to the things which are not seen, and not present, as being real and eternal. We pass through this world as men on pilgrimage. We traverse an enemy's country. Going from one manifestation to another, we are as birds migrating on the wing from one region to another: there is no rest for us by the way. We are to keep ourselves as loose as we can from this country through which we make our pilgrim way; for we are strangers and foreigners, and here we have no continuing city. We hurry through this Vanity Fair: before us lies the Celestial City and the coming of the Lord who is the King thereof. As voyagers cross the Atlantic, and so pass from shore to shore, so do we speed over the waves of this ever-changing world to the glory land of the bright appearing of our Lord and Savior Jesus Christ.

Already I have given to you, in this description of our position, the very best argument for a holy life. If it be so, my brethren, you are not of the world even as Jesus is not of the world. If this be so, that before you blazes the supernatural splendor of the second advent, and behind you burns the everlasting light of the Redeemer's first appearing, what manner of people ought you to be? If, indeed, you be but journeying through this present world, suffer not your hearts to be defiled with its sins; learn not the manner of speech of these aliens through whose country you are passing. Is it not written, "The people shall dwell alone, and shall not be reckoned among the nations"? "Come ye out from among them, and be ye separate, touch not the unclean thing," for the Lord has said, "I will be a Father unto you, and ye shall be my sons and daughters." They that lived before the coming of Christ had responsibilities upon them, but not such as those which rest upon you who have seen the face of God in Jesus Christ, and who expect to see that face again. You live in light which renders their brightest knowledge a comparative darkness: walk as children of light. You stand between two mornings, between which there is no evening. The glory of the Lord has risen upon you once in the incarnation and atonement of your Lord: that light is shining more and more, and soon there will come the perfect day, which shall be ushered in by the second advent. The sun shall no more go down, but it shall unveil itself, and shed an indescribable splendor upon all hearts that look for it. "Put on therefore the armor of light." What a grand expression! Helmet of light, breastplate of light, shoes of light—everything of light. What a knight must he be who is clad, not in steel, but in light, light which shall flash confusion on his foes! There ought to be a holy light about you, O believer in Jesus, for there is the appearing of grace behind you, and the appearing of glory before you. Two manifestations of God shine upon you. Like a wall of fire the Lord's appearings are round about you: there ought to be a special glory of holiness in the midst. "Let your light so shine before men, that they may see your good works, and glorify your Father which is in heaven." That is the position of the righteous according to my text, and it furnishes a loud call to holiness.

2. Second, I have to call your attention to *the instruction* which is given to us by the grace of God which has appeared unto all men.

Our translation runs thus: "The grace of God hath appeared to all men, teaching us that, denying ungodliness and worldly lusts, we should live soberly, righteously, and godly, in this present world." A better translation would be: "The grace of God that brings salvation has appeared to all men, disciplining us in order that we may deny ungodliness and worldly lusts." Those of you who know a little Greek will note that the word which in our version is rendered "teaching" is a scholastic term, and has to do with the education of children; not merely the teaching, but the training and bringing of them up. The grace of God has come to be a schoolmaster to us, to teach us, to train us, to prepare us for a more developed state. Christ has manifested in his own person that wonderful grace of God which is to deal with us as with sons, and to educate us unto holiness, and so to the full possession of our heavenly heritage. We are the many sons who are to be brought to glory by the discipline of grace.

So then, first of all, *grace has a discipline.* We generally think of law when we talk about schoolmasters and discipline; but grace itself has a discipline and a wonderful training power too. The manifestation of grace is preparing us for the manifestation of glory. What the law could not do, grace is doing. The free favor of God instills new principles, suggests new thoughts, and by inspiring us with gratitude, creates in us love to God and hatred of that which is opposed to God. Happy are they who go to school to the grace of God! This grace of God entering into us shows us what was evil even more clearly than the commandment does. We receive a vital, testing principle within, whereby we discern between good and evil. The grace of God provides us with instruction, but also with chastisement, as it is written, "As many as I love I rebuke and chasten." As soon as we come under the conscious enjoyment of the free grace of God, we find it to be a holy rule, a fatherly government, a heavenly training. We find, not self-indulgence, much less licentiousness; but on the contrary, the grace of God both restrains and constrains us; it makes us free to holiness and delivers us from the law of sin and death by "the law of the spirit of life in Christ Jesus."

Grace has its discipline, *and grace has its chosen disciples,* for you cannot help noticing that while the eleventh verse says that, "the grace of God that brings salvation has appeared to all men," yet it is clear that this grace of God has not exercised its holy discipline upon all men, and therefore the text changes its "all men" into "us." Usually in Scripture when you get a generality you soon find a particularity near it. The text has it, "teaching us that, denying ungodliness and worldly lusts, we should live soberly, righteously, and godly, in this present world." Thus you see that grace has its own disciples. Are you a disciple of the grace of God? Did you ever come and submit yourself to it? Have you learned to spell that word "faith"? Have you childlike trust in Jesus? Have you learned to wash in the laver of atonement? Have you learned those holy exercises which are taught by the grace of God? Can you say that your salvation is of grace? Do you know the meaning of that text, "By grace are ye saved through faith; and that not of yourselves: it is the gift of God"? If so, then you are his disciples, and the grace of God which has appeared so conspicuously has come to discipline you. As the disciples of grace, endeavor to adorn its doctrine. According to the previous verses, even a slave might do this. He might be an ornament to the grace of God. Let grace have such an effect upon your life and character that all may say, "See what grace can do! See how the grace of God produces holiness in believers!" All along I wish to be driving at the point which the apostle is aiming at: that we are to be holy—holy because grace exercises a purifying discipline, and because we are the disciples of that grace.

The discipline of grace, according to the apostle, has three results—denying, living, looking. You see the three words before you. The first is "denying." When a young man comes to college he usually has much to unlearn. If his education has been neglected, a sort of instinctive ignorance covers his mind with briars and brambles. If he has gone to some faulty school where the teaching is flimsy, his tutor has first of all to fetch out of him what he has been badly taught. The most difficult part of the training of young men is not to put the right thing into them, but to get the wrong thing out of them. A man proposes to teach a language in six months, and in the end a great thing is done if one of his pupils is able to forget all his nonsense in six years. When the Holy Spirit comes into the heart, he finds that we know so much already of what it were well to leave unknown; we are self-conceited, we are puffed up. We have learned lessons of worldly wisdom and carnal policy, and these we need to unlearn and deny. The Holy Spirit works this denying in us by the discipline of grace.

What have we to deny? First, we have to deny ungodliness. That is a lesson which many of you have great need to learn. Listen to working men. "Oh," they say, "we have to work hard, we cannot think about God or religion." This is ungodliness! The grace of God teaches us to deny this; we come to loathe such atheism. Others are prospering in the world, and they cry, "If you had as much business to look after as I have, you would have no time to think about your soul or another world. Trying to battle with the competition of the times leaves me no opportunity for prayer or Bible reading; I have enough to do with my daybook and ledger." This also is ungodliness! The grace of God leads us to deny this; we abhor such forgetfulness of God. A great work of the Holy Spirit is to make a man godly, to make him think of God, to make him feel that this present life is not all, but that there is a judgment to come, wherein he must give an account before God. God cannot be forgotten with impunity. If we treat him as if he were nothing, and leave him out of our calculations for life, we shall make a fatal mistake. O my hearer, there is a God, and as surely as you live, you are accountable to him. When the Spirit of God comes with the grace of the gospel, he removes our inveterate ungodliness, and causes us to deny it with joyful earnestness.

We next deny "worldly lusts": that is, the lusts of the present world or age, which I described to you just now as coming in between the two appearings. This present age is as full of evil lusts as that in which Paul wrote concerning the Cretans. The lust of the eye, the lust of the flesh, and the pride of life are yet with us. Wherever the grace of God comes effectually, it makes the loose liver deny the desires of the flesh; it causes the man who lusted after gold to conquer his greediness; it brings the proud man away from his ambitions; it trains the idler to diligence, and it sobers the wanton mind which cared only for the frivolities of life. Not only do we leave these lusts, but we deny them. We have an abhorrence of those things wherein we formerly placed our delight. Our cry is, "What have I to do any more with idols?" To the worldling we say, "These things may belong to you; but as for us, we cannot own them; sin shall no more have dominion over us. We are not of the world, and therefore its ways and fashions are none of ours." The period in which we live shall have no paramount influence over us, for our truest life is with Christ in eternity; our conversation is in heaven. The grace of God has made us deny the prevailing philosophies, glories, maxims, and fashions of this present world. In the best sense we are nonconformists. We desire to be crucified to the world and the world to us. This was a great thing for grace to do among the degraded sensualists of Paul's day, and it is not a less glorious achievement in these times.

But then, brethren, you cannot be complete with a merely negative religion; you must have something positive; and so the next word is *living*—that "we should live soberly, righteously, and godly, in this present world." Observe, brethren, that the Holy Ghost expects us to live in this present world, and therefore we are not to exclude ourselves from it. This age is the battlefield in which the soldier of Christ is to fight. Society is the place in which Christianity is to exhibit the graces of Christ. If it were possible for these good sisters to retire into a large house and live secluded from the world, they would be shirking their duty rather than fulfilling it. If all the good men and true were to form a select colony, and do nothing else but pray and hear sermons, they would simply be refusing to serve God in his own appointed way. No, you have to live soberly, godly, righteously in this world, such as it is at present. It is of no use for you to scheme to escape from it. You are bound to breast this torrent, and buffet all its waves. If the grace of God is in you, that grace is meant to be displayed, not in a select and secluded retreat but in this present world. You are to shine in the darkness like a light.

This life is described in a threefold way. You are, first, to live "soberly"— that is, for yourself. "Soberly" in all your eating and your drinking, and in the indulgence of all bodily appetites—that goes without saying. Drunkards and gluttons, fornicators and adulterers, cannot inherit the kingdom of God. You are to live soberly in all your thinking, all your speaking, all your acting. There is to be sobriety in all your worldly pursuits. You are to have yourself well in hand: you are to be self-restrained. I know some brethren who are not often sober. I do not accuse them of being drunk with wine; but they are mentally intoxicated: they have no reason, no moderation, no judgment. They are all spur and no rein. Right or wrong, they must have that which they have set their hearts upon. They never look round to take the full bearing of a matter: they never estimate calmly; but with closed eyes they rush on like bulls. Alas for these unsober people! They are not to be depended on, they are everything by turns, and nothing long. The man who is disciplined by the grace of God becomes thoughtful, considerate, self-contained; and he is no longer tossed about by passion, or swayed by prejudice. There is only one insobriety into which I pray we may fall; and truth to say, that is the truest sobriety. Of this the Scripture says, "Be not drunk with wine, wherein is excess; but be filled with the Spirit." When the Spirit of God takes full possession of us, then we are borne along by his sacred energy, and are filled with a divine enthusiasm which needs no restraint. Under all other influences we must guard ourselves against yielding too completely, that thus we may live "soberly."

As to his fellowmen the believer lives "righteously." I cannot understand that Christian who can do a dirty thing in business. Craft, cunning, over-reaching, misrepresentation, and deceit are no instruments for the hand of godly men. I am told that my principles are too angelic for business life—that a man cannot be a match for his fellowmen in trade, if he is too Puritanic. Others are up to tricks, and he will be ruined if he cannot trick them in return. O my dear hearers, do not talk in this way. If you mean to go the way of the devil, say so, and take the consequences; but if you profess to be servants of God, deny all partnership with unrighteousness. Dishonesty and falsehood are the opposites of godliness. A Christian man may be poor, but he must live righteously: he may lack sharpness, but he must not lack integrity. A Christian profession without uprightness is a lie. Grace must discipline us to righteous living.

Toward God we are told in the text that we are to be *godly*. Every man who has the grace of God in him indeed and of a truth will think much of God, and will seek first the kingdom of God and his righteousness. God will enter into all his calculations, God's presence will be his joy, God's strength will be his confidence, God's providence will be his inheritance, God's glory will be the chief end of his being, God's law the guide of his conversation. Now, if the grace of God, which has appeared so plainly to all men, has really come with its sacred discipline upon us, it is teaching us to live in this three-fold manner.

Once more, there is looking, as well as living. One work of the grace of God is to cause us to be "looking for that blessed hope of the glorious appearing of the great God and our Savior Jesus Christ." What is that "blessed hope"? Why, first, that when he comes we shall rise from the dead, if we have fallen asleep; and that, if we are alive and remain, we shall be changed at his appearing. Our hope is that we shall be approved of him and shall hear him say, "Well done, good and faithful servant." This hope is not of debt, but of grace: though our Lord will give us a reward, it will not be according to the law of works. We expect to be like Jesus when we shall see him as he is. When Jesus shines forth as the sun, "then shall the righteous shine forth as the sun in the kingdom of our Father." Our gain by godliness cannot be counted down into the palm of our hand. It lies in the glorious future; and yet to faith it is so near that at this moment I almost hear the chariot of the coming One. The Lord comes, and in the coming of the Lord lies the great hope of the believer, his great stimulus to overcome evil, his incentive to perfect holiness in the fear of the Lord. Oh, to be found blameless in the day of the manifestation of our Lord! God grant us this! Do you not see, brethren, how the discipline of the doctrine of grace runs toward the separating of us from sin, and the making us to live unto God?

3. Lastly, and briefly, the text sets forth certain of *our encouragements*. I will only briefly hint at them.

In this great battle for right and truth and holiness, what could we do, my brethren and my sisters, if we were left alone? But our first encouragement is that grace has come to our rescue; for in the day when the Lord Jesus Christ appeared among men, he brought for us the grace of God to help us to overcome all iniquity. He that struggles now against inbred sin has the Holy Spirit within him to help him. He that goes forth to fight against evil in other men by preaching the gospel has that same Holy Ghost going with the truth to make it like a fire and like a hammer. I would ground my weapons, and retreat from a fight so hopeless were it not that the Lord of hosts is with us, the God of Jacob is our refuge. The grace of God that brings salvation from sin has flashed forth conspicuously like the lightning which is seen from one part of the heaven to the other, and our victory over darkness is insured. However hard the conflict with evil, it is not desperate. We may hope on and hope ever. A certain warrior was found in prayer, and when his king sneered, he answered that he was pleading with his majesty's august ally. I question whether God is the ally of anybody when he goes forth with gun and sword; but in using those weapons which are "not carnal, but mighty through God to the pulling down of strongholds," we may truly reckon upon our august ally. Speak the truth, man, for God speaks with you! Work for God, woman, for God works in you to will and to do of his own good pleasure. The appearance of the grace of God in the person of Christ is encouragement enough to those who are under the most difficult circumstances, and have to contend for righteousness against the deadliest odds. Grace has appeared; wherefore let us be of good courage!

A second encouragement is that another appearing is coming. He who bowed his head in weakness, and died in the moment of victory, is coming in all the glory of his endless life. Do not question it, the world is not going to darken into an eternal night: the morning comes as well as the night, and though sin and corruption abound, and the love of many waxes cold, these are but the tokens of his near advent who said that it would be so before his appearing. The right with the might and the might with the right shall be: as surely as God lives, it shall be so. We are not fighting a losing battle. The Lord must triumph. Oh, if his suffering life and cruel death had been the only appearing, we might have feared; but it is not: it is but the first, and the prefatory part of his manifestation. He comes! He comes! None can hinder his coming! Every moment brings him nearer; nothing can delay his glory. When the hour shall strike he shall appear in the majesty of God to put an end to the dominion of sin, and bring in endless peace. Satan shall be bruised under our feet shortly; wherefore comfort one another with these words, and then prepare for further battle. Grind your swords, and be ready for close fighting! Trust in God, and keep your powder dry. Ever this our war cry, "He must reign." We are looking for the appearing of the great God and Savior Jesus Christ.

Another encouragement is that we are serving a glorious Master. The Christ whom we follow is not a dead prophet like Muhammad. Truly we preach Christ crucified; but we also believe in Christ risen from the dead, in Christ gone up on high, in Christ soon to come a second time. He lives, and he lives as the great God and our Savior. If indeed you are soldiers of such a captain throw fear to the winds. Can you be cowards when the Lord of hosts leads you? Dare you tremble when at your head is the Wonderful, the Counselor, the mighty God, the everlasting Father, the Prince of peace? The trumpet is already at the lip of the archangel; who will not play the man? The great drum which makes the universe to throb, summons you to action.

> *Stand up, stand up for Jesus,*
> *Ye soldiers of the cross;*
> *Lift high his royal banner,*
> *It must not suffer loss.*

His cross is the old cross still, and none can overthrow it. Hallelujah, hallelujah to the name of Jesus!

Then come the tender thoughts with which I finish, the memories of what the Lord has done for us to make us holy: "Who gave himself for us." Special redemption, redemption with a wondrous price—"who gave himself for us." Put away that trumpet and that drum; take down the harp and gently touch its sweetest strings. Tell how the Lord Jesus loved us, and gave himself for us. O sirs, if nothing else can touch our hearts this must: "Ye are not your own, ye are bought with a price."

And he gave himself for us with these two objects: first, redemption, that he might redeem us from all iniquity; that he might break the bonds of sin asunder, and cast the cords of depravity far from us. He died—forget not that—died that your sins might die, died that every lust might be dragged into captivity at his chariot wheels. He gave himself for you that you might give yourselves for him.

Again, he died that he might purify us—purify us unto himself. How clean we must be if we are to be clean unto him. The holy Jesus will only commune with that which he has purified after the manner of his own nature; purified unto himself. He has purified us to be wholly his: no human hand may use the golden cup, no human incense may burn in the consecrated censer. We are purified unto himself, as the Hebrew would put it, to be his *segullah*, his peculiar possession. The translation "peculiar people" is unfortunate, because "peculiar" has come to mean odd, strange, singular. The passage really means that believers are Christ's own people, his choice and select portion. Saints are Christ's crown jewels, his box of diamonds; his very, very, very own. He carries his people as lambs in his bosom; he engraves their names on his heart. They are the inheritance to which he is the heir, and he values them more than all the universe beside. He would lose everything else sooner than lose one of them. He desires that you, who are being disciplined by his grace, should know that you are altogether his. You are Christ's men. You are each one to feel, "I do not belong to the world; I do not belong to myself; I belong only to Christ. I am set aside by him for himself only, and his I will be." The silver and the gold are his, and the cattle upon a thousand hills are his; but he makes small account of them, "the Lord's portion is his people."

The apostle finishes up by saying that we are to be a people "zealous of good works." Would to God that all Christian men and women were disciplined by divine grace till they became zealous for good works! In holiness zeal is sobriety. We are not only to approve of good works, and speak for good works, but we are to be red-hot for them. We are to be on fire for everything that is right and true. We may not be content to be quiet and inoffensive, but we are to be zealous of good works. Oh, that my Lord's grace would set us on fire in this way! There is plenty of fuel in the church, what is wanted is fire. A great many very respectable people are, in their sleepy way, doing as little as they can for any good cause. This will never do. We must wake up. Oh, the quantity of ambulance work that Christ's soldiers have to do! One half of Christ's army has to carry the other half. Oh, that our brethren could get off the sick list! Oh, that all of us were ardent, fervent, vigorous, zealous! Come, Holy Spirit, and quiet us! We may not go about to get this by our own efforts and energies, but God will work it by his grace. Grace given us in Christ is the fountainhead of all holy impulse. O heavenly grace, come like a flood at this time and bear us right away!

Oh, that those of you who have never felt the grace of God may be enabled to believe in the Lord Jesus Christ as to his first appearing! Then, trusting in his death upon the cross, you will learn to look for his second coming upon the throne, and you will rejoice therein. Unto his great name be glory forever and ever! Amen.

The Watchword for Today: "Stand Fast"

❧

Delivered on Lord's Day morning, April 17, 1887, at the Metropolitan Tabernacle, Newington. No. 1959.

For our conversation is in heaven, from whence also we look for the Savior, the Lord Jesus Christ: who shall change our vile body, that it may be fashioned like unto his glorious body, according to the working whereby he is able even to subdue all things unto himself. Therefore, my brethren dearly beloved and longed for, my joy and crown, so stand fast in the Lord, my dearly beloved.
—PHILIPPIANS 3:20–4:1

Every doctrine of the Word of God has its practical bearing. As each tree bears seed after its kind, so does every truth of God bring forth practical virtues. Hence you find the apostle Paul very full of *therefores*—his therefores being the conclusions drawn from certain statements of divine truth. I marvel that our excellent translators should have divided the argument from the conclusion by making a new chapter where there is least reason for it.

Last Lord's Day I spoke with you concerning the most sure and certain resurrection of our Lord Jesus: now there is a practical force in that truth, which constitutes part of what is meant by "the power of his resurrection." Since the Lord has risen, and will surely come a second time, and will raise the bodies of his people at his coming, there is something to wait for, and a grand reason for steadfastness while thus waiting. We are looking for the coming of our Lord and Savior Jesus Christ from heaven, and that he shall "fashion anew the body of our humiliation, that it may be conformed to the body of his glory"; therefore let us stand fast in the position which will secure us this honor. Let us keep our posts until the coming of the great Captain shall release the sentinels. The glorious resurrection will abundantly repay us for all the toil and travail we may have to undergo in the battle for the Lord. The glory to be revealed even now casts a light upon our path, and causes sunshine within our hearts. The hope of this happiness makes us even now strong in the Lord, and in the power of his might.

Paul was deeply anxious that those in whom he had been the means of kindling the heavenly hope might be preserved faithful until the coming of Christ. He trembled lest any of them should seem to draw back, and prove traitors to their Lord. He dreaded lest he should lose what he hoped he had gained, by their turning aside from the faith. Hence he beseeches them to "stand fast." He expressed in the sixth verse of the first chapter his conviction that he who had begun a good work in them would perform it, but his intense love made him exhort them, saying, "Stand fast in the Lord, my dearly beloved." By such exhortations final perseverance is promoted and secured.

Paul has fought bravely; and in the case of the Philippian converts he believes that he has secured the victory, and he fears lest it should yet be lost. He reminds me of the death of that British hero, Wolfe, who on the heights of Quebec received a mortal wound. It was just at the moment when the enemy fled, and when he knew that they were running, a smile was on his face, and he cried, "Hold me up. Let not my brave soldiers see me drop. The day is ours. Oh, do keep it!" His sole anxiety was to make the victory sure. Thus warriors die, and thus Paul lived. His very soul seems to cry, "We have won the day. Oh, do keep it!" O my beloved hearers, I believe that many of you are "in the Lord," but I entreat you to "stand fast in the Lord." In your case, also, the day is won; but oh, do keep it! There is the pith of all I have to say to you this morning: may God the Holy Spirit write it on your hearts! Having done all things well thus far, I entreat you to obey the injunction of Jude, to "keep yourselves in the love of God," and to join with me in adoring him who alone is able to keep us from falling, and to present us faultless before his presence with exceeding great joy. Unto him be glory forever. Amen.

In leading out your thoughts I will keep to the following order:

First, it seems to me from the text that *the apostle perceived that these Philippian Christians were in their right place:* they were "in the Lord," and in such a position that he could safely bid them "stand fast" in it. Second, *he longed for them that they should keep their right place*—"Stand fast in the Lord, my dearly beloved"; and then, third, *he urged the best motives for their keeping their place.* These motives are contained in the first two verses of our text, upon which we will enlarge further on.

1. Paul joyfully perceived that *his beloved converts were in their right place.*

It is a very important thing indeed that we should begin well. The start is not everything, but it is a great deal. It has been said by the old proverb, that "well begun is half done"; and it is certainly so in the things of God. It is vitally important to enter in at the strait gate; to start on the heavenly journey from the right point. I have no doubt that many slips and falls and apostasies among professors are due to the fact that they were not right at first: the foundation was always upon the sand, and when the house came down at last, it was no more than might have been expected. A flaw in the foundation is pretty sure to be followed by a crack in the superstructure. Do see to it that you lay a good foundation. It is even better to have no repentance than a repentance which needs to be repented of: it is better to have no faith than a false faith: it is better to make no profession of religion than to make an untruthful one. God give us grace that we may not make a mistake in learning the alphabet of godliness, or else in all our learning we shall blunder on and increase in error. We should early learn the difference between grace and merit, between the purpose of God and the will of man, between trust in God and confidence in the flesh. If we do not start aright, the further we go the further we shall be from our desired end, and the more thoroughly in the wrong shall we find ourselves. Yes, it is of prime importance that our new birth and our first love should be genuine beyond all question.

The only position, however, in which we can begin aright is to be "in the Lord." This is to begin as we may safely go on. This is the essential point. It is a very good thing for Christians to be in the church; but if you are in the church before you are in the Lord you are out of place. It is a good thing to be engaged in holy work; but if you are in holy work before you are in the Lord you will have no heart for it, neither will the Lord accept it. It is not essential that you should be in this church or in that church; but it is essential that you should be "in the Lord"; it is not essential that you should be in the Sabbath school nor in the working meeting nor in the Tract Society; but it is essential to the last degree that you should be in the Lord. The apostle rejoiced over those that were converted at Philippi because he knew that they were in the Lord. They were where he wished them to remain, therefore he said, "Stand fast in the Lord."

What is it to be "in the Lord"? Well, brethren, *we are in the Lord vitally and evidently when we fly to the Lord Jesus by repentance and faith*, and make him to be our refuge and hiding place. Is it so with you? Have you fled out of self? Are you trusting in the Lord alone? Have you come to Calvary, and beheld your Savior? As the doves build their nests in the rock, have you thus made your home in Jesus? There is no shelter for a guilty soul but in his wounded side. Have you come there? Are you in him? Then keep there. You will never have a better refuge; in fact, there is no other. No other name is given under heaven among men whereby we must be saved. I cannot tell you to stand fast in the

Lord, unless you are there: hence my first inquiry is—Are you in Christ? Is he your only confidence? In his life, his death, and his resurrection do you find the grounds of your hope? Is he himself all your salvation, and all your desire? If so, stand fast in him.

Next, these people, in addition to having fled to Christ for refuge, were now *in Christ as to their daily life*. They had heard him say, "Abide in me"; and therefore they remained in the daily enjoyment of him, in reliance upon him, in obedience to him, and in the earnest copying of his example. They were Christians, that is to say, persons upon whom was named the name of Christ. They were endeavoring to realize the power of his death and resurrection as a sanctifying influence, killing their sins and fostering their virtues. They were laboring to reproduce his image in themselves, that so they might bring glory to his name. Their lives were spent within the circle of their Savior's influence. Are you so, my dear friends? Then stand fast. You will never find a nobler example; you will never be saturated with a diviner spirit than that of Christ Jesus your Lord. Whether we eat or drink, or whatsoever we do, let us do all in the name of the Lord Jesus, and so live in him.

These Philippians had, moreover, realized that they were *in Christ by a real and vital union with him*. They had come to feel, not like separated individualities, copying a model, but as members of a body made like to their head. By a living, loving, lasting union they were joined to Christ as their covenant head. They could say, "Who shall separate us from the love of God which is in Christ Jesus our Lord?" Do you know what it is to feel that the life which is in you is first in Christ, and still flows from him, even as the life of the branch is mainly in the stem? "I live; yet not I, but Christ liveth in me." This is to be in Christ. Are you in him in this sense? Forgive my pressing the question. If you answer me in the affirmative, I shall then entreat you to "stand fast" in him. It is in him, and in him only, that spiritual life is to be sustained, even as only from him can it be received. To be engrafted into Christ is salvation; but to abide in Christ is the full enjoyment of it. True union to Christ is eternal life. Paul, therefore, rejoiced over these Philippians, because they were joined unto the Lord in one spirit.

This expression is very short, but very full. "In Christ." Does it not mean that we are in Christ as the birds are in the air which buoys them up and enables them to fly? Are we not in Christ as the fish are in the sea? *Our Lord has become our element*, vital, and all surrounding. In him we live and move and have our being. He is in us, and we are in him. We are filled with all the fullness of God, because in Christ does all fullness dwell, and we dwell in him. Christ to us is all; he is in all; and he is all in all! Jesus to us is everything in everything. Without him we can *do* nothing, and we *are* nothing. Thus are we emphatically in him. If you have reached this point, "stand fast" in it. If you dwell in the secret place of the tabernacles of the most High, abide under the shadow of the Almighty. Do you sit at his table, and eat of his dainties? Then prolong the visit, and think not of removal. Say in your soul—

> Here would I find a settled rest,
> While others go and come;
> No more a stranger, or a guest,
> But like a child at home.

Has Jesus brought you into his green pastures? Then lie down in them. Go no further, for you will never fare better. Stay with your Lord, however long the night, for only in him have you hope of morning.

You see, then, that these people were where they should be—in the Lord, and that this was the reason why the apostle took such delight in them. Kindly read the first verse of the fourth chapter, and see how he loves them, and joys over them. He heaps up titles of love! Some dip their morsel in vinegar, but Paul's words were saturated with honey. Here we not only have sweet words, but they mean something: his love was real and fervent. The very heart of Paul is written out large in this verse—"Therefore, my brethren dearly beloved and longed for, my joy and crown, so stand fast in the Lord, my dearly beloved." Because they were in Christ, therefore first of all they were Paul's *brethren*. This was a new relationship, not earthly, but heavenly. What did this Jew from Tarsus know about the Philippians? Many of them were Gentiles. Time was when he would have called them dogs, and despised them as the uncircumcised; but now he says, "my brethren." That poor word has become very hackneyed. We talk of brethren without particularly much of brotherly love, but true brothers have a love for one another which is very unselfish and admirable, and so there is between real Christians a brotherhood which they will neither disown nor dissemble nor forget. It is said of our Lord, "For this cause he is not ashamed to call them brethren"; and surely they need never be ashamed to call one another brethren. Paul, at any rate, looks at the jailer, that jailor who had set his feet in the stocks, and he looks at the jailer's family, and at Lydia, and many others; in fact, at the whole company that he had gathered at Philippi, and he salutes them lovingly as "my brethren." Their names were written in the same family register, because they were in Christ and therefore had one Father in heaven.

Next, the apostle calls them "my *dearly beloved*." The verse almost begins with this word, and it quite finishes with it. The repetition makes it mean, "my doubly dear ones." Such is the love which every true servant of Christ will have for those who have been begotten to the faith of Christ by his means. Oh yes, if you are in Christ his ministers must love you. How could there be a lack of affection in our hearts toward you, since we have been the means of bringing you to Jesus? Without cant or display we call you our "dearly beloved."

Then the apostle calls them his *"longed for,"* that is, his most desired ones. He first desired to see them converted; after that he desired to see them baptized; then he desired to see them exhibiting all the graces of Christians. When he saw holiness in them, he desired to visit them and commune with them. Their constant kindness created in him a strong desire to speak with them face to face. He loved them, and desired their company, because they were in Christ. So he speaks of them as those for whom he longed. His delight was in thinking of them and in hoping to visit them.

Then he adds, "my joy and crown." Paul had been the means of their salvation, and when he thought of that blessed result he never regretted all that he had suffered: his persecutions among the Gentiles seemed light indeed since these priceless souls were his reward. Though he was nothing but a poor prisoner of Christ, yet he talks in right royal style: they are his crown. They were his *stephanos*, or crown given as a reward for his life race. This among the Greeks was usually a wreath of flowers placed around the victor's brow. Paul's crown would never fade. He writes as he felt the amaranth around his temples: even now he looks upon the Philippians as his chaplet of honor: they were his joy and his crown; he anticipated, I do not doubt, that throughout eternity it would be a part of his heaven to see them amid their blessedness, and to know that he helped to bring them to that felicity by leading them to Christ. O beloved, it is indeed our highest joy that we have not run in vain, neither labored in vain: you who have been snatched as "brands from the burning," and are now living to the praise of our Lord Jesus Christ, you are our prize, our crown, our joy.

These converts were all this to Paul simply because they were "in Christ." They had begun well, they were where they should be, and he, therefore, rejoiced in them.

2. But second, it was for this reason that *he longed that they should keep there.*

He entreated them to stand fast. "So stand fast in the Lord, my dearly beloved." The beginning of religion is not the whole of it. You must not suppose that the sum of godliness is contained within the experience of a day or two or a week or a few months or even a few years. Precious are the feelings which attend conversion; but dream not that repentance, faith, and so forth, are for a season, and then all is done and done with. I am afraid there are some who secretly say, "Everything is now complete; I have experienced the necessary change, I have been to see the elders and the pastor, and I have been baptized, and received into the church, and now all is right forever." That is a false view of your condition. In conversion you have started in the race, and you must run to the end of the course. In your confession of Christ, you have carried your tools into the vineyard, but the day's work now begins. Remember, "He that shall endure unto the end, the same shall be saved." Godliness is a lifelong business. The working out of the salvation which the Lord himself works in you is not a matter of certain hours, and of a limited period of life. Salvation is unfolded throughout all our sojourn here. We continue to repent and to believe, and even the process of our conversion continues as we are changed more and more into the image of our Lord. Final perseverance is the necessary evidence of genuine conversion.

In proportion as we rejoice over converts, we feel an intense bitterness when any disappoint us, and turn out to be merely temporary camp followers. We sigh over the seed which sprang up so speedily, but which withers so soon because it has neither root nor depth of earth. We were ready to say, "Ring the bells of heaven"; but the bells of heaven did not ring because these people talked about Christ, and said they were in Christ; but it was all a delusion. After a while, for one reason and another, they went back; "they went out from us, but they were not of us; for if they had been of us, they would no doubt have continued with us: but they went out, that they might be made manifest that they were not all of us." Our churches suffer most seriously from the great numbers who drop out of their ranks, and either go back to the world, or else must be pursuing a very secret and solitary path in their way to heaven, for we hear no more of them. Our joy is turned to disappointment, our crown of laurel becomes a circle of faded leaves, and we are weary at the remembrance of it. With what earnestness, therefore, would we say to you who are beginning the race, "Continue in your course. We beseech you turn not aside, neither slacken your running, till you have won the prize"!

I heard an expression yesterday which pleased me much. I spoke about the difficulty of keeping on. "Yes," answered my friend, "and it is harder still to keep on keeping on." So it is. There is the pinch. I know lots of fellows who are wonders at the start. What a rush they make! But then there is no stay in them; they soon lose breath. The difference between the spurious and the real Christian lies in this staying power. The real Christian has a life within him which can never die, an incorruptible seed which lives and abides forever; but the spurious Christian begins after a fashion, but ends almost as soon as he begins. He is esteemed a saint; but turns out a hypocrite. He makes a fair show for a while, but soon he quits the way of holiness, and makes his own damnation sure. God save you, dear friends, from anything which looks like apostasy. Hence I would with all my might press upon you these two most weighty words: "Stand fast."

I will put the exhortation thus: "Stand fast *doctrinally.*" In this age all the ships in the waters are pulling up their anchors: they are drifting with the tide; they are driven about with every wind. It is your wisdom to put down more anchors. I have taken the precaution to cast four anchors out of the stern, as well as to see that the great bower anchor is in its proper place. I will not budge an inch from the old doctrine for any man. Now that the cyclone is triumphant over many a bowing wall and tottering fence, those who are built upon the one foundation must prove its value by standing fast. We will hearken to no teaching but that of the Lord Jesus. If you see a truth to be in God's Word, grasp it by your faith; and if it be unpopular, grapple it to you as with hooks of steel. If you are despised as a fool for holding it, hold it the more. Like an oak, take deeper root, because the winds would tear you from your place. Defy reproach and ridicule, and you have already vanquished it. Stand fast, like the British squares in the olden times. When fierce assaults were made upon them, every man seemed transformed to rock. We might have wandered from the ranks a little in more peaceful times, to look after the fascinating flowers which grow on every side of our march; but now we know that the enemy surrounds us, we keep strictly to the line of march, and tolerate no roaming. The watchword of the host of God just now is "Stand fast!" Hold you to the faith once delivered to the saints. Hold fast the form of sound words, and deviate not one jot or tittle therefrom. Doctrinally stand fast!

Practically, also, abide firm in the right, the true, the holy. This is of the utmost importance. The barriers are broken down; they would amalgamate church and world: yes, even church and stage. It is proposed to combine God and devil in one service; Christ and Belial are to perform on one stage. Surely now is the time when the lion shall eat straw like the ox, and very dirty straw too. So they say; but I repeat to you this word, "Come out from among them, and be ye separate, and touch not the unclean thing." Write "holiness unto the Lord" not only on your altars, but upon the bells of the horses; let everything be done as before the living God. Do all things unto holiness and edification. Strive together to maintain the purity of the disciples of Christ; and take up your cross, and go without the camp bearing his reproach. If you have already stood apart in your decision for the Lord, continue to do so. Stand fast. In nothing moved by the laxity of the age, in nothing affected by the current of modern opinion, say to yourself, "I will do as Christ bids me to the utmost of my ability. I will follow the Lamb whithersoever he goes." In these times of worldliness, impurity, self-indulgence, and error, it becomes the Christian to gather up his skirts and keep his feet and his garments clean from the pollution which lies all around him. We must be more Puritanic and precise than we have been. Oh, for grace to stand fast!

Mind also that you stand fast *experimentally*. Pray that your inward experience may be a close adhesion to your Master. Do not go astray from his presence. Neither climb with those who dream of perfection in the flesh, nor grovel with those who doubt the possibility of present salvation. Take the Lord Jesus Christ to be your sole treasure, and let your heart be ever with him. Stand fast in faith in his atonement, in confidence in his divinity, in assurance of his second advent. I pine to know within my soul the power of his resurrection, and to have unbroken fellowship with him. In communion with the Father and the Son let us stand fast. He shall fare well whose heart and soul, affections and understanding are wrapped up in Christ Jesus, and in none beside. Concerning your inward life, your secret prayer, your walk with God, here is the watchword of the day: "Stand fast."

To put it very plainly, "Stand fast *in the Lord,*" *without wishing for another trust*. Do not desire to have any hope but that which is in Christ. Do not entertain the proposition that you should unite another confidence to your confidence in the Lord. Have no hankering after any other fashion of faith except the faith of a sinner in his Savior. All hope but that which is set before us in the gospel and brought to us by the Lord Jesus is a poisoned delicacy, highly colored, but by no means to be so much as tasted by those who have been fed upon the bread of heaven. What need we more than Jesus? What way of salvation do we seek but that of grace? What security but the precious blood? Stand fast; and wish for no other rock of salvation save the Lord Jesus.

Next, stand fast *without wavering in our trust*. Permit no doubt to worry you. Know that Jesus can save you, and, what is more, know that he has saved you. So commit yourself to his hands, that you are as sure of your salvation as of your existence. The blood of Jesus Christ this day cleanses us from all sin; his righteousness covers us, and his life quickens us into newness of life. Tolerate no doubt, mistrust, suspicion, or misgiving. Believe in Christ up to the hilt. All for myself, I will yield to be lost forever if Jesus does not save me. I will have no other string to my bow, no second door of hope, or way of retreat. I could risk a thousand souls on my Lord's truth and feel no risk. Stand fast, without wishing for another trust, and without wavering in the trust you have.

Moreover, stand fast *without wandering into sin*. You are tempted this way and that way: stand fast. Inward passions rise; lusts of the flesh rebel, the devil hurls his fearful suggestions; the men of your own household tempt you: stand fast. Only so will you be preserved from the torrents of iniquity. Keep close to the example and spirit of your Master; and having done all, still stand.

As I have said, stand fast without wandering, so next I must say stand fast *without wearying*. You are a little tired. Never mind, take a little rest and brush up again. "Oh," you say, "this toil is so monotonous." Do it better, and that will be a change. Your Savior endured his life and labor without this complaint, for zeal had eaten him up. "Alas!" you cry, "I cannot see results." Never mind; wait for results, even as the husbandman waits for the precious fruits of the earth. "Oh, sir, I plod along and make no progress." Never mind, you are a poor judge of your own success. Work on, for in due season you shall reap if you faint not. Practice perseverance. Remember that if you have the work of faith and the labor of love, you must complete the trio by adding the patience of hope. You cannot do without this last. "Be ye steadfast, unmovable, always abounding in the work of the Lord, forasmuch as ye know that your labor is not in vain in the Lord." I am reminded of Sir Christopher Wren, when he cleared away old St. Paul's to make room for his splendid pile. He was compelled to use battering rams upon the massive walls. The workmen kept on battering and battering. An enormous force was brought to bear upon the walls for days and nights, but it did not appear to have made the least impression upon the ancient masonry. Yet the great architect knew what he was at: he bade them keep on incessantly, and the ram fell again and again upon the rocky wall, till at length the whole mass was disintegrating and coming apart; and then each stroke began to tell. At a blow it reeled, at another it quivered, at another it moved visibly, at another it fell over amid clouds of dust. These last strokes did the work. Do you think so? No, it was the combination of blows, the first as truly as the last. Keep on with the battering ram. I hope to keep on until I die. And, mark you, I may die and I may not see the errors of the hour totter to their fall, but I shall be perfectly content to sleep in Christ, for I have a sure expectation that this work will succeed in the end. I shall be happy to have done my share of the work, even if I personally see little apparent result. Lord, let your work appear unto your servants, and we will be content that your glory should be reserved for our children. Stand fast, my brethren, in incessant labors, for the end is sure.

And then, in addition to standing fast in that respect, stand fast *without warping*. Timber, when it is rather green, is apt to go this way or that. The spiritual weather is very bad just now for green wood: it is one day damp with superstition, and another day it is parched with skepticism. Rationalism and ritualism are both at work. I pray that you may not warp. Keep straight; keep to the truth, the whole truth, and nothing but the truth; for in the Master's name we bid you "Stand fast in the Lord."

Stand fast, for there is great need. Many walk of whom I have told you often, and now tell you even weeping, that they are the enemies of the cross of Christ.

Paul urged them to stand fast because, even in his own case, spiritual life was a struggle. Even Paul said, "Not as though I had already attained." He was pressing forward; he was straining his whole energy by the power of the Holy Ghost. He did not expect to be carried to heaven on a featherbed; he was warring and agonizing. You, beloved, must do the same. What a grand example of perseverance did Paul set to us all! Nothing enticed him from his steadfastness. "None of these things move me," said he, "neither count I my life dear unto me." He has entered into his rest, because the Lord his God helped him to stand fast, even to the end. I wish I had power to put this more earnestly, but my very soul goes forth with it. "Stand fast in the Lord, my dearly beloved."

3. Third, *the apostle urged the best motives for their standing fast.*

He says, "Stand fast *because of your citizenship.*" Read the twentieth verse: "For our citizenship is in heaven." Now, if you are what you profess to be, if you are in Christ, you are citizens of the New Jerusalem. Men ought to behave themselves according to their citizenship, and not dishonor their city. When a man was a citizen of Athens, in the olden time, he felt it incumbent upon him to be brave. Xerxes said, "These Athenians are not ruled by kings: how will they fight?" "No," said one, "but every man respects the law, and each man is ready to die for his country." Xerxes soon had to know that the like obedience and respect of law ruled the Spartans, and that these, because they were of Sparta, were all brave as lions. He sends word to Leonidas and his little troop to give up their arms. "Come and take them," was the courageous reply. The Persian king had myriads of soldiers with him, while Leonidas had only three hundred Spartans at his side; yet they kept the pass, and it cost the eastern despot many thousands of men to force a passage. The sons of Sparta died rather than desert their post. Every citizen of Sparta felt that he must stand fast: it was not for such a man as he to yield. I like the spirit of Bayard, that "knight without fear and without reproach." He knew not what fear meant. In his last battle, his spine was broken, and he said to those around him, "Place me up against a tree, so that I may sit up and die with my face to the enemy." Yes, if our backs were broken, if we could no more bear the shield or use the sword, it would be incumbent upon us, as citizens of the New Jerusalem, to die with our faces toward the enemy. We must not yield, we dare not yield, if we are of the city of the great King. The martyrs cry to us to stand fast; the cloud of witnesses bending from their thrones above beseech us to stand fast; yes, all the hosts of the shining ones cry to us, "Stand fast." Stand fast for God, and the truth, and holiness, and let no man take your crown.

The next argument that Paul used was *their outlook*. "Our conversation is in heaven; from whence also we look for the Savior, the Lord Jesus Christ." Brethren, Jesus is coming. He is even now on the way. You have heard our tidings till you scarcely credit us; but the word is true, and it will surely be fulfilled before long. The Lord is coming indeed. He promised to come to die, and he kept his word: he now promises to come to reign, and be you sure that he will keep his tryst with his people. He is coming. Ears of faith can hear the sound of his chariot wheels; every moment of time, every event of providence is bringing him nearer. Blessed are those servants who shall not be sleeping when he comes nor wandering from their posts of duty; happy shall they be whom their Lord shall find faithfully watching and standing fast in that great day!

To us, beloved, he is coming, not as Judge and destroyer, but as *Savior*. We look for the Savior, the Lord Jesus Christ. Now, if we do look for him, let us "stand fast." There must be no going into sin, no forsaking the fellowship of the church, no leaving the truth, no trying to play fast and loose with godliness, no running with the hare and hunting with the hounds. Let us stand so fast in singleness of heart that, whenever Jesus comes, we shall be able to say, "Welcome, welcome, Son of God!"

Sometimes I wait through the weary years with great comfort. There was a ship some time ago outside a certain harbor. A heavy sea made the ship roll fearfully. A dense fog blotted out all buoys and lights. The captain never left the wheel. He could not tell his way into the harbor, and no pilot could get out to him for a long time. Eager passengers urged him to be courageous and make a dash for the harbor. He said, "No; it is not my duty to run so great a risk. A pilot is required here, and I will wait for one if I wait a week." The truest courage is that which can bear to be charged with cowardice. To wait is much wiser than when you cannot hear the foghorn and have no pilot yet to steam on and wreck your vessel on the rocks. Our prudent captain waited his time, and at last he espied the pilot's boat coming to him over the boiling sea.

When the pilot was at his work the captain's anxious waiting was over. The church is like that vessel, she is pitched to and fro in the storm and the dark, and the pilot has not yet come. The weather is very threatening. All around the darkness hangs like a pall. But Jesus will come, walking on the water, before long; he will bring us safe to the desired haven. Let us wait with patience. Stand fast! Stand fast! for Jesus is coming, and in him is our sure hope.

Further, there was another motive. *There was an expectation.* "He shall change our vile body," or rather, "body of our humiliation." Only think of it, dear friends! No more headaches or heartaches, no more feebleness and fainting, no more inward tumor or consumption; but the Lord shall transfigure this body of our humiliation into the likeness of the body of his glory. Our frame is now made up of decaying substances, it is of the earth earthy. "So to the dust return we must." This body groans, suffers, becomes diseased, and dies: blessed be God, it shall be wonderfully changed, and then there shall be no more death, neither sorrow nor crying, neither shall there be any more pain. The natural appetites of this body engender sad tendencies to sin, and in this respect it is a "vile body." It shall not always be so; the great change will deliver it from all that is gross and carnal. It shall be pure as the Lord's body! Whatever the body of Christ is now, our body is to be like it. We spoke of it last Sunday, you know, when we heard him say, "Handle me." We are to have a real, corporeal body as he had for substance and reality; and, like his body, it will be full of beauty, full of health and strength; it will enjoy peculiar immunities from evil, and special adaptations for good. That is what is going to happen to me and to you; therefore let us stand fast. Let us not willfully throw away our prospects of glory and immortality. What! Relinquish resurrection? Relinquish glory? Relinquish likeness to the risen Lord? O God, save us from such a terrible piece of apostasy! Save us from such immeasurable folly! Suffer us not to turn our backs in the day of battle, since that would be to turn our backs from the crown of life that fades not away.

Last, the apostle urges us to stand fast because of *our resources.* Somebody may ask, "How can this body of yours be transformed and transfigured until it becomes like the body of Christ?" I cannot tell you anything about the process; it will all be accomplished in the twinkling of an eye, at the last trump. But I can tell you by what power it will be accomplished. The omnipotent Lord will lay bare his arm and exercise his might, "according to the working whereby he is able even to subdue all things unto himself." O brethren, we may well stand fast since we have infinite power at our backs. The Lord is with us with all his energy, even with his all-conquering strength, which shall yet subdue all his foes. Do not let us imagine that any enemy can be too strong for Christ's arm. If he is able to subdue all things unto himself, he can certainly bear us through all opposition. One glance of his eye may wither all opposers, or, better still, one word from his lips may turn them into friends. The army of the Lord is strong in reserves. These reserves have never yet been fully called out. We, who are in the field, are only a small squadron, holding the fort; but our Lord has at his back ten thousand times ten thousand who will carry war into the enemy's camp. When the Captain of our salvation comes to the front, he will bring his heavenly legions with him. Our business is to watch until he appears upon the scene, for when he comes, his infinite resources will be put in marching order. I like that speech of Wellington (who was so calm amid the roar of Waterloo), when an officer sent word, "Tell the commander in chief that he must move me, I cannot hold my position any longer, my numbers are so thinned." "Tell him," said the great general, "he *must* hold his place. Every Englishman today must die where he stands, or else win the victory." The officer read the command to stand, and he did stand till the trumpet sounded victory. And so it is now. My brethren, we must die where we are rather than yield to the enemy. If Jesus tarries we must not desert our posts. Wellington knew that the heads of the Prussian columns would soon be visible, coming in to ensure the victory; and so by faith we can perceive the legions of our Lord approaching: in serried ranks his angels fly through the opening heaven. The air is teeming with them. I hear their silver trumpets. Behold, he comes with clouds! When he comes he will abundantly recompense all who stood fast amid the rage of battle. Let us sing, "Hold the fort, for I am coming."

"He Cometh with Clouds"

Delivered at the Metropolitan Tabernacle, Newington. No. 1989.

Behold, he cometh with clouds; and every eye shall see him, and they also which pierced him: and all kindreds of the earth shall wail because of him. Even so, Amen. —REVELATION 1:7

In reading the chapter we observed how the beloved John saluted the seven churches in Asia with, "Grace and peace be unto you." Blessed men scatter blessings. When the *benediction* of God rests on us we pour out benedictions upon others.

From benediction John's gracious heart rose into *adoration* of the great King of saints. As our hymn puts it, "The holy to the holiest leads." They that are good at blessing men will be quick at blessing God.

It is a wonderful doxology which John has given us: "Unto him that loved us, and washed us from our sins in his own blood, and hath made us kings and priests unto God and his Father; to him be glory and dominion forever and ever. Amen." I like the Revised Version for its alliteration in this case, although I cannot prefer it for other reasons. It runs thus: "Unto him that *loveth* us, and *loosed* us from our sins by his blood." Truly our Redeemer has loosed us from sin; but the mention of his blood suggests washing rather than loosing. We can keep the alliteration and yet retain the meaning of cleansing if we read the passage, "Unto him that loved us, and laved us." *Loved* us, and *laved* us: carry those two words home with you: let them lie upon your tongue to sweeten your breath for prayer and praise. "Unto him that loved us, and laved us, be glory and dominion forever and ever."

Then John tells of the dignity which the Lord has put upon us in making us kings and priests, and from this he ascribes royalty and dominion unto the Lord himself. John had been extolling the great King, whom he calls, "the Prince of the kings of the earth." Such indeed he was, and is, and is to be. When John had touched upon that royalty which is natural to our divine Lord, and that dominion which has come to him by conquest, and by the gift of the Father as the reward of all his travail, he then went on to note that he has "made us kings." Our Lord's royalty he diffuses among his redeemed. We praise him because he is in himself a king, and next, because he is a king maker, the fountain of honor and majesty. He has not only enough of royalty for himself, but he hands a measure of his dignity to his people. He makes kings out of such common stuff as he finds in us poor sinners. Shall we not adore him for this? Shall we not cast our crowns at his feet? He gave our crowns to us, shall we not give them to him? "To him be glory and dominion forever and ever. Amen." King by thy divine nature! King by filial right! King maker, lifting up the beggar from the dunghill to set him among princes! King of kings by the unanimous love of all your crowned ones! you are he whom your brethren shall praise! Reign forever and ever! Unto you be hosannas of welcome and hallelujahs of praise. Lord of the earth and heaven, let all things that be, or ever shall be, render unto you all glory in the highest degree. Brethren, do not your souls take fire as you think of the praises of Emmanuel? Fain would I fill the universe with his praise. Oh, for a thousand tongues to sing the glories of the Lord Jesus! If the Spirit who dictated the words of John has taken possession of our spirits, we shall find adoration to be our highest delight. Never are we so near to heaven as when we are absorbed in the worship of Jesus, our Lord and God. Oh, that I could now adore him as I shall do when, delivered from this encumbering body, my soul shall behold him in the fullness of his glory!

It would seem from the chapter that the adoration of John was increased by his expectation of the Lord's second coming; for he cries, "Behold, he cometh with clouds." His adoration awoke his expectation, which all the while was lying in his soul as an element of that vehement heat of reverent love which he poured forth in his doxology. "Behold, he cometh," said he, and thus he revealed one source of his reverence. "Behold, he cometh," said he, and this exclamation was the result of his reverence. He adored until his faith realized his Lord and became a second and nobler sight.

I think, too, that his reverence was deepened and his adoration was rendered more fervent by his conviction of the speediness of his Lord's coming. "Behold, he cometh" or is coming: he means to assert that he is even now on his way. As workmen are moved to be more diligent in service when they hear their master's footfall, so, doubtless, saints are quickened in their devotion when they are conscious that he whom they worship is drawing near. He has gone away to the Father for a while, and so he has left us alone in this world; but he has said, "I will come again and receive you unto myself," and we are confident that he will keep his word. Sweet is the remembrance of that loving promise. That assurance is pouring its savor into John's heart while he is adoring; and it becomes inevitable, as well as most meet and proper, that his doxology should at its close introduce him to the Lord himself, and cause him to cry out, "Behold, he cometh." Having worshiped among the pure in heart, he sees the Lord: having adored the King, he sees him assume the judgment seat, and appear in the clouds of heaven. When once we enter upon heavenly things, we know not how far we can go nor how high we can climb. John who began with blessing the churches now beholds his Lord.

May the Holy Ghost help us reverently to think of the wondrous coming of our blessed Lord, when he shall appear to the delight of his people and the dismay of the ungodly!

There are three things in the text. They will seem commonplace to some of you, and, indeed, they are the commonplace of our divine faith, and yet nothing can be of greater importance. The first is, *our Lord Jesus comes*: "Behold, he cometh with clouds." The second is, *our Lord Jesus Christ's coming will be seen of all*: "Every eye shall see him, and they also which pierced him." And, in the third place, *this coming will cause great sorrow*: "All kindreds of the earth shall wail because of him."

1. May the Holy Spirit help us while, in the first place, we remember that *our Lord Jesus Christ comes!*

This announcement is thought worthy of a note of admiration. As the Latins would say, there is an *Ecce* placed here: "Behold, he cometh." As in the old books the printers put hands in the margin pointing to special passages, such is this "Behold!" It is a *nota bene* calling upon us to note well what we are reading. Here is something which we are to *hold* and *behold*. We now hear a voice crying, "Come and see!" The Holy Spirit never uses superfluous words, nor redundant notes of exclamation; when he cries, "Behold!," it is because there is reason for deep and lasting attention. Will you turn away when he bids you pause and ponder, linger, and look? O you that have been beholding vanity, come and behold the fact that Jesus comes. You that have been beholding this, and beholding that, and thinking of nothing worthy of your thoughts; forget these passing sights and spectacles, and for once behold a scene which has no parallel. It is not a monarch in her jubilee, but the King of kings in his glory. That same Jesus who went up from Olivet into heaven is coming again to earth in like manner as his disciples saw him go up into heaven. Come and behold this great sight. If ever there was a thing in the world worth looking at, it is this. Behold and see if there was ever glory like unto his glory! Hearken to the midnight cry, "Behold, the bridegroom cometh!" It has practically to do with you. "Go ye forth to meet him." This voice is to you, O sons of men. Do not carelessly turn aside; for the Lord God himself demands your attention: he commands you to "Behold!" Will you be blind when God bids you behold? Will you shut your eyes when your Savior cries, "Behold"? When the finger of inspiration points the way, will not your eye follow where it directs you? "Behold, he cometh." O my hearers, look hither, I beseech you.

If we read the words of our text carefully, this "Behold" shows us first, that this coming is to be vividly realized. I think I see John. He is in the spirit; but on a sudden he seems startled into a keener and more solemn attention. His mind is more awake than usual, though he was ever a man of bright eyes that saw afar. We always liken him to the eagle for the height of his fight and the keenness of his vision; yet on a sudden, even he seems startled with a more astounding vision. He cries out, "Behold! Behold!" He has caught sight of his Lord. He says not, "He will come by and by," but, "I can see him; he is now coming." He has evidently realized the second advent. He has so conceived of the second coming of the Lord that it has become a matter of fact to him; a matter to be spoken of and even to be written down. "Behold, he cometh!" Have you and I ever realized the coming of Christ so fully as this? Perhaps we believe that he will come. I should hope that we all do that. If we believe that the Lord Jesus has come the first time, we believe also that he will come the second time; but are these equally assured truths to us? Peradventure we have vividly realized the first appearing: from Bethlehem to Golgotha, and from Calvary to Olivet we have traced the Lord, understanding that blessed cry, "Behold the Lamb of God, which taketh away the sin of the world!" Yes, the Word was made flesh and dwelt among us, and we beheld his glory, the glory as of the only begotten of the Father, full of grace and truth. But have we with equal firmness grasped the thought that he comes again without a sin offering unto salvation? Do we now say to each other, as we meet in happy fellowship, "Yes, our Lord comes"? It should be to us not only a prophecy assuredly believed among us, but a scene pictured in our souls, and anticipated in our hearts. My imagination has often set forth that dread scene: but better still, my faith has realized it. I have heard the chariot wheels of the Lord's approach, and I have endeavored to set my house in order for his reception. I have felt the shadow of that great cloud which shall attend him, damping the ardor of my worldliness. I hear even now in spirit the sound of the last trumpet, whose tremendous blast startles my soul to serious action and puts force into my life. Would God that I lived more completely under the influence of that august event!

Brothers and sisters, to this realization I invite you. I wish that we could go together in this, until as we went out of the house we said to one another, "Behold, he cometh!" One said to his fellow, after the Lord had risen, "The Lord has risen indeed." I want you tonight to feel just as certain that the Lord is coming indeed, and I would have you say as much to one another. We are sure that he will come, and that he is on the way; but the benefit of a more vivid realization would be incalculable.

This coming is to be zealously proclaimed, for John does not merely calmly say, "He cometh," but he vigorously cries, "Behold, he cometh." Just as the herald of a king prefaces his message by a trumpet blast that calls attention, so John cries, "Behold!" As the old town crier was inclined to say, "Oh yes! Oh yes! Oh yes!" or to use some other striking formula by which he called upon men to note his announcement, so John stands in the midst of us, and cries, "Behold, he cometh!" He calls attention by that emphatic word "behold." It is no ordinary message that he brings, and he would not have us treat his word as a commonplace saying. He throws his heart into the announcement. He proclaims it loudly, he proclaims it solemnly, and he proclaims it with authority: "Behold, he cometh."

Brethren, no truth ought to be more frequently proclaimed, next to the first coming of the Lord, than his second coming; and you cannot thoroughly set forth all the ends and bearings of the first advent if you forget the second. At the Lord's Supper, there is no discerning the Lord's body unless you discern his first coming; but there is no drinking into his cup to its fullness, unless you hear him say, "Until I come." You must look forward, as well as backward. So must it be with all our ministries; they must look to him on the cross and on the throne. We must vividly realize that he, who has once come, is coming yet again, or else our testimony will be marred, and one-sided. We shall make lame work of preaching and teaching if we leave out either advent.

And next, *it is to be unquestionably asserted*. "Behold, he cometh." It is not, "Perhaps he will come"; nor, "Perhaps he may yet appear." "Behold, he cometh" should be dogmatically asserted as an absolute certainty, which has been realized by the heart of the man who proclaims it. "Behold, he cometh." All the prophets say that he will come. From Enoch down to the last that spoke by inspiration, they declare, "The Lord cometh with ten thousands of his saints." You shall not find one who has spoken by the authority of God, who does not, either directly or by implication, assert the coming of the Son of man, when the multitudes born of woman shall be summoned to his bar, to receive the recompense of their deeds. All the promises are travailing with this prognostication, "Behold, he cometh." We have his own word for it, and this makes assurance doubly sure. He has told us that he will come again. He often assured his disciples that if he went away from them, he would come again to them; and he left us the Lord's Supper as a parting token to be observed until he comes. As often as we break bread we are reminded of the fact that, though it is a most blessed ordinance, yet it is a temporary one, and will cease to be celebrated when our absent Lord is once again present with us.

What, dear brethren, is there to hinder Christ from coming? When I have studied and thought over this word, "Behold, he cometh," yes, I have said to myself, indeed he does; who shall hold him back? His heart is with his church on earth. In the place where he fought the battle he desires to celebrate the victory. His delights are with the sons of men. All his saints are waiting for the day of his appearing, and he is waiting also. The very earth in her sorrow and her groaning travails for his coming, which is to be her redemption. The creation is made subject to vanity for a little while; but when the Lord shall come again, the creation itself also shall be delivered from the bondage of corruption into the glorious liberty of the children of God. We might question whether he would come a second time if he had not already come the first time; but if he came to Bethlehem, be assured that his feet shall yet stand upon Olivet. If he came to die, doubt not that he will come to reign. If he came to be despised and rejected of men, why should we doubt that he will come to be admired in all them that believe? His sure coming is to be unquestionably asserted.

Dear friends, this fact that he will come again, *is to be taught as demanding our immediate interest.* "Behold, he cometh with clouds." Behold, look at it; meditate on it. It is worth thinking of. It concerns yourself. Study it again and again. "He cometh." He will so soon be here that it is put in the present tense: "He cometh." That shaking of the earth; that blotting out of sun and moon; that fleeing of heaven and earth before his face—all these are so nearly here that John describes them as accomplished. "Behold, he cometh."

There is this sense lying in the background—that *he is already on the way.* All that he is doing in providence and grace is a preparation for his coming. All the events of human history, all the great decisions of his august majesty whereby he rules all things—all these are tending toward the day of his appearing. Do not think that he delays his coming, and then upon a sudden he will rush hither in hot haste. He has arranged for it to take place as soon as wisdom allows. We know not what may make the present delay imperative; but the Lord knows, and that suffices. You grow uneasy because nearly two thousand years have passed since his ascension, and Jesus has not yet come; but you do not know what had to be arranged for, and how far the lapse of time was absolutely necessary for the Lord's designs. Those are no little matters which have filled up the great pause: the intervening centuries have teemed with wonders. A thousand things may have been necessary in heaven itself before the consummation of all things could be arrived at. When our Lord comes it shall be seen that he came as quickly as he could, speaking after the manner of his infinite wisdom; for he cannot behave himself otherwise than wisely, perfectly, divinely. He cannot be moved by fear or passion so as to act hastily as you and I too often do. He dwells in the leisure of eternity, and in the serenity of omnipotence. He has not to measure out days, and months, and years, and to accomplish so much in such a space or else leave his lifework undone; but according to the power of an endless life he proceeds steadily on, and to him a thousand years are but as one day. Therefore be assured that the Lord is even now coming. He is making everything tend that way. All things are working toward that grand climax. At this moment, and every moment since he went away, the Lord Jesus has been coming back again. "Behold, he cometh!" He is on the way! He is nearer every hour! And we are told that *his coming will be attended by a peculiar sign*. "Behold, he cometh *with clouds*." We shall have no need to question whether it is the Son of man who has come, or whether he is indeed come. This is to be no secret matter: his coming will be as manifest as yonder clouds. In the wilderness the presence of Jehovah was known by a visible pillar of cloud by day, and an equally visible pillar of fire by night. That pillar of cloud was the sure token that the Lord was in his holy place, dwelling between the cherubim. Such is the token of the coming of the Lord Christ.

> *Every eye the cloud shall scan,*
> *Ensign of the Son of man.*

So it is written, "And then shall appear the sign of the Son of man in heaven: and then shall all the tribes of the earth mourn, and they shall see the Son of man coming in the clouds of heaven with power and great glory." I cannot quote at this time all those many passages of Scripture in which it is indicated that our Lord will come either sitting upon a cloud, or "with the clouds," or "with the clouds of heaven"; but such expressions are abundant. Is it not to show that his coming will be majestic? He makes the clouds his chariots. He comes with hosts of attendants, and these of a nobler sort than earthly monarchs can summon to do them homage. With clouds of angels, cherubim and seraphim, and all the armies of heaven he comes. With all the forces of nature, thundercloud and blackness of tempest, the Lord of all makes his triumphant entrance to judge the world. The clouds are the dust of his feet in that dread day of battle when he shall ease him of his adversaries, shaking them out of the earth with his thunder, and consuming them with the devouring flame of his lightning. All heaven shall gather with its utmost pomp to the great appearing of the Lord, and all the terrible grandeur of nature shall then be seen at its full. Not as the Man of sorrows, despised and rejected of men, shall Jesus come, but as Jehovah came upon Sinai in the midst of thick clouds and a terrible darkness, so shall he come, whose coming shall be the final judgment.

The clouds are meant to set forth the *might*, as well as the majesty, of his coming. "Ascribe ye strength unto God: his excellency is over Israel, and his strength is in the clouds." This was the royal token given by Daniel the prophet in his seventh chapter, at the thirteenth verse, "I saw in the night visions, and, behold, one like the Son of man came with the clouds of heaven." Not less than divine is the glory of the Son of God, who once had not where to lay his head. The sublimest objects in nature shall most fitly minister to the manifest glory of the returning King of men. "Behold, he cometh"; not with the swaddling bands of his infancy, the weariness of his manhood, the shame of his death, but with all the glorious tapestry of heaven's high chambers. The hanging of the divine throne room shall aid his state.

The clouds, also, denote *the terror of his coming to the ungodly*. His saints shall be caught up together with him in the clouds, to meet the Lord in the air; but to those that shall remain on earth the clouds shall turn their blackness and horror of darkness. Then shall the impenitent behold this dread vision— the Son of man coming in the clouds of heaven. The clouds shall fill them with dread, and the dread shall be abundantly justified, for those clouds are big with vengeance, and shall burst in judgment on their heads. His great white throne, though it be bright and lustrous with hope to his people, will with its very brightness and whiteness of immaculate justice strike dead the hopes of all those who trusted that they might live in sin and yet go unpunished. "Behold, he cometh. He cometh with clouds."

I am in happy circumstances tonight, because my subject requires no effort of imagination from me. To indulge fancy on such a theme would be a wretched profanation of so sublime a subject, which in its own simplicity should come home to all hearts. Think clearly for a moment, till the meaning becomes real to you. Jesus Christ is coming, coming in unwonted splendor. When he comes he will be enthroned far above the attacks of his enemies, the persecutions of the godless, and the sneers of skeptics. He is coming in the clouds of heaven, and we shall be among the witnesses of his appearing. Let us dwell upon this truth.

2. Our second observation is this: *our Lord's coming will be seen of all.*

"Behold, he cometh with clouds, *and every eye shall see him, and they also which pierced him.*"

I gather from this expression, first, that *it will be a literal appearing, and an actual sight.* If the second advent was to be a spiritual manifestation, to be perceived by the minds of men, the phraseology would be, "Every mind shall perceive him." But it is not so: we read, "Every eye shall see him." Now, the mind can behold the spiritual, but the eye can only see that which is distinctly material and visible. The Lord Jesus Christ will not come spiritually, for in that sense he is always here, but he will come really and substantially, for every eye shall see him, even those unspiritual eyes which gazed on him with hate, and pierced him. Go not away and dream, and say to yourself, "Oh, there is some spiritual meaning about all this." Do not destroy the teaching of the Holy Ghost by the idea that there will be a spiritual manifestation of the Christ of God, but that a literal appearing is out of the question. That would be altering the record. The Lord Jesus shall come to earth a second time as literally as he has come a first time. The same Christ who ate a piece of a broiled fish and of a honeycomb after he had risen from the dead; the same who said, "Handle me, and see; for a spirit hath not flesh and bones, as ye see me have"—this same Jesus, with a material body, is to come in the clouds of heaven. In the same manner as he went up he shall come down. He shall be literally seen. The words cannot be honestly read in any other way.

"Every eye shall see him." Yes, I do literally expect to see my Lord Jesus with these eyes of mine, even as that saint expected who long ago fell asleep, believing that though the worms devoured his body, yet in his flesh he should see God, whom his eyes should see for himself, and not another. There will be a real resurrection of the body, though the moderns doubt it: such a resurrection that we shall see Jesus with our own eyes. We shall not find ourselves in a shadowy, dreamy land of floating fictions, where we may perceive, but cannot see. We shall not be airy nothings, mysterious, vague, impalpable; but we shall literally see our glorious Lord, whose appearing will be no phantom show, or shadow dance. Never day more real than the day of judgment; never sight more true than the Son of man upon the throne of his glory. Will you take this statement home, that you may feel the force of it? We are getting too far away from facts nowadays, and too much into the realm of myths and notions. "Every eye shall see him," in this there shall be no delusion.

Note well that *he is to be seen of all kinds of living men:* every eye shall see him: the king and the peasant, the most learned and the most ignorant. Those that were blind before shall see when he appears. I remember a man born blind who loved our Lord most intensely, and he was inclined to glory in this, that his eyes had been reserved for his Lord. Said he, "The first whom I shall ever see will be the Lord Jesus Christ. The first sight that greets my newly opened eyes will be the Son of man in his glory." There is great comfort in this to all who are now unable to behold the sun. Since "every eye shall see him," you also shall see the King in his beauty. Small pleasure is this to eyes that are full of filthiness and pride: you care not for this sight, and yet you must see it whether you please or do not please. You have thus far shut your eyes to good things, but when Jesus comes you *must* see him. All that dwell upon the face of the earth, if not at the same moment, yet with the same certainty, shall behold the once crucified Lord. They will not be able to hide themselves, nor to hide him from their eyes. They will dread the sight, but it will come upon them, even as the sun shines on the thief who delights in the darkness. They will be obliged to own in dismay that they behold the Son of man: they will be so overwhelmed with the sight that there will be no denying it.

He will be seen of those who have been long since dead. What a sight that will be for Judas and for Pilate and for Caiaphas and for Herod! What a sight it will be for those who, in their lifetime, said that there was no Savior, and no need of one; or that Jesus was a mere man, and that his blood was not a propitiation for sin! Those that scoffed and reviled him have long since died, but they shall all rise again and rise to this heritage among the rest—that they shall see him whom they blasphemed sitting in the clouds of heaven. Prisoners are troubled at the sight of the judge. The trumpet of assize brings no music to the ears of criminals. But you must hear it, O impenitent sinner! Even in your grave you must hear the voice of the Son of God and live and come forth from the tomb, to receive the things done in your body, whether they were good or bad. Death cannot hide you, nor the vault conceal you, nor rottenness and corruption deliver you. You are bound to see in your body the Lord who will judge both you and your fellows.

It is mentioned here that he will especially be seen by those that pierced him. In this is included all the company that nailed him to the tree, with those that took the spear and made the gash in his side; indeed, all that had a hand in his cruel crucifixion. It includes all of these, but it comprehends many more besides. "They also who pierced him" are by no means a few. Who have pierced him? Why those that once professed to love him and have gone back to the world. Those that once ran well, "What did hinder them?" And now they use their tongues to speak against the Christ whom once they professed to love. They also have pierced him whose inconsistent lives have brought dishonor upon the sacred name of Jesus. They also have pierced him, who refused his love, stifled their consciences, and refused his rebukes. Alas, that so many of you should be piercing him now by your base neglect of his salvation! They that went every Sunday to hear of him and that remained hearers only, destroying their own souls rather than yield to his infinite love—these pierced his tender heart. Dear hearers, I wish I could plead effectually with you tonight, so that you would not continue any longer among the number of those that pierced him. If you will look at Jesus now, and mourn for your sin, he will put your sin away; and then you will not be ashamed to see him in that day. Even though you did pierce him, you will be able to sing, "Unto him that loved us, and washed us from our sins in his own blood." But, remember, if you persevere in piercing him, and fighting against him, you will still have to see him in that day, to your terror and despair. He will be seen by you and by me, however ill we may behave. And what horror will that sight cost us!

I felt unfit to preach to you tonight; but last Lord's Day I said that I would preach tonight if I could possibly manage it. It seemed barely possible, but I could not do less than keep my word; and I also longed to be with you, for your sakes; for perhaps there may not remain many more occasions on which I shall be permitted to preach the gospel among you. I am often ill; who knows how soon I shall come to my end? I would use all that remains to me of physical strength and providential opportunity. We never know how soon we may be cut off, and then we are gone forever from the opportunity of benefiting our fellowmen. It were a pity to be taken away with one opportunity of doing good unused. So would I earnestly plead with you under the shadow of this great truth: I would urge you to make ready, since we shall both behold the Lord in the day of his appearing. Yes, I shall stand in that great throng. You also will be there. How will you feel? You are not accustomed, perhaps, to attend a place of worship; but you will be there, and the spot will be very solemn to you. You may absent yourself from the assemblies of the saints, but you will not be able to absent yourself from the gathering of that day. You will be there, one in that great multitude; and you will see Jesus the Lord as truly as if you were the only person before him, and he will look upon you as certainly as if you were the only one that was summoned to his bar.

Will you kindly think of all this as I close this second head? Silently repeat to yourself the words, "Every eye shall see him, and they also that pierced him."

3. And now I must close with the third head, which is a painful one, but needs to be enlarged upon: *his coming will cause great sorrow.*

What does the text say about his coming? "All kindreds of the earth shall wail because of him."

"All kindreds of the earth." Then *this sorrow will be very general.* You thought, perhaps, that when Christ came, he would come to a glad world, welcoming him with song and music. You thought that there might be a few ungodly persons who would be destroyed with the breath of his month, but that the bulk of mankind would receive him with delight. See how different— "All kindreds of the earth," that is, all sorts of men that belong to the earth; all earthborn men, men out of all nations and kindreds and tongues shall weep and wail, and gnash their teeth at his coming. O sirs, this is a sad out- look! We have no smooth things to prophesy. What think you of this?

And, next, *this sorrow will be very great.* They shall *"wail."* I cannot put into English the full meaning of that most expressive word. Sound it at length, and it conveys its own meaning. It is as when men wring their hands and burst out into a loud cry; or as when eastern women, in their anguish, rend their gar- ments, and lift up their voices with the most mournful notes. All the kindreds of the earth shall wail: wail as a mother laments over her dead child; wail as a man might wail who found himself hopelessly imprisoned and doomed to die. Such will be the hopeless grief of all the kindreds of the earth at the sight of Christ in the clouds: if they remain impenitent, they shall not be able to be silent; they shall not be able to repress or conceal their anguish, but they shall wail or openly give vent to their horror. What a sound that will be which will go up before high heaven when Jesus sits upon the cloud, and in the fullness of his power summons them to judgment! Then "they shall wail because of him."

Will your voice be heard in that wailing? Will your heart be breaking in that general dismay? How will you escape? If you are one of the kindreds of the earth and remain impenitent, you will wail with the rest of them. Unless you now fly to Christ, and hide yourself in him, and so become one of the kin- dred of heaven—one of his chosen and blood-washed ones, who shall praise his name for washing them from their sins—unless you do this, there will be wailing at the judgment seat of Christ, and you will be in it.

Then it is quite clear that men will not be universally converted when Christ comes; because, if they were so, they would not wail. Then they would lift up the cry, "Welcome, welcome, Son of God!" The coming of Christ would be as the hymn puts it—

> *Hark, those bursts of acclamation!*
> *Hark, those loud triumphant chords!*
> *Jesus takes the highest station.*
> *Oh, what joy the sight affords!*

These acclamations come from his people. But according to the text the multitude of mankind will weep and wail, and therefore they will not be among his people. Do not, therefore, look for salvation to some coming day, but believe in Jesus now, and find in him your Savior at once. If you joy in him now, you shall much more rejoice in him in that day, but if you will have cause to wail at his coming, it will be well to wail at once.

Note one more truth. It is quite certain that when Jesus comes in those latter days *men will not be expecting great things of him.* You know the talk they have nowadays about "a larger hope." Today they deceive the people with the idle dream of repentance and restoration after death, a fiction unsupported by the least tittle of Scripture. If these kindreds of the earth expected that when Christ would come they would all die out and cease to be, they would rejoice that thereby they escaped the wrath of God. Would not each unbeliever say, "It were a consummation devoutly to be wished"? If they thought that at his coming there would be a universal restoration and a general jail delivery of souls long shut up in prison, would they wail? If Jesus could be supposed to come to proclaim a general restoration, they would not wail, but shout for joy. Ah no! It is because his coming to the impenitent is black with blank despair that they will wail because of him. If his first coming does not give you eternal life, his second coming will not. If you do not hide in his wounds when he comes as your Savior, there will be no hiding place for you when he comes as your Judge. They will weep and wail because, having rejected the Lord Jesus, they have turned their backs on the last possibility of hope.

Why do they wail *because of him*? Will it not be because they will see him in his glory, and they will recollect that they slighted and despised him? They will see him come to judge them, and they will remember that once he stood at their door with mercy in his hands and said, "Open to me," but they would not admit him. They refused his blood: they refused his righteousness: they trifled with his sacred name; and now they must give an account for this wickedness. They put him away in scorn, and now, when he comes, they find that they can trifle with him no longer. The days of child's play and of foolish delay are over; and now they have solemnly to give in their life's account. See, the books are opened! They are covered with dismay as they remember their sins, and know that they are written down by a faithful pen. They must give an account; and unwashed and unforgiven they cannot render that account without knowing that the sentence will be, "Depart, ye cursed." This is why they weep and wail because of him.

O souls, my natural love of ease makes me wish that I could preach pleasant things to you; but they are not in my commission. I need scarce wish, however, to preach a soft gospel, for so many are already doing it to your cost. As I love your immortal souls, I dare not flatter you. As I shall have to answer for it in the last great day, I must tell you the truth.

Ye sinners seek his face
Whose wrath ye cannot bear.

Seek the mercy of God tonight. I have come here in pain to implore you to be reconciled to God. "Kiss the Son lest he be angry, and ye perish from the way, when his wrath is kindled but a little. Blessed are all they that put their trust in him."

But if you will not have my Lord Jesus, he comes all the same for that. He is on the road now, and when he comes you will wail because of him. Oh, that you would make him your friend, and then meet him with joy! Why will you die? He gives life to all those who trust him. Believe, and live.

God save your souls tonight, and he shall have the glory. Amen.

Preparation for the Coming of the Lord

~~~

Delivered on Lord's Day morning, September 22, 1889, at the Metropolitan Tabernacle, Newington. No. 2105.

And now, little children, abide in him; that, when he shall appear, we may have confidence, and not be ashamed before him at his coming. —1 JOHN 2:28

Our first anxious desire is that our hearers would come to Christ. We lay ourselves out to lift him up, as Moses lifted up the serpent in the wilderness, and to bid men look to him and live. There is no salvation except by faith in the Lord Jesus Christ. He said, "Look unto me, and be ye saved, all the ends of the earth: for I am God, and there is none else."

When men have looked to Jesus, our next anxiety is that they may be in Christ, the city of refuge. We long to speak of them as "men in Christ Jesus." My beloved hearers, you must be in living, loving, lasting union with the Son of God, or else you are not in a state of salvation. That which begins with coming to Christ, as the engrafted branch is bound to the vine, continues in your growing into him and receiving of his life. You must be in Christ as the stone is in the building, as the member is in the body.

When we have good hope that our hearers have come to Christ, and are "in Christ," a further anxiety springs up in our hearts that they may "abide" in Christ. Our longing is that, despite temptations to go away from him, they may always remain at his feet; that, notwithstanding the evil of their nature, they may never betray their Master, but may faithfully hold to him. We would have them mindful of that precept, "As ye have received Christ Jesus the Lord, so walk ye in him." Oh, that they may be rooted in him, and built up in him, and may always be in union with him! Then shall we present them to our Lord in the day of his appearing with exceeding great joy.

To this third anxiety of the minister of Christ I would give my mind this morning. John says, "Little children, abide in him." How sweetly those words must have flowed from the lips and the pen of such a venerable saint! I think he is in this the echo of the Lord Jesus; for in the fifteenth chapter of the Gospel of John, the Lord Jesus said, "Abide in me, and I in you. As the branch cannot bear fruit of itself, except it abide in the vine, no more can you, except you abide in me. If you abide in me, and my words abide in you, you shall ask what you will, and it shall be done unto you." That word, "abide," was a very favorite one with the Lord Jesus, and it became equally dear to that disciple whom Jesus loved. In our Authorized Version, the translators have interpreted it sometimes "remain," and sometimes "continue"; but it is not very wise of them to have so changed the rendering. It is one of the virtues of the Revised Version that it generally translates the same Greek word by the same English word. This may not be absolutely requisite, for a little variety may be tolerated; but it is eminently instructive, since it allows us to see in our own mother tongue where the Holy Spirit used the same word; and if the translation be correct in one case, we may naturally conclude it will not be incorrect in another. "Abide" is one of John's special words.

May the Lord help us to consider these blessed words! Better still, may he write them on our hearts, and may we fulfill their teaching!

First, notice *to what he urges them*—"abide in him"; second, *under what character he addresses them*—"little children"; and third, *by what motive he exhorts them*—"that, when he shall appear, we may have confidence, and not be ashamed before him at his coming."

1. First, then, observe *to what he urges them*: "abide in him."

By this he meant one thing; but that thing is so comprehensive that we may better understand it by viewing it from many sides.

He meant fidelity to the truth taught by our Lord. We are sure he meant this, because, a little previously, in the twenty-fourth verse, he had said, "If that which ye have heard from the beginning shall remain in you, ye also shall continue in the Son, and in the Father." Beloved, you have believed in the Lord Jesus Christ unto the salvation of your souls. You have trusted in him as the Son of God, the appointed Mediator, and the effectual sacrifice for your sin. Your hope has come from a belief in Christ as God has borne witness to him. Abide in the truth which you received from the beginning; for in your earliest days it worked salvation in you. The foundation of your faith is not a changeable doctrine: you rest on a sure word of testimony. Truth is, in its very nature, fixed and unalterable. You know more about it than you did; but the thing itself is still the same, and must be the same. Take care that you abide in it. You will find it difficult to do so, for there is an element of changeableness about yourself: this you must overcome by grace. You will find many elements of seduction in the outside world. There are men whose business it is to shake the faith of others, and thereby to gain a repute for cleverness and depth of thought. Some seem to think it an ambition worthy of a Christian to be always questioning, or, as the apostle puts it, to be "ever learning, and never able to come to the knowledge of the truth." To throw doubt into minds which, by a gracious certainty, have been made blessed, is their chosen life-work. Therefore, you will be often led to try your foundation, and at times you will tremble as you cling to it. Hearken, then, to this word from the mouth of your Lord: "abide in him." Keep you where you were as to the truth which you believe. That which has justified you, will sanctify you. That which has, in a measure, sanctified you, will yet perfect you. Make no change as to the eternal verities upon which you ground your hope. As a stone, you are built on the foundation; abide there. As a branch, you have been grafted into the stem; abide there. As a member, you are in the body; abide there; it is all over with you if you do not. Abide in that holy mold of doctrine into which you were at first delivered. Let no man deceive you with vain words, though there are many abroad in these days who "would deceive, if it were possible, the very elect." Abide in Jesus, by letting his words abide in you. Believe what you have found to be the means of your quickening. Believe it with a greater intensity and a greater practicalness; but "cast not away your confidence, which hath great recompense of reward."

Next, he means "abide in him" *as to the uniformity of your trust.* When you first enjoyed a hope, you rested upon Christ alone. I think I heard the first infant prattle of your faith when it said,

> *I'm a poor sinner and nothing at all,*
> *But Jesus Christ is my all in all.*

At the first, you had no experience upon which you could rely, you had no inward graces upon which you could depend: you rested wholly upon Christ and his finished work. You rested in no degree upon the works of the law, nor upon your own feelings, nor upon your own knowledge, nor upon your own resolves. Christ was all. Do you not remember how you used to tell others that the gospel precept was "only believe"? You cried to them, "Trust in Jesus; get out of yourselves; find all your wants provided for in him." Now, beloved, you have experience; thank God for it. Now you have the graces of the Spirit; thank God for them. Now you know the things of God by the teaching of the Holy Spirit; be grateful for that knowledge. But do not now fly in the face of your Savior by putting your experience, or your graces, or your knowledge, where he and he alone must be. Depend today as simply as you depended then. If you have some idea that you are hastening toward perfection, take care that you do not indulge a vain conceit of yourself; but even if it be true, still mix not your perfection with his perfection, nor your advance in grace with the foundation which he has laid for you in his blood and righteousness. "Abide in him." He is that good ship into which you have entered that he may bear you safe to the desired haven. Abide in the vessel: neither venture to walk on the water, like Peter, nor think to swim by your own strength; but "abide in him," and you shall weather every storm. Only as you keep to your first simple confidence in the perfect work of the Lord Jesus can you have peace and salvation; as it is written, "Thou wilt keep him in perfect peace, whose mind is stayed on thee; because he trusteth in thee."

Moreover, abide in the Lord Jesus Christ in making him the constant object of your life. As you live by Christ, so live for Christ. Ever since you trusted in Christ as dying for you, you have felt that if he died for you, then you died in him, that henceforth your life might be consecrated to him. You are not your own, but you are Christ's, and Christ's only. The first object of your being is to honor and serve him who loved you and gave himself for you. You have not followed after wealth or honor or self-pleasing, but you have followed Jesus: take heed that you "abide in him" by continuing to serve him. "Love not the world, neither the things that are in the world. If any man love the world, the love of the Father is not in him. For all that is in the world, the lust of the flesh, and the lust of the eyes, and the pride of life, is not of the Father, but is of the world. And the world passes away, and the lust thereof: but he that does the will of God abides forever." You may wisely continue where you are, for you have chosen the right pursuit, and you have entered upon the right road. That crown which glitters in your eye at the end of the race is worthy of all your running. You could not have a nobler motive power than the constraining love of Christ. To live for Christ is the highest style of living: continue in it more and more. If the Lord changes your circumstances, still live for Christ. If you go up, take Christ up with you: if you go down, Christ will go down with you. If you are in health, live for Christ earnestly; if you are bound to a sick bed, live for Christ patiently. Go about your business and sing for Jesus; or if he bids you stay at home, and cough away your life, then sicken for Jesus; but let everything be for him. For you, "excelsior" means higher consecration, more heavenly living.

Surely, we should also understand by "abide in him," that we are to persevere in our obedience to our Lord. The next verse is, "If ye know that he is righteous, ye know that everyone that doeth righteousness is born of him." What your Lord bids you, continue to do. Call no man "master," but in all things submit your thoughts, your words, and your acts to the rule of the Lord Jesus. Obey him by whose obedience you are justified. Be precise and prompt in your execution of his commands. If others reckon you morbidly conscientious, heed not their opinion, but "abide in him." The rule of the master is always binding on all his disciples, and they depart from him in heart when they err from his rule. Reverence for the precept is as much included in our homage of Christ as credence of the doctrine. If you have been upright in your dealings, be upright; be accurate to the penny in every payment. If you have been loving and generous, continue loving and generous; for your Lord's law is love. If you have closely imitated the Lord Jesus, go on to copy him still more minutely. Seek no new model; pray the Holy Spirit to work you to the selfsame thing. To you, as a soldier, your Captain's word is law:

> Yours is not to reason why,
> Yours is but to dare and die.

"Abide in him." I know you might be rich by doing that un-Christly act; scorn to win wealth in such a way. I know you may involve yourself in persecution if you follow your Lord closely. Accept such persecution gladly, and rejoice in it, for his name's sake. I know that a great many would say that for charity's sake you had better make compromises, and keep in union with evil doctrine and worldly practice; but you know better. Be it yours to follow the Lamb whithersoever he goes; for this is what his beloved apostle means when he says, "Abide in him."

But I have not completed the full description yet; I fear I am not able to do so, by reason of my shallow knowledge and forgetfulness. *Continue in spiritual union with your Lord.* All the life you have is life derived from him; seek no other. You are not a Christian except as Jesus is the Christ of God to you; you are not alive unto God, except as you are one with the risen Lord. You are not saved, except as he is your Savior; nor righteous, save as he is your Righteousness. You have not a single pulse of heavenly desire, nor a breath of divine life in you, but what was first given you from him, and is daily given to you by him. Abide in this vital union. Do not try to lead an independent life. "Abide in him," in complete dependence from day to day upon the life which is treasured up in him on your behalf.

Let your life "abide in him" in the sense of being directed by him. The head directs all the members. The order which lifts my hand, or spreads my palm, or closes my fist, or lowers my arm, comes from the brain, which is the headquarters of the soul. Abide in your Lord by implicitly owning his headship. Let every regulation of your life come from him who is the head, and let it be obeyed as naturally as the desires of the mind coming from the brain are obeyed by every part of the body. There is no war between the hand and the foot, for they abide in the head, and so are ruled without force, and guided without violence. If the leg were to set up an independent authority over itself, instead of obeying the head, what strange walking we should see! Have you never met with afflicted people in whom the nerves have lost vigor, and the muscles seem to jerk at random, and throw out a leg or an arm without reason? Such movements are painful to see, and we know that such a man is diseased. Do not desire to be without law to Christ. Let that mind be in you which was also in Christ Jesus: in that respect "abide in him."

"Abide in him" as the element of your life. Let him encompass you as the air surrounds you on all sides. As a fish, whether it be the tiniest sprat or the hugest whale, abides in the sea, so do you abide in Christ. The fish does not seek the sky or the shore, it could not live out of the element of water; and even so, I beseech you, do not seek to live in the world and in its sins; for as a Christian you cannot live there: Christ is your life. There is room enough for you in the Lord Jesus Christ, for he is the infinite God. Go not out of him for anything. Seek not pleasure outside of Christ, nor treasure outside of Christ; for such pleasure or treasure would be ruinous. Have neither want, nor will, nor wish, beyond your Lord. Let him draw a line around you, and do you abide within that circle.

"Abide in him" in the sense of being at home in him. What a world of meaning I intend by that word "being at home in Christ"! and yet this is the sense of the word "abide in him." I was speaking yesterday to a friend who had bought a pleasant house, with a large garden; and he said to me, "I now feel as if I had a home. I have lived in London for years, and I have changed from one house to another with as little regret as a man feels in changing an omnibus; but I have always longed for the home feeling which hung about my father's house in the country. Why, there we loved the cozy rooms, and the lookouts from the little windows, and the corner cupboards in the kitchen. As for the garden and the field, they yielded us constant delight, for there was that bush in the garden where the robin had built, and the tree with the black-bird's nest. We knew where the pike lay in the pool, and where the tortoise had buried itself for the winter, and where the first primroses would be found in the spring. There is a vast difference between a house and a home." That is what John means with regard to Christ: we are not merely to call on him, but to abide in him. Do not go to Jesus one day and to the world another day: do not be a lodger with him, but abide in him. My friend spoke of changing from one omnibus to another, and I fear that some change from Christ to the world when the day changes from Sunday to Monday; but it should not be so. Say with Moses, "Lord, thou hast been our dwelling place in all generations." Your cross is the rooftree of the family of love; within the thorn hedge of your suffering love our whole estate is shut in; your name is named on our abiding place. We are not to you as tenants with a lease, but we have a freehold in you. We can truly say and sing—

> Here would I make a settled rest
> While others go and come:
> No more a stranger or a guest,
> But like a child at home.

Lord Jesus, I am at home nowhere but in you; but in you I abide. Wherever else I lodge, I have in due time to shift my quarters. Whatever else I have, I lose it, or leave it; but you are the same, and you change not. What a comfort to have our Lord himself to be our chosen dwelling place in time and in eternity!

Now I think I have come nearer to the full sense of my text. "Abide in him" means, hold fast to him, live in him, let all your noblest powers be drawn forth in connection with him, as a man at home is all there. Feel at ease in fellowship with him. Say, "Return unto thy rest, O my soul; for the Lord hath dealt bountifully with thee."

Why does the apostle urge us to abide in Christ? Is there any likelihood of our going away? Yes; for in this very chapter he mentions apostates, who from disciples had degenerated into antichrists, of whom he says, "They went out from us, but they were not of us; for if they had been of us they would, no doubt, have continued with us." "Abide in him," then, and do not turn aside unto crooked ways, as many professors have done. The Savior once said to his apostles, "Will ye also go away?," and they answered him with that other question, "Lord, to whom shall we go?" I hope your heart is so conscious that he has the words of eternal life that you could not dream of going elsewhere.

"But surely it is implied in these warnings that saints do leave their Lord and perish?" I answer, "No." Carefully observe the provision which is made against that fatality—provision to enable us to carry out the precept of the text. Will you open your Testaments, and just look at the verse which immediately precedes my text? What do you see? "Ye shall abide in him. And now, little children, abide in him." There is a promise made to those who are in Christ that they shall "abide in him"; but that promise does not render the precept unnecessary; for the Lord deals with us as with reasonable beings, not as with sticks and stones; and he secures the fulfillment of his own promise that we shall abide in him, by impressing upon our hearts his sacred precept, whereby he bids us "abide in him." The force he uses to effect his purpose is instruction, heart winning, and persuading. We abide in him, not by a physical law, as a mass of iron abides on the earth; but by a mental and spiritual law, by which the greatness of divine love and goodness holds us fast to the Lord Jesus. You have the guarantee that you shall abide in Christ in the covenant engagement, "I will put my fear in their hearts, that they shall not depart from me." What a blessed promise that is! You are to take care that you abide in Christ as much as if all depended upon yourself; and yet you can look to the promise of the covenant, and see that the real reason for your abiding in Christ lies in the operation of his unchanging love and grace.

Moreover, brethren, if you are in Christ Jesus, you have the Holy Ghost given you to enable you to abide in him. Read the twenty-seventh verse: "But the anointing which ye have received of him abideth in you, and ye need not that any man teach you: but as the same anointing teacheth you of all things, and is truth, and is no lie, and even as it hath taught you, ye shall abide in him."

The Holy Ghost brings the truth home to your heart with savor and unction, endearing it to your inmost soul. The truth has so saturated you through the anointing, that you cannot give it up. Has not your Lord said, "The water that I shall give him shall be in him a well of water springing up unto everlasting life"? Thus, you see that what is commanded in one Scripture is promised and provided for in another. To his people, God's commandings are enablings. As he bids you abide in him, so by that very bidding he causes you to abide in him to his praise and glory.

2. Second, notice *under what character John addresses these believers.*

He says, "And now, *little children.*" This indicates *the apostle's love to them.* John lived to a great age; and the tradition is, that they used to carry him into the assembly, and, when he could do nothing else, he would lift his hand, and simply say, "Little children, love one another." Here, to show his tender concern for those to whom he wrote, he called them "little children." He could not wish them a greater blessing out of the depth of his heart's affection, than that they should faithfully abide in Christ.

Next, by this he suggests their near and dear relation to their Father in heaven. You are the children of God; but as yet you are little ones, therefore do not leave your Father's house, nor run away from your elder brother's love. Because you are little children, you are not of traveling years, therefore stay at home and abide in your Lord.

Does he not hint at their feebleness? Even if you were grown and strong, you would not be wise to gather all together and wander away into the far country; but as you are so young, so dependent, so feeble, it is essential that you abide in him. Shall a babe forsake its mother? What can you do apart from God? Is he not your life, your all?

Does not the apostle also gently hint at *their fickleness*? You are very change-able, like little babes. You are apt to be hot and cold in half an hour. You are this and that, and fifty other things, in the course of one revolving moon. But, lit-tle children as you are, be faithful to one point—abide in your Savior. Change not toward your Redeemer. Stretch out your hands and clasp him and cry,

> *My Jesus, I love thee, I knew thou art mine,*
> *For thee all the follies of sin I resign.*

Surrender yourself to him by an everlasting covenant never to be can-celed. Be his forever and ever.

Did not this remind them of their daily dependence upon the Lord's care, as little children depend on their parents? Why, beloved, the Lord has to nurse you. He feeds you with the unadulterated milk of the Word; he comforts you as a mother does her child; he carries you in his bosom, he bears you all your days. Your new life is as yet weak and struggling; do not carry it into the cold atmosphere of distance from Jesus. Little children, since you derive all from Jesus, abide in him. To go elsewhere will be to wander into a howling wilder-ness. The world is empty; only Christ has fullness. Away from Jesus you will be as a child deserted by its mother, left to pine, and starve, and die; or as a lit-tle lamb on the hillside without a shepherd, tracked by the wolf, whose teeth will soon extract its heart's blood. Abide, O child, with your mother! Abide, O lamb, with your shepherd!

We may all come under John's description at this time. The beloved John speaks unto us as unto little children, for we are none of us much more. We are not such wonderfully knowing people as certain of our neighbors; we are not such learned scientists and acute critics as they are; neither have we their marvelous moral consciousness, which is superior to inspiration itself; there-fore we are bound by our very feebleness to venture less than they do. Let the men of the world choose what paths they will, we feel bound to abide in Christ because we know no other place of safety. They may push off into the sea of speculation; our smaller boats must hug the shore of certainty. To us, however, it is no small comfort that the Lord has revealed to babes the things which are hidden from the wise and prudent. Those who become as little chil-dren enter into the kingdom of heaven.

Cling to the Lord Jesus in your feebleness, in your fickleness, in your noth-ingness; and abidingly take him to be everything to you. "The coneys are but a feeble folk, yet make they their houses in the rocks"; be you like them. Abide in the rifts of the Rock of ages, and let nothing tempt you to quit your stronghold. You are no lion, able to fight your foes, and deliver yourself by main strength; you are only a little coney, and you will be wise to hide rather than fight. "Little children, abide in him."

3. I now come to my last point, which is most important, for it finds steam wherewith to drive the engine. Third, we shall consider *by what motive John exhorts us to this pleasant and necessary duty of abiding in Christ.*

Kindly look at the text, for there is in it a little word to be noticed. The apostle exhorts us *by a motive in which he takes his share.* Let me read it: "Now, little children, abide in him; that, when he shall appear, you may have confidence." No, no. Look at that little word: it runs thus, "that *we* may have confidence." The beloved John needed to have confidence at the appearing of the Lord, and confidence fetched from the same source as that to which he directed his little children. They must abide in Christ, that they might have confidence, and the dearest of the apostles must practice the same abiding. How wisely, and yet how sweetly, he puts himself upon our level in this matter!

Notice, further, that the motive is one *drawn from Jesus.* John does not drive believers with the lash of the law, but he draws them with the cords of love. I never like to see God's children whipped with rods gathered from the thorny sides of Sinai. We have not come to Mount Sinai, but to Mount Zion. When a man tries to pommel me to my duty by the law, I kick at the goad like a bullock unaccustomed to the yoke; and rightly so, "For you are not under the law, but under grace." The motive which sways a freeborn heir of heaven is fetched from grace, and not from law; from Jesus, and not from Moses. Christ is our example, and our motive also, blessed be his name!

The motive is drawn from our Lord's expected advent. Notice how John puts it. He uses two words for the same thing: "when he shall appear" and "at his coming." The second advent may be viewed in two lights. First, as the appearing of one who is here already, but is hidden; and next, as the coming of one who is absent. In the first sense, we know that our Lord Jesus Christ abides in his church; according to his word, "Lo, I am with you always, even unto the end of the world." Yet, though spiritually present, he is unseen. Our Lord will, on a sudden, be "manifested," as the Revised Version has it. The spiritual and secret presence of Christ will become a visible and manifest presence in the day of his appearing.

The apostle also uses the term "at his coming" or "his presence." This is the same thing from another point of view. In a certain evident sense our Lord is absent: "He is not here, for he is risen." He has gone his way unto the Father. In that respect he will come a second time, "without a sin offering, unto salvation." He who has gone from us will so come in like manner as he was seen to go up into heaven. There is thus a difference of aspect between the second advent when it is described as "his appearing" and "his coming." John pleads the glorious manifestation of our Lord under both of these views as a reason for abiding in him.

As to our Lord's "appearing," he would have us abide in Christ, that we may have confidence when he appears. Confidence at his appearing is the high reward of constant abiding in Christ. The apostle keeps most prominent "the appearing" as an argument. A thousand things are to happen at our Lord's appearing; but John does not mention one of them. He does not hold it up as a thing to be desired that we may have confidence amid the wreck of matter and the crash of worlds, when the stars shall fall like autumn leaves, when the sun shall be turned into darkness, and the moon into blood; when the graves shall be opened, and the dead shall rise, or when the heavens, being on fire, shall be dissolved, and the elements shall melt with fervent heat, the earth also, and the works that are therein, shall be burned up. Those will be direful times, days of terror and dismay; but it is not of these that he speaks particularly; for he regards all these events as swallowed up in the one great fact of the glorious appearing of our Lord and Savior Jesus Christ.

His desire is that we may have confidence if he appear on a sudden. What does he mean by having confidence when he shall appear? Why, this: that if you abide in him when you do not see him, you will be very bold should he suddenly reveal himself. Before he appears, you have dwelt in him, and he has dwelt in you; what fear could his appearing cause you? Faith has so realized him, that if suddenly he were to appear to the senses, it would be no surprise to you; and, assuredly, it would cause you joy rather than dismay. You would feel that you at last enjoyed what you had long expected, and saw somewhat more closely a friend with whom you had long been familiar. I trust, beloved, that some of us live in such a style that if, on a sudden, our Lord were to appear, it would cause no alarm to us. We have believed him to be present, though unseen, and it will not affect our conduct when he steps from behind the curtain and stands in the open light. O Lord Jesus, if you were now to stand in our midst, we should remember that we had your presence before, and lived in it, and now we should only be the more assured of that which we before knew by faith. We shall behold our Lord with confidence, freedom, assurance, and delight, feeling perfectly at home with him. The believer who abides in his Lord would be but little startled by his sudden appearing; he is serving his Lord now, and he would go on serving him; he loves him now, and he would go on loving him, only as he would have a clearer view of him, he would feel a more intense consecration to him.

The word translated "confidence" means freedom of speech. If our divine Lord were to appear in a moment, we should not lose our tongue through fear, but should welcome him with glad acclaim. To desert our Lord would rob us of that ease of mind which is shown by free speech; but to cleave to him will secure us confidence. We now speak to him in secret, and he speaks again to us; we shall not cease to speak in tones of reverent love when he appears. I have preached concerning my Lord, while he is not seen, those truths which I shall not blush to own before his face. If my Lord and Master were, at this instant, to appear in his glory in this tabernacle, I dare with confidence hand in to him the volumes of my sermons, in proof that I have not departed from his truth, but have heartily continued in him. I ought to improve in many things, but I could not improve upon the gospel which I have preached among you. I am prepared to live by it, to die by it, or to meet my Lord upon it if he should this day appear. O my hearers, if you are in Christ, see to it that you so abide in him that, should he suddenly appear, you would behold him with confidence. If we abide in him, if he were to unveil his majestic face, we might be overcome with rapture, but our confidence in him would grow stronger, our freedom with him would be even more enlarged, and our joy in him would be made perfect. Has he not prayed for us that we may be with him, and behold his glory; and can we be afraid of the answer to his loving prayer? If you abide in Christ, the manifestation of Christ will be your manifestation, and that will be a matter of delight, and not of fear.

Beloved, if you do not abide in him, you will have no confidence. If I were to compromise the truth, and then my Lord were to appear, could I meet him with confidence? If, to preserve my reputation, or be thought liberal minded, I played fast and loose with the gospel, how could I see my Lord's face with confidence? If any of you have failed to serve your Master; if you have preferred gain to godliness, and pleasure to holiness; if he were suddenly to shine forth in his glory, what confidence could you have in meeting him? A good man was asked, one day, "If the Lord were now to appear, how would you feel?" He replied. "My brother, I should not be afraid; but I think I should be ashamed." He meant that he was not afraid of condemnation, but he blushed to think how little he had served his Lord. In this case it was genuine humility. I pray you, get not only beyond being afraid, but may the Lord make you so to abide in him that you would not even be ashamed at his appearing!

The other point is, that you should "not be ashamed before him at his coming." That means, that having regarded him as being absent, you have not so lived that, if he should suddenly be present in person, you would be ashamed of your past life. What must it be to be driven with shame away from his presence into everlasting contempt? The text may have such a meaning. What have you been doing while he has been absent? This is a question for a servant to answer at his Lord's arrival. You are left in his house to take care of it while he is in the far-off country; and if you have been beating his servants, and eating and drinking with the drunken, you will be greatly ashamed when he returns. His coming will be in itself a judgment. "Who may abide the day of his coming? And who shall stand when he appears?" Blessed is that man who, with all his faults, has been so sanctified by grace that he will not be ashamed at his Lord's coming. Who is that man? It is the man who has learned to abide in Christ. What is the way to prepare for Christ's coming? By the study of the prophecies? Yes, if you are sufficiently instructed to be able to understand them. "To be prepared for the Lord's coming," some enthusiasts might say, "had I not better spend a month in retirement, and get out of this wicked world?" You may, if you like; and especially you will do so if you are lazy. But the one scriptural prescription for preparing for his coming is this: "abide in him." If you abide in the faith of him, holding his truth, following his example, and making him your dwelling place, your Lord may come at any hour, and you will welcome him. The cloud, the great white throne, the blast of trumpets, the angelic attendants of the last assize, the trembling of creation, and the rolling up of the universe as a worn-out vesture, will have no alarms for you; for you will not be ashamed at his coming.

The date of that coming is concealed. When he shall come, no man can tell. Watch for him, and be always ready, that you may not be ashamed at his advent. Should a Christian man go into worldly assemblies and amusements? Would he not be ashamed should his Lord come and find him among the enemies of the cross? I dare not go where I should be ashamed to be found should my Lord come on a sudden. Should a Christian man ever be in a passion? Suppose his Lord should there and then come; would he not be ashamed at his coming? One here says of an offender, "I will never forgive her; she shall never darken my doors again." Would you not be ashamed if the Lord Jesus came, and found you unforgiving? Oh, that we may abide in him, and never be in such a state that his coming would be unwelcome to us! Beloved, so live from day to day in duty and in devotion, that your Lord's coming would be timely. Go about your daily business and abide in him, and then his coming will be a glorious delight to you. I called to see one of our friends, and she was whitening the front steps of the house. She apologized very much, and said that she felt ashamed of being caught in such a position; but I assured her that I should like my Lord to come and find me, just as I found her, doing my daily work with all my heart. We are never in better trim for seeing our Master than when we are faithfully doing his work. There is no need for a pious smartening up; he that abides in Christ always wears garments of glory and beauty; he may go in with his Lord into the wedding whenever the midnight cry is heard. Abide in him, and then none can make you ashamed. Who shall lay anything to your charge?

He will come—behold, he is coming even now. Hear you not the sounding of his chariot wheels? He may arrive before yon sun goes down. "In such an hour as ye think not, the Son of man cometh." When the world is eating and drinking, marrying and giving in marriage, he will bring destruction upon the ungodly. Be you so engaged, day by day, that you will not be taken at unawares. What will it be to be caught up together with the saints in the clouds, to meet the Lord in the air? What will it be to see him come in the glory of the Father, and all his holy angels with him? What will it be to see him reign upon the earth, with his ancients gloriously? Can you imagine the millennial splendor, the age of gold, the halcyon days of peace? As for the judgment of the world, know you not that the saints shall judge angels? They shall appear as assessors with Christ, and the Lord shall bruise Satan under their feet. Glory awaits us, and nothing but glory, if we abide in Christ. Therefore, keep your garments unspotted, your loins girded, your lamps trimmed, and your lights burning, and you yourselves as men that look for your Lord, that, when he comes, you may have confidence, and not shame. May the Holy Spirit, without whom this cannot be, be freely given to us this day, that we may abide in the Lord! And you who have never trusted in Christ for salvation, may you come to him, and then "abide in him" from this good hour! To his name be glory! Amen.

Watching for Christ's Coming

Intended for reading on Lord's Day, April 2, 1893; delivered on Lord's Day evening, April 7, 1889, at the Metropolitan Tabernacle, Newington. No. 2302.

Blessed are those servants, whom the lord when he cometh shall find watching: verily I say unto you, that he shall gird himself, and make them to sit down to meat, and will come forth and serve them. And if he shall come in the second watch, or come in the third watch, and find them so, blessed are those servants. —LUKE 12:37–38

I am about to speak of the second coming of Christ; and I felt thankful that my dear brother's prayer, although we had not been in consultation with one another upon the matter, was in every way so suitable to the subject upon which I am to speak. He led us in prayer to think of our coming Lord; so that I trust you are on the margin of the subject now, and that you will not have to make any very great exertion of mind to plunge into midstream, and be carried away with the full current of thought concerning the second advent of the Savior. It is a very appropriate topic when we come to the Lord's table; for, as that prayer reminded us, the Lord's Supper looks backward and is a memorial of his agony; but it looks forward and is an anticipation of his glory. Paul wrote to the church at Corinth, "For as often as ye eat this bread, and drink this cup, ye do show the Lord's death till he come." By looking forward, in a right state of heart, to that second coming of Christ which is the joy of his church, you will be also in a right state of heart for coming to the communion table. May the Holy Ghost make it to be so!

The posture at the communion table, as you know, according to our Lord's example, was not that of kneeling, but that of reclining. The easiest position which you can assume is the most fitting for the Lord's Supper; and yet remember that the supper was no sooner finished than "they sang a hymn," and when that hymn was concluded, they went out into the Mount of Olives to the agonies of Gethsemane. It often seems to me as if now, after finding rest at the table by feeding upon Christ, whose real presence we have, not after a carnal sort, but after a spiritual sort, after that, we sing a hymn, as if we would go out to meet our Lord in his second coming, not going to the Mount of Olives to see him in a bloody sweat, but to hear that word of the angel, "This same Jesus, which is taken up from you into heaven, shall so come in like manner as ye have seen him go into heaven." I do not think we ought to feel at all surprised if we were to go out from the table of fellowship tonight, and meet our Lord at once; no, we should be always waiting for his appearing, ever expecting him, not knowing at what hour the Master of the house shall come. The world does not expect him; it goes on with its eating and drinking, its marrying and giving in marriage; but his own family should expect him. When he will return from the wedding, I trust that he will not find the door shut against him, but that we shall be ready to open to our Lord immediately he knocks. That is the object of the few words that I shall have to say tonight, to stir you up, and my own heart also, to be ever watching for Christ's second coming.

1. First, *the Lord will come*. He that has come once is to come again; he will come a second time. The Lord will come.

He will come again, for *he has promised to return*. We have his own word for it. That is our first reason for expecting him. Among the last of the words which he spoke to his servant John are these, "Surely I come quickly." You may read it, "I am coming quickly. I am even now upon the road. I am traveling as fast as wisdom allows. I am always coming and coming quickly." Our Lord has promised to come, and to come in person. Some try to explain the second coming of Christ as though it meant the believer dying. You may, if you like, consider that Christ comes to his saints in death. In a certain sense, he does; but that sense will never bear out the full meaning of the teaching of the second advent with which the Scripture is full. No, "the Lord himself shall descend from heaven with a shout, with the voice of the archangel, and with the trump of God." He who went up to heaven will come down from heaven, and stand in the latter day upon the earth. Every redeemed soul can say with Job, "Though after my skin worms destroy this body, yet in my flesh shall I see God: whom I shall see for myself, and mine eyes shall behold, and not another." Christ will as certainly be here again in glory as he once was here in shame, for he has promised to return.

Moreover, *the great scheme of redemption requires Christ's return*. It is a part of that scheme that, as he came once with a sin offering, he should come a second time without a sin offering, that, as he came once to redeem, he should come a second time to claim the inheritance which he has so dearly bought. He came once, that his heel might be bruised; he comes again, to break the serpent's head, and, with a rod of iron, to dash his enemies in pieces, as potters' vessels. He came once, to wear the crown of thorns; he must come again, to wear the diadem of universal dominion. He comes to the marriage supper; he comes to gather his saints together; he comes to glorify them with himself on this same earth where once he and they were despised and rejected of men. Make you sure of this, that the whole drama of redemption cannot be perfected without this last act of the coming of the King. The complete history of paradise regained requires that the New Jerusalem should come down from God out of heaven, prepared as a bride adorned for her husband; and it also requires that the heavenly bridegroom should come riding forth on his white horse, conquering and to conquer, King of kings and Lord of lords, amid the everlasting hallelujahs of saints and angels. It must be so. The man of Nazareth will come again. None shall spit in his face then; but every knee shall bow before him. The crucified shall come again; and though the nail prints will be visible, no nails shall then fasten his dear hands to the tree; but instead thereof, he shall grasp the scepter of universal sovereignty; and he shall reign forever and ever. Hallelujah!

When will he come? Ah, that is the question, the question of questions! He will come in his own time. *He will come in due time.* A brother minister, calling upon me, said, as we sat together, "I should like to ask you a lot of questions about the future." "Oh, well!" I replied, "I cannot answer you, for I daresay I know no more about it than you do." "But," said he, "what about the Lord's second advent? Will there not be the millennium first?" I said, "I cannot tell whether there will be the millennium first; but this I know, the Scripture has left the whole matter, as far as I can see, with an intentional indistinctness, that we may be always expecting Christ to come, and that we may be watching for his coming at any hour and every hour. I think that the millennium will commence after his coming, and not before it. I cannot imagine the kingdom with the King absent. It seems to me to be an essential part of the millennial glory that the King shall then be revealed; at the same time, I am not going to lay down anything definite upon that point. He may not come for a thousand years; he may come tonight. The teaching of Scripture is, first of all, 'In such an hour as ye think not the Son of man cometh.' It is clear that, if it were revealed that a thousand years must elapse before he would come, we might very well go to sleep for that time, for we should have no reason to expect that he would come when Scripture told us he would not."

"Well," answered my friend, "but when Christ comes, that will be the general judgment, will it not?" Then I quoted these texts, "The dead in Christ shall rise first." "But the rest of the dead lived not again until the thousand years were finished. This is the first resurrection." I said, "There is a resurrection from among the dead to which the apostle Paul labored to attain. We shall all rise; but the righteous shall rise a thousand years before the ungodly. There is to be that interval of time between the one and the other; whether that is the millennial glory, or not, this deponent says not, though he thinks it is. But this is the main point, the Lord shall come. We know not when we are to expect his coming; we are not to lay down, as absolutely fixed, any definite prediction or circumstance that would allow us to go to sleep until that prediction was fulfilled, or that circumstance was apparent."

"Will not the Jews be converted to Christ, and restored to their land?" inquired my friend. I replied, "Yes, I think so. Surely they shall look on him whom they have pierced, and they shall mourn for him, as one mourns for his only son; and God shall give them the kingdom and the glory, for they are his people, whom he has not forever cast away. The Jews, who are the natural olive branches, shall yet be grafted into their own olive tree again, and then shall be the fullness of the Gentiles." "Will that be before Christ comes, or after?" asked my friend. I answered, "I think it will be after he comes; but whether or no, I am not going to commit myself to any definite opinion on the subject."

To you, my dear friends, I say, read for yourselves and search for yourselves; for still this stands first and is the only thing that I will insist upon tonight: the Lord will come. He may come now; he may come tomorrow; he may come in the first watch of the night, or the second watch, or he may wait until the morning watch; but the one word that he gives to you all is, "Watch! Watch! Watch!," that whenever he shall come, you may be ready to open to him, and to say, in the language of the hymn we sang just now—

> Hallelujah!
> Welcome, welcome, Judge divine!

So far I know that we are scriptural, and therefore perfectly safe in our statements about the Lord's second advent.

Brethren, I would be earnest on this point, *for the notion of the delay of Christ's coming is always harmful,* however you arrive at it, whether it be by studying prophecy, or in any other way. If you come to be of the opinion of the servant mentioned in the forty-fifth verse, you are wrong: "If that servant say in his heart, 'My lord delayeth his coming'; and shall begin to beat the menservants and maidens, and to eat and drink, and to be drunken; the lord of that servant will come in a day when he looketh not for him, and at an hour when he is not aware, and will cut him in sunder, and will appoint him his portion with the unbelievers." Do not, therefore, get the idea that the Lord delays his coming, and that he will not or cannot come as yet. Far better would it be for you to stand on the tiptoe of expectation, and to be rather disappointed to think that he does not come. I do not wish you to be shaken in mind so as to act fanatically or foolishly, as certain people did in America, when they went out into the woods with ascension dresses on, so as to go straight up all of a sudden. Fall into none of those absurd ideas that have led people to leave a chair vacant at the table, and to put an empty plate, because the Lord might come and want it; and try to avoid all other superstitious nonsense. To stand stargazing at the prophecies, with your mouth wide open, is just the wrong thing; far better will it be to go on working for your Lord, getting yourself and your service ready for his appearing, and cheering yourself all the while with this thought, "While I am at work, my Master may come. Before I get weary, my Master may return. While others are mocking at me, my Master may appear; and whether they mock or applaud, is nothing to me. I live before the great Taskmaster's eye, and do my service knowing that he sees me, and expecting that, by and by, he will reveal himself to me, and then he will reveal me and my right intention to misrepresenting men." That is the first point, brethren, the Lord will come. Settle that in your minds. He will come in his own time, and we are always to be looking for his appearing.

2. Now, second, *the Lord bids us watch for him.*

That is the marrow of the text: "Blessed are those servants, whom the lord when he cometh shall find watching."

Now what is this watching? Not wishing to use my own words, I thought that I would call your attention to the context. The first essential part of this watching is that we are not to be taken up with present things. You remember that the twenty-second verse is about not taking thought what you shall eat, or what you shall drink; you are not to be absorbed in that. You who are Christians are not to live the fleshly, selfish life that asks, "What shall I eat and drink? How can I store up my goods? How can I get food and raiment here?" You are something more than dumb, driven cattle, that must think of hay and water. You have immortal spirits. Rise to the dignity of your immortality. Begin to think of the kingdom, the kingdom so soon to come, the kingdom which your Father has given you, and which, therefore, you must certainly inherit, the kingdom which Christ has prepared for you, and for which he is making you kings and priests unto God, that you may reign with him forever and ever. Oh, be not earthbound! Do not cast your anchor here in these troubled waters. Build not your nest on any of these trees; they are all marked for the ax, and are coming down; and your nest will come down, too, if you build it here. Set your affection on things above, up yonder—

> Up where eternal ages roll,
> Where solid pleasures never die,
> And fruits eternal feast the soul;

there project your thoughts and your anxieties, and have a care about the world to come. Be not anxious about the things that pertain to this life. "Seek ye first the kingdom of God, and his righteousness; and all these things shall be added unto you."

Reading further down, in the thirty-fifth verse, you will notice that watching implies *keeping ourselves in a serviceable condition:* "Let your loins be girded about." You know how the Orientals wear flowing robes, which are always getting in their way. They cannot walk without being tripped up; so that, if a man has a piece of work on hand, he just tucks in his robe under his girdle, ties his girdle up tightly, and gets ready for his task; as we should say in English, turning the Oriental into the western figure, rolling up your shirtsleeves, and preparing for work. That is the way to wait for the Lord, ready for service, that, when he comes, he may never find you idle. I called to see a sister one morning; and when I called, she was cleaning the front steps with some whitening, and she said, "Oh, my dear pastor, I am sorry that you should call upon me just now! I would not have had you see me like this on any account." I answered, "That is how I like to see you, busy at your work. I should not have liked to have come in, and caught you talking to your neighbor over the back palings. That would not have pleased me at all. May your Lord, when he comes, find you just so, doing your duty!" You see exactly what is meant; you are to be doing your duty; you are to be engaged about those vocations to which God has called you. You are to be doing it all out of love to Christ, and as service for him. Oh, that we might watch in that style, with our loins girded about! Work and wait and watch! Can you put those three things together? Work and wait and watch! This is what your Master asks of you.

And next, he would have us wait with our lights burning. If the Master comes home late, let us sit up late for him. It is not for us to go to bed till he comes home. Have the lights all trimmed; have his chamber well lit up; have the entrance hall ready for his approach. When the King comes, have your torches flaming, that you may go out to meet the royal bridegroom, and escort him to his home. If we are to watch for the Lord, as we ought, it must be with lamps burning. Are you making your light to shine among men? Do you think that your conduct and character are an example that will do your neighbors good, and are you trying to teach others the way of salvation? Some professors are like dark lanterns, or candles under a bushel. May we never be such! May we stand with our lamps trimmed, and our lights burning, and we ourselves like unto men that wait for their Lord; not walking in darkness, nor concealing our light, but letting it shine brightly! That is the way to watch for Christ, with your girdle tight about you because you are ready for work, and your lamp flaming out with brightness because you are anxious to illuminate the dark world in which you live.

To put it very plainly, I think that watching for the coming of the Lord means acting just as you would wish to be acting if he were to come. I saw, in the orphanage schoolroom, that little motto, "What would Jesus do?" That is a very splendid motto for our whole life. "What would Jesus do in such a case and in such a case?" Do just that. Another good motto is, "What would Jesus think of me if he were to come?" There are some places into which a Christian could not go, for he would not like his Master to find him there. There are some kinds of amusements into which a believer would never enter, for he would be ashamed for his Master to come and find him there. There are some conditions of angry temper, of pride, petulance, or spiritual sloth, in which you would not like to be if you felt that the Master was coming. Suppose an angel's wing should brush your cheek just as you have spoken some unkind word, and a voice should say, "Your Master is coming," you would tremble, I am sure, to meet him in such a condition. O beloved, let us try every morning to get up as if that were the morning in which Christ would come; and when we go up to bed at night, may we lie down with this thought, "Perhaps I shall be awakened by the ringing out of the silver trumpets heralding his coming. Before the sun arises, I may be startled from my dreams by the greatest of all cries, 'The Lord is come! The Lord is come!'" What a check, what an incentive, what a bridle, what a spur, such thoughts as these would be to us! Take this for the guide of your whole life. Act as if Jesus would come during the act in which you are engaged; and if you would not wish to be caught in that act by the coming of the Lord, let it not be your act.

The second verse of our text speaks about the Master coming in the second watch, or in the third watch. *We are to act as those who keep the watches of the age for Christ.* Among the Romans, it was as it is on board ship; there were certain watches. A Roman soldier, perhaps, stood on guard for three hours, and when he had been on the watch for three hours, there came another sentry who took his place, and the first man retired, and went back to the barracks, and the fresh sentinel stood in his place during his allotted time. Brethren, we have succeeded a long line of watchmen. Since the days of our Lord, when he sent out the chosen twelve to stand upon the citadel, and tell how the night waxed or waned, how have the watchers come and gone! Our God has changed the watchers, but he has kept the watch. He still sets watchmen on the walls of Zion, who cannot hold their peace day or night, but must watch for the coming of their master, watch against evil times, watch against error, and watch for the souls of men. At this time, some of us are called to be specially on the watch, and dare we sleep? After such a line of lynx-eyed watchmen, who counted not their lives dear unto them that they might hold their post, and watch against the foe, shall we be cravens, and be afraid; or shall we be sluggards, and go to our beds? By him that lives and was dead and is alive forevermore, we pray that we may never be guilty of treason to his sacred name and truth; but may we watch on to the last moment when there shall ring out the clarion cry, "Behold, the bridegroom cometh; go ye out to meet him." People of the tabernacle, you are set to watch tonight just as they did in the brave days of old! Whitefield and Wesley's men were watchers; and those before them, in the days of Luther and of Calvin, and backward even to the days of our Lord. They kept the watches of the night, and you must do the same, until—

> Upstarting at the midnight cry,
> "Behold your heavenly bridegroom nigh,"

you go forth to welcome your returning Lord.

We are to wait with one object in view, namely, *to open the door to him, and to welcome him*: "that when he cometh and knocketh, they may open unto him immediately." Perhaps you know what it is to go home to a loving, tender wife and children who are watching for you. You have been on a journey; you have been absent for some little time; you have written them letters which they have greatly valued; you have heard from them; but all that is nothing like your personal presence. They are looking out for you; and if, perchance, the boat should fail you, or the train be late, if you arrived at eleven or twelve o'clock at night, you would not expect to find the house all shut up, and nobody watching for you. No, you had told them that you would come, and you were quite sure that they would watch for you. I feel rebuked myself, sometimes, for not watching for my Master, when I know that, at this very time, my dogs are sitting against the door, waiting for me; and long before I reach home, there they will be, and at the first sound of the carriage wheels, they will lift up their voices with delight because their master is coming home. Oh, if we loved our Lord as dogs love their masters, how we should catch the first sound of his coming, and be waiting, always waiting, and never happy

until at last we should see him! Pardon me for using a dog as a picture of what
you ought to be; but when you have attained to a state above that, I will find
another illustration to explain my meaning.

3. Now, lastly, *there is a reward for watchers.*

Their reward is this, "Blessed are those servants, whom the lord when he
cometh shall find watching."

They have a present blessedness. It is a very blessed thing to be on the watch
for Christ, it is a blessing to us now. How it detaches you from the world! You
can be poor without murmuring; you can be rich without worldliness; you
can be sick without sorrowing; you can be healthy without presumption. If
you are always waiting for Christ's coming, untold blessings are wrapped up
in that glorious hope. "Every man that hath this hope in him purifieth himself
even as he is pure." Blessednesses are heaped up one upon another in that
state of heart in which a man is always looking for his Lord.

But what will be the blessedness when Jesus does come? Well, a part of
that blessedness will be *in future service.* You must not think that, when you
have done working here, you Sunday school teachers, and those of us who
preach and teach, that the Master will say, "I have discharged you from my service. Go and sit on a heavenly mount, and sing yourselves away forever and
ever." Not a bit of it. I am but learning how to preach now; I shall be able to
preach by and by. You are only learning to teach now; you will be able to teach
by and by. Yes, to angels and principalities and powers, you shall make known
the manifold wisdom of God. I sometimes aspire to the thought of a congregation of angels and archangels, who shall sit and wonder, as I tell what God
has done for me; and I shall be to them an everlasting monument of the grace
of God to an unworthy wretch, upon whom he looked with infinite compassion and saved with a wonderful salvation. All those stars, those worlds of
light, who knows how many of them are inhabited? I believe there are regions
beyond our imagination to which every child of God shall become an everlasting illumination, a living example of the love of God in Christ Jesus. The
people in those far distant lands could not see Calvary as this world has seen
it; but they shall hear of it from the redeemed. Remember how the Lord will
say, "Well done, thou good and faithful servant: thou hast been faithful over a
few things, I will make thee ruler over many things." He is to keep on doing
something, you see. Instead of having some little bit of a village to govern, he
is to be made ruler over some great province. So it is in this passage. Read the
forty-fourth verse: "Of a truth I say unto you, that he will make him ruler over
all that he hath." That is, the man who has been a faithful and wise steward of

God here will be called of God to more eminent service hereafter. If he serves his Master well, when his Master comes, he will promote him to still higher service. Do you not know how it used to be in the Spartan army? Here is a man who has fought well, and been a splendid soldier. He is covered with wounds on his breast. The next time that there is a war, they say, "Poor fellow, we will reward him! He shall lead the way in the first battle. He fought so well before, when he met one hundred with a little troop behind him; now he shall meet ten thousand with a larger troop." "Oh!" say you, "that is giving him more work." That is God's way of rewarding his people, and a blessed thing it is for the industrious servant. His rest is in serving God with all his might. This shall be our heaven, not to go there to roost, but to be always on the wing; forever flying, and forever resting at the same time. "They do his commandments, hearkening unto the voice of his word." "His servants shall serve him: and they shall see his face." These two things blended together make a noble ambition for every Christian.

May the Lord keep you waiting, working, watching, that when he comes, you may have the blessedness of entering upon some larger, higher, nobler service than you could accomplish now, for which you are preparing by the lowlier and more arduous service of this world! God bless you, beloved, and if any of you do not know my Lord, and therefore do not look for his appearing, remember that he will come whether you look for him or not; and when he comes, you will have to stand at his bar. One of the events that will follow his coming will be your being summoned before his judgment seat, and how will you answer him then? How will you answer him if you have refused his love and turned a deaf ear to the invitations of his mercy? If you have delayed and delayed and delayed and delayed, how will you answer him? How will you answer him in that day? If you stand speechless, your silence will condemn you, and the King will say, "Bind him hand and foot, and take him away." God grant that we may believe in the Lord Jesus unto life eternal, and then wait for his appearing from heaven, for his love's sake! Amen.

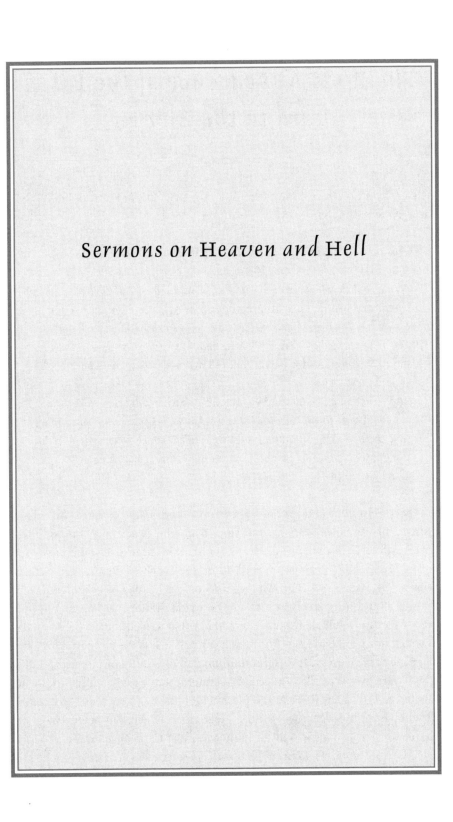

Sermons on Heaven and Hell

The First Appearance of the Risen Lord to the Eleven

⚜

Delivered on Lord's Day morning, April 10, 1887, at the Metropolitan Tabernacle, Newington. No. 1958.

And as they thus spake, Jesus himself stood in the midst of them, and saith unto them, "Peace be unto you." But they were terrified and affrighted, and supposed that they had seen a spirit. And he said unto them, "Why are ye troubled? and why do thoughts arise in your hearts? Behold my hands and my feet, that it is I myself: handle me, and see, for a spirit hath not flesh and bones, as ye see me have." And when he had thus spoken, he showed them his hands and his feet. And while they yet believed not for joy, and wondered, he said unto them, "Have ye here any meat?" And they gave him a piece of a broiled fish, and of an honeycomb. And he took it, and did eat before them. And he said unto them, "These are the words which I spake unto you while I was yet with you, that all things must be fulfilled, which were written in the law of Moses, and in the prophets, and in the psalms, concerning me."
—LUKE 24:36–44

This, beloved friends, is one of the most memorable of our Lord's many visits to his disciples after he had risen from the dead. Each one of these appearances had its own peculiarity. I cannot at this time give you even an outline of the special colorings which distinguished each of the many manifestations of our risen Lord. The instance now before us may be considered to be the fullest and most deliberate of all the manifestations, abounding beyond every other in "infallible proofs." Remember that it occurred on the same day in which our Lord had risen from the dead, and it was the close of a long day of gracious appearings. It was the summing up of a series of interviews, all of which were proofs of the Lord's resurrection. There was the empty tomb and the grave clothes left therein: the place where the Lord lay was accessible to all who chose to inspect it—for the great stone which had been sealed and guarded was rolled away. This in itself was most impressive evidence. Moreover, the holy women had been there and had seen a vision of angels, who said that Jesus was alive. Magdalene had enjoyed a special interview. Peter and John had been into the empty tomb and had seen for themselves. The report was current that "the Lord was risen indeed, and had appeared unto Simon." It was a special thing that he should appear unto Simon for the disciples painfully knew how Simon had denied his Master, and his appearance unto Simon seemed to have struck them as peculiarly characteristic: it was so like the manner of our Lord.

They met together in their bewilderment: the eleven of them gathered, as I suppose, to a social meal, for Mark tells us that the Lord appeared unto them "as they sat at meat." It must have been very late in the day, but they were loath to part, and so kept together till midnight. While they were sitting at meat, two brethren came in who, even after the sun had set, had hastened back from Emmaus. These newcomers related how one who seemed a stranger had joined himself to them as they were walking from Jerusalem, had talked with them in such a way that their hearts had been made to burn, and had made himself known unto them in the breaking of bread at the journey's end. They declared that it was the Lord who had thus appeared unto them, and, though they had intended to spend the night at Emmaus, they had hurried back to tell the marvelous news to the eleven. Hence the witness accumulated with great rapidity; it became more and more clear that Jesus had really risen from the dead. But as yet the doubters were not convinced, for Mark says: "After that he appeared in another form unto two of them, as they walked, and went into the country. And they went and told it unto the residue: neither believed they them."

Everything was working up to one point: the most unbelieving of them were being driven into a corner. They must doubt the truthfulness of Magdalene and the other saintly women; they must question the veracity of Simon; they must reject the two newly arrived brethren, and charge them with telling idle tales, or else they must believe that Jesus was still alive, though they had seen him die upon the cross. At that moment the chief confirmation of all presented itself; "for Jesus himself stood in the midst of them." The doors were shut; but, despite every obstacle, their Lord was present in the center of the assembly. In the presence of one whose loving smile warmed their hearts, their unbelief was destined to thaw and disappear. Jesus revealed himself in all the warmth of his vitality and love, and made them understand that it was none other than his very self, and that the Scriptures had told them it should be so. They were slow of heart to believe all that the prophets had spoken concerning him, but he brought them to it by his familiar communion with them. Oh, that in a like way he would put an end to all our doubts and fears!

Brethren, though you and I were not at that interview, yet we may derive much profit from it while we look at it in detail, anxiously desiring that we may in spirit see and look upon and handle the Word of life manifested in the flesh. Oh, to learn all that Jesus would teach us, as we now in spirit take our places at that midnight meeting of the chosen ones!

In this wonderful manifestation of our Lord to his apostles, I notice three things worthy of our careful observation this morning. This incident teaches us *the certainty of the resurrection of our Lord;* second, it shows us a little of *the character of our risen Master;* and, third, it gives us certain hints as to *the nature of our own resurrection,* when it shall be granted us. Oh, that we may be counted worthy to attain to the resurrection from among the dead!

1. First, then, let us see here *the certainty of our Lord's resurrection.*

We have often asserted, and we affirm it yet again, that no fact in history is better attested than the resurrection of Jesus Christ from the dead. The common mass of facts accepted by all men as historical are not one tenth as certainly assured to us as this fact is. It must not be denied by any who are willing to pay the slightest respect to the testimony of their fellowmen, that Jesus, who died upon the cross and was buried in the tomb of Joseph of Arimathea, did literally rise again from the dead.

Observe that when this person appeared in the room, the first token that it was Jesus was his speech: *they were to have the evidence of hearing:* he used the same speech. No sooner did he appear than he spoke. He was never dumb, and it was natural that the great teacher and friend should at once salute his followers, from whom he had been so painfully parted. His first accents must have called to their minds those cheering notes with which he had closed his last address. They must have recognized that charming voice. I suppose its tone and rhythm to have been rich with a music most sweet and heavenly. A perfect voice would naturally be given to a perfect man. The very sound of it would, through their ears, have charmed conviction into their minds with a glow of joy, had they not been frozen up in unbelief. "Never man spoke like this man": they might have known him by his speech alone. There were tones of voice as well as forms of language which were peculiar to Jesus of Nazareth.

What our Lord said was just like him; it was all of a piece with his former discourse. Among the last sounds which lingered in their ears was that word— "Peace I leave with you, my peace I give unto you: not as the world giveth, give I unto you"; and now it must surely be the same person who introduces himself with the cheering salutation, "Peace be unto you." About the Lord there were the air and style of one who had peace himself and loved to communicate it to others. The tone in which he spoke peace tended to create it. He was a peacemaker, and a peace giver, and by this sign they were driven to discern their leader.

Do you not think that they were almost persuaded to believe that it was Jesus when he proceeded to chide them in a manner more tender than any other chiding could have been? How gentle the accents when he said, "Why are ye troubled? And why do thoughts arise in your hearts?" Our Lord's chidings were comforts in disguise. His upbraidings were consolations in an unusual shape. Did not his upbraiding on this occasion bring to their minds his question upon the sea of Galilee when he said to them, "Why are ye fearful, O ye of little faith?" Did they not also remember when he came to them walking on the water, and they were afraid that he was a spirit, and cried out for fear; and he said to them, "It is I; be not afraid"? Surely they remembered enough of these things to have made sure that it was their Lord, had not their spirits been sunken in sorrow. Our Lord had never been unwisely silent as to their faults. He had never passed over their errors with that false and indulgent affection which gratifies its own ease by tolerating sin; but he had pointed out their faults with the fidelity of true love; and now that he thus admonished them, they ought to have perceived that it was none other than he.

When Jesus came at last to talk to them about Moses and the prophets and the psalms, he was upon a favorite topic. Then the eleven might have nudged each other and whispered, "It is the Lord." Jesus had, in his later hours, been continually pointing out the Scriptures which were being fulfilled in himself, and at this interview he repeated his former teaching. This is assuredly none other than he who always spoke his Father's mind and will and constantly did honor to the Holy Ghost by whom the sacred books were inspired. Thus in his tones and topics our Lord gave clear indications that it was himself who had suddenly appeared in that little assembly.

I want you to notice that this evidence was all the better, because they themselves evidently remained the same men as they had been. "They were terrified and affrighted, and supposed that they had seen a spirit"; and thus they did exactly what they had done long before when he came to them walking on the waters. In the interval between his death and his appearing, no change has come over them. Nothing has happened to them to elevate them as yet out of their littleness of mind. The Holy Spirit was not yet given, and therefore all that they had heard at the Last Supper, and seen in Gethsemane, and at the cross had not yet exercised its full influence upon them: they were still childish and unbelieving. The same men, then, are looking at the same person, and they are in their ordinary condition; this argues strongly for the correctness of their identification of their well-beloved Lord. They are not carried away by enthusiasm, nor wafted aloft by fanaticism, they are not even as yet upborne by the Holy Spirit into an unusual state of mind, but they are as slow of heart and as fearful as ever they were.

If *they* are convinced that Jesus has risen from the dead, depend upon it, it must be so. If they go forth to tell the tidings of his resurrection, and to yield up their lives for it, you may be sure that their witness is true, for they are not the sort of men to be deceived. In our day there has been a buzz about certain miracles of faith, but the statements usually come from persons whose impartiality is questionable—credulous persons who saw what they evidently wished to see. I know several good people who would not willfully deceive, who nevertheless upon some points are exceedingly unreliable, because their enthusiasm is prepared to be imposed upon. Any hawker of wonders would expect them to be buyers, they have a taste for the marvelous. As witnesses, the evidence of such people has no value in it as compared with that of these eleven men, who evidently were the reverse of credulous or excitable. In the apostles' case the facts were tested to the utmost, and the truth was not admitted till it was forced upon them. I am not excusing the unbelief of the disciples, but I claim that their witness has all the more weight in it, because it was the result of such cool investigation. These apostles were in special manner to be witnesses of the resurrection, and it makes assurance doubly sure to us when we see them arrive at their conclusion with such deliberate steps. These were men like ourselves, only perhaps a little less likely to be deceived: they needed to be convinced by overwhelming witness, and they were so: ever afterward they declared boldly that their crucified Lord had indeed risen from the dead.

Thus far in the narrative they had received the evidence of their ears, and that is by no means weak evidence, but now *they are to have the evidence of sight;* for the Savior says to them, "Behold my hands and my feet, that it is I myself"; "and when he had thus spoken, he showed them his hands and his feet." John says also "his side," which *he* specially noted because he had seen the piercing of that side, and the outflow of blood and water. They were to see and identify that blessed body which had suffered death. The nail prints were visible, both in his hands which were open before them, and also in his feet which their condescending Lord deigned to expose to their deliberate gaze. There was the mark of the gash in his side; and this the Lord Jesus graciously bared to them, as afterward he did more fully to Thomas, when he said, "Reach hither thy hand, and thrust it into my side." These were the marks of the Lord Jesus, by which his identity could be verified. Beyond this there was the general contour of his countenance, and the fashion of the whole man by which they could discern him. His body, though it was now in a sense glorified, was so far veiled as to its new condition that it retained its former likeness: they might perceive that the Lord was no longer subject to the pains and infirmities of our ordinary mortality—else his wounds had not been healed so soon; but yet there remained sure marks by which they knew that it was Jesus, and no other. He looked like a lamb that had been slain: the signs of the Son of man were in his hands and feet and side. Their sight of the Lord was not a hasty glimpse, but a steady inspection, for John in his first epistle writes, "Which we have seen and looked upon." This implies a lengthened looking, and such the Lord Jesus invited his friends to take. They could not have been mistaken when they were afforded such a view of those marks by which his identity was established. The same Christ that died had risen from the dead, the same Jesus that had hung upon the cross now stood in the midst of those who knew him best. It was the same body, and they identified it, although a great change had doubtless come over it since it was taken down from the tree.

Furthermore, that they might be quite sure, *the Lord invited them to receive the evidence of touch or feeling*. He called them to a form of examination, from which, I doubt not, many of them shrank; he said, "Handle me. Handle me, and see; for a spirit hath not flesh and bones, as ye see me have." Writers have remarked upon the use of the word "bones," instead of blood, in this case; but I do not think that any inference can be safely drawn therefrom. It would have been barely possible for the disciples to have discovered by handling that the Lord had blood, but they could by handling perceive that he had bones; hence the expression is natural enough, without our imputing to it a meaning which it may never have been intended to convey. The Savior had a reason, no doubt, other than some have imagined, for the use of the terms "a spirit hath not flesh *and bones* as ye see me have." The Savior had not assumed a phantom body: there was bone in it as well as flesh; it was to the full as substantial as ever. He had not put on an appearance, as angels do when they visit the sons of men. No, his body was solid substance, which could be handled. "Handle me, and see that it is I myself." He bade them see that it was flesh and bone, such as no spirit has. There were the substantial elements of a human frame in that body of Christ which stood in the midst of the eleven. Jesus cried, "Handle me, and see."

Thus our Lord was establishing to the apostles, not only his identity, but also his substantial corporeal existence: he would make them see that he was a man of flesh and bones, and not a ghost, airy and unsubstantial. This should correct a certain form of teaching upon the resurrection which is all too common. I was present some years ago at the funeral of a man of God for whom I had much respect. In the chapel a certain excellent doctor of divinity gave us an address before the interment, in which he informed us as to the condition of his departed friend. He said that he was not in the coffin: indeed, there was nothing of him there. This I was sorry to hear, for if so I was ignorantly mourning over a body which had no relation to my friend. The preacher went on to describe the way in which the man of God had ascended to heaven at the moment of death, his spirit fashioning for itself a body as it passed through the air. I believed in my friend's being in heaven, but not in his being there in a body. I knew that my friend's body was in the coffin, and I believed that it would be laid in the tomb, and I expected that it would rise again from the grave at the coming of the Lord. I did not believe that my friend would weave for himself a filmy frame, making a second body, nor do I believe it now, though I heard it so affirmed.

I believe in the resurrection of the dead. I look to see the very body which was buried raised again. It is true that as the seed develops into the flower, so the buried body is merely the germ out of which will come the spiritual body; yet still it will not be a second body, but the same body, as to identity. I shall enter into no dispute about the atoms of the body, nor deny that the particles of our flesh, in the process of their decay, may be taken up by plants and absorbed into the bodies of animals, and all that; I do not care one jot about identity of atoms; there may not be a solitary ounce of the same matter, but yet identity can be preserved; and it must be preserved if I read my Bible aright. My body today is the same as that which I inhabited twenty years ago, and yet all its particles are different: even so the body put into the grave and the body that rises from it are not two bodies, but one body. The saints are not at the coming of their Lord to remain disembodied spirits, nor to wear freshly created bodies, but their entire manhood is to be restored, and to enjoy endless bliss. Well said the patriarch of old, "in my flesh shall I see God." "He which raised up the Lord Jesus shall raise up us also by Jesus."

I cannot see how the doctrine of Christ goes beyond the doctrine of Plato and others if it be not a doctrine which respects this body. The immortality of the soul was accepted and known as a truth before the faith of Christ was preached, for it is dimly discoverable by the light of nature; but the resurrection of the body is a revelation peculiar to the Christian dispensation, at which the wise men of the world very naturally mocked, but which it ill becomes Christian men to spirit away. The body which is buried shall rise again. It is true it is sown a natural body and shall be raised a spiritual body, but it will be truly a body, and the same *it* which was sown shall be raised. It is true it is sown in weakness and raised in power, but the same *it* is thus raised. It is true that it is sown in weakness to be raised in power, and sown a corruptible body, to be raised in incorruption, but in each case it is the same body, though so gloriously changed. It will be of a material substance also; for our Savior's body was material, since he said, "Handle me, and see that it is I myself; for a spirit hath not flesh and bones, as ye see me have."

Still further to confirm the faith of the disciples, and to show them that their Lord had a real body, and not the mere form of one, *he gave them evidence which appealed to their common sense*. He said, "'Have ye any meat?' And they gave him a piece of a broiled fish, and of an honeycomb. And he took it, and did eat before them." This was an exceedingly convincing proof of his unquestionable resurrection. In very deed and fact, and not in vision and phantom, the man who had died upon the cross stood among them.

Let us just think of this and rejoice. This resurrection of our Lord Jesus is a matter of certainty; for, if you spirit this away, you have done away with the gospel altogether. If he is not risen from the dead, then is our preaching vain, and your faith is also vain; you are yet in your sins. Justification receives its seal in the resurrection of Jesus Christ from the dead; not in his appearing as a phantom, but in his very self being loosed from death, and raised to a glorious life. This is God's mark of the acceptance of the work of the great substitute, and of the justification of all for whom his atoning work was performed.

Note well that this is also our grand hope concerning those that are asleep. You have buried them forever if Christ was not raised from the dead. They have passed out of your sight, and they shall never again have fellowship with you, unless Jesus rose again from the dead; for the apostle makes the resurrection of all who are in Christ to hinge upon the resurrection of Christ. I do not feel it necessary, when I talk with the bereaved, to comfort them at all concerning those that are asleep in Christ, as to their souls: we know that they are forever with the Lord, and are supremely blessed, and, therefore, we need no further comfort. The only matter upon which we need consolation is that poor body, which once we loved so well, but which now we must leave in the cold clay. The resurrection comes in as a final undoing of all that death has done. "They shall come again from the land of the enemy." Jesus says, "Thy dead men shall live, together with my dead body shall they arise." If we question the resurrection of Christ, then is the whole of our faith questioned, and those who have fallen asleep in Christ have perished, and we are left just where others were before Christ brought this divine truth to light. Only as we are sure of the resurrection of Jesus can we cry, "O death, where is thy sting? O grave, where is thy victory?"

2. Second, will you follow me while I very briefly set forth *our Lord's character when risen from the dead?*

What is he now that he has quit death, and all that belongs to it? What is he now that he shall hunger no more, neither thirst any more? He is much the same as he used to be; indeed he is altogether what he was, for he is "the same yesterday, today, and forever."

Notice, first, that in this appearance of Christ we are taught that *he is still anxious to create peace in the hearts of his people.* No sooner did he make himself visible than he said, "Peace be unto you." Beloved, your risen Lord wants you to be happy. When he was here on earth, he said, "Let not your hearts be troubled": he says just the same to you today. He takes no delight in the distresses of his people. He would have his joy to be in them, that their joy may be full. He bids you rejoice in him evermore. He whispers to you this morning, as you sit in the pew, "Peace be unto you." He has not lost his tender care over the least of the flock; he would have each one led by the still waters and made to lie down in green pastures.

Note again, that *he has not lost his habit of chiding unbelief, and encouraging faith;* for as soon as he has risen, and speaks with his disciples, he asks them, "Why are ye troubled? And why do thoughts arise in your hearts?" He loves you to believe in him, and be at rest. Find if you can, beloved, one occasion in which Jesus inculcated doubt, or bade men dwell in uncertainty. The apostles of unbelief are everywhere today, and they imagine that they are doing God service by spreading what they call "honest doubt." This is death to all joy! Poison to all peace! The Savior did not so. He would have them take extraordinary measures to get rid of their doubt. "Handle me," he says. It was going a long way to say that, but he would sooner be handled than his people should doubt! Ordinarily it might not be meet for them to touch him. Had he not said to the women, "Touch me not"? But what may not be allowable ordinarily becomes proper when necessity demands it. The removal of their doubt as to our Lord's resurrection needed that they should handle him, and therefore he bids them do so. O beloved, you that are troubled and vexed with thoughts, and therefore get no comfort out of your religion because of your mistrust, your Lord would have you come very near to him, and put his gospel to any test which will satisfy you. He cannot bear you to doubt. He appeals tenderly, saying, "O thou of little faith, wherefore didst thou doubt?" He would at this moment still encourage you to taste and see that the Lord is good. He would have you believe in the substantial reality of his religion and handle him and see: trust him largely and simply, as a child trusts its mother and knows no fear.

Notice, next, that when the Savior had risen from the dead, and a measure of his glory was upon him, *he was still most condescendingly familiar with his people.* He showed them his hands and his feet, and he said, "Handle me, and see." When he was on earth, before his passion, he was most free with his disciples: no affectation of dignity kept him apart from them. He was their Master and Lord, and yet he washed their feet. He was the Son of the Highest, but he was among them as one that served. He said, "Suffer little children to come unto me." He is the same today.

> *His sacred name a common word*
> *On earth he loves to hear;*
> *There is no majesty in him*
> *Which love may not come near.*

Though he reigns in the highest heavens, his delights are still with the sons of men. Still he will permit us to sit at his feet, or even to lean our head upon his bosom. Jesus will hear us tell out our griefs; he will regard our cry when we are not pleading about a sword in our bones, but only concerning a thorn in our flesh. Jesus is still the brother born for adversity; he still manifests himself to us as he does not unto the world. Is not this clear, and also very pleasant to see, as we study this interview?

The next thing is that *the risen Lord was still wonderfully patient,* even as he had always been. He bore with their folly and infirmity; for "while they yet believed not for joy, and wondered," he did not chide them. He discerned between one unbelief and another, and he judged that the unbelief which grew out of wonder was not so blamable as that former unbelief which denied credible evidence. Instead of rebuke he gives confirmation. He says, "Have ye here any meat?" and he takes a piece of broiled fish, and of a honeycomb, and eats it. Not that he needed food. His body could receive food, but it did not require it. Eating was his own sweet way of showing them that if he could he would solve all their questions. He would do anything in his great patience that they might be cured of their mistrust. Just so today, beloved, Jesus does not chide you, but he invites you to believe him: he invites you, therefore, to sup with him and eat bread at his table. "He will not always chide, neither will he keep his anger forever"; but in his great mercy he will use another tone, and encourage you to trust him. Can you hold back? Oh, do not so.

Observe that our Savior, though he was risen from the dead, and there-fore in a measure in his glory, *entered into the fullest fellowship with his own.* Peter tells us that they did eat and drink with him. I do not notice in this narrative that he drank with them, but he certainly ate of such food as they had, and this was a clear token of his fellowship with them. In all ages eating and drink-ing with one another has been the most expressive token of communion, and so the Savior seems to say to us today, "I have eaten with you, my people, since I have quitted the grave. I have eaten with you through the eleven who repre-sented you. I have eaten, and I will still eat with you, till we sit down together at the marriage supper of the Lamb. If any man open unto me, I will come in to him, and will sup with him, and he with me." Yes, the Lord Jesus is won-derfully near to us still, and he waits to grant us the highest forms of fellow-ship which can be known on this side the gate of pearl. In this let our spirits quietly rejoice.

Let me call your attention to the fact that when Jesus had risen from the dead *he was just as tender of Scripture as he was before his decease.* I have dwelt for two Sunday mornings upon the wonderful way in which our Lord always magnified the Scriptures; and here, as if to crown all, he told them that "'all things must be fulfilled which were written in the law of Moses, and in the prophets, and in the psalms concerning' himself; and he opened their under-standing that they might understand the Scriptures, and said unto them, 'Thus it is written, and thus it behooved Christ to suffer, and to rise from the dead.'" Find Jesus where you may, he is the antagonist of those who would lessen the authority of holy Scripture. "It is written" is his weapon against Satan, his argument against wicked men. The learned at this hour scoff at the Book, and accuse of bibliolatry those of us who reverence the divine Word; but in this they derive no assistance from the teaching or example of Jesus. Not a word derogatory of Scripture ever fell from the lips of Jesus Christ; but evermore he manifested the most reverent regard for every jot and tittle of the inspired vol-ume. Since our Savior, not only before his death, but after it, took care thus to commend the Scriptures to us, let us avoid with all our hearts all teaching in which holy Scripture is put into the background. Still the Bible, and the Bible alone, should be and shall be the religion of Protestants, and we will not budge an inch from that standpoint, God helping us.

Once again, our Savior, after he had risen from the dead, *showed that he was anxious for the salvation of men;* for it was at this interview that he breathed upon the apostles, and bade them receive the Holy Ghost, to fit them to go forth and preach the gospel to every creature. The missionary spirit is the spirit of Christ—not only the spirit of him that died to save, but the spirit of him who has finished his work, and has gone into his rest. Let us cultivate that spirit, if we would be like the Jesus who has risen from the dead.

3. I can stay no longer, because I would draw your attention, in the third place, to the light which is thrown by this incident upon *the nature of our own resurrection.*

First, I gather from this text that our nature, *our whole humanity, will be perfected at the day of the appearing of our Lord and Savior Jesus Christ,* when the dead shall be raised incorruptible, and we that may then be alive shall be changed. Jesus has redeemed not only our souls, but our bodies. "Know ye not that your bodies are the temples of the Holy Ghost?" When the Lord shall deliver his captive people out of the land of the enemy, he will not leave a bone of one of them in the adversary's power. The dominion of death shall be utterly broken. Our entire nature shall be redeemed unto the living God in the day of the resurrection. After death, until that day, we shall be disembodied spirits; but in the adoption, to wit, the redemption, of the body, we shall attain our full inheritance. We are looking forward to a complete restoration. At this time the body is dead because of sin, and hence it suffers pain, and tends to decay; but the spirit is life because of righteousness: in the resurrection, however, the body shall be quickened also, and the resurrection shall be to the body what regeneration has been to the soul. Thus shall our humanity be completely delivered from the consequences of the fall. Perfect manhood is that which Jesus restores from sin and the grave; and this shall be ours in the day of his appearing.

I gather next that in the resurrection *our nature will be full of peace.* Jesus Christ would not have said, "Peace be unto you," if there had not been a deep peace within himself. He was calm and undisturbed. There was much peace about his whole life; but after the resurrection his peace becomes very conspicuous. There is no striving with scribes and Pharisees, there is no battling with anybody after our Lord is risen. A French author has written of our Lord's forty days on earth after the resurrection under the title of "The Life of Jesus Christ in Glory." Though rather misleading at first, the title is not so inaccurate as it appears; for his work was done, and his warfare was accomplished, and our Lord's life here was the beginning of his glory. Such shall be our life, we shall be flooded with eternal peace, and shall never again be tossed about with trouble and sorrow and distress and persecution. An infinite serenity shall keep our body, soul, and spirit throughout eternity.

When we rise again *our nature will find its home amid the communion of saints.* When the Lord Jesus Christ had risen again his first resort was the room where his disciples were gathered. His first evening was spent among the objects of his love. Even so, wherever we are we shall seek and find communion with the saints. I joyfully expect to meet many of you in heaven, and to know you, and commune with you. I should not like to float about in the future state without a personality in the midst of a company of undefined and unknown beings. That would be no heaven to me. No, brethren, we shall soon perceive who our comrades are, and we shall rejoice in them, and in our Lord. There could be no communion among unknown entities. You cannot have fellowship with people whom you do not recognize; and therefore it seems to me most clear that we shall in the future state have fellowship through recognition, and our heavenly bodies shall help the recognition and share in the fellowship. As the risen Christ wends his way to the upper room of the eleven, so will you by force of holy gravitation find your way to the place where all the servants of God shall gather at the last. Then shall we be truly at home, and go no more out forever.

Furthermore, I see that in that day *our bodies will admirably serve our spirits.* For look at our Lord's body. Now that he is risen from the dead he desires to convince his disciples, and his body becomes at once the means of his argument, the evidence of his statement. His flesh and bones were text and sermon for him. "Handle me," says he, "and see." Ah brethren! Whatever we may have to do in eternity, we shall not be hindered by our bodies as we now are. Flesh and blood hamper us, but "flesh and bones" shall help us. I want to speak sometimes, and my head aches, or my throat is choked, or my legs refuse to bear me up: but it is not so in the resurrection from the dead. A thousand infirmities in this earthly life compass us about; but our risen body shall be helpful to our regenerated nature. It is only a natural body now, fit for our soul; but hereafter it shall be a spiritual body, adapted to all the desires and wishes of the heaven-born spirit; and no longer shall we have to cry out, "The spirit indeed is willing, but the flesh is weak." We shall find in the risen body a power such as the spirit shall wish to employ for the noblest purposes. Will not this be well?

In that day, beloved, when we shall rise again from the dead, *we shall remember the past.* Do you not notice how the risen Savior says, "These are the words which I spoke unto you, while I was yet with you." He had not forgotten his former state. I think Dr. Watts is right when he says that we shall "with transporting joys recount the labors of our feet." It is rather a small subject, and probably we shall far more delight to dwell on the labors of our Redeemer's hands and feet; but still we shall remember all the way whereby the Lord our God led us, and we shall talk to one another concerning it. In heaven we shall remember our happy Sabbaths here below, when our hearts burned within us while Jesus himself drew near. Since Jesus speaks after he has risen of the things that he said while he was with his disciples, we perceive that the river of death is not like the fabled Lethe, which caused all who drank thereof to forget their past. We shall arise with a multitude of hallowed memories enriching our minds. Death will not be oblivion to us, for it was not so to Jesus. Rather shall we meditate on mercies experienced, and by discoursing thereon we shall make known to principalities and powers the manifold wisdom of God.

Observe that our Lord, after he had risen from the dead, *was still full of the spirit of service*, and therefore he called others out to go and preach the gospel, and he gave them the Spirit of God to help them. When you and I are risen from the dead, we shall rise full of the spirit of service. What engagements we may have throughout eternity we are not told, because we have enough to do to fulfill our engagements now; but assuredly we shall be honored with errands of mercy and tasks of love fitted for our heavenly being; and I doubt not it shall be one of our greatest delights while seeing the Lord's face to serve him with all our perfected powers. He will use us in the grand economy of future manifestations of his divine glory. Possibly we may be to other dispensations what the angels have been to this. Be that as it may, we shall find a part of our bliss and joy in constantly serving him who has raised us from the dead.

There I leave the subject, wishing that I could have handled it much better. Think it over when you are quiet at home, and add this thought to it, that you have a share in all that is contained in resurrection. May the Holy Ghost give you a personal grip of this vital truth! You yourself shall rise from the dead; therefore, be not afraid to die.

If any of my hearers have no share in our Lord's resurrection, I am truly sorry for them. O my friend, what you are losing! If you have no share in the living Lord, may God have mercy upon you! If you have no share in Christ's rising from the dead, then you will not be raised up in the likeness of his glorified body. If you do not attain to that resurrection from among the dead, then you must abide in death, with no prospect but that of a certain fearful looking for of judgment, and of fiery indignation. Oh, look to Jesus, the Savior! Only as you look to him can there be a happy future for you. God help you to do so at once, for his dear name's sake! Amen.

Great Difference

Delivered on Lord's Day morning, May 19, 1878, at the Metropolitan Tabernacle, Newington. No. 1415.

Where is the God of judgment? —MALACHI 2:17

Then shall ye return, and discern between the righteous and the wicked,
between him that serveth God and him that serveth him not. —MALACHI 3:18

You were not here, I am thankful to say, last Sabbath evening, for it was
your duty and privilege to stay away to give others an opportunity of hearing;
but my subject then was our heavenly Father, who makes his sun to rise upon
the evil and upon the good, and sends rain upon the just and upon the unjust.
Then I set forth the universal benevolence of God and the way in which he
stays the operations of justice to give space for forbearance and longsuffering.
Now this fact, this gracious fact, which ought to lead man to repentance, has
through the perversity of human nature been used for quite another purpose.
Men have said, "He blesses the evil as well as the good. The sun shines on all
alike; the rain indiscriminately enriches the field of the churl and the pasture
of the generous heart; where is the God of judgment? Is there such a God? Is
it not one and the same whether we fear him or disregard him?" Side by side
with this has run another circumstance perhaps even more readily misunderstood. God is in this life preparing his people for a better world and part of that
process is effected by trial and affliction, so that it frequently happens that the
godly are in adversity while the wicked are in prosperity. Having no such
designs toward them as toward his people, the Lord permits the wicked to
enjoy themselves while they may; so that oftentimes they are as bullocks fattened in rich pastures, but they forget that they are fattened for the slaughter;
while the righteous are brought very low, are often in poverty, frequently in
sickness, and not seldom in despondency of spirit, but all to prepare them for
the glory land. From the trials of the godly, which are all sent in wisdom and
in love, shortsighted man has inferred that God has no regard to human character and even treats those worst who serve him best. In Malachi's days the
blaspheming crew even said that God takes sides with the wicked, and they
wearied God by saying, "Everyone that doeth evil is good in the sight of the

Lord, and he delighteth in them." Then again they uttered the old rude but plainspoken question, "Where is the God of judgment?"

Truly brethren, in looking with these poor eyes upon the affairs around us, they do appear to be a great tangle and snarl, a mixed medley of strange accidents. We see the true princes of the earth walking in the dust and beggars riding upon horses. We mourn as we see servants of God and heirs of heaven lying, like Lazarus, sick at the gate of the ungodly miser, while the vicious libertine is rioting in luxury and drinking full bowls of pleasure. Until we perceive the clue, providence is a labyrinth into whose center we can never penetrate. But there is a clue which opens all its secrets. There is a God of judgment, not sitting in heaven in blind indifference, but looking down upon the sons of men and working out purposes of righteousness at all times.

At this time I purpose to speak upon the fact that God does put a difference between the righteous and the wicked, and makes no mistake between Egypt and Israel. The Lord knows them that are his, and in his dealings, which we cannot always understand, he nevertheless has not confounded his people with the world, nor does the rod of the wicked rest upon the lot of the righteous. He has a right hand of acceptance for them that fear him, he has a left hand of punishment for those that fear him not. This distinction is not so apparent yet as it shall be, but we shall now trace the gradual widening of the division between the two classes, and show that still there is a God of judgment, and that by and by even the blindest eye shall be able to discern between the righteous and the wicked, between him that serves God and him that serves him not.

1. First, then, *there are signs of separation* between the righteous and the wicked.

The first sign is seen in the evident difference of *character*. "They that feared the Lord" are spoken of. That is to say, there are still some on the face of the earth who believe that there is a God, who believe in the revelation which he has given, who accept the atonement which he has provided, and who delight to be obedient to the will which he has declared. How came they to fear the Lord? The answer is, it is a gift of his grace and a work of his Spirit wherever it is found. It makes a distinction very deep, and very vital, and consequently very lasting, for it shall continue throughout eternity. Let us bless God that in the worst times he still has a remnant according to the election of grace, and when blasphemers grow bold in sin and say, "Where is the God of judgment?," there are at least a few hidden ones who nevertheless look up and behold the Lord exalted above the rage of his foes. There will always be a band who bow the knee and worship the most High, because their hearts stand in awe of him. God is beginning to separate his chosen from the world, when he gives them an inward sense of his presence, and a consequent holy fear and sacred awe of him. The dividing work begins here, in the bent and current of the heart.

This difference in real character soon shows itself in a remarkable change of *thought* and meditation. According to the passage before us, those who are said to "fear the Lord" are also described as those who "thought upon his name." Their thoughts are not always toward the transient things of this world, but they are much engaged with the eternal God and his truth: they are not always groveling after the creature, but soaring toward the Creator. The Hebrew word has the idea of "counting": they reckon the Lord as the chief consideration when they count up their arguments for action. Others do not take him into the reckoning, they act as if there were no God at all: but the righteous make much of him, and account him to be the greatest factor in all their calculations; they fall back upon God in trouble, and joy most of all in him when they are glad. They reckon not without the Lord of hosts; they say, "The best of all is, God is with us." And concerning any action, if it be contrary to his mind, they reject it; if it be according to his will they think upon him, and they delight to carry it out. This makes a great difference in their course of life, and also in their happiness. Dear hearers, I trust there are many among you who can truly say that your meditation of God has been very sweet, you have been glad in the Lord. This, then, is working out a distinction between you and the wicked who forget God. You fear the Lord, and you take delight in meditating upon him in secret, but this the worldling cannot understand.

This makes a distinction between you and the careless, which does not long exist without operating in a further direction: you grow weary of their frivolous conversation, and they cannot endure your serious observations, and so two parties are formed, as of old there were two lines, the sons of God and the children of Cain. You will soon see Ishmael and Isaac, Esau and Jacob living over again if you watch the thoughtless worldling and the pious Christian, and mark how much they differ. Hence there grows out of this difference of thought and feeling a separation as to society. "Then they that feared the Lord spoke often one to another," which shows that they often met, and that they delighted in one another's company. Each man felt himself feeble in the midst of the ungodly, and therefore he sought out a brother that he might be strengthened by association. Each man felt himself to be like a sheep in the midst of wolves, but knowing the nature of sheep to be gregarious, each one sought to his fellow, that they might make up a flock, hoping that, as a flock, they might gather round the good Shepherd. Yes, and in the ungodliest times there are not only gracious people here and there, but these chosen souls by some means or other make mutual discoveries, and come together and so form the visible church of the living God.

In Rome in the days of the Caesars, when to be a Christian meant to be condemned to die without mercy, if believers could not meet in their houses they would meet in the abodes of the dead, in the catacombs: but they must meet. It is the nature of God's children that they do not like going to heaven alone, but prefer to go up to the temple in bands and companies, and the more the merrier, as the proverb has it, for they delight to go with the multitude that keep holy day, and they rejoice to fly in flocks like doves to their windows. There is a divine sweetness in Christian communion, and every true saint delights in it. The essence of our religion is love, and he that loves not the brethren loves not God, and lacks an essential point of the Christian character. By the exercise of holy brotherhood, the Lord continues to call out his own people, and thus to create a manifest separation. Likeness of character and thought produce a mutual attractiveness, and so a corporate body is formed, and the solitary secret ones become manifest in the mass. The chosen stones are quarried and are built into the similitude of a palace; what if I say that they come together bone to his bone to fashion the spiritual body of the Lord Jesus Christ?

This distinct association leads on to a peculiar *occupation*: for "they that feared the Lord *spoke* often one to another." They heard others speak against the Lord, and they resolved to speak too. Of others the Lord complained, "'Your words have been stout against me,' saith the Lord," and these men felt that it would be a shame if *they* were silent. They did not cast their pearls before swine, yet they wore their pearls where those who were not swine, but saints, could see them. In society where truth would be appreciated, they were not backward to declare it: they "spoke often one to another." It was a time of noise and tumult, it was a time of speaking very bitterly against the Lord: therefore when they met together they spoke for the Lord, and each one opened his mouth, that the Lord might not lack for witnesses. I take it that the expression means that they renewed and *repeated their testimony*. They "spoke often one to another." They said, "Ah, we can answer what the ungodly are saying, our experience testifies that they speak not aright. It is not a vain thing to serve God. How do you find it, brother?" Then the brother would say, "I find it exceedingly comforting and cheering to my soul. They have said, 'What profit is it that we have kept his ordinances?' but I have found it exceedingly profitable, for in keeping his commandments there is great reward." Then a third would say, "It has enriched our souls to walk according to the mind of God, and in the blessed ordinances of his house our souls have been fed and exceedingly nourished." A fourth would add, "The ungodly say it is in vain that we have walked mournfully before the Lord of hosts: do you find it so, brother?" The reply would be, "No, my mournful days have often been most profitable, like the days of shower and cloud, which have most to do with the harvest." "Besides," said another, "we do not walk mournfully before the Lord as a rule, for we rejoice before him, yes, in his name we do exceedingly rejoice." Thus, you see, by their testimony the one to the other they supported each other's minds against the popular infidelities of the time; they set their thoughtful experience against the vicious falsehoods of unbelieving men, and so they both honored God and benefited each other.

When they "spoke often one to another," I have no doubt *they expressed their affection* one for the other. They said, "Let us not marvel if the world hate us: did not our Master say, 'It hated me before it hated you'?" Did he not tell us to beware of man; did he not remind us that our worst enemies should be those of our own household. "Yes, brethren," they would say one to another, "let us love one another, for love is of God." The elders would speak like John the divine and say, "Little children, love one another," and the younger ones would respond by acts and words of loving respect to the older saints. Their mutual expressions of love would increase love. As when we lay live coals together they burn the better, so loving intercommunications increase the heat of affection till it glows like coals of juniper, which have a most vehement flame.

No doubt, for we know by what we see, this speaking one to another *assisted each other's faith.* One might be weak, but they were not all weak at once; one and another would be strong just then. We all have our ups and downs, but the mercy is that when one is sinking another is rising. It will frequently happen that if the sun does not shine on my side of the hedge it is shining on yours, and you can tell me that the sun is not snuffed out, but that it will shine on me too by and by. Commerce makes nations rich, and Christian intercourse makes believers grow in grace. Speaking often one to another with the view of helping the weak hands and confirming the feeble knees is a means of great blessing to the souls of Christians. When they met, one would tell what he knew which his brother might not know, and a third would say, "I can confirm that statement and add something more," and so the first speaker would learn as well as teach. Then a fourth brother would say, "But there is yet another truth which stands in relation to that which you have stated, do not overlook it." Thus by communion in experience, and each one expressing what the Lord had written upon his heart, the whole would be edified in righteousness.

Now, beloved, it is in proportion as the children of God speak often one to another in this way that the church is brought out into a visible condition. A silent church might grope through the world unobserved, but a speaking church, speaking often within itself, is of necessity soon heard beyond the doors of the house in which it dwells. Soon does the sound of gospel music steal over hill and dale. "Their sound hath gone forth throughout all the earth, and their words unto the end of the world." The speaking together of assembled saints at Pentecost led to the gift of tongues, and then they spoke so that every man in his own language heard the wonderful works of the Lord. An increase of private communion among the saints would lead to a fuller public communication to the outside, and the world would receive a blessing.

Thus I have shown you that the Lord thus gradually begins to separate a people to himself. The fear of the Lord in the heart, and the thought of God in the mind lead to association in persons of similar mold: hence arises the church. Then the interchange of expression between the godly makes them zealous, and this leads to public testimony, and the people of God are revealed. You will say that this does not prove that God is dealing differently with them from other men. "Where is the God of judgment?" is the question; and how is it to be answered? My reply is, but in all this the Lord is putting a difference. To work his fear in the heart is an act of sovereign grace, but to enable the soul to find deep enjoyment in meditating upon divine things is a reward as well as a gift of grace, and a reward more valuable than if he gave the God-fearing man wealth and fame.

Christian society is also no small token of the divine favor, and is another reward of the God-fearing. I do not know how you find it, but I can truly assert that my choicest delights are with the people of God. What a deal some of us owe to Christian fellowship! People whom we should never have known and never have thought of speaking to are now our choicest friends, and have been and are incalculably helpful to us. Christian love has enlarged our family circle wonderfully. We have come to be intertwisted the one with the other, and the separate threads have ceased to be such, for they have become a three-fold cord which cannot be broken, and this is no small gift of divine grace. Moreover, the communications which have arisen out of this society, in which we have edified one another, have they not been very precious to us? Can you not say you had rather dwell for a day in the courts of the Lord than reign in the tents of wickedness for ages? Is it not so that when we are able to rejoice together, and tell out our experience, we find a pleasure which makes the wilderness and the solitary place to be glad?

Best of all, it is in the midst of these communications, where holy society yields us gracious fellowship, that God himself is found. This is the grand distinction in God's relation to the universe at this present time, that he is with his people, and they know it; while he is far from the wicked. The Lord hearkened and heard of old, and he hearkens and hears still; and the Lord answers out of his holy place the prayers of his children, and sends tokens of acceptance to those who praise and magnify his name. "The Lord of hosts is with us, the God of Jacob is our refuge." Oh come, let us exult before him, for he is not far away, nor has he hidden his face from us, but he dwells between the cherubim and shines forth among his saints in the person of his dear Son, and manifests himself to us as he does not to the world. Even now Israel in Egypt is not Egypt, for God is pitying the sighs and cries of his people. Israel in the Arabian desert is not Arabian, for, lo, the fiery cloudy pillar, like an uplifted standard, gathers around it a separated people. Lo, "The people shall dwell alone, and shall not be reckoned among the nations." Even now the faithful in going out from the world and being separate find the promise fulfilled: "I will dwell in them, and walk in them; and I will be their God, and they shall be my people." There is the first answer to the question, "Where is the God of judgment?" The separation is already beginning; there are signs of it now.

2. Second, *there are preparations for a final separation,* and these are at this moment proceeding.

What these preparations are we learn from the sixteenth verse: "The Lord hearkened and heard it, and a book of remembrance was written before him for them that feared the Lord, and that thought upon his name." There is a day coming in which he will separate the two sorts of men the one from the other, as a shepherd divides the sheep from the goats. The great net is now dragging the sea bottom: the day comes when the net shall be hauled in, and drawn to shore. What a medley it contains of good and bad fish, of creeping things, and weeds, and shells, and stones: this mass must be parted. Then will come the putting of the good into vessels and the casting of the bad away. When that is done it will be executed with great solemnity and care. There will be great discrimination used in the dividing of the righteous from the wicked, and as at a trial *everything proceeds upon evidence,* the separating work is being prepared for us every day, because the evidence is being collected and recorded. The evidence in favor of the righteous might be forgotten if it were not duly preserved, in order that in the day when the separation shall be consummated there may be no mistake, and nobody may be able to challenge the decision of the great Judge.

Recollect this, dear friends, that *evidence is being written down in a book—evidence of fidelity to God* in evil times. When others were thinking against God, and speaking against God, there were some who spoke on his behalf, because they feared him, and thought upon his name, and their singular conduct was reported upon and chronicled. God's gracious eye never overlooks one single act of decision for him in the midst of blasphemy and rebuke. If the timid girl in the midst of a Christless family still patiently endures reproach, and holds on to her Master's truth, though she cannot speak eloquently, behold it is written in the book. Though her tears may often be her strongest expressions, they are in the book also, and shall not be forgotten. When the workman in the shop speaks a word against filthy language, a word for the sacredness of the Sabbath, a word for his Lord, it is all written in the book of remembrance. A commission is instituted for the collection of evidence as to those that fear the Lord, and think upon his name. Are you, dear friends, furnishing evidence, do you think, evidence which will prove that you are truly godly? Do you clearly stand out from among your fellows, and are you manifestly separate, so that even Satan himself at the last great day will not be able to challenge the evidence that will be given, that you did indeed fear the Lord when others reviled him?

This evidence is being taken by the Lord himself. There is much consolation in this, because others might be prejudiced, and give an unfavorable view of what we do, but when the Lord himself bears witness the truth will be manifested. "The Lord hearkened and heard." It is a very strong expression; he not only "hearkened" as one trying to hear, but he did actually hear all that was said. What a witness God will be in favor of his saints! If we really fear him and think upon his name, he will set our holy fear and our godly thought and our gracious talk in evidence on our behalf. He reads our motives, and these are a deep and vital part of character. Others might err, but he cannot: what he hears is accurately heard and correctly understood. Evidence is being collected, then, by a witness who is truth itself.

This evidence is before God's eye at all times. If you notice, "the book of remembrance was written *before him*," as if while every item was being put down, the book lay open before his gaze. From him the record is no more concealed than the act itself: past deeds of virtue are present to his eye. Every recorded act of grace is especially noticed by the Lord, every separate word of faithfulness and act of true God-fearing life is noted, weighed, estimated, valued, and safely preserved in memory to justify the verdict of the last grand dividing day. Do think of it, then, beloved, all that divine grace is working in you of humble faithfulness to God is being recorded. No annual report will proclaim it, it will never be printed in the magazine, nor advertised through the newspapers so as to bring you renown; but a book of remembrance is written before the Lord himself. There it lies before him whose single approval is more than fame. There, read a page, "Such a one thought upon my name; So-and-So spoke to his brother concerning me, and helped to the mutual edification of the body and to the bearing of powerful testimony for the truth against the assaults of error."

This evidence, moreover, dear friends, *is of a spiritual kind;* and this is one reason why it is taken down by God and by no one else, for it is evidence concerning the state of the heart in reference to God, and who is to form that estimate, but the Lord who searches the heart. Who is to know the thoughts of the mind, save God alone? There is an ear that hears thought: though it is not indicated by a sound so loud as the tick of a clock, nor so audible as the chirping of a little bird, yet every thought is vocal to the mind of the most High, and it is written down in the remembrance book. Certain great actions which every man applauds may never go into that book, because they were done from motives of ostentation; but the thought which nobody could have known and which must otherwise have remained in oblivion, is recorded of the Lord, and shall be published at the last assize. Perhaps it ran thus, "What can I do for Jesus? How can I help his poor people? How can I cheer such-and-such a languishing spirit? How can I defeat error? How can I win a wandering soul for my Master?" Such thoughts as these are reckoned worthy of record, and they are supplying evidence which in his gracious love the Lord is collecting, that the sentence of his great tribunal may be justified to all.

That evidence concerns apparently little things, for it mentions that "they spoke one to another." Of course people will gossip when they get together: what is there in talk? Oh, but what sort of gossip was it? That is the question. For a holy theme turns gossip into heavenly fellowship. It is written, they "thought upon his name." Surely it is not much to think. Ah brethren, thinking and speaking are two very powerful forces in the world, and out of them the greatest actions are hatched. Thoughts and words are the seeds of far-reaching deeds, and God takes care of these embryos and germs: men do not even know of them, and if they did know would not esteem them, but they are put down in the book of remembrance which lies always open before the most High.

Now, all this is going on every day and every night as certainly as time's sands drop through the hourglass. Letter after letter, and stroke by stroke, the story is being written in the book of remembrance, and though men see it not the evidence is being gathered up to be used in that dread solemnity, in which, amid the pomp of angels, the great Infallible shall separate the blessed of his Father from those who are accursed. Thus every day the God of judgment is working toward the time when even the most careless shall discern between the righteous and the wicked.

3. This brings us to the third point that *in that separation great principles will be manifested*. I shall only have time to mention them rapidly.

First, the principle of *election* will be displayed. God will have a people who are more his than other men can be. "'They shall be mine,' saith the Lord of hosts, 'in that day.'" "All souls are mine," says God, and his witness is true, but he rejects some souls because of sin, and says, "Ye are not my people." As for his chosen, they are his portion, his peculiar treasure, his regalia, his crown jewels, and they shall be his forever. Then will special love and peculiar choice be manifest, for in the day of the separation it shall be seen that the Lord knows them that are his, and while he counts others to be as mere stones of the field, he has set his heart upon the saints who are the gems of his crown.

But then will come as the next principle the fact of *essential value*: namely, that the Lord's people are not only his, but they are his *jewels*. There is something in them which grace has put there, which makes them to be more precious than other men. "The righteous is more excellent than his neighbor": God's grace makes his children to be purer, holier, heavenlier than the rest of mankind; and they are rightly divided from the impure and worthless mass. They will at the last by evidence be proved to have been jewels among men, and nobody shall be able to question their worth. They shall be confessed by all men to have been precious stones and pebbles, gold and dross.

Then will come up the next principle of *open acknowledgment*. They were the Lord's, and they shall be owned as such. "'They shall be mine,' saith the Lord of hosts, 'in that day.'" He himself will declare the fact, for it is written, "He is not ashamed to call them brethren," and in that day the Lord Jesus will say, "Here am I, and the children that thou hast given me." Oh, what a joy it will be to be thus openly confessed by Jesus himself! Now, we are unknown if we be God's people, for the world knows us not because it knew not our Master himself; for we are dead and our life is hid with Christ in God; but when he who is our life shall appear then shall we also appear with him in glory. "Then shall thy righteousness shine forth as the sun in the kingdom of their

Father." Then shall be carried out the principle that there is nothing hid which shall not be known; and those who were secretly servants of the Lord shall have evidence of that fact read aloud before assembled worlds, and God, the Judge of all, shall not be ashamed to declare, "They are mine; they are my peculiar treasure."

But even in their case the principle of *mercy* will be conspicuous. I want you to notice very specially. "When I make up my jewels they shall be mine, and I will spare them." Sparing applies to those who under another mode of judgment would not escape. Had it been a question of merit as under law, they would have been doomed as well as others, but the Lord says, "I will spare them." O God, even though you have made your chosen to be your treasure, yet you do spare them, for the evidence does not prove them meritorious, but shows that they were saved in Christ Jesus, and therefore taught to fear you. When the apostle had received great kindness from a friend whom he had valued, he offered a prayer for him, which you may be sure would be a very earnest and comprehensive one, but it was this: "The Lord have mercy upon him in that day." That is all we can expect, and, blessed be God, it is all we need. The matter of justice is settled by our great substitute, and to us mercy comes freely. The brightest saint that ever reflected the image of Christ on earth will have to be saved by mercy from first to last. "I will spare them," says he, for he might have dealt otherwise with them had he taken them on grounds of law, and judged them apart from the mercy which flows through the atoning sacrifice. True, they were jewels, and they were the Lord's own treasure, but if he had laid up their sins in evidence instead of their marks of grace, if that book of remembrance which is written before him had contained an account of their shortcomings and their transgressions as the basis of judgment, it would have gone otherwise with them, but now he calls to remembrance their godly fear, their sacred thoughts, and their holy conversation, and therefore he spares them.

They will be dealt with on the principle of *relationship* also. "I will spare them as a man spareth his own that serveth him." You spare your son when you know he is doing his best to serve you. He has made a blunder, and if he had been a mere hired servant, you might have been angry, but you say, "Ah, I know my boy was doing all he could, and he will do better soon, and therefore I cannot be severe. I see that he is imperfect, but I see equally well that he loves me, and acts like a loving son." The word here used signifies pity or compassion, "Like as a father pitieth his children, so the Lord pitieth them that fear him." He will even at the last look upon us with a love which has pity mingled with it, for we shall need it in that day. He will "remember that we are dust," and will accept us, though cognizant of all the faults there were, and of all the infirmities that there had been: he will accept us still, because we are his own sons in Christ Jesus, and by grace desire to serve him. We do not serve him to become sons, but because we are sons. It is a sweet name for a child of God: a son-servant, one who is a servant to his father, and therefore, because he is his son, serves not for wage, nor of compulsion, but out of love. Such service is mentioned as evidence of sonship, and not as a claim; and we shall be saved through grace, our holy service of sonship being the proof of that grace.

Beloved, on these principles will God make the final division. He will say, "You are mine: I chose you. You are my saints, and there is a gracious excellence in you. I acknowledge you as mine, and I am not ashamed to do so, for you bear my nature. I chose you in mercy, and in consequence of my having chosen you, I have made you to be my son-servants, and so I accept your holy conversation as the token of your sincere love to me, and I receive you into my glory to be mine forever and ever.

4. And now, last, comes the sure truth that *the separation itself will be clear to all.*

Then shall you mourn, you sorcerers and adulterers, you that oppress the hireling and turn aside the stranger from his right, you false swearers and enemies of God. You now can go on your way and say, "God cares nothing about righteous or wicked, he deals with all alike, or even smites his children worst of all"; but you shall look another way by and by. Compelled to turn your heads in another direction from that of this poor fleeting world, you shall see something that will astound you; for though you wish it not, even you and much more the godly shall then "discern between the righteous and the wicked, between him that serveth God and him that serveth him not."

The division will be sharp and decisive. Wherever you read in the Bible you find only two classes; you never read of three; but you find the righteous and the wicked, him that fears God and him that fears him not. A certain order of persons puzzle us in making division here below, because we do not know to which party they belong; but when the book of remembrance is finished and shall be opened, there will be no sort of difficulty in knowing them; the two classes shall roll apart like the two portions of the Red Sea when Moses lifted up his rod, and there shall be a space between. On which side, my dear hearer, you that are halting between two opinions—on which side will you be? There will be no borderland, no space for noncommittal and neutrality; you will then be among the fearers of God or among those that fear not his name. Who may abide the day of his coming? That coming may be very speedy, for none of us knows the day nor the hour when the Son of man shall appear.

The separation will be sharp and decisive, there will be no undecided ones left. And *it will obliterate a host of pretensions,* for the day comes that shall burn as an oven, and all the proud shall be as stubble. The Pharisee who thought he took his place among those that were the jewels of creation will find that the coming of the Lord will burn up his phylacteries and his broad hems, and utterly consume all his boasting as to fasting thrice in the week and taking mint and anise and cumin, for these things were never written in the book, nor worth recording there. What was put there was fearing the Lord, and thinking upon his name, and speaking one to another; but ceremonials and niceties of observance are not thought worth a stroke of the recording pen. There is nothing in the book to act as evidence for the proud, but everything to condemn him; and therefore the day shall burn him up and utterly consume him and his hopes.

That division will be *universal,* for all they that do wickedly shall be as stubble, not one of them escaping. Though they hid their wickedness and bore a good name, though they concealed their sin even from those who watched them, they entered the church and gained honors in it, as Judas did in the college of the apostles; yet that day shall discover all that do wickedly. Talk how they may, and speak as they please, their outward conduct will be the index of their inner alienation from God, and in the hour of their judgment the fire shall consume them from off the earth.

Then shall both classes perceive that the distinction *involves two very different fates.* Once the righteous were in the fire, and according to the third chapter and the third verse, the Lord sat as a refiner and purified them in a furnace like silver, but now the tables are turned, and the proud, and they that do wickedly, are in a more terrible fire. The day shall burn as an oven! The righteous were profited by their fire, for they were good metal, and to part with the dross was no loss, but the wicked are such base metal that they shall utterly fail in the testing fire. The tables will be turned again, for the righteous were under the feet of the wicked—they ridiculed and mocked them, and called them "cants and hypocrites"; but then the ungodly shall be laid low, and the righteous shall tread them as ashes under their feet. The cause of evil will be a worn-out thing, it will be burned up, and there will be nothing left of it upon the earth but memories of its former power and of the fire by which it perished. That day comes, and let the mighty ones among the sons of men who rebel against God know it: they shall no more be able to resist the terror of his presence than the stubble is able to stand against the blazing fire. When they pine forever in the place where their worm dies not and their fire is not quenched, they will know the God of judgment, and see how utterly he consumed them out of the land.

Look at the lot of the righteous. When Christ the Sun of righteousness shall arise upon the earth and gild it with his own light, there shall be a new heaven and a new earth, and the righteous shall go forth and leap for joy, like cattle which formerly had been penned in the stall. No works of the ungodly shall be left. As far as this world is concerned, they shall be utterly and altogether gone. There shall then be no tavern songs or alehouse ribaldry; there shall be no village profligate around whom shall gather the youth of the hamlet to be led away by his libidinous and blasphemous words; there shall then be no shameless reviler who shall provide a hall where blasphemers may congregate to try which can utter the blackest profanities against the Lord of hosts. There shall be no shrine of virgin, or of saint or idol or image or crucifix. Superstition shall be swept away. There shall be no congregations where pretended preachers of the gospel shall deal out new philosophies and suggest newly invented skepticisms, or which at least they hoped men would accept as new, though they were the old errors of the past picked from off the dunghill upon which they had been thrown by disgusted ages. Sin shall all be gone and not a trace of it shall be left, but here shall dwell righteousness and peace; the meek shall inherit the earth, and the saints shall stand each one in his lot, for the Lord himself shall reign among his ancients gloriously. From every hill and every vale shall come up the one song of glory unto the most High and every heart that beats shall magnify his name, who at last has answered the question, "Where is the God of judgment?" Then, cast into the nethermost hell, in the place appointed for the devil and his angels, the ungodly shall never ask again, "Where is the God of judgment?," and saints triumphant in their Lord, with whom they shall reign forever in eternity, shall also perceive that he "discerneth between the righteous and the wicked, between him that serveth God and him that serveth him not." Beloved hearer, where? oh, where will you be? Where shall I be—"in that day"?

The Plumb Line

Published on Thursday, October 6, 1904; delivered on Lord's Day evening, August 27, 1876, at the Metropolitan Tabernacle, Newington. No. 2904.

> *Thus he showed me: and, behold, the LORD stood upon a wall made by a plumb line, with a plumb line in his hand. And the LORD said unto me, "Amos, what seest thou?" And I said, "A plumb line." Then said the LORD, "Behold, I will set a plumb line in the midst of my people Israel: I will not again pass by them anymore."* —AMOS 7:7–8

God usually speaks by men according to their natural capacity. Amos was a herdsman. He was not a man of noble and priestly rank, like Ezekiel, nor a man of gigantic intellect and mighty eloquence, like Isaiah. He was a simple herdsman, and therefore God did not cause him to see the visions of Isaiah, or dazzle his mind with the wondrous revelations that were given to Ezekiel. God's rule is, "Every man in his own order," and if we depart from that, we get out of place ourselves, and we are apt to try to make others do that which they are not fit to do, and then blame them when they fail to accomplish what they should never have attempted. God always uses his servants in the best possible way, and as they ought to be used; so, when the herdsman Amos had a vision, he simply saw a piece of string with a plumb of lead at the bottom of it—a plumb line— a thing which he could easily understand. There was a mystery about the vision, but the vision itself was not mysterious. It was a very simple emblem indeed, exactly suited to the mind of Amos, just as the visions of Ezekiel and Isaiah were adapted to the more poetic minds of men of another class.

You and I, dear brethren, may be very thankful if God should use us as he did Amos; and, if he does, we must not be aping the Isaiahs and Ezekiels. If we see a plumb line, let us preach about a plumb line; and if God should ever enable us to understand the visions of Zechariah or Ezekiel, then let us preach about them. Let every preacher or teacher testify according to the measure of light and grace that God has given him; then we shall do well. Amos can see a plumb line, and he sees it well; and when he has seen it, he tells what he has seen, and leaves God to set his seal upon his testimony.

Now, on this occasion, we have nothing before us but this plumb line, but there is a great deal to be learned from it. The first thing is this, *the plumb line is used in construction*; second, *the plumb line is used for testing what is built*; and, third, it appears from the text that *the plumb line is used in the work of destruction*, for the casting down of that which is found not to be straight.

1. First, *the plumb line is used in construction.*

We are told, in the text, that "the Lord stood upon a wall made by a plumb line," that is to say, a wall which had been constructed with the help of a plumb line; and, therefore, he tested it with that which was supposed to have been used in its construction, which was a fair and proper thing to do. If the wall only professed to be run up without a plumb line, then it might be hard to try it with the plumb line; but as it was a wall which professed to have been constructed according to the rules of the builder's art, it was fair and reasonable that it should be tested by the plumb line.

First, then, dear friends, a plumb line is used in building when it is done as it ought to be; and I remind you that *God always uses it in his building.* Everything that God builds is built plumb and straight and square and fair. You see that rule at work in nature; there is nothing out of proportion there. Those who understand these things, and look deeply into them, will tell you that the very form and size of the earth have a connection with the blooming of a flower or the hanging of a dewdrop upon a blade of grass; and that, if the sun were larger or smaller than it is, or if the material of which the earth is formed were more dense, or different in any degree from what it is, then everything, the most magnificent and the most minute, would be thrown out of gear.

Someone of old used to say that God is the great arithmetician, the great master of geometry; and so he is. He never makes any mistakes in his calculations; there is not anything in the world that he has made in a careless manner. The mixing of the component parts of the air we breathe is managed with consummate skill; and if you could resolve a drop of water into its original elements, you would be struck by the wisdom with which God has adapted the proportions of each particle so as to make a liquid which man can drink. Everything is done by order and rule, as in the changes of the various seasons, the movements of the heavenly bodies, and the arrangements of divine providence. God always has the plumb line in his hand. He never begins to build, as a careless workman would, that which might turn out to be right or might turn out to be wrong; but he makes sure work of all that he does.

In spiritual matters, it is very manifest that, whenever God is dealing with souls, he always uses the plumb line. In beginning with us, he finds that the very foundation of our nature is out of the perpendicular; and, therefore, he does not attempt to build upon it, but commences his operations by digging it out. The first work of divine grace in the soul is to pull down all that nature has built up. God says, "I cannot use these stones in my building. This man has been behaving himself admirably in some respects, and he thinks that he is building up a temple to my honor and glory with his own natural virtues, his own good works, and other things of a like character. But all this must be dug out." The man has taken a great deal of pains in putting it together, but it must all come out, and there must be a great hole left; the man must feel himself emptied, and abased, and humbled in the sight of God; for, if God is to be everything to the man, then he himself must be nothing; and if Christ is to be his Savior, he must be a complete Savior, from beginning to end. So the foundation of human merit must be cleared right out and flung away, for God could not build squarely upon it. With such a foundation as that, the plumb line would never mark a perpendicular wall.

After all human merit has been flung out, the Lord begins his gracious work by laying the foundation stone of a simple faith in Jesus Christ, and that faith, though simple, is very real. When a man professes to convert his fellowman, he only gives him a fictitious faith which is of no value to him; but when God saves a sinner, he gives him real faith. There may be little knowledge of the truth, but the little that the man knows is truth; and faith, though it be but as a grain of mustard seed, if it be of the right sort, is better than that faith which is as big as a mountain, yet all of the wrong sort, which will not stand in the time of testing. But the faith which the Holy Spirit gives is the faith of God's elect, the real faith which will endure even the tests which God applies to it.

Side by side with that faith, God puts true repentance. When a man attempts to convert his fellowman, he gives him a sham repentance, or perhaps he tells him that there is no need of any repentance at all. Certain preachers have been telling us, lately, that it is a very easy matter to obtain salvation, and that there is no need of repentance; or if repentance is needed, it is merely a change of mind. That is not the doctrine that our fathers used to preach, nor the doctrine that we have believed. That faith, which is not accompanied by repentance, will have to be repented of; so, whenever God builds, he builds repentance fair and square with faith. These two things go together; the man just as much regrets and grieves over the past as he sees that past obliterated by the precious blood of Jesus. He just as much hates all his sin as he believes that his sin has been all put away.

The Lord never builds anything falsely in any man or teaches him to reckon that to be true which is not true; but he builds with facts, with substantial verities, with true grace, and with a real and lasting work in the soul.

When the Lord builds in a man, he builds with the plumb line in the sense of always building up that which is toward holiness. Have any of you fallen into sin, rest assured that God did not build you in that way. Have sinful desires and lustings after evil been excited within you by any doctrine to which you have listened? Then you may be sure that it was not of God. "By their fruits shall ye know them" is an infallible test of doctrines as well as of disciples; and if any of you have embraced any form of doctrine which hinders you from being watchful, prayerful, careful, and anxious to avoid sin, you have embraced error and not truth, for all God's building tends toward holiness, toward carefulness, toward a gracious walk to the praise and glory of God. When the Lord builds a man up, he makes him conscientious, makes him jealous of himself, makes him detect the very shadow of sin, so that, before the sin itself comes upon him, he holds up his all-covering shield of faith, that he may be preserved from its deadly assaults. You may always know God's building because it is pure building, clean building; but if anybody builds you up in such a style that you can talk of sin as a trifle, and think that you may indulge in it, at least in a measure, with impunity, that is certainly not God's building.

And, blessed be his name, when our souls are really given up into the Lord's hands, he will continue to build in us until he has built us up to perfection. There will come a day when sin, which now makes its nest in this mortal body of ours, shall find this body dissolving and crumbling back to the earth of which it was made; and then our emancipated spirits, delivered from the last taint and trace of sin—free from even the tendency to evil—shall soar away to be with Christ, which is far better, and to wait for the trumpet of the resurrection, when the body itself shall also be delivered from corruption, for the grave is a refining pot; and, at the coming of Christ, our body shall be pure and white, like the garments of a bride arrayed to meet her bridegroom, and the soul, reunited with the body, shall have triumphed over every sin. This is the way that God builds. He does not build us up so that we can go to heaven with our sin still working in us. He does not build us up to be temples for him to dwell in, and let the devil also dwell in us. Antinomian building is not according to the fashion of God's building; but God builds up surely, solidly, truthfully, sincerely, and until we have reached that state of perfection which makes us fit for heaven.

Now, beloved, as God thus uses the plumb line in his building, I gather that *we also should use the plumb line in our building*. First, with regard to the uplifting of our own soul, I would urge upon myself first, and then upon you next, the constant use of the plumb line. It is very easy to seek after speed, but to neglect to ensure certainty. There is such a thing as being in a dreadful hurry to do what had better never be done, or else be done in a very different style. We see some people who become Christians in about two minutes; and I am devoutly thankful when that is really the case. We see some others become full-grown Christians in about two days, and instructors of others in the course of a week; and, very speedily, they attain to such vast dimensions that there is no ordinary church that is big enough to hold them. That is very quick work; that is the way that mushrooms grow, but it is not the way that oaks grow. I urge you all to remember that, often, the proverb, "the more haste, the less speed," is true in spiritual things as well as in temporal. My dear brother, if you only grow an inch in the course of ten laborious years, yet that growth is real, it is better than appearing to grow six feet in an hour, when that would only be disease puffing you up and blowing you out. Often and often, the soul needs to use the plumb line to see whether that which is built so very quickly is really built perpendicularly, or whether it does not lean this way or that. As the work goes on, we should frequently stop and say to ourselves, "Now, is this right? Is this real? Is this true?" Many a time, if we did that, we should have to fall upon our knees, and cry, "O Lord, deliver me from exalting myself above measure and counting myself to be rich and increased with goods, when, all the while, I am wretched and miserable and poor and blind and naked."

I would like you young men who are here to use the plumb line when you begin your spiritual life-building. I mean this: your father and mother are members of a certain church, but do not you, therefore, go and join that church without a thorough investigation of the principles on which it is founded. Use the plumb line to see whether it is all straight and square. Try all the doctrines that are taught and do not embrace that which is popular, but that which is biblical. Then try with the plumb line the ordinances of the church; do not submit to them simply because other people do so, but use the plumb line of Scripture to test them all. You know that, as a body, we are not afraid that you will ever read your Bible too much. We, as Baptists, have no objection to your bringing everything that is taught to the test of the Bible, for we know that we should be the gainers if you were to do that; but, instead of using the plumb line of the Bible, many people have a newly invented test—the Book of Common Prayer or Minutes of the Conference or something else equally valueless. Now, whatever respect I have for books of that sort, I prize my Bible infinitely above them all, and above all the volumes of decretals of popes and councils and conferences put together. I should not like to feel that I had been building and building and building and building, and yet that there had been a radical error in the whole structure, for I had commenced with a mistake, and I had been building myself up, not in the most holy faith of the apostles, but in the most mischievous error of my own notions. Do, I pray you, apply the Bible plumb line continually to all your beliefs and views and practices.

But, even before you do that, use the gospel plumb line to see whether you really were ever born again, for our Lord Jesus said to Nicodemus, "Except a man be born again, he cannot see the kingdom of God." Do test yourselves as to whether you have really believed in Jesus Christ, for "without faith it is impossible to please God"; and if you have believed in him, take care that, while you think you are getting more faith, more love, more patience, more of every grace, you keep the plumb line going; otherwise, you may get a great deal into the structure that you will have to take out again, and you will get the building out of the perpendicular, and the whole of it may come down with a crash.

And this plumb line is also to be used upon all work that is done on behalf of other people. There is much teaching which has been given with a pure motive, but which, nevertheless, cannot endure this test. There are some little sects, still existing upon the face of the earth, that were formed with much labor by their originators; but they are evidently not gold or silver or precious stones, for they are passing away with the lapse of time. I would like, as a minister of the gospel, to do for God that which will endure the supreme test of the day of judgment. I should not like to build up a great church here, and then, when I was dead and gone, for it to be scattered to the four winds, and to learn in heaven that I had been mistaken except as to the matter of my own salvation; and that, consequently, while some good was done, there was ill done as well. No; we must constantly use the plumb line, so that what we build may be perpendicular, and may stand the test of the ages, and the test of God's great judgment seat. Look to it, sirs, you who are diligent, that you are diligent in spreading truth and not error. See to it, you who count up your many converts, that they are real converts, and not the mere fruit of excitement. See to it, you who plod on from day to day so industriously seeking to save souls, that they are really saved and truly brought to Christ; for, if not, your work will be in vain. Churches that are built in a hurry will come down in a hurry; wood, hay, and stubble, that look all right in the building, will look terrible in the burning, when the day of the trial by fire shall come.

So that is our first point, that the plumb line is to be used in the construction of the building.

2. Second, *the plumb line is to be used for testing the building when it is built.*

Do not let us judge either ourselves or one another simply by the eye. I have frequently thought that a building was out of the perpendicular when it was not; and I have sometimes thought it perpendicular when it really was not so. The human eye is readily deceived, but the plumb line is not; it drops straight down, and at once shows whether the wall is upright or not. *We must continually use upon ourselves the plumb line of God's Word.* Here is a wall that needs to be tested—the wall of self-righteousness. This man thinks he is all right. He never did anything very wrong. Moreover, he is religious in his way. He says that he has kept the law from his youth up. That is a fine piece of wall, is it not?—with some very handsome stones inlaid therein with fair colors. You are very proud of it, my dear friend; but if I put the Bible plumb line to your life, you will be astonished to find how much out of the perpendicular it is. The plumb line is according to this standard, "If any man will be saved by his own works, he must keep the law of the Lord perfectly; for he who is guilty of the breach of any one of God's commandments, has broken the whole law: 'therefore by the deeds of the law there shall no flesh be justified in his sight.'" That condemns your wall, does it not?—because you have not at all times kept the whole law in the fullness of the meaning which Christ gave to it. If you are to be saved by works, there must not be a single flaw in the whole wall of your life. If there is, it is not in the perpendicular.

Here is another wall, built by a man who says that he is doing his best, and trusting to Christ to make up for his deficiencies. Well, my dear friend, your wall is sadly out of the perpendicular, because there is a text which says, "Christ is all"; and I know that the Lord Jesus Christ will never be willing to be put side by side with such a poor creature as you are, to be jointly used with yourself to your soul's salvation. Remember that in the gospel plan it is not Christ and Co.; it must be all Christ, or no Christ at all. So, if you are depending partly upon self, and partly upon him, my plumb line shows that your wall is out of the perpendicular, and that it will have to come down.

Another man is depending upon rites and ceremonies. Now, there are some very strong texts in Scripture concerning that matter. Here is one: "To obey is better than sacrifice, and to hearken than the fat of rams." Will you come before God bringing the blood of beasts or costly offerings? Has he not told you that, to come before him with a broken and a contrite heart, and, especially, to come unto him through the merit of the one great sacrifice offered by his Son, is the only acceptable way of approaching him? The most gorgeous ceremonies in the whole world cannot save a single soul. That wall is out of the perpendicular and must come down.

Here is another man, who says, "I am, as often as I can be, a hearer of the Word." I am glad that you are; but if you are only a hearer, and not a doer of the Word, your wall is out of the perpendicular; for, if it is good to hear what is right, it is better still to do it; and your condemnation will be all the more terrible if you have known what you ought to do, and yet have not done it. There are many of you who come here and who have been coming for a long time who, I hope, will be led to do much more than simply come to hear; for I trust that you will be led by the Holy Spirit to lay hold on eternal life. If not, your wall will not endure the test of the Bible plumb line, which plainly shows that you are quite out of the perpendicular.

There are many other bowing walls besides those I have mentioned, but I cannot stop to try them now. I would, however, most earnestly urge you all to remember that, if you do not test yourself by the plumb line of God's Word, *if you are God's servant, you will be tried and tested.* Have you never known what it is to be laid aside, on a bed of sickness, and to have everything about you tried? In times of acute pain, I have had every morsel of what I thought to be gold and silver put into the fire, piece by piece, by the Master himself, until he has put it all in. Thank God, some of it has been proved to be gold, and has come out all the brighter for the testing; but, oh, how much of it has proved to be alloy or even worthless dross! You can have a great deal of patience when you have not any pain; and you can have a great deal of joy in the Lord when you have got joy in your worldly prosperity; and you can have any quantity of it when you have no troubles to test its reality. But the real faith is that which will endure the trial by fire. The real patience is that which will bear intense agony without a murmur of complaint. The Lord will test and try you, my brother, sooner or later, if you are his. He will be sure to use the plumb line, so you had better use it yourself. It may save you much anxiety in the future if you stop now to question yourself and to inquire whether these things be real and true to you or not.

And remember, once more, that *God will use the plumb line, at the last great day, to test everything.* How many of us could hear, without a tremor, the intimation that God had summoned us to appear before his bar? O my brethren and sisters, if the great scales of divine justice were swinging from this ceiling now, and the Judge of all said to you, "Step in, and let me see what is your weight," is there one of us who could solemnly and sincerely rise and say, "Lord, I am ready for the weighing"? Yes; I trust that many could say, each one for himself or herself, "There is not anything good in me, but my hope is fixed on Christ alone; and though I am not what I ought to be, nor what I want to be, nor what I shall be, yet 'by the grace of God I am what I am.' My profession of being a Christian is not a lie; it is not a pretense; it is not a piece of religious masquerade; it is true, great God; it is true." My brother, my sister, if you can say that, you may step into the scales without any fear, for the contrite and believing heart can endure being weighed. But into the scales you will have to go whether you are ready or not. Your building will all have to be tested and tried. Some of you have built fine mansions and towers and palaces; but the plumb line will be applied to them all, and it is God himself who will use the plumb line in every case. No counterfeit will be allowed to pass the pearly gates, nor anything that defiles or works abomination or makes a lie. At the last great day, none shall pass from beneath the eye of the Judge of all without due examination. He will not suffer even one of the guilty to escape, nor condemn any one of those who have been absolved for Christ's sake. It will be a right and just judgment that will be given in that day; but judgment there will be.

3. My last point is this, *the plumb line is used in the work of destruction.*

When a city wall was to be battered down, the general would sometimes say, "This wall is to be taken down to this point," and then the plumb line was hung down to mark how far they were to go with the work of destruction. They thus marked out that part which might be spared and that which must be destroyed.

Now, in the work of destruction, God always uses the plumb line, and *he goes about that work very slowly.* He shows that he does not like it. When the Lord is going to save a sinner, he has wings to his feet; but when he is going to destroy a sinner, he goes with leaden footsteps, waiting, and warning many times, and while he waits and warns, sighing, and crying, "How shall I give thee up?" He even goes so far as to use an oath, saying, "As I live, saith the Lord God, I have no pleasure in the death of the wicked; but that the wicked turn from his way and live." God never brings men to judgment, as the infamous Judge Jeffreys did, in a great haste. He would hurry them off to the gallows with indecent speed; but, at the last great day, there will be a solemn and stately pomp about the whole dread assize, the sounding of the trumpet, the bursting of the graves, the setting up of the great white throne, the opening of the books, and the majestic appearance of him from whose face heaven and earth will flee away. And when the judgment begins, it will not be without due order, nor will it be without keen perception of all differences. There will hang the infallible plumb line. That which is perpendicular will be declared to be perpendicular, and that which bows will be shown tottering to its fall; for, before the Judge's eye, and before the eyes of the assembled universe, shall hang a plumb line, with these words above it: "He which is filthy, let him be filthy still; . . . and he that is holy, let him be holy still."

The whole judgment shall be according to the plumb line. *Not a soul, in that great day, will be sent to hell who does not deserve to go there.* If there be any man who can plead that it would be unjust to condemn him—if he can truthfully prove that he has been obedient up to the measure of his light, if he can prove that justice is on his side—God will not do an unjust turn to him, or to any other man. Those awful gates, which grind upon their iron hinges, never yet opened to receive a soul damned unjustly. It would be impossible, in the very nature of things, for such a thing to happen. If any man could truly say, "This is unjust," he would have taken away the sting of hell, for this is the essence and the soul of helldecretal—"I am wrong and can never get right. I am wrong and do not want to get right. I am so wrong that I love the wrong and make evil to be my good, and good to be my evil. I hate God, for it is impossible, while I am in such a state as this, that I can be otherwise than unhappy; and this is the greatest hell that can happen to a man, not to love God, and not to love right." That is the flame of hell, the worm that gnaws forever—that being out of gear with God—that being out of harmony with the most High forever. I imagine that there needs to be no fiercer hell than that. So, the final judgment will be according to the plumb line, so that no one will be condemned unjustly.

You talk to me about the fate of the heathen who have never heard the gospel, and I reply, "I know very little about them; but I know that God is just, so I leave them in his hands, knowing that the Judge of all the earth will do right." There will not be one pang, to a soul in hell, more than that soul deserves, not a single spasm of despair, or a sinking in hopelessness, that is imposed by the arbitrary will of God. It will be a terrible reaping for them, when they reap sheaves of fire; but they will only reap what they have sown. There will be an awful pouring out of divine vengeance upon the vessels of wrath fitted to destruction; but no one will be able to say that the judgment is unjust. The lost will themselves feel that they only have to eat as they baked and to drink as they brewed. It will all be just to them; and this is what will make the teeth of the serpent of hell, and the flame of its fire—that it is all just—that if I were myself judge, I must condemn myself to what I have to suffer. Think of that, and escape from the wrath to come.

And as that plumb line hangs there, in that great day of account, *there will be differences made between some lost men and other lost men.* All hell is not the same hell, any more than all flesh is the same flesh. That man knew his Lord's will and did it not; lay on the lashes to the full that the law allows. That other man did not obey his Lord's will, but, then, he did not know it, so he shall be beaten with few stripes. Few will be too many for anyone to bear; so do not run the risk of them. But, oh, the many stripes, what will they be. There are the lost that perished in Sodom and Gomorrah—those filthy beings whose sins we dare not think upon. There they are, and there is the hell they suffer. There hangs the plumb line; and, by his unerring justice, God awards their doom. But what will he award to you and you and you, who have heard the gospel simply and plainly preached, and yet have rejected Christ? You will have to go lower down in hell than the inhabitants of Sodom and Gomorrah, for God's plumb line tells us that sin against light is the worst of sin, and that the willful rejection of the atoning blood flowing from the loving Savior's wounds is the climax of all iniquity. That is how the plumb line will work.

And when you come up, you rich man, who have spent your money in sin, and when you come up, you poor man, who work so hard, there shall be a difference between the one of you and the other, between the seducer, whom the world allows to enter into her drawing room, and the poor girl whom he led astray; for, though both are guilty, God will make a difference, not as men make it here, but quite the other way. The man of talent and of rank and of position who frittered away his whole existence in the life of a butterfly, there will be a difference between his sentence and that of the obscure, uneducated individual who did sin, but not as he did who had the greater gifts. To put one talent in a napkin brings its due punishment; but to bury or misuse ten talents shall bring a tenfold doom; for there will hang that plumb line, and by the rules of infinite justice everything shall be determined.

"This is dreadful talk," some of you may be saying. It is; it is; and it is a dreadful business altogether for the lost, that being driven from God's presence when you die, hearing him say, "Depart, ye cursed, into everlasting fire, prepared for the devil and his angels." You do not like to hear about this, and I do not like to preach about it; only I must do so, lest you come unto that place of torment because I failed to warn you. Then might you say, in your despair, "O cursed preacher! O unfaithful minister! You tried to tickle our ears with pleasant things, but you left out all allusions to the wrath to come. You toned down the truth, you softened it, and now we are ruined forever through your wicked desire to please our foolish ears. O sirs, you will never be able truthfully to say that, for I do pray you to escape from that awful future. Run no risk of it. I think every one of you would like to have his house insured against fire, and to know that, as far as proper title deeds go, whatever you have is held on a good tenure. Then, I implore you, make sure work for eternity by laying hold on Christ Jesus. Yield yourself up to him, that he may make you right where you are wrong, put you in gear with God, and set you running parallel with the will of the most High; that he, indeed, may build you up on the perpendicular, on the solid foundation of his eternal merits by faith, through the power of the ever-blessed Spirit, that you may be so built that, when God himself holds the plumb line, it may hang straight down, and he will be able to say, "It is all right." Happy will you be if you hear his verdict, "Well done, good and faithful servant; thou hast been faithful in a few things, I will make thee ruler over many things. Enter thou into the joy of thy Lord."

May God grant this mercy to every one of you, for Jesus Christ's sake! Amen.

Preparation for Heaven

Published on Thursday, November 16, 1916; delivered at the Metropolitan Tabernacle, Newington. No. 3538.

Now he that hath wrought us for the selfsame thing is God, who also hath given unto us the earnest of the Spirit. —2 CORINTHIANS 5:5

How very confidently Paul contemplates the prospect of death! He betrays no trembling apprehensions. With the calmness and serenity, not merely of resignation and submission, but of assurance and courage, he appears joyous and gladsome, and even charmed with the hope of having his body dissolved, and being girded about with the new body which God has prepared for his saints. He that can talk of the grave and of the hereafter with such intelligence, thoughtfulness, faith, and strong desire as Paul did is a man to be envied. Princes might well part with their crown for such a sure and certain hope of immortality. Could emperors exchange their treasures, their honors, and their dominions, to stand side by side with the humble tentmaker in his poverty, they would be great gainers. Were they but able to say with him, "We are always confident, and willing rather to be absent from the body, and to be present with the Lord," they might well barter earthly rank for such a requital.

This side heaven, what can be more heavenly than to be thoroughly prepared to pass through the river of death? On the other hand, what a dreary and dreadful state of mind must they be in who, with nothing before them but to die, have no hope and see no outlet—the pall and the shroud their last adorning; the grave and the sod their destination. Without hope of rising again in a better future or realizing a better heritage than that which should know us no more before long; no prospects of seeing God face to face with rejoicing—well may men dislike any reference to death. So they shrink from the thought of it; far less can they tolerate its being talked of in common conversation. No marvel that they recoil from the shade of mortality when they are so ill prepared to face the reality of the soul's departure. But, dear friends, since it is so desirable to be ready to depart, it cannot be inexpedient sometimes to talk about it; and on my part the more so, because there is a proneness in all our minds to start aside from that grave topic which, as God shall help us, shall be our subject this evening—preparation for the great hereafter. "For," says the apostle, "God hath wrought us for this selfsame thing"; he has prepared us for the dropping of the present body, and the putting on of the next, and he has "given us the earnest of his Spirit."

Our three departments of meditation will be—*the work of preparation itself*; *the Author of it*; and *the seal which he sets to it,* the possession of which may resolve all scruples as to whether we are prepared or not.

1. *The work of preparation* stands first.

Is it not almost universally admitted that some preparation is absolutely essential? Whenever the death of a friend or comrade is announced, you will hear the worst instructed say, "I hope, poor man, he was prepared." It may be but a passing reflection or a common saying. Yet everybody will give expression to it, "I hope he was ready." Whether the words be well understood or not, I do not know; but the currency given to them proves a unanimous conviction that some preparation is necessary for the next world. And, in truth, this doctrine is in accordance with the most elementary facts of our holy religion. Men by nature need something to be done for them before they can enter heaven and something to be done in them, something to be done with them, for by nature they are enemies to God. Dispute it as you will, God knows best. He declares that we are enemies to him and alienated in our hearts. We need, therefore, that some ambassador should come to us with terms of peace and reconcile us to God. We are debtors as well as enemies to our Creator—debtors to his law. We owe him what we cannot pay, and what he cannot pardon. He must exact obedience, and we cannot render it. He must, as God, demand perfection of us, and we, as men, cannot bring him that perfection.

Some mediator, then, must come in to pay the debt for us, for we cannot pay it, neither can we be exempted from it. There must be a substitute who shall stand between us and God, one who shall undertake all our liabilities and discharge them, and so set us free, that the mercy of God may be extended to us. In addition to this, we are all criminals. Having violated the law of God, we are condemned already. We are not, as some vainly pretend, introduced to this world on probation; but our probation is over; we have forfeited all hope; we have broken the law and the sentence is gone out against us, and we stand by nature as condemned criminals, tenants of this world during the reprieve of God's mercy, in fear of a certain and terrible execution, unless someone come in between us and that punishment; unless some gracious hand bring us a free pardon; unless some voice divine plead and prevail for us that we may be acquitted. If this be not done for us, it is impossible that we should entertain any well-grounded hope of entering heaven.

Say, then, brethren and sisters, has this been done for you? I know that many of you can answer, "Blessed be God, I have been reconciled to him through the death of his Son; God is no enemy of mine, nor I of his; there is no distance now between me and God; I am brought near to him and made to feel that he is near to me and that I am dear to him." Full many here present can add, "My debts to God are paid; I have looked to Christ, my substitute; I have seen him enter into suretyship engagements for me, and I am persuaded that he has discharged all my liabilities; I am clean before God's bar; faith tells me I am clean." And, brethren, you know that you are no longer condemned. You have looked to him who bore your condemnation, and you have drunk in the spirit of that verse, "There is, therefore, now no condemnation to them that are in Christ Jesus, who walk not after the flesh, but after the Spirit." Surely this is a preparation for heaven. How could we enter there if our debts were not discharged? How could we obtain the divine favor eternally if we were still condemned criminals? How could we dwell forever in the presence of God if we were still his enemies? Come, let us rejoice in this: that he has worked us for this selfsame thing having championed our cause from the cradle to the grave.

Preparation for heaven consists still further in *something that must be worked in us,* for observe, brethren, that if the Lord were to blot out all our sins, we should still be quite incapable of entering heaven unless there was a change wrought in our natures. According to this Book, we are dead by nature in trespasses and sins—not some of us, but all of us; the best as well as the worst; we are all dead in trespasses and sins. Shall dead men sit at the feasts of the eternal God? Shall there be corpses at the celestial banquets? Shall the pure air of the New Jerusalem be defiled with the putrefaction of iniquity? It must not, it cannot be. We must be quickened; we must be taken from the corruption of our old nature into the incorruption of the new nature, receiving the incorruptible seed which lives and abides forever. Only the living children can inherit the promises of the living God, for he is not the God of the dead, but of the living; we must be made living creatures by the new-creating power of grace or else we cannot be made meet for glory.

By nature we are all worldly. Our thoughts go after earthly things. We "mind earthly things," as the apostle says. We seek after the world's joys; the world's maxims govern us; the world's fears alarm us; the world's hopes and ambitions excite us. We are of the earth earthy, for we bear the image of the first Adam. But, brethren, we cannot go to heaven as worldly men; for there would be nothing there to gratify us. The gold of heaven is not for barter to use, nor for covetousness to hoard. The rivers of heaven are not for commerce, neither are they to be defiled by men. The joys and glories of heaven are all spiritual, all celestial.

> *Pure are the joys above the skies*
> *And all the region peace.*

Such peace is of a heavenly kind and for heavenly minds. Carnal spirits, greedy, envious spirits—what would they do in heaven? If they were in the place called heaven, they could not be in the state called heaven, and heaven is more a state than a place. Though it is probably both, yet it is mainly the former, a state of happiness, a state of holiness, a state of spirituality, which it would not be possible for the worldly to reach. The incongruity of such a thing is palpable. Therefore, you see, brethren, the Holy Spirit must come and give us new affections. We must have a fresh object set before us. In fact, instead of minding the things that are seen, we must come to love and to aspire to the things that are not seen. Our affections, instead of going downward to things of earth, must be allured by things that are above, where Christ sits at the right hand of God.

In addition to our spiritual death and worldliness, we are all unholy by nature. Not one of us is pure in the sight of God. We are all defiled and all defiling, but in heaven they are "without fault before the throne of God." No sin is tolerated there; no sin of thought or word or deed. Angels and glorified spirits delight to do God's will without hesitation, without demur, without omission; and we, like them, must be holy, or we cannot enter into their sacred fellowship.

> *Those holy gates forever bar*
> *Pollution, sin, and shame.*
> *None shall obtain admission there*
> *But followers of the Lamb.*

But what a change must come over the carnal man to make him holy! Through what washings he must pass! What can wash him white, indeed, but that far-famed blood of the Son of God? Through purification he must pass! What, indeed, can purify him at all but the refining energy of God the Holy Ghost? He alone can make us what God would have us to be, renewed in his image in holiness and righteousness.

That a great change must be wrought in us, even ungodly men will confess, since the idea of the heaven of the Scriptures has always been repulsive, never agreeable, to unconverted men and women. When Muhammad would charm the world into the belief that he was the prophet of God, the heaven he pictured was not at all the heaven of holiness and spirituality. His was a heaven of unbridled sensualism, where all the passions were to be enjoyed without let or hindrance for endless years. Such the heaven that sinful men would like; therefore, such the heaven that Muhammad painted for them and promised to them.

Men in general, be they courtly, or be they coarse in their habits, when they read of heaven in the Scriptures with any understanding of what they read, curl their lips and ask contemptuously, "Who wants to be everlastingly psalm singing? Who could wish to be always sitting down with these saints talking about the mighty acts of the Lord and the glorious majesty of his kingdom?" Such people cannot go to heaven, it is clear; they have not character or capacity to enter into its enjoyment. I think Whitefield was right. Could a wicked man be admitted into heaven, he would be wretched there; being unholy, he must be unhappy. From sheer distaste for the society of heaven, he might fly to hell for shelter. With the tumult of evil passions in his breast, he could not brook the triumph of righteousness in the city of the blessed. There is no heaven for him who has not been prepared for it by a work of grace in his soul. So necessary is this preparation—a preparation for us, and a preparation in us.

And if we ever have such a preparation, beyond all question we must have it on this side of our death. It can only be obtained in this world. The moment one breathes his last, it is all fixed and settled. As the tree falls, so it must lie. While the nature is soft and supple, it is susceptible of impression, stamp what seal you may upon it; once let it grow cold and hard, fixed and frigid, you can do so no more, it is proof against any change. While the iron is flowing into the mold, you can fashion it into what implement you please; let it grow cold, in vain you strive to alter its form. With pen of liquid ink in your hand, you write what you will on the paper, but the ink dries, the impress remains, and where is the treachery that shall tamper with it? Such is this life of yours. It is over, all over with you for eternity, beyond alteration or emendation, when the breath has gone from the body. Your everlasting state is fixed then.

> There are no acts of pardon passed
> In the cold grave to which we haste;

> *But darkness, death, and long despair*
> *Reign in eternal silence there.*

We have no intimation in the Word of God that any soul dying in unbelief will afterward be converted to the faith. Nor have we the slightest reason to believe that our prayers in this world can at all affect those who have departed this life. The masses of priests are fictions, without the shadow of divine authority. Purgatory, or "pick-purse," as old Latimer used to call it, is an invention for making fat larders for priests and monks, but the Scriptures of truth give it no countenance. The Word of God says, "He that is holy, let him be holy still; he that is filthy, let him be filthy still." Such as you are when death comes to you, such will judgment find you, and such will the eternal reward or the eternal punishment leave you, world without end. Preparation is needed, and the preparation must be found before we die.

Moreover, we ought to know—for *it is possible for a man to know whether he is thoroughly prepared.* Some have said not, but they have usually been persons very little acquainted with the matter. The writings of those grand old divines of the Puritan period abundantly prove how thoroughly they enjoyed the assurance of faith. They did not hesitate to express themselves in such language as the apostle used: "We *know* that if this earthly house of our tabernacle be dissolved, we have a house not made with hands, eternal in the heavens." They were apt to speak as Job does when he says, "I know that my Redeemer liveth." And indeed, many of the children of God among us at this present time are favored with a confident, unstaggering confidence that, let their last hour come when it may, or let the Lord himself descend from heaven with a shout, there will be nothing but joy and peace for them—no cause of trembling, nothing that can give them dismay. Why, some of us live from year to year in constant assurance of our preparation for the bliss that awaits and the rest that remains for God's people.

Beloved, God has not so left us in such a dubious case that we always need to be inquiring, "Am I his, or am I not?" He has given us good substantial grounds to go upon to make sure work of it. He tells us that "he that believeth and is baptized shall be saved"; if we have been obedient to these two commands, we shall be saved, for our God keeps his word. He tells us that such believers, patiently continuing in well doing, inherit eternal life. If we are kept by his grace, walking in his fear, we may rest assured that we shall come to the ultimate end of such a life, namely, the glory which abides for the faithful. We need not harbor endless questionings. What miserable work it is to stand in any doubt on this matter. Let us not be satisfied till we are sure and confident that heaven will be ours.

Alas, how many put off all thoughts of being prepared to die! They are prepared for almost anything except the one thing for which it is most needful to be ready. If the summons should come to some of you at this moment, how dread it would be! Were we to see an angel hovering in the air, and should we have intelligence by a message from the clouds that someone of us must, on a sudden, leave his body behind him and appear before God, what cowering down, what trembling, what muttering of forgotten prayers there would be with some of you! You are not ready. You never will be ready, I fear. The carelessness in which you have lived so long has become habitual. One would think you had resolved to die in your sins.

Have you never heard the story of Archaeus, the Grecian despot, who was going to a feast, and on the way a messenger brought him a letter, and seriously importuned him to read it? It contained tidings of a conspiracy that had been formed against him, that he should be killed at the feast. He took the letter and put it into his pocket. In vain the messenger urged that it was concerning serious matters. "Serious matters tomorrow," said Archaeus, "feasting tonight." That night the dagger reached his heart while he had about him the warning which, had he heeded it, would have averted the peril. Alas, too many men say, "Serious things tomorrow"! They have no misgiving that, when their sport is over, they will have alike the leisure and the leanings for these weighty matters. Were it not wiser, sirs, to let these grave affairs come first? Might ye not, then, find some better sport of nobler character than all the froth and frivolity to which fashion leads on? A holy merriment and a sacred feasting that well become immortal spirits. How vain and groveling the mirth which reduces men to children, pleased with a rattle, tickled with a straw; then brings them down to driveling fools and degrades them often till they become worse than brutes. I wish I could imprint a solemn thought on the mind of some careless individuals. You care not that time is short, that life is precarious, that opportunities cross your path at lightning speed, that hope flatters those on whom the fangs of death are fixed; that there is no vestibule in which to fit your frame of mind, that the shock will always come sudden at last. What sentence more trite; what sentiment more prevalent; yet what solemnity more neglected than this: "Prepare to meet your God"! Propound it, profess it, preach it as we may, the most of men are unprepared. They know the inevitable plight, they see the necessity of preparation, but they postpone and procrastinate instead of preparing. God grant you may not trifle, any of you, until your trembling souls are launched into that sphere unknown, but not unfeared, and read your doom in hell.

2. Now, *as to the Author of this preparation for death*, the text says, "he that hath wrought us for the selfsame thing is God."

It is God alone, then, who makes men fit for heaven. He works them to the selfsame purpose. Who made Adam fit for paradise but God? And who must make us fit for the better paradise above but God? That we cannot do it ourselves is evident. According to the Scriptures, we are dead in trespasses and sins. Can the dead start from the grave of their own accord? Do you think to see coffins opened and gravestones uplifted by the natural energy of corpses? Such things were never dreamed of. The dead shall surely rise, but they shall rise because God raises them. They cannot vitalize their inert frames, neither can the dead in sin quicken themselves and make themselves fit for the presence of God. Conversion, which prepares us for heaven, is a new creation. That word "creation" puts all the counsel, the conceit, and the contrivance of man into the background. If anyone says that he can make a new heart, let him first go and make a fly. Not until he has created such a winged insect let him presume to tell us that he can make a man a new creature in Christ Jesus. And yet to make a fly would not demonstrate that a fly could make itself, and it would offer but a feeble pretext for that wonderful creation which is supposed in a man's making himself a new heart. The original creation was the work of God, and the new creation must likewise be of God. To take away a heart of stone and give a heart of flesh is a miracle. Man cannot do it; if he attempts it, it shall be to his own shame and confusion. The Lord must make us anew. Have not we, who know something of the Lord's working in us, this selfsame thing, been made to feel that it is all of his grace? What first made us think about eternal things? Did we, the stray sheep, come back to the fold of our own accord? No; far from it.

> *Jesus sought me when a stranger,*
> *Wandering from the fold of God.*

And ever since, we have been living men in Christ Jesus. To whom must we ascribe our preservation and our progress? Must we not attribute every victory over sin, and every advance in the spiritual life, to the operation of God and nothing at all to ourselves?

A poor simpleton once said, "'Twas God and I did the work." "Well, but Charlie, what part did you take in it?" "Sure, then," said he, "I did all I could to stop the Lord, and he beat me." I suppose, did we tell the simple truth, we should say much the same. In the matter of our salvation we do all we can to oppose it—our old nature does—and he overcomes our evil propensities. From first to last, Jesus Christ has to be the Author and the Finisher of our salvation, or it never would have been begun, and it never would have been completed. Think, beloved, of what fitness for heaven is. To be fit for heaven a man must be perfect. Go, you who think you can prepare yourselves, be perfect for a day. The vanity of your own mind, the provocation of this treacherous world, and the subtle temptation of the devil, would make short work of your empty pretensions. You would be blown about like chaff. Creature perfection, indeed! Was ever anything so absurd? Men have boasted of attaining it, but their very boastings have proved that they possessed it not. He that gets nearest to perfection is the very man who sighs and cries over the abiding infirmities of his flesh. No, if perfection is to be reached—and it must be, or we shall not be fit for heaven—by the operation of God it must be wrought. Man's work is never perfect; it is always marred on the wheel. His best machinery may still be improved upon; his finest productions of art might still be excelled. God alone is perfect, and he alone is the perfecter. Blessed be God, we can heartily subscribe to this truth: "He that hath wrought us for the selfsame thing is God."

But what shall I say to those of you, my friends, who have no acquaintance with God? You certainly cannot be fitted for heaven. Your cause is not committed to him. He is doing nothing for you. He has not begun the good work in you. You live in this world as if there were no God. The thought, the stupendous thought, of his "being" does not affect you. You would not act any differently if there were twenty Gods or if there were no God. You utterly ignore his claims on your allegiance and your responsibility to his law. Virtually in thought and deed you are without God in the world. Poor forlorn creature, you have forgotten your Creator. Poor wandering soul, you have fallen out of gear with the universe; you have become alienated from the great Father who is in heaven. I tremble at the thought. To be on the wide sea without rudder or compass; to be lost in the wilderness, where there is no way! Cheerless as your condition is, remember this: though you see not God, God sees you. God sees you now; he hears you now. If you breathe but a desire toward him, that desire shall be accepted and fulfilled. He will yet begin to work in you that gracious preparation which shall make you meet to be a partaker of the inheritance of the saints in light.

3. And now, third: *let the seal of this preparation* be briefly but attentively considered.

The apostle says, "He that hath wrought us for the selfsame thing is God, who also hath given unto us the earnest of the Spirit." Masters frequently pay during the week a part of the wages which will be due on Saturday night. God gives his Holy Spirit, as it were, to be a part of the reward which he intends to give to his people, when, like hirelings, they have fulfilled their day. Our country friends just before harvest go out into the fields, and they pick half a dozen ears that are ripe, braid the ends, and hang them up over the mantel as a kind of earnest of the harvest. So God gives us his Holy Spirit to be in our hearts as an earnest of heaven; and as the ears of wheat are of the same quality and character as the harvest, so the gift of the Holy Spirit is the antepast of heaven. When you have him, you have a plain indication to your soul of what heaven will be. You have a part of heaven—"a young heaven," as Dr. Watts somewhere calls it, within you.

Ask yourself, then, dear hearer, this question, "Have I received the earnest of the Spirit?" If so, you have the preparation for heaven; if not, you are still a stranger to divine things, and you have no reason to believe that the heaven of the saints will be your heritage. Come, now, have you received the Holy Spirit? Do you reply, "How may I know?" Wherever the Holy Spirit is, he works certain graces in the soul—repentance, to wit. Have you ever repented of sin? I mean, do you hate it? Do you shun it? Do you grieve to think you should once have loved it? Is your mind altogether changed with regard to sin, so that what once seemed pleasure now is pain, and all the sweetness of sin is poison to your taste? Where the Holy Spirit is, repentance is followed by the whole train of graces, all in a measure, not any in perfection, for there is always room to grow in grace and in the knowledge of Jesus Christ. Such is patience, which submits to the Lord's will; such, too, the gracious disposition of forgiveness, which enables us to bear injuries and to forgive those that vex us; such, likewise, that holy courage which is not ashamed to own our Lord, or to defend his cause. In fact, where the Holy Ghost is bestowed, all the graces of the Spirit will be communicated in some degree. Though they will all need to grow, yet there will be the seeds of them all. Where the Holy Spirit is, there will be the joy.

No delight can be more animating or more elevating than that which springs from the indwelling of God in the soul. Think of God coming to abide in this poor bosom! Why, were a cross of diamonds or pearls glittering on your breast, some might envy you the possession of such a treasure; but to have God within your breast is infinitely better. God dwells in us, and we in him. Oh! sacred mystery! Oh! birth of joy unspeakable! Oh! well of bliss divine that makes earth like heaven! Have you ever had this joy—the joy of knowing that you are pardoned; the joy of being sure that you are a child of God; the joy of being certain that all things work together for your good; the joy of expecting that before long, and the sooner the better, you shall be forever beyond gunshot of fear and care and pain and want? Where the Spirit of God is, there is more or less of this joy, which is the earnest of heaven.

This gift, moreover, will be conspicuously evidenced by a living faith in the Lord Jesus Christ. The Holy Ghost is not in you if you rely on anything but Jesus; but if, as a poor guilty sinner, you have come to him, partaken of his gracious pardon, kissed his blessed feet, and are now depending upon him alone, you have received the Holy Ghost, and you have got the antepast of heaven.

Brethren and sisters, it is intensely desirable that we should seek more to be consciously filled with the Holy Spirit. We get easily contented with a little spiritual blessedness. Let us grow more covetous of the best gifts. Let us crave to be endued with the Holy Spirit and to be baptized in the Holy Ghost and in fire. The more we get of him, the more assurance we shall have of heaven for our peace, the more foretastes of heaven for our happiness, and the more preparation for heaven in lively hope.

Thus have I shown you the need of preparation, the Author of preparation, and the great seal which proves the verity of that preparation. If your honest conscience allows your humble claim to have received this sacred token of salvation, how happy you would be! Do not be afraid to be happy. Some Christians seem to court the gloom of despondency as if they dared not bask in the sunshine of heaven. I have sometimes heard people say that they have not enjoyed themselves. No, dear friends; pity, I think, if any of us ever should. It would be a poor kind of enjoyment if we merely enjoyed ourselves. But oh! it is delightful when you can enjoy your God, and when you can enjoy the mercies that are in him and the promises that are in him and the blessings which through him come to you. When you gather round the table of the Lord's love, do not be afraid to partake of the feast. There is nothing put there to be looked at. There is no confectionery spread out for show. If you dare conclude that you are living in Christ, and living on Christ, do not be afraid to sing as you go home—

> Now I can read my title clear
> To mansions in the skies;
> I bid farewell to every fear,
> And wipe my weeping eyes.

It will be a blessing to your family for you to be happy. You may find that something has gone wrong while you have been away. Go home as happy as you can be, and you will be better able to bear the cares and vexations that must and will befall you. Keep your spirit well worked up to the fear of the

Lord and the enjoyment of his presence. Then, if some little cross matter should come to disquiet you, you can say, "Who am I that I should be vexed and chafed, or lose my temper, or be cast down about such a matter as this? This is not my sphere of well-being; this is not my heaven; this is not my God."

> *If thou shouldst take them all away,*
> *Yet should I not repine;*
> *Before they were possess'd by me*
> *They were entirely thine.*
>
> *Nor would I speak a murmuring word,*
> *Though the whole world were gone,*
> *But seek enduring happiness*
> *In thee, and thee alone.*

But oh! suppose you feel persuaded and honestly admit that you are not prepared to die, not made meet for heaven. Do not utterly despair, but be grateful that you live where the gospel is preached. "Faith cometh by hearing, and hearing by the Word of God." Be much in hearing the Word, and be much in earnest prayer that the hearing may be blessed to your soul. Above all, give diligence to that divine command which bids you trust in Jesus Christ, whom he has sent. Eternal life lies in the nutshell of that one sentence, "Believe in the Lord Jesus Christ, and thou shalt be saved." All that is asked of you—and even that grace gives you—is simply to trust in him who, as Son of God, died for the sins of men. God give you that faith, and then may you meet death with joy or look forward to the coming of the Lord with peace, whichever may be your lot. Amen.

The Strait Gate

Published on Thursday, April 19, 1917; delivered at the Metropolitan Tabernacle, Newington. No. 3560.

Strive to enter in at the strait gate; for many, I say unto you, will seek to enter in, and shall not be able. —LUKE 13:24

The precepts of our Lord Jesus Christ are dictated by the soundest wisdom. He has given us divine prescriptions for the health of our souls, and his commandments, though clothed with sovereign authority, are spoken in such infinite kindness that we may regard them as the advice of a true and faithful friend. This is not a legal but a gospel exhortation: "Strive to enter in at the strait gate." He himself is the only gate, or the door, by which we can find admission, and the way to enter in through Jesus Christ is not by working, but by believing. Then, as to the strife we are urged to carry on, it is an earnest endeavor to steer clear of all the rocks and shoals and quicksands of popular fallacies and deceitful traditions, and to sail in the deep waters, with his covenant for our chart, and his Word for our compass, in simple obedience to his statutes, trusting to him as our pilot, whose voice we always hear, though his face we cannot see. The storm signal may well rouse your fears; the cry of peril had need excite your caution. The mere mention sounds like a menace. "Many shall seek to enter in, and shall not be able." Listen to that warning, lest you be among the "many" that founder—perhaps you shall be among the few that escape. Hearken to what Jesus tells you shall come to pass with the multitude, that it may never come to pass with you as individuals.

1. Mark now, first, *a gate which it is most desirable to enter.*

Surely "many" would not seek to enter if they were not convinced of the desirableness of passing through it. The very fact that so many, although they fail, will at least seek to enter, proves that there is a desire, a reason, and a motive why men should aim to enter.

This gate—that is, Christ—it is most desirable for us to pass through, *because it is the gate of the city of refuge.* Cities of refuge were appointed for manslayers, that when they were pursued by the avenger of blood, they might pass the gate and be secure within the sanctuary or city. The gospel of Jesus

Christ is intended as a refuge for those who have broken the law of God, whom vengeance is pursuing, who will certainly be overtaken, to their eternal destruction, unless they fly to Christ and find shelter in him. Outside of Christ the sword of fire pursues us swift and sharp. From God's wrath there is but one escape, and that is by a simple faith in Christ. Believe in him, and the sword is sheathed, and the energy and the love of God will become your everlasting portion; but refuse to believe in Jesus, and your innumerable sins, written in his book, shall be laid at your door in that day when the pillars of heaven shall reel, and the stars shall fall like withered fig leaves from the tree.

Oh! who would not wish to escape from the wrath to come! Mr. Whitefield, when preaching, would often hold up his hands and cry, "Oh! the wrath to come! the wrath to come! the wrath to come!" There is more weight and meaning in these words than tongue can tell or heart conceive. The wrath to come! the wrath to come! When past that gate, like Noah after he had passed into the ark, you are safe from the overwhelming deluge; you are sheltered from the devouring conflagration which shall consume the earth; you are rescued from the death and the doom that await the countless multitudes of the impenitent. Who would not wish to enter where there is salvation, the only place where salvation can be found?

It is desirable to enter this gate *because it is the gate of a home.* There is sweet music in that word "home." Jesus is the home of his people's hearts. We are at rest when we get to Christ. We have all we want when we have Jesus. Happiness is the portion of the Christian in this life while he lives upon his Savior. I have seen outside the night refuges crowds of persons waiting an hour beforehand, till the doors were opened. Poor souls! Shivering in the cold, but in expectation of being warmed and comforted in a little time for a little while, when they should be admitted. What think you, O homeless men and women—were there a permanent home for you, a home from which you never could be banished, a home into which you could be introduced as dear children, would it not be worth your while to wait long at the door, and to knock again and again right vehemently, could you but ultimately gain admission? Jesus is a home for the homeless, a rest for the weary, a comfort for the comfortless.

Is your heart broken? Jesus can comfort you. Have you been banished from your family, or one by one have the dear ones been taken to their last resting place? Do you feel solitary, friendless, cheerless, accounting "the black flowing river" to be preferred before this troubled stream of life, and that pitiless society of men and women, eager all for gain and gaiety, caring nothing of your griefs or your groans? Oh, come to Jesus! Trust in him, and he will light up a star in the black midnight sky; he will kindle a fire in your hearts that shall make them glow with joy and comfort, even now. It were worthwhile to be a Christian, irrespective of the hereafter. Such present comfort as a belief in Jesus imparts is an inestimable compensation. This is the gate of refuge, and it is the gate of a home.

Moreover, it *leads to a blessed feast*. We read just now of the supper that was spread. Jesus does not feed our bodies, but he does what is better, he feeds our minds. A hungry stomach is terrible, but a hungry heart is far more dreadful, for a loaf of bread will fill the one, but what can satisfy the other? Oh! when the heart gets craving and pining and yearning after something it cannot get, it is like the sea that cannot rest; it is like the grave that never can be filled; it is like the horse leech, whose daughters cry, "Give, give, give." Happy the man who believes in Jesus, for he becomes at once a contented man. Not only does he find rest in Christ, but joy and gladness, peace and abiding satisfaction are the portion of his lot. I tell you what I do know—and I would not lie, even for the Lord himself—I tell you that there is a mirth to be found in faith in Christ which cannot be matched. Speak you of their buoyant spirits who make merry in the dance or of the festive glee of those that are filled with wine? It is but the crackling of a handful of thorns under a pot—how soon it is gone! But the joy of the man who meditates on the love of Christ which embraces him, on the blood of Christ which cleanses him, on the arm of Christ which upholds him, on the hand of Christ which leads him, on the crown of Christ which is to be his portion—the joy of such a man is constant, deep, overflowing, beyond the power of expression.

The meanest Christian in all the world, bedridden, living on parish allowance, full of pains and ready to die, when his heart is stayed upon Christ, would not change places with the youngest, brightest, richest, noblest spirit to be found outside the church of God. No, kings and emperors, boast no more of your beggarly crowns; their glitter will soon fade; your purple robes will soon be moth-eaten; your silver shall soon be cankered; of your palace, not a stone shall be left upon its fellow. Bitter shall be the dregs of your wine cups, and all your music shall end in discord. I tell you that the poorest of all the company of the faithful in Christ Jesus excel you, and "would not change their blest estate for all that earth calls good or great." So abundantly worthwhile is it to come to Christ for the happiness, as well as the repose, which we find in him.

Well likewise, dear friends, may men desire to pass through the strait gate, knowing it is *the gate which leads to paradise*. There was one gate of paradise through which our father—Adam—and our mother—Eve—went weeping as they left the garden all behind them, to wander into the desert world. Can you picture them to yourselves, with the cherubim behind them and the flaming sword bidding them begone, for paradise was no place for rebels? Men have wandered up and down the world since then to find the gate of paradise, that they might enter yet again. They have scaled the peaks of Sinai, but they have not found it there. They have traversed the tracks of the wilderness, weary and footsore, jaded and faint, but they have found no gate to paradise anywhere in all their expeditions. The scholar has searched for it in the ancient books; the astronomer has hunted for it among the stars; sages, as they were called, have sought to find it by studying their arts; and fools have tried to find it among their viols and their bowls.

But there is only one gate. See, there it is. It is in the form of a cross, and he that will find the gate of heaven finds the cross and the man that did hang thereon. Happy he who can come up to it and pass through it, reposing all his confidence in the atonement once made by the Man of suffering on Calvary's tree. On earth he is saved, and in the article of death he shall pass through that gate of pearl unchallenged, walk the streets of gold unabashed, and bow before the excellent glory without a fear. He is free of heaven. The cross is a mark of a citizen of the skies. Having truly believed in Jesus, everlasting felicity is his beyond all doubt. Who, then, would not pass through the strait gate?

And who would not wish to pass through it when he considers what will be the lot of those outside the gate? How we tremble at the thought of that outer darkness, where shall be weeping and wailing and gnashing of teeth! There are many inquiries nowadays about eternal punishment. O men and brethren, do not rashly or carelessly challenge the bitter experience of such condemnation! Speculate as you will about the doctrine, but I pray you do not trifle with the reality. To be lost forever, let that mean what it may, will be more than you can bear though your ribs were iron and your bones were brass. Tempt not the avenging angel. Beware that you forget not God, lest he tear you in pieces, and there be none to deliver. By the living God, I pray you fear and tremble, lest you be found out of Christ in the day of his appearing. Rest not, be not patient, much less merry, till you are saved. To be in danger of hellfire is a peril that no heart can adequately realize, no language fitly paint. Oh! I beseech you, halt not, give yourself no rest, till you have got beyond that danger! Flee for your lives, for the fiery shower will soon descend! Escape! God, in his mercy, quicken your pace that you may escape full soon, lest the hour of mercy cease and the day of judgment come! Surely these are reasons enough for wanting to pass in at the strait gate.

2. Observe still further what our Lord tells us. *There is a crowd of people who will seek to enter and will not be able.*

Who are these? If you look closely at *the crowd who this day seek to pass,* I think you will see a considerable difference between seeking and striving. You are not merely advised to seek; you are urgently bidden to strive. Striving is a more vehement exercise than seeking. Are you among those who coolly seek admission because, indeed, they suppose it is the proper thing? Many there be who come up to the gate of mercy and seek to enter, not striving, not particularly anxious, certainly far enough from being agitated. And when they look at the gate they object to the lintel because it is too low, nor will they deign to stoop. There is no believing in Jesus with a proud heart. He that trusts Christ must feel himself to be guilty and acknowledge it. He never will savingly believe till he has been thoroughly convinced of sin. But many say, "I will never stoop to that. Unless I have something to do in the work, and share some of the merit, I cannot enter." No, sirs, some of you are quite unable to believe in Christ because you believe in yourselves. As long as a man thinks himself a fine fellow, how can he think well of Jesus? You eclipse the sun; you hold up your own little hands before the sunlight; how can you expect to see? You are too good to go to heaven or, at least, too good in your own apprehension. O man! I pray God prick that bubble, that blown-up bladder, and let out the gas, that you may discern what you really are, for you are nothing, after all, but a poor worm, contemptible, notwithstanding your conceit and pride, in spite of your poverty, an arrogant worm, that dares to lift up its head when it has nothing to glory in. Oh! bow yourself in lowly self-abhorrence, else you may seek to enter, but shall not be able!

Some are unable to enter *because the pride of life will not let them.* They come to this gate in their carriage and pair, and expect to drive in, but they cannot get admission. There is no different way of salvation for a peer of the realm than for a pauper in the workhouse. The greatest prince that ever lived must trust Jesus just as the meanest peasant does. I recollect a minister once telling me that he attended the bedside of a very proud woman, of considerable wealth, and she said to him, "Do you think, sir, that when I am in heaven, such a person as Betty-My-Maid will be in the same place as I am? I never could endure her company here. She is a good servant in her way, but I am sure I could not put up with her in heaven." "No, madam," said he, "I do not suppose you will ever be where Betty will be." He knew Betty to be one of the humblest and most consistent of Christian women anywhere, and he might have told her proud mistress that in the sight of God meekness is preferable to majesty. The Lord Jesus, in the day of his coming, will wipe out all such distinctions as may very properly exist on earth, though they cannot be recognized beyond the skies. O rich man, glory not in your riches! All your wealth, if you could take it with you, would not buy a single paving stone in the streets of heaven. This poor stuff—do not trust in it. Oh! lay it aside as a crown of glorying and pass humbly through the gate with Lazarus!

Some are unable to enter *because they carry contraband goods with them.* When you land in France, there stands the gendarme, who wants to see what you are carrying in that basket. If you attempt to push by, you will soon find yourself in custody. He must know what is there; contraband goods cannot be taken in. So at the gate of mercy which is Christ, no man can be saved if he desire to keep his sins. He must give up every false way. "Oh!" says the drunkard, "I'd like to get to heaven, but I must smuggle in this bottle somehow." "I would like to be a Christian," says another; "I do not mind taking Dr. Watts's hymns with me, but I should like sometimes to sing a Bacchanalian song, or a lightsome serenade." "Well," cries another, "I enjoy myself on Sunday with God's people, but you must not deny me the amusements of the world during the week; I cannot give them up." Well, then, you cannot enter, for Jesus Christ never saves us in our sins; he saves us from our sins. "Doctor," says the fool, "make me well, but I'd like to keep my fever." "No," says the doctor, "how can you be well while you keep the fever?" How can a man be saved from his sins while he clings to his sins? What is salvation but to be delivered from sin? Sin lovers may seek to be saved, but they shall not be able; while they hug their sins, they cannot have Christ. Some of you are in this grievous predicament. You have been attending this house of prayer a good long time. I do not know what hinders you, but this I do know, there is a worm somewhere eating out the heart of that fair-looking apple. Some private sin that you pamper is destroying your souls. Oh! that you had grace to give it up, and to come in by the strait gate, trusting in Jesus Christ!

Not a few are unable to enter in because *they want to postpone the matter until tomorrow.* Today, at any rate, you are engaged with other plans and projects. "A little longer let me revel in some of the sensual enjoyments of life, and afterward I will come in." Procrastinators are among the most hopeless of people. He that has "tomorrow" quivering on his lips is never likely to have grace reigning in his heart.

Others, and these are in the worst plight of all, *think that they are in,* and that they have entered. They mistake the outside of the gate for the inside. A strange mistake to fall into, but many do thus delude themselves. They rub their backs against the posts, and then they tell us they are as near heaven as anybody else. They have never passed the threshold; they have never found shelter in Christ, albeit they may have felt wonderfully excited at a revival meeting, and sung as loudly and lustily as any of the congregation: "I do believe, I will believe." There is a considerable show of reformation about them. Although they have not got a new garment, they have mended up the old one. They are not new creatures, but still they are better behaved creatures than they were before. And they are "all right." Be not deceived, my dear friends; do beware of mistaking a work of nature for the operation of God's grace. Do not be taken in by the devil's counterfeits. They are well made; they look like genuine; when they are brand new they shine and glitter like fine gold, but they will not stand the test; every one of them will have a nail driven through them one day; they will never pass current with God. If you have a religion, let it be real and true, not feigned and hypocritical. Of all cheats, the man who cheats himself is certainly the least wise, and, as I think, he is the least honest. Do not play the knave with your own soul. Suspect yourself too much rather than too little. Better journey to heaven in terror of hell than dream of the happy land while drifting in the other direction. "Ah! that deceit should steal such gentle shapes!" Be on your guard, every one of you. Let not any man deceive himself.

Thus it is that a crowd—I had almost said a countless crowd—of people nowadays seek to enter in, but for manifold reasons they are not able to do so. And yet there is a more appalling aspect to the same fact. "Many, I say unto you, *will* seek to enter in, and shall not be able." *The dying are not able.* Panic-stricken, the dying man sends for the minister whom he never went to hear when his health was good and hours hung heavy on his hands. The charm of Sundays lay in their dissipation; an excursion up the river or a cheap trip to Brighton and back; anything—everything sooner than hear the gospel. He never read his Bible; he never prayed. Now the doctor shakes his head and the nurse suggests that they "fetch a clergyman." Poor soul! She means right; but what, think you, can he do? What can we ministers do for you? What can any man do for his fellow creature? "None of us can by any means redeem his brother, nor give to God a ransom for him." He begins to seek, when, alas! he cannot think, poor fellow, for he is in *articulo mortis*, with the throes of his last struggle. His head swims, pains grow at his vitals, a glassy film is over his eyes, rambling words fall from his lips. Could he think, he has got something else to think about than the dread future that awaits him. Look at his weeping wife. See those dear children, brought in to get a last kiss from their father. Were his mind more vigorous, it were not likely to be taken up with spiritual thoughts; there is too much in the solemn farewell to occupy the moments left in preparation for the future. "Pray for me, sir," he says, with fainting, failing breath. Yes, he is seeking to enter in. In ninety-nine cases out of a hundred, I fear the answer is, he shall not be able. Little hope have I for deathbed repentances. Never trust to them, I beseech you. Such a vestibule as a deathbed you may never have. To die in the street may be your lot. Should you have a deathbed, you will have something else to think about besides religion. Oh! how often have I heard Christian men say, when they have been dying, "Ah sir, if I had a God to seek now, what a misery it would be! What a blessing it is that, with all the cares that now come upon me, I have a sure and certain hope in Christ, for I found him years ago." O dear hearers, do not be among those who postpone and procrastinate, till, in a dying hour, after a fashion you seek to enter and find you shall not be able.

Some years ago I was awakened about three o'clock in the morning by a sharp ring of the doorbell. I was urged without delay to visit a house not very far off London Bridge. I went, and up two pairs of stairs I was shown into a room, the occupants of which were a nurse and a dying man. There was nobody else. "O sir," said she, "Mr. So-and-So, about half an hour ago, begged me to send for you." "What does he want?" I asked. "He is dying, sir," she replied. I said, "I see that. What sort of a man was he?" "He came home last night, sir, from Brighton. He had been out all day. I looked for a Bible, sir, but there is not one in the house; I hope you have got one with you." "Oh!" I said, "a Bible would be of no use to him now; if he could understand me, I could tell him the way of salvation in the very words of Holy Scripture." I spoke to him, but he gave me no answer. I spoke again; still there was no reply. All sense had fled. I stood a few minutes gazing at his face, till I perceived he was dead; his soul had departed. That man in his lifetime had been inclined to jeer at me. In strong language he had often denounced me as a hypocrite. Yet he was no sooner smitten with the darts of death than he sought my presence and my counsel, feeling no doubt in his heart that I was a servant of God, though he did not care to own it with his lips. There I stood, unable to help him. Promptly as I had responded to his call, what could I do but look at his corpse and go home again? He had, when too late, sighed for the ministry of reconciliation, sought to enter in, but he was not able. There was no space left in him then for repentance; he had wasted the opportunity. Therefore, I pray and beseech you, my dear hearers, by the near approach of death—it may be much nearer than you think—give earnest heed to these things. I look round on this building and note the pews and sittings from which hearers, whose faces were once familiar to us, have gone—some to glory, some I know not where. God knows. Oh! let not the next removal, if it be yours, vacate the seat of a scoffer or of a neglecter or of one who, having been touched in his conscience, silenced the secret monitor and would not turn. As the Lord lives, you must turn or burn; you must either repent or be ruined forever. May God give you wisdom to choose the better part!

It appears from Scripture that *even after death there will be some who will seek to enter and shall not be able.* I do not attempt to explain what I cannot understand, but I find the Master represents those on the left hand asking a question, "When saw we thee hungry, and fed thee not?" as if they had some glimmering hope that the sentence upon them might be reversed. And I read in another place of those who will come and knock at the door, and say, "Lord, Lord, open to us." But the Master of the house, having already risen up and shut to the door, will answer, "Verily, I say unto you, I know you not." Is there, then, such a thing as prayer in hell? When the soul has passed out of the body without hope, will it seek for hope hereafter? Perhaps so. Did not the rich man pray to Abraham to send Lazarus? It is but natural to expect that, as they doubted God's promises on earth, they may doubt God's threatenings in hell, and may hope, perhaps, that there will be a way of escape. They will seek, they will seek, but they shall not be able, not able to enter heaven. They said they were not able on earth; they shall find they are not able in hell. *Non possumus* is the sinner's cry. "We are not able to leave our sins; we are not able to believe; we are not able to be serious; we are not able to be prayerful"; and then, how it will be thrown back into their teeth! Not able to enter heaven; not able to escape from torment; not able to live; not able to die; not able, because the gate of heaven admits no sinner who has not been washed in the Redeemer's blood. Back with you, sir! You would not come to the fountain, you would not wash. Back with you.

You are not able; not able, because heaven is a prepared place for a prepared people, and you never thought of preparation. Away with you, sir! How can you enter when you are not prepared? Heaven is a place for which a fitness is needed. Men cannot enjoy that which would be contrary to their natures. Away with you, sirs! You could not enjoy heaven if you were admitted, for you are not changed in heart. Away with you! What, do you linger? Do you cry? Do you pray? Do you weep? Do you entreat? Away with you! No, the angels shall sweep you away, for is it not written: You yourselves shall be thrust out—unceremoniously driven and scourged away from the gate of glory, because you would not come to the gate of grace. These are terrible things to utter.

I well might shrink from speaking thus, were it not that fidelity to your souls makes such demands that I must ring the warning. If you die without faith in Christ, behold there is *a gulf fixed* between you and heaven. I do not know what that means, but I know what idea it gives to me, and should give to you. Between heaven and hell there is no traffic. None ever passed from hell to heaven.

> *There are no acts of pardon passed*
> *In the cold grave to which we haste;*
> *But darkness, death, and long despair*
> *Reign in eternal silence there.*

They would fain pass the gulf—were it fire, they could be glad to pass it; were it full of torments, many and manifold as a Spanish Inquisition could invent, they would be glad to bear them; could they but hope to cross the gulf. But no, the voice is heard—an angel's voice: "He that is filthy, let him be filthy still; he that is unjust, let him be unjust still." The wax has cooled; you cannot alter the impression. The die is cast; you cannot remold it. The tree has fallen; there it lies.

I wish I could speak now in words that should burn their way right into your inmost hearts. Alas! I cannot. I must, however, just repeat the text again, and leave it with you. Many shall seek in that dread day to enter, but shall not be able. Oh! enter then, enter you! Enter now, while yet the gate stands open wide, and mercy bids you come! Make haste to enter while yet the avenging angel lingers, and the angel of mercy stands with outstretched arms and cries, "Whosoever will, let him come and take of the water of life freely." May God, the ever-blessed Spirit, without whom no warning can be effectual, and no invitation can be attractive, sweetly constrain you to trust Christ tonight.

Here is the gospel in a few words. Jesus suffered the wrath and torment we justly merited. He doubtless bore the penalty of your transgressions, if you penitently believe in his sacrifice. When you trust in him for pardon, 'tis proof your sins were laid on him for judgment. You are, therefore, a forgiven man, a pardoned woman; you are saved—saved forever. If you have a simple, childlike trust, you may go home, singing for joy of heart, knowing that you have already entered the strait gate, and before you lie grace on earth and glory in heaven. May God bless you richly, and may you adore him gratefully, for his dear name's sake. Amen.

A Last Lookout

Delivered at the Metropolitan Tabernacle, Newington. No. 989.

The time of my departure is at hand. —2 TIMOTHY 4:6

So near, so very near the change—his removal from this to another world; and so very conscious of it; yet Paul looked back with calm satisfaction; he looked forward with sweet assurance; and he looked round with deepest interest on the mission that had engaged his life. As you must have noticed while we were reading the chapter, in his case "the ruling passion was strong in death." Writing what he well knows is the last letter he shall ever write, its main topic is care for the church of God—anxiety for the promotion of the truth—zeal for the furtherance of the gospel. When he is dead and gone from the post of service, the scene of suffering, the field of enterprise, on whom shall his mantle fall? He desires that in Timothy he may find a worthy successor, strong in the faith, sincere of heart, and having dauntless courage withal, one who will wield the sword and hold the banner when his hand is palsied in death.

Men have usually shown us what lies at the bottom of their heart when they have come to die. Often their last expiring expressions have been indicative of their entire character. Certainly you have before you in the last sentences of Paul's pen a fair epitome of his entire life. He is trusting in the Savior; he is anxious to show his love for that Savior. The welfare of the Christian church and the advancement of the holy cause of the gospel are uppermost in his mind. May it be yours and mine to live wholly for Christ and to die also for him. May this ever be foremost in our thoughts: "How can I advance the kingdom of our Lord and Savior? By what means can I bless his church and people?" It is very beautiful to observe the way in which Paul describes his death in this verse. According to our translation, he speaks of it as an offering. "I am now ready," says he, "to be offered." If we accept this version, he may be supposed to mean that he felt as one standing like a bullock or a lamb, ready to be laid on an altar. He foresaw he would die a martyr's death. He knew he could not be crucified as his brother Peter had been, for a Roman citizen was, as a rule, exempt from that ignominious death. He expected to die in some other manner. Probably he guessed it would be by the sword, and so he describes himself as waiting for the sacrificial knife to be used, that he might be presented as a sacrifice.

So I say the words of our translation would lead us to think. But the original is far more instructive. He here likens himself, in the Greek, not to an offering, but to the drink offering. Every Jew would know what that meant. When there was a burnt sacrifice offered, the bullock or the victim then slain was the main part of the sacrifice. But sometimes there was a little, what if I say an unimportant, supplement added to that sacrifice—a little oil and a little wine were poured on to the altar or the bullock, and thus a drink offering was said to be added to the burnt offering. Now Paul does not venture to call himself an offering—Christ is his offering. Christ is, so to speak, the sacrifice on the altar. He likens himself only to that little wine and oil poured out as a supplement thereto, not necessary to its perfection, but tolerated in performing a vow, or allowed in connection with a freewill offering, as you will find if you refer at leisure to the fifteenth chapter of Numbers, from the fourth to the eighth verses. The drink offering was thus a kind of addendum, by which the person who gave it showed his thankfulness. So Paul is resolved to show his thankfulness to Christ, the great sacrifice, and he is willing that his blood should be poured as a drink offering on the altar where his Lord and Master was the great burnt offering. He rejoices when he can say, "I am ready to be presented as a drink offering unto God."

We have mainly to do with the second description which he gives of his death. What does he say when the hour that this grim monster must be grappled with is at hand? I do not find him sad. Those who delight in gloomy poetry have often represented death in terrible language. "It is hard," says one—

> To feel the hand of death arrest one's steps,
> Throw a chill blight on all one's budding hopes,
> And hurl one's soul untimely to the shades.

And another exclaims—

> O God, it is a fearful thing
> To see the human soul take wing,
> In any shape, in any mood!
> I've seen it rushing forth in blood,
> I've seen it on the breaking ocean,
> Strive with a swollen, convulsive motion.

Not so the apostle Paul. I do not even hear him speak of flying through the gate as our grand old poet has described death. He does not say, "The hour of my dissolution is at hand"—a very proper word if he had used it; but he is not looking so much at the process as at the result of his dying. He does not even say, "The hour of my death is at hand," but he adopts a beautiful expression, "the time of my departure"—words which are used sometimes to signify the departure of a vessel from the port; the pulling up of the anchor so that it looses its moorings, when about to put out to sea—so he feels himself like a ship lying at the harbor for a while—but he says, "The time for pulling up the anchor, the time for letting loose the cable, and cutting from the mooring is at hand; I shall soon be launched upon my voyage." And he knew right well where that voyage would end, in the fair havens of the port of Peace in the better country, whither his Lord had gone before him.

Now we will proceed very briefly to say a word about *departure*; and then a shorter word still about the time of our departure; and then a little more about *the time* of our departure *being at hand*—trying here, especially, to bring forward some lessons which may be of practical usefulness to each one of us.

1. First, then, dear brethren, let us think a little about *our departure*.

It is quite certain we shall not dwell here forever: we shall not live here below as long as the first man did, or as those antediluvian fathers, who tarried some eight or nine hundred years. The length of human life then led to greatness of sin. Monstrosities of evil were ripened through the long continuance of physical strength and the accumulating force of eager passions. All things considered, it is a mercy that life is abridged and not prolonged to a thousand years. Amid the sharp competition of man with man, and class with class, there is a bound to every scheme of personal aggrandizement, a limit to all the spoils of individual despotism, a restraint upon the hoardings of anyone's avarice. It is well, I say, that it should be so. The narrow span of life clips the wings of ambition and balks it of its prey. Death comes in to deprive the mighty of his power, to stay the rapacity of the invader, to scatter abroad the possessions of the rich. The most reprobate men must end their career after they have had their threescore years and ten or their fourscore years of wickedness.

And as for the good and godly, though we mourn their exit, especially when we think that they have been prematurely taken from us, we remember how the triumphs of genius have been for the most part achieved in youth, and how much the world has been enriched by the heads and hearts of those who have but sown the seeds of faith and left others to reap the fruits. If into less than the allotted term they have crowded the service of their generation, we may save our tears, for our regrets are needless. The summons will reach each one of us before long. We cannot stop here as long as the gray fathers of our race: we expect, and it is meet that we should prepare, to go. The world itself is to be consumed one day. "The elements shall melt with fervent heat." The land on which we stand we are apt to call *terra firma*, but beneath it is probably an ocean of fire, and it shall itself feel the force of the ocean. We must not marvel, the house being so frail, that the tenants are unsettled and migratory. Certainly, whether we doubt it or not, we shall have to go. There will be a departure for us.

Beloved believer in Christ Jesus, to you the soft term "departure" is not more soft than the truth it represents. To die is to depart out of this world unto the Father. What say you about your departure? What say you of that from which you go, and what think you of that land to which you go? Well, of the land from which we go, my brethren, we might say many hard things if we would, but I think we had better not. We shall speak more correctly if we say the hard things of ourselves. This land, my brethren, has been a land of mercy to us: there have been sorrows in it; but in bidding it farewell, we will do it justice and speak the truth concerning it. Our sorrows have usually sprung up in our own bosoms, and those that have come from the soil itself would have been very light if it had not been for the plague of our hearts, which made us vex and fret over them. Oh, the mercy you and I have enjoyed even in this life! It has been worthwhile to live for us who are believers. Even had we to die like a dog dies, it has been worthwhile to live for the joy and blessedness which God has made to pass before us. I dare not call that an evil country in which I have met my Savior and received the pardon of my sin. I dare not call that an ill life in which I have seen my Savior, though it be through a glass darkly. How shall I speak ill of that land where Zion is built, beautiful for situation, the joy of the whole earth, the place of our solemn assemblies, where we have worshiped God? No; cursed of old as the earth was to bring forth the thorn and the thistle, the existence of the church of God in that land seems to a great degree to have made reparation for the blight to such as know and love the Savior.

Oh, have we not gone up to the house of God in company with songs of ecstatic joy, and have we not when we have gathered round the table of the Lord—though nothing was upon it but the type and emblem—have we not felt it a joyous thing to be found in the assembly of the saints, and in the courts of the Lord's house even here? When we loose our cable and bid farewell to earth, it shall not be with bitterness in the retrospect. There is sin in it, and we are called to leave it; there has been trial in it, and we are called to be delivered from it; there has been sorrow in it, and we are glad that we shall go where we shall sorrow no more. There have been weakness and pain and suffering in it, and we are glad that we shall be raised in power; there has been death in it, and we are glad to bid farewell to shrouds and to knells; but for all that there has been such mercy in it, such loving-kindness of God in it, that the wilderness and the solitary place have been made glad, and the desert has rejoiced and blossomed as a rose. We will not bid farewell to the world, execrating it, or leaving behind us a cold shudder and a sad remembrance, but we will depart, bidding adieu to the scenes that remain and to the people of God that tarry therein yet a little longer, blessing him whose goodness and mercy have followed us all the days of our life, and who is now bringing us to dwell in the house of the Lord forever.

But, dear brethren, if I have had to speak in a somewhat apologetic manner of the land from which we depart, I shall need to use many apologies for my own poor talk about the land to which we are bound. Ah, where do you go, spirit loosened from your clay—do you know? Where do you go? The answer must be, partly, that we know not. None of us have seen the streets of gold of which we sang just now; those harpings of the harpers, harping with their harps, have never fallen on these ears; eye has not seen it, ear has not heard it: it is all unrevealed to the senses; flesh and blood cannot inherit it, and, therefore, flesh and blood cannot imagine it. Yet it is not unknown, for God has revealed it unto us by his Spirit. Spiritual men know what it is to feel the spirit, their own newborn spirit, living, glowing, burning, triumphing within them. They know, therefore, that if the body should drop off, they would not die. They feel there is a life within them superior to blood and bone and nerve and sinew. They feel the life of God within them, and none can dispute it. Their own experience has proven to them that there is an inner life.

Well, then, when that inner life is strong and vigorous, the spirit often reveals to it what the world of spirits will be. We know what holiness is, do we not, brethren? Are we not seeking it? That is heaven—perfect holiness is heaven. We know what peace means; Christ is our peace. Rest—he gives us rest: we find *that* when we take his yoke. Rest is heaven. And rest in Jesus tells us what heaven is. We know, even today, what communion with God is. If anyone should say, "I do not know it," I should reply to him thus: Suppose I said to you, "You know not what it is to eat and drink": the man would tell me that I belied him, for he knew, as he knew his own existence, what it was to eat and drink; and, as surely as I live, I have communion with God. I know it as certainly as you know that I have declared it to you. Well, friends, that is heaven. It has but to be developed from the germ to the produce, and there is heaven in its full development.

Communion with saints in like manner—know we not what that is? Have we not rejoiced in each other's joys, been made glad with the experience of our brethren? That, too, carried to perfection, will be heaven. Oh, to throw yourself into the bosom of the Savior and lie there taken up with his mind and his love, yielding all things to his supremacy, beholding your King in him! When you have been in that state you have had an antepast of heaven. Your view may have been but as one seeing a man's face in shadow yet you would know that man again even by the shadow; so know we what heaven is. We shall not be strangers in a strange land when we get there. Though, like the Queen of Sheba, we shall say, "The half has not been told me," yet we shall reflect on it thus: "I did surmise there would be something of this sort. I did know from what I felt of its buddings in my soul below that the full-blown flower would be somewhat of this kind." Where away, then, spirit that is departing to soar through tracks to yourself unknown? Your answer is, "I am away: away to the throne of him whose cross first gave me life and light and hope. I am away to the very bosom of my Savior, where I hope to rest and to have fellowship with the church of the Firstborn, whose names are written in heaven." This is your departure that you have in near prospect.

Suppose, dear friend, the thought of departing from this world to the glory world should ever startle you, let me remind you that you are not the first that ever went that way. Your vessel is in the pool, as it were, or in the dock; she is going out on her voyage; oh, but you will not go alone, nor have to track your course through paths unnavigated or unknown before! When the Portuguese captain first went by the Cape of Storms it was a venturous voyage, and he called it the Cape of Good Hope when he had rounded it. When Columbus first went in search of the New World, his was a brave spirit that dared cross the unnavigated Atlantic. But oh, there are tens of thousands that have gone where you go. The Atlantic that severs us from Canaan is white with the sails of the vessels that are on voyage there. Fear not, they have not been wrecked; we hear good news of their arrival; there is good hope for you. There are no icebergs on the road, no mists, no counter currents, and no sunken vessels or quicksands; you have but to cut your moorings, and with Christ on board you shall be at your desired haven at once.

Remember, too, your Savior went that way. Have you to depart? So Christ departed too. Some of my brethren are always so pleased—pleased as some children are with a new toy—at the idea that they shall never die; that Christ will come, it may be, before the time of their decease; for, "we shall not all sleep, but we shall all be, changed." Well, let him come, yes, let him come;

come quickly. But if I had my choice, were it permitted me to choose, I would prefer to pass through the portals of the grave. Those that are alive and remain unto the coming of the Lord will not prevent, go before, or steal a march on them which are asleep. But surely they will lack one point of conformity to their Lord, for he disdained not to sojourn awhile in the tomb, though it was impossible that he should be held of death. Let the seal of death, then, be set upon this face of mine, that my fate in the matter may be like his. Enoch and Elijah were exempt from this privilege—privilege, I call it—of conformity to his death. But it is safe to go by the beaten track and desirable to travel by the ordinary route to the heavenly city. Jesus died. Through the valley of shadows, the vale of death shades, there are the footprints of Emmanuel all the way along: go down into it and fear not. Do you consider, too, dear brethren and sisters, that we may well look forward to our departure and look forward to it comfortably too? Is it not expedient by reason of nature? Is it not desirable by reason of grace? Is it not necessary by reason of glory?

I say, is not our departure needful by reason of nature? Men are not, when they come to hoary age, what they were in the prime of their days. The staff is needed for the foot, and the glass is wanted for the eye; and after a certain number of years, even those on whom Time has gently laid his hand find the taste is gone. They might proclaim, like old Barzillai, that they know not what they eat or drink. The hearing fails, the daughters of music are silent, the whole tenement gets very crazy. Oh, it were a melancholy thing if we had to continue to live! Perhaps there is no more hideous picture than that which the satirist drew of men who lived on to six or seven hundred years of age—that strange satirical man, Swift. Be thankful that we do not linger on in imbecility. Kind nature says we may depart; she gives us notice, and makes it welcome by the decays that come upon us. Besides, grace desires it; for it were a poor experience of his kindness as our best and truest friend that did not make us long to see our Savior's face. It is no mere driveling sentiment, I hope, when we join to sing—

> *Father, I long, I faint to see*
> *The place of thine abode;*
> *I'd leave thy earthly courts, and flee*
> *Up to thy seat, my God!*

I must confess there was one verse in the hymn we sang just now which I could not quite chime in with. I am not eagerly wishing to go to heaven this night. I have a great deal more to do here; therefore I do not want to take a hasty leave of all below. To full many of us, I suppose, there are times of quiet contemplation and times of rapt devotion, when our thoughts surmount these lower skies, and look within the veil and then, oh, how we wish to be there! Yet there are other times; times of strenuous activity when we buckle on the armor and press to the front; and then we see such a battle to be waged, such a victory to be won, such a work to be worked, that we say: "Well, to abide in the flesh, to continue with you all for the joy and furtherance of your faith, seems more loyal to Christ, more needful for you, and more in accord with our present feelings." I think it is idle for us to be crying to go home; it is too much like the lazy workman that wants Saturday night to come when it is only Tuesday morning. Oh no; if God spare us to do a long life's work, so much the better. At the same time, as a spark flies upward to the sun, the central source of flame, so does the newborn spirit aspire toward heaven, toward Jesus, by whom it was kindled. And, I add, that glory demands it, and makes our departure needful. Is not Christ in heaven praying that we may be with him where he is? Are there not the saints in heaven, of whom it is said, they without us cannot be perfect? The circle of the skies cannot be completed until all the redeemed be there. The grand orchestra of glory misses some notes as yet. What if the bass be full, there are wanting still some trebles and tenors! There are some sopranos that will be requisite to swell the enchanting melodies and consummate the worship of the Eternal! What, therefore, nature prepares for, grace desires, and glory itself demands, we have no just cause to shudder at. Our departure need not make us afraid.

2. Having thus occupied so much time on this first point, I have little or no room to enlarge on the second. *The time of our departure,* though unknown to us, is fixed by God, unalterably fixed; so rightly, wisely, lovingly settled, and prepared for, that no chance or haphazard can break the spell of destiny.

The wisdom of divine love shall be proven by the carefulness of its provision. Perhaps you will say: "It is not easy to discern this; the natural order of things is so often disturbed by casualties of one kind or another." Let me remind you, then, that it is through faith, only through faith, we can understand these things; for it is as true now of the providence of God as it was of old of the creation of God that "*things* which are seen were not made of things which do appear." Because the *mode* of your departure is beyond your own knowledge, it does not follow that the time of your departure is not foreseen by God. "Ah but," say you, "it seems so shocking for anyone to die suddenly, unexpectedly, without warning, and so come to an untimely end!" I answer you thus. If you take counsel with death, your flesh will find no comfort; but if you trust in God, your faith will cease to parley with these feverish anxieties, and your spirit will enjoy a sweet calm.

Dire calamities befell Job when he was bereaved of his children and his servants, his herds and his flocks. Yet he took little heed of the different ways in which his troubles were brought about—whether by an onslaught of the Sabeans or by a raid of the Chaldeans, whether the fire fell from heaven or the wind came from the wilderness, it mattered little. Whatever strange facts broke on his ear, one thought penetrated his heart, and one expression broke from his lips. "The Lord gave, and the Lord hath taken away; blessed be the name of the Lord." So, too, beloved, when the time of your departure arrives—be it by disease or decay, be it by accident or assault, that your soul quits its present tenement—rest assured that "thy times are in his hand"; and know of a surety that "all his saints are in his hand" likewise.

Besides this, dear friends, since the time of our departure must come, were the manner of it at our own disposal, I think we should most of us say, "What I shall choose, I know not." Fevers and agues, the pangs and tortures of one malady and another, or the delirium incident to sickness, are not so much to be preferred to the shock of a disaster or the terror of a wreck at sea, because one is the prolonging of pain, and the other the dispatch of fate, that we need to covet, and desire weeks or months spent in the vestibule of the grave. Rather should we say, "Let the Lord do with me as seems him good." To live in constant communion with God is a sure relief from all these bitter frettings. Those who have walked with him have often been favored with such presentiments of their departure as no physician could give them. Survivors will tell you that though death seemed to come suddenly to the godly merchant, he had in the last acts of his life appeared to expect and prepare for it, and even to have taken an affecting farewell of his family while in the vigor of health, as though he were aware that he was setting out on his last journey, which a few hours afterward it proved to be. So, too, the minister of Christ has sometimes fallen, expiring in his pulpit with a *nunc dimittis*, "Now lettest thou thy servant depart in peace," on his lips—secretly, but surely, made ready to depart and to be with his Lord. There is a time to depart; and God's time to call me is my time to go.

3. Now, to our third point—*the time is at hand*. "The time of my departure is at hand."

In a certain sense, every Christian here may say this; for whatever interval may interpose between us and death, how very short it is! Have you not all a sense that time flows faster than it did? In our childish days, we thought a year was quite a period of time, a very epoch in our career; now as for weeks—one can hardly reckon them! We seem to be traveling by an express train, flying along at such a rate that we can hardly count the months. Why, the past year only seemed to come in at one door and go out at the other; it was over so soon. We shall soon be at the terminus of life, even if we live for several years; but in the case of some of us, God knows of whom, this year, perhaps this month, will be our last. I think tomorrow night we shall have to report at the church meeting the deaths of nine members of this church within the last eight or nine days. Since these have gone, some of us may expect to follow them. There are those who will evidently go; disease has set in upon them. Some of those disorders that in this land seem to be always fatal, tell these dear friends that the time of their departure is undoubtedly at hand. And then old age, which comes so gracefully and graciously to many of our matrons and our veterans, shows, past all dispute, "the time of your departure is at hand." The lease of your life is almost up. Not indeed that I would address myself to such special cases only. I speak to every brother and sister in Christ here. "The time of our departure is at hand." What then, dear friends?

Is not this a reason for surveying our condition again? If our vessel is just launching, let us see that she is seaworthy. It would be a sad thing for us to be near departing, and yet to be just as near discovering that we are lost. Remember, dear friends, it is possible for anyone to maintain a decent Christian profession for fifty years, and be a hypocrite after all; possible to occupy an office in the church of God, and that of the very highest, and yet to be a Judas; and one may not only serve Christ, but suffer for him too, and yet, like Demas, may not persevere to the end; for all that looks like grace is not grace. Where true grace is, there it will always be; but where the semblance of it is, it will oftentimes suddenly disappear. Search yourself, good brother; set your house in order, for you must die and not live. Have you the faith of God's elect? Are you built on Christ? Is your heart renewed? Are you verily an heir of heaven? I charge every man and woman within this place, since the time of his departure may be far nearer than he thinks, to take stock and reckon up and see whether he be Christ's or no.

But if the time of my departure be at hand, and I am satisfied that it is all right with me, is there not a call for me to do all I can for my household? Father, the time of your departure is at hand; is your wife unsaved? Will you pass another night without lovingly speaking to her of her soul? Are those dear boys unregenerate? Is that girl still thoughtless? The time of your departure is at hand. You can do little more for the lads and lasses; you can do little more for the wife and the brother. Oh! do what you can now. Sister, you are consumptive; you will soon be gone. You are the only Christian in the family. God sent you there to be a missionary. Do not have to say, when you are dying, "The last hope of my family is going out, for I have not cared for their souls." Masters, you that have servants about you, you must soon be taken away. Will you not do something for their souls? I know if there were a mother about to go to Australia, and she had to leave some of her children behind, she would fret if she thought, "I have not done all that needs to be done for those poor children. Who will care for them now their mother is gone?" Well, but to have neglected something necessary for their temporal comfort would be little in comparison with not having cared for their souls! Oh, let it not be so! Let it not be a thorn in your dying pillow that you did not fulfill the relations of life while you had the opportunity. "The time of my departure is at hand."

Then there is a third lesson. Let me try to finish all my work, not only as regards my duty to my family, but in respect to all the world so far as my influence or ability can reach. Rich men, be your own executors. Do what you can with your substance while it is your own. Men of talent, speak for Jesus before your tongue has ceased to articulate and becomes a piece of clay. George Whitefield may supply us with a fine model of this uniform consistency. He was so orderly and precise in his habits, and so scrupulous and holy in his life, that he used to say he would not like to go to bed if there were a pair of gloves out of place in the house, much less were his will not made or any part of his duty unfulfilled to the best of his knowledge. He wished to have all right, and to be fully prepared for whatever might happen, so that, if he never woke again from the slumbers of the night, nobody would have cause to reflect upon anything he had left undone, entailing needless trouble on his wife or his children. Such care bestowed on what some account to be trifles is a habit; worthy of our imitation. The main work of life may be sadly spoiled by negligence in little things. This is a striking test of character. "He that is faithful in that which is least is faithful also in much: and he that is unjust in the least is unjust also in much." Oh then! time is fleeting, dispatch is urgent; gather up your thoughts, quicken your hands, speed your pace, for God commands you to make haste. If you have anything to do, you must do it soon. The wheels of eternity are sounding behind you. Press on! If you are to run a race you must run it fast, for death will soon overtake you. You may almost feel the hot breath of the white horse of death upon your cheeks already. O God, help us to do something ere we go hence and be no more seen. It was grand of the apostle that in the same breath, when he said, "The time of my departure is at hand," he could also say, "I have fought a good fight, I have finished my course, I have kept the faith." So may we be able to say when the time of our departure has arrived.

If the time of our departure is at hand, let it cheer us amid our troubles. Sometimes, when our friends go to Liverpool to sail for Canada or any other distant region, on the night before they sail they get into a very poor lodging. I think I hear one of them grumbling, "What a hard bed! What a small room! What a bad lookout." "Oh," says the other, "never mind, brother; we are not going to live here; we are off tomorrow." Consider in like manner, you children of poverty, this is not your rest. Put up with it; you are away tomorrow. You sons of sorrow, you daughters of weakness, you children of sickness, let this cheer you:

> The road may be rough,
> But it cannot be long
> And I'll smooth it with hope,
> And cheer it with song.

Oftentimes when I have been traveling on the Continent, I have been obliged to put up at a hotel that was full, where the room was so inconvenient that it scarcely furnished any accommodation at all. But we have said, "Oh, never mind: we are off in the morning! What matters it for one night?" So, as we are soon to be gone and the time of our departure is at hand, let us not be ruffling our tempers about trifles, nor raise evil spirits around us by caviling and finding fault. Take things as you find them, for we shall soon be up and away.

And if the time of my departure is at hand, I should like to be on good terms with all my friends on earth. Were you going to stop here always, when a man treated you badly, apart from a Christian spirit, you might as well have it out with him; but as we are going to stop such a little while, we may well put up with it. It is not desirable to be too ready at taking an offense. What if my neighbor has an ugly temper, the Lord has to put up with him, and so I may. There are some people with whom I would rather dwell in heaven forever than abide with them half an hour on earth. Nevertheless, for the love of the brethren, and for the peace of the church, we may tolerate much during the short time we have to brook with peevish moods and perverse humors. Does Christ love them, and shall not we? He covers their offenses; why, then, should we disclose them or publish them abroad? If any of you have any grievances with one another, if there is any bickering or jealousy between you, I should like you to make it up tonight, because the time of your departure is at hand.

Suppose there is someone you spoke harshly to, you would not like to hear tomorrow that he was dead. You would not have minded what you said to him if he had lived, but now that the seal is set upon all your communications one with another, you could wish that the last impress had been more friendly. There has been a little difference between two brothers—a little coldness between two sisters. Oh, since one or other of you will soon be gone, make it up! Live in love, as Christ loved you and gave himself for you. If one of you were going to Australia tomorrow, never to come back again, and you had had a little tiff with your brother, why, I know before you started, you would say, "Come, brother, let us part good friends." So now, since you are so soon to depart, end all strife, and dwell together in blessed harmony till the departure actually occurs.

If the time of my departure is at hand, then let me guard against being elated by any temporal prosperity. Possessions, estates, creature comforts dwindle into insignificance before this outlook. Yes, you may have procured a comfortable house and a delightful garden, but it is not your rest: your tenure is about to expire. Yes, you may say, "God did prosper me last year, the bank account did swell, the premises were enlarged, and the business thrived beyond all expectation." Ah! hold them loose. Do not think that they are to be your heaven. Be very jealous lest you should get your good things here, for if you do you will not have them hereafter. Be not lifted up too much when you grasp the pain, of which you must so soon quit your hold. As I said of the discomfort of the hotel, we did not think much of it, because we were going away. So, if it happens to be very luxurious, do not be enamored of it, for you must go tomorrow. "These are the things," said one, when he looked at a rich man's treasures, "that make it hard to die." But it need not be so if you hold them as gifts of God's kindness, and not as gods to be worshiped with self-indulgence. You may take leave of them with composure, "knowing in yourselves that you have in heaven a better and an enduring substance."

Last, if the time of our departure is at hand, let us be prepared to bear our testimony. We are witnesses for Christ. Let us bear our testimony before we are taken up and mingle with the cloud of witnesses who have finished their course and rested from their labors. Do you say, "I hope to do that on my dying bed"? Brother, do it now: do it now, for you may never have opportunity to do it then. Mr. Whitefield was always desirous that he might bear a testimony for Christ in the hour of death; but he could not do so at that momentous crisis, for as you well know, he was suddenly taken ill after preaching and very soon expired. Was this to be grievously deplored? Ah no. Why, dear friends, he had borne so many testimonies for his Lord and Master while he was alive, there was no need to add anything in the last few moments before his death, or to supply the deficiencies of a life devoted to the proclamation of the gospel. Oh, let you and me bear our testimony now! Let us tell to others wherever we can what Christ has done for us. Let us help Christ's cause with all our might while it is called today. Let us work for Jesus while we can work for him. As to thinking we can undo the effect of our idleness by the spasmodic effort of our dying breath, that were a vain hope indeed compared with living for Jesus Christ. Your dying testimony, if you are able to bear it, will have the greater force if it is not a sickly regret, but a healthy confirmation of your whole career.

I only wish these words about departure were applicable to all here. "Precious in the sight of the Lord is the death of his saints." But, "'As I live,' says the Lord God, 'I have no pleasure in the death of the wicked, but that the wicked turn from his ways, and live.'" O unconverted man, the time for letting loose your cable draws nigh; it is even at the door. You must shortly set sail for a far country. Alas, then yours is not the voyage of a passenger, with a sweeter clime, a happier home, a brighter prospect in view. Your departure is the banishment of a convict, with a penal settlement looming in the distance; fear all rife and hope all blank, for the term of your banishment is interminable. I fear there are some of you who may depart before long full of gloom with a fearful looking for of judgment and of fiery indignation. I seem to see the angel of death hovering over my audience. He may, perhaps, select for his victim an unconverted soul. If so, behind that death angel attends there something far more grim. Hell follows death to souls that love not Christ. Oh, make haste, make haste! Seek Christ. Lay hold on eternal life; and may infinite mercy save you, for Jesus Christ's sake. Amen and amen.

A Precious Promise for a Pure People

Published on Thursday, December 14, 1916, at the Metropolitan Tabernacle, Newington. No. 3542.

Thine eyes shall see the king in his beauty. —ISAIAH 33:17

No doubt these words originally had a timely and strictly literal meaning for the people of Jerusalem. When the city was besieged by Sennacherib, the inhabitants saw Hezekiah in garb of mourning. How had he rent his clothes in sorrow! But the day would come, according to prophecy, when Sennacherib must fall. Those who counted the resources and estimated the strength or the weakness of the city would be far away; and then there would be times of liberty. The people would be able to travel to the utmost ends of Palestine, so they would see the land that is very far off. Hezekiah himself would come out in his robes of excellency and majesty on a joyful occasion to praise the Lord, and thus would the people's eyes see the king in his beauty.

The passage, however, has been frequently used with quite another import, and that properly enough if it be thoroughly understood that it is by way of accommodation we take it, and that it is typically we trace it out. Have we not by faith seen our King in his robes of mourning? Have we not seen Jesus in the sorrowful weeds of affliction and humiliation while here below? Our faith has gazed upon him in the rent garments of his passion. We have beheld him in his agony and bloody sweat, in his crucifixion and his death. Well, now, another and a brighter view awaits us. Our eyes shall one day see the King in a more glorious array. We shall behold him as John saw him on Patmos. We shall behold the King in his beauty, and then we shall enter and enjoy the land which is at present very far off.

I think it meet and right to take such a word as this tonight when there are so many in our midst who are seeking and finding the Savior; because it is very certain that not long after their conversion they will have to encounter some of the difficulties of the way. Sometimes within a few hours of their starting on pilgrimage, they are met by some of the dragons, or they fall into some Slough of Despond, or they are surprised by some Hill Difficulty; therefore, they ought to be stimulated with encouragements; they need to be cheered and consoled by the prospect which lies before them. You will recol-

lect how Christian is represented by Bunyan in his famous allegory to be reading in his book as he went along concerning the blessed country, the celestial
land where their eyes should behold the King in his beauty, and this beguiled
the roughness of the road, and made the pilgrim hasten on with more alacrity
and less weariness.

Now I am going to turn over one of the elementary pages of this book. I
want to show the young convert a vision pleasing and profitable for all Christians, young or old, the glory that awaits him, the rest which is secured by the
promise of God to every pilgrim who continues in the blessed road and holds
on and holds out to the end. Your eyes, beloved, you who have lately been converted to God, if by divine grace your conversion prove genuine, your eyes
shall one day behold the King in his beauty. This may well inspire you with
courage and dispose you to endure with patience all the difficulties of the way.
When God brought his servant Abraham into the separated position of a
stranger in a strange land, it was not long before he said to him, "Lift up now
thine eyes, and look to the north, and to the south, and to the east, and to the
west, for all this land will I give to thee and to thy seed forever," as if to solace
and cheer him in the place of his sojourn by the picture and the promise that
greeted him. In like manner, you children of faithful Abraham, you who have
left all for Christ's sake, look upon your future heritage from the spot of your
present exile, and your hearts will exceedingly rejoice.

We shall notice, first, *the object to be seen*—the King in his beauty! Then,
second, *the nature of this vision,* for our eyes shall see the admirable spectacle;
and, third, we shall draw your attention to *those to whom this favor will be
granted.* The context will help us to discover of whom it is the Lord speaks
when he says, "Thine eyes shall see the king in his beauty." Not all eyes, but
your eyes shall see the King in his beauty. What is this vision which is here
promised to God's people? They are to see the King.

1. They are to see *the King in his beauty.*

The King—a sweet title which belongs to our Lord Jesus Christ as his
exclusive prerogative, crowned with the thorn crown once, but now wearing
the diadem of universal monarchy. Other kings there are, but theirs is only a
temporary title to temporal precedence among the sons of men. I had almost
said theirs was a mimic sovereignty. He is the real King—the King of kings—
the King that reigns forever and forever. He is King, for he is God. Jehovah
reigns. The Maker of the earth must be her King. He in whose hands are the
deep places of the earth, and the strength of the hills; he by whom all things
exist and all things consist; he must of necessity reign. The government shall

be upon his shoulders. His name shall be called Wonderful, Counselor, the mighty God. From the very fact that he is the Son of God, the express image of his Father's glory, he must be King. Because he condescended to veil himself in our flesh, he derives a second title to the kingdom—he is King now by his merits. "Wherefore God also has highly exalted him, and given him a name which is above every name, that at the name of Jesus every knee should bow, of things in heaven, and things in earth, and things under the earth." For the suffering of death, he was made for a little while lower than the angels; but now, seeing he has been obedient even unto death, even the death of the cross, he has obtained a more excellent name than the angels, and he is crowned with glory and honor.

He is Head over all things now. In him dwells all the fullness of the Godhead bodily. We rejoice to reflect upon him as King by nature, and then as King by due desert over a kingdom which he has inherited by right divine. He is King at this time by virtue of the conquests he has made, having spoiled the principalities and powers of darkness. In this world he fought the battle, and so bravely did he fight it out that he could say, "It is finished." He made an end of sin; he made reconciliation for iniquity; he trampled death and hell beneath his feet, and now he is King by force of arms. He entered into the strong man's house, wrestled with him, and vanquished him, for he is stronger than he; he has led captivity captive, and he has ascended upon high—King of kings and Lord of lords. He reigns supremely, moreover, in some of our hearts. We have yielded to the sway of his love. We rejoice to crown him. We never feel happier than when our hearts and tongues are singing—

> *Bring forth the royal diadem*
> *And crown him Lord of all.*

I trust there are many more among you who have not yet yielded that yet yield your hearts to his power. Fresh provinces shall be added to his empire; new cities of Mansoul will open their gates that the Prince Emmanuel may ride in, and may sit in triumph there. Oh! that it may be so, for a multitude that no man can number shall cheerfully, joyfully own his sway, and kiss the Son lest he be angry. But mark, the limit of his power is not according to the will of man, for where he does not reign by the joyful consent of his people and the mighty conquest of his love, he still exercises absolute dominion. Even the wicked are his servants. They shall be made in some way or other to subserve his glory, for he must reign till he has put all enemies under his feet. Why do the heathen rage, and the people imagine a vain thing? The King is anointed upon God's holy hill of Zion. King he is. He has a bit in the mouth of his most violent adversaries, and he turns them about according to his own will. What though with mingled cruelty and rage men attack the gospel of Christ, they strive in vain to thwart the divine decree. In ways mysterious and unknown to us, the Lord asserts his own supremacy. He reigns even where the rulers conspire, and the people rebel against him.

Beloved, the sovereignty of our Lord Jesus Christ, to which he is entitled by inheritance, is due to him for his merits and in the equitable claim of his conquests—this reign of Christ extends over all things. He is the universal Lord. In this world he is regent everywhere. By him all things exist and consist. When I think of him, it seems to me that the sea roars to his praise, and the trees of the wood rejoice in his presence. There is not a dewdrop that twinkles on the flower at sunrise but reflects his bounty; there is not an avalanche that falls from its alp with thundering crash but resounds with tokens of his power. The great Shepherd reigns. The Lord is King. As Joseph was made ruler over all the land of Egypt, even so, according unto the word of Jesus, all the people are ruled. He has all things put under his feet; for it was of him the prophet sang of old, "Thou hast made him a little"—(or as the margin has it, a little while)—"lower than the angels, and hast crowned him with glory and honor; thou hast put all things under his feet, all sheep and oxen, yea, and the beasts of the field; the fowl of the air, and the fish of the sea, and whatsoever passeth through the paths of the seas." Though we see not yet all things put under man, yet we see Jesus, who, for the suffering of death, was made, for a little while, lower than the angels, crowned with glory and honor. At this hour he rules on earth. Death and hell are under his scepter. Satan, and the spirits that have followed his leadership, bite their iron bonds while they confess the power of the Lord divine to be paramount. He can crush his enemies and break them with a rod of iron as a potter's vessel. His mighty power is felt and feared.

But oh! yonder, up in heaven, where the full beams of his glory are unveiled, he reigns in matchless splendor. The angels worshiped him when he was brought forth as the only begotten into the world. So spoke the oracle, "Let all the angels of God worship him." Seraphim and cherubim, are they not his messengers? He makes them like flames of fire. The redeemed by blood, what could they do? What is their joy, their occupation, their delight, but to sing forever, "Worthy is the Lamb that was slain to receive honor, and glory, and dominion, and power"? Oh! tell us not of emperors; there is but one imperial brow! Tell us not of monarchs, for the crown belongs to the blessed and only potentate. He alone is King. As such, we think of him and long for his appearing, when we shall hail him the King in his beauty. I love to see his courtiers. That is a happy hour in which I can talk with one who has my Master's ear. I love to see the skirts of his garment as I come in fellowship with him to his table. I love to tread his courts; I love to hear his voice, even though I cannot yet see the face of him that speaks with me. But to see the King—to see the King himself! Oh! joy unspeakable! It is worth worlds even to have a good hope of beholding a sight so resplendent with glory.

Note well the promise, "Thine eyes shall see the king in his *beauty.*" Does not this suggest to us that the King has been seen, though not in his beauty? He was seen on earth as the prophet foretold, "despised and rejected of men, a man of sorrows, and acquainted with grief." And as seen then, we are told there is no beauty that we should desire him. There was a time when many were astonished at him. His visage was more marred than any man and his form more than the sons of men; that was in the day of his humiliation.

But we are yet to see the King in his beauty, and I know, beloved, that in part that vision does beam, even now, upon spirits before the throne. I would not exactly say that they have eyes, for they have left these organs of sense behind them. They have not received the fullness of this promise, yet in a measure they see the beauty of the King, that beauty which his Father has put upon him now that he has ascended up on high and returned to the Father, having obeyed all his precepts and fulfilled all his will. His father has already rewarded him. He sits enthroned on the right hand of the Majesty on high; he is adored and worshiped. It is no small sight for our disimprisoned spirits to behold him and adore. But remember the spirits in heaven, without us, cannot be made perfect, so says the apostle. They are waiting for the adoption—to wit, the redemption of the body—waiting for the trumpet of resurrection. It is then, I think, that this blessed hope will be fully verified, "Thine eyes shall see the king in his beauty." As Job puts it, "I know that my Redeemer liveth, and that he shall stand at the latter day upon the earth; and though, after my skin worms destroy this body, yet in my flesh shall I see God, whom I shall see for myself, and mine eyes shall behold, and not another." Our bodies shall be raised from the dead.

> *These eyes shall see him in that day,*
> *The God that died for me;*
> *And all my rising bones shall say—*
> *Lord, who is like to thee?*

From the dark chambers of the grave, we shall come forth with all the blood-bought company of the faithful. Then we shall see the King in his beauty. What beauty that will be! We steadfastly look for his appearing when he shall come the second time. This personal manifestation must be welcome to the saints. To see him then must be to see his beauty. Our senses, relieved of infirmity, will be endowed with full capacity, our graces being increased and our spirits lively and vigorous to appreciate his wonderful person. As God and Man we do now believe in him; but how little can our faith anticipate the vision! We acknowledge the mystery which is as yet unveiled. How little are we affected by the wonderful information which must astonish angels—that the infinite can be joined with the finite, that the Godhead can be in perfect union with the manhood, the bush of the manhood burning with the glow of the Godhead, yet not thereby consumed. 'Tis matchless that the Eternal should link himself with finite flesh; that he should hang upon his mother's breast, who bears up the columns of the universe. Strange conjunction! Till we wake up in his likeness, we shall never thoroughly understand it. Oh! how amazement will resolve itself into admiration as we gaze upon him who has a nature that we have been familiar with, the proper divinity which no man has seen or can see! What grandeur to behold! What rapture to experience when our eyes see the King in his beauty! The sight will overwhelm us.

But in other respects than that which is essential to his kingly dignity, the spectacle will be illustrious. In the hour of conquest he will take possession of a throne which no rival dare dispute. Judas will be there, but he will not think of betraying him. Pilate will be there, but he will not think of questioning him. The Jews will be there, but they will not cry, "Crucify him." The Romans will be there, but they will not think of hauling him away to execution. His enemies in that day shall lick the dust. They shall be like chaff before the whirlwind in the day of his coming. And what will be the splendor of his glory when he shall be proclaimed King of kings in his beauty, with all the insignia of his royal power!

He will have the beauty of state pageant too, for he will assume office as Judge of quick and dead. Then will the trumpet sound, and all the solemn pomp of the great assize will encircle him round about. The vivid lightning will flash through the universe, and the roar of his thunder shall awake the dead, while an irresistible summons shall compel them to appear before his dread tribunal. From his searching gaze no creature shall be hid, and every eye shall see him. They also that pierced him, and all the kindreds of the earth, shall weep and wail because of him. But to us that awful pomp will not be appalling, but a fit accessory on which his royal beauty is displayed. We shall admire the hand that holds the scepter, for we shall recognize it as the same hand that was once pierced for us. We shall admire the voice that condemns the wicked and bids them, "Depart!," for that voice shall pronounce our welcome, saying, "Come, you blessed." We shall admire the Shepherd's crook with which he shall separate the sheep and the goats, for it will apportion us to eternal bliss, though it shall dismiss the goats to their eternal doom. Thrice happy and most blessed shall we be in that day. Terror and trouble shall be the lot of the world; trust and triumph shall then be the portion of the saints. He shall be admired in all them that believed; and when that final judgment shall have fulfilled its destined purpose, he shall be in his beauty seen as the conqueror of all evil, the conqueror of sin, of death, and hell. The last enemy that shall be destroyed is death. How shall we see him in his beauty when death itself shall die!

I cannot attempt to describe that beauty. It is far too dazzling for me to picture. I have dreamed of it sometimes in sacred soliloquies. My faith has tried to realize the facts which are revealed unto us by his Spirit. Still the tongue cannot tell so much as the heart has conceived. There are unspeakable words which greet us in seasons of rapture which it is not lawful to utter. Whenever we are caught up to the third heaven in rapturous meditation, we have but small news to tell to men. But how inconceivable to us now is the glory of Christ as it shall be when all his people are present with him in heaven!

I have not touched upon the millennial age or the latter-day glory. Your thoughts can fill up the vacancy. But what will be the beauty of Christ in heaven in that day "when he shall make up his jewels"! What are the jewels of our King but his redeemed people? What will be the ornaments of his state but those for whom he shed his blood? And when they are all there, then we shall see the King in his beauty with all his jewels. Beauty! A shepherd's beauty lies much in his simple garb; a mother's beauty—very much of it is to be seen as she appears in the center of a happy and lovely family. So, beyond all doubt, the beauty of Christ will be most conspicuous when all his saints are with him. I was in company with some good people lately, who were discussing the question whether we should see the saints in heaven. I do not know whether they settled the question to their satisfaction, but I settled it very well to mine. I expect to see and know all the saints, to recognize them, and rejoice with them, and that without the slightest prejudice to my being wholly absorbed in the sight of my Lord. Let me explain to you how this can be. When I went the other day into a friend's drawing room, I observed that on all sides there were mirrors. The whole of the walls were covered with glass, and everywhere I looked I kept seeing my friend. It was not necessary that I should fix my eyes upon him, for all the mirrors reflected him. Thus, brethren, it seems to me that every saint in heaven will be a mirror of Christ, and that as we look upon all the loved ones, gazing round upon them all, we shall see Christ in every one of them; so we shall still be seeing the Master in the servants, seeing the head in all the members. It is I in them, and they in me. Is it not so? It will be all the Master. This is the sum total of heaven. "Thine eyes shall see the king in his beauty," and they shall see the beauty of the King in all his people. Nor does it appear that the manifestation shall be ever withdrawn, or that we shall ever leave off seeing the beauty of our King. There is the mercy. "Thine eyes shall see the king in his beauty," on and on, and on still, and on, forever on, discerning more and more of the beauty, the inexhaustible beauty and splendor of the Sun of righteousness world without end. The theme grows upon us. We must curb ourselves. We can but skim the surface as the swallow does the brook.

2. Now, as to *the nature of this vision,* we know it is in the future.

"Thine eyes *shall* see the king in his beauty." You poor sinners must be content with seeing the King in his majesty. Happy souls who come to see Jesus on the cross! Oh! it is joy for them to look unto him and be saved! Behold the Lamb of God—behold the Lamb slain from the foundation of the world. Poor sin-sick soul, are you looking to Jesus to be saved? If it be so in the present, then in the future you shall see him in his beauty. It will be a vision for all. Their natural sense shall discern the real Savior, "Thine eyes shall see the king in his beauty." It is not merely your spiritual perception, but your natural eyes. Does not Job express this conviction, "whom mine eyes shall see"? Oh yes! not as it now is with this flesh and blood, but still with this body! I call you a vile body sometimes, my poor flesh and blood, and so you are. Yet in your origin there was something good, and in your destiny there is something better, "Bone of thy bone, and flesh of thy flesh." Born of a woman as you were and fed on bread as you must be, and though the worms devour you, yet shall you rise again. Oh body! you are even now the temple of God. Know you not that your *bodies* are the members of Christ? Know you not that your body is the temple of the Holy Ghost? These eyes shall see him. They may be weeping eyes, aching eyes, weary eyes, and sleepy eyes, yes, or even blind eyes, or your failing eyes on which the curtain is being drawn about you—your eyes shall see the King. When heaven is in sight there will be no need for glasses to assist your vision. Your eyes all strengthened to bear the light, as the eagle's eye, when the sun shines in his strength—"Thine eyes shall see the King in his beauty."

It will be a personal vision. "Whom mine eyes shall see, and not another." It shall not be somebody else repeating another's testimony, "Yes, I see him." I like to hear what John saw, but I like better to have John's privilege; we shall be like John, and shall ourselves behold him. Can you realize it? You recollect in Bunyan's *Pilgrim's Progress* how Mercy laughed in her sleep, and Christiana asked her what made her laugh so. Mercy replied that she had seen a beautiful vision. Is it not enough to make us laugh in our sleep, to think that "thine eyes shall see the king in his beauty"? To think that this head shall wear a crown; that these hands shall grasp the palms; that these feet shall stand on the transfigured globe; that these ears shall hear the symphonies of eternity; and that this tongue shall help to swell the everlasting chorus. Oh! who would not rejoice? This is the wine which, as it goes down, makes the lips of him who drinks to speak. Oh! that we may all have a personal sight of the King in his beauty!

And *it will be a near sight,* because it will be clear and distinct. "Thine eyes shall see the king in his beauty." This does not imply a distant view of a remote object; a dim vision of the dazzling splendor; but you shall behold him in such close proximity that you can discern every feature of his person, every phase of his comeliness. You shall discern all the insignia of his offices, his conquests, his titles, his dominion, and his glory. Now you only see a picture of him reflected as in a glass darkly, then you shall see him face to face. Oh! that the curtain might be drawn up, the veil rent, the vision unfolded!

It will be a delightful sight. When he shall appear in his beauty, we cannot wear the vestments of our mourning and sorrow. As he is, so are we in this world. As he shall be revealed, so shall we be also in that world. "It doth not yet appear what we shall be, but we know that when he shall appear we shall be like him, for we shall see him as he is." Thus we shall be beautiful when we shall see him in his beauty. He shall say to us, "Thou art all fair, my love; there is not a spot in thee." Oh! the delight, the pure unclouded joy, reflective as the light of heaven. What an introduction to eternal felicity this will be when your eyes shall see the King in his beauty! There is no period, no finale, no end put to it.

This is no transient spectacle. His beauty never fades. Our festival can never terminate. Long as he appears in his beauty we shall see him, and be enamored of his loveliness. Is it not written, "Because I live, ye shall live also"? Without his people, without the complement of his saints with him, he would not be a full Christ at any time. "Know ye not that the church is the fullness of him who filleth all in all?" So all his disciples must be forever with him, and they must forever see his face and be partakers of his glory.

We find a remarkably full description of these people. Read the fifteenth verse [Isa. 33]. Their ordinary gait distinguishes them. *"He that walketh righteously."* "The pure in heart shall see God"; but if your deportment disgraces you, how deep will be your dishonor. Unholy creatures will never see a holy God. It is not possible. O sinners, what think you of this? You must be changed; you must be cleansed; you must be converted; the Holy Ghost must regenerate you; otherwise, you cannot walk uprightly or stand in the presence of the King in his beauty.

Next to this they are known by their tongues: *"and speaketh uprightly."* No liar shall enter into heaven. Those who talk lasciviously, those who swear profanely, the singers of idle songs, those who lend their lips to slander, backbite their neighbors, and circulate evil reports in malice—these and such as these can have no inheritance in the kingdom of God. Oh! may the Lord wash your tongues, rinse your mouths, and make them sweet and clean; else you will never sing the songs of heaven. "He that walketh righteously and speaketh uprightly" is so far approved.

But let him take heed to his commercial character; for it is further said, *"he that despiseth the gain of oppressions,"* or, as the margin has it, of deceit. A man that gets money by squeezing others, by oppressing the poor by hard bargains, shall not enjoy the beatific vision. If you buy and sell and get gain by lying, by false pretenses, by tricks of trade—yes, even by the customs that are commonly allowed, though they would look fraudulent if thoroughly exposed, you shall have no inheritance in the kingdom of God. How can you be gracious when you are not honest? He that is not able to hold the scales lightly, measure out an even yard, or make out a bill equitably, may well tremble at being poised in the balances of the sanctuary. When such as these are weighed, they will be found wanting. Thorough integrity must stand the test of disinterestedness.

"He that shaketh his hands from holding of bribes." Some men cannot help preferring coin to conscience. This is the way of bribery. Palm oil was largely used when Isaiah wrote. It is much in vogue still; perhaps not so much in this country as in others; but there are plenty of ways of receiving bribes besides selling one's vote at the polling booth. How many men are bribed by a smile or a crown—bribed to Sabbath breaking—bribed to the follies of the world—bribed to I know not what of error! But drop a shilling into a conscientious man's hand, and he shakes it from his hand; he does not like the touch of it; he is like Paul, who shook off the viper into the fire. So the man who is to see the King in his beauty shakes his hand from holding bribes.

Moreover, *"he stoppeth his ears from hearing of blood."* He does not like to hear of cruelty, of outrage, or wantonly causing pain. He stops his ears, he will not listen to any proposal either to gratify a resentment or to seek a personal advantage whereby his neighbor would be injured. In this wicked world it is often wise to stop one's ears. A deaf ear is a great blessing when there is base conversation in the neighborhood.

The good man who thus keeps guard over his hands and his feet, his tongue and his ears, is likewise known by his eyes. *"He shutteth his eyes from seeing evil."* He shuns the temptations to which a vain curiosity would expose him. Oh! if our mother Eve had shut her eyes when the serpent pointed out yon rosy apple on the tree! Oh! that she had shut her eyes to it! Oh! that she had said, "No, I will not even look at it." Looking leads to longing, and longing leads to sin. Do you say, "There can be no harm in looking, just to see for yourself; are we not told to prove all things?" "Just come here, young man," says the tempter; "you do not know what life is; one evening will suffice to show you a little gaiety, and let you see how the frolic is carried on. You need not share in it, you know. You may learn a thing or two you never dreamed of before. Surely a man is not to go through the world a baby. Just come for an hour or two and look on." "Ah no," says the man, whose eyes are to see the King in his beauty, "the tree of knowledge of good and evil never brought any man good yet, so please let me alone. I shut my eyes from the sight of it. I do not want to participate, even as a spectator. I do not care to look upon that which God will not look upon without abhorrence. I know that his love has put my sins behind his back; what, then, he puts behind his back shall I put before my face? That were ingratitude indeed!

Perhaps you say, "Well, if this is the character of such as shall see the King in his beauty, I shall never come up to the standard." "No, but you must, else you will never enjoy the beatific vision." "But I cannot convert myself after this fashion." I know you cannot, but there is One who can. Has not Jesus Christ come into the world to make us new creatures? It is his object and intent. "Behold, I make all things new." He changes a man, gives him new desires, new longings, and new hopes. And he can change you. Let me ask you, have you ever seen, by faith, the King? Have you ever looked to Jesus on the cross, and did you ever recognize that Jesus Christ, if he is to be your Savior, must be your King? You say you have believed in Jesus. Yes, but did you take him to be your King? Did you mean to obey him as well as to trust him? Did you intend to serve him as well as to lean upon him? Remember you cannot have a half of Christ. You cannot have him as your Redeemer, but not as your Ruler. You must take him as he is. He is a Savior, but he saves his people from their sins. Now, if you have ever seen Christ as your Savior, you have seen beauty in him; he is lovely in your eyes, for the loveliest sight in the world to a sinner is his Savior. "What is the latest news," said a certain squire to a companion, accustomed to hunt with him, who had come up to the metropolis—

"what is the latest news you have heard in London?" "The latest news, and the best news I have ever heard," was the quick reply, "is that Jesus Christ came into the world to save sinners." "Tom," says he, "I think you are mad." "William," said Tom, "I know you are. I only wish you were cured of your insanity as, by the grace of God, I have been." Oh! that we did but all of us know Jesus Christ in his beauty, and could, every one of us, rejoice in him, as those do that are charmed by the sight. If you have not your eyes opened, you cannot see the King in his beauty. But if they are opened now, so that you greet Jesus as your King and see beauty in him, then, whatever your former life may have been, its sins are forgiven—they are blotted out.

Your Savior's sacrifice, that offered such satisfaction to God for your sins, shall give sweet solace to your conscience. By the gracious help of the Holy Spirit, you shall start a fresh career and begin a new life. Be it so; and you will henceforth shut your eyes from seeing, stop your ears from hearing, shake your hands from all iniquity, and turn aside your feet from it, to live the life you live in the flesh by the faith of the Son of God, to his honor and glory. So shall your eyes, poor sinner—weeping, sorrowing, mournful eyes as they may now be—your eyes shall see the King in his beauty. The Lord grant that we, all of us, may have a present earnest and a future fruition of this delightful promise, for his name's sake. Amen.

The Earnest of Heaven

⮜꧑⮞

Delivered on Sunday morning, February 3, 1861, at Exeter Hall, Strand. No. 358.

That holy Spirit of promise, which is the earnest of our inheritance.
—EPHESIANS 1:13–14

So then, heaven, with all its glories, is an *inheritance*! Now, an inheritance is not a thing which is bought with money, earned by labor, or won by conquest. If any man has an inheritance, in the proper sense of that term, it came to him by birth. It was not because of any special merit in him, but simply because he was his father's son that he received the property of which he is now possessed. So is it with heaven. The man who shall receive this glorious heritage will not obtain it by the works of the law, nor by the efforts of the flesh; it will be given to him as a matter of most gracious right, because he has been "begotten again unto a lively hope, by the resurrection of Jesus Christ from the dead"; and has thus become an heir of heaven by blood and birth.

They who come unto glory are sons; for is it not written, "The captain of our salvation brings many sons unto glory"? They come not there as servants; no servant has any right to the inheritance of his master; let him be ever so faithful, yet he is not his master's heir. But because you are sons—sons by God's adoption, sons by the Spirit's regeneration—because by supernatural energy you have been born again—you become inheritors of eternal life, and you enter into the many mansions of our Father's house above. Let us always understand, then, when we think of heaven, that it is a place which is to be ours, and a state which we are to enjoy as the result of birth—not as the result of work. "Except a man be born again, he cannot see the kingdom of God," that kingdom being an inheritance, but until he has the new birth, he can have no claim to enter it.

But is it possible for us, provided that heaven be our inheritance, and we are God's sons—is it possible for us to know anything whatever of that land beyond the flood? Is there power in human intellect to fly into the land of the hereafter and reach those islands of the happy, where God's people rest in the bosom of their God eternally? We are met at the outset with a rebuff which staggers us. "Eye hath not seen, nor ear heard, neither hath entered into the heart of man, the things which God hath prepared for them that love him." If we paused here we might give up all idea of beholding from our houses of clay that goodly land and Lebanon, but we do not pause, for like the apostle, we go on with the text, and we add "But he hath revealed it unto us by his Spirit." It *is* possible to look within the veil; God's Spirit *can* turn it aside for a moment, and bid us take a glimpse, though it be but a distant one, at that unutterable glory. There are Pisgahs even now on the surface of the earth, from the top of which the celestial Canaan can be beheld; there are hallowed hours in which the mists and clouds are swept away, and the sun shines in his strength, and our eye, being freed from its natural dimness, beholds something of that land which is very far off, and sees a little of the joy and blessedness which is reserved for the people of God hereafter.

Our text tells us that the Holy Spirit is the earnest of the inheritance, by which I understand, that he is not only the pledge, for a pledge is given for security, but when the thing pledged is given, then the pledge itself is restored—but he is an earnest, which is a pledge and something more. An earnest is a part of the thing itself; it is not only a pledge of the thing, for security, but it is a foretaste of it for present enjoyment. The word in the Greek has a stronger force than our word "pledge." Again I repeat it: if I promise to pay to a man somewhat, I may give him land or property in pledge, but if instead thereof I pay him a part of the sum which I have promised, that is a pledge, but it is more—it is *an earnest*, because it is a part of the thing itself. So the Holy Spirit is a pledge to God's people. Inasmuch as God has given them the graces of the Spirit, he will give them the glory that results therefrom.

But he is more: he is a foretaste—he is a sweet antepast of heaven, so that they who possess the Spirit of God possess the first tastes of heaven; they have reaped the firstfruits of the eternal harvest; the first drops of a shower of glory have fallen upon them; they have beheld the first beams of the rising sun of eternal bliss; they have not merely a pledge for security—they have an earnest, which is security and foretaste combined. Understand, then, for this is what I am about to speak of this morning: by the Holy Spirit there is given to the people of God even now, experiences, joys, and feelings, which prove that they shall be in heaven—which do more, which *bring heaven down to them, and make them already able to guess in some measure what heaven must be.* When I have enlarged upon that theme, I shall take the black side of the picture, and remark that *it is possible for men on earth to have both a pledge and an earnest of those eternal pains which are reserved for the impenitent:* a dark subject, but may God grant it may be for our profit and arousing.

1. First, then, *there are some works of the Spirit which are peculiarly an earnest to the child of God, of the blessings of heaven.*

And, first, *heaven is a state of rest.* It may be because I am constitutionally idle, that I look upon heaven in the aspect of rest with greater delight than under any other view of it, with but one exception. To let the head which is so continually exercised, for once lie still—to have no care, no trouble, no need to labor, to strain the intellect, or vex the limbs! I know that many of you, the sons of poverty and of toil, look forward to the Sabbath day, because of the enjoyments of the sanctuary, and because of the rest which it affords you. You look for heaven as Watts did in his song:

> There shall I bathe my weary soul
> In seas of heavenly rest,
> And not a wave of trouble roll
> Across my peaceful breast.

"There remains therefore a rest to the people of God." 'Tis not a rest of sleep, but yet a rest as perfect as though they slept; it is a rest which puts from them all carking [burdensome] care, all harrowing remorse, all thoughts of tomorrow, all straining after a something which they have not as yet. They are runners no more—they have reached the goal; they are warriors no more—they have achieved the victory; they are laborers no more—they have reaped the harvest. "'They rest,' saith the Spirit, 'they rest from their labors, and their works do follow them.'" My beloved, did you ever enjoy on certain high days of your experience, a state of perfect rest? You could say you had not a wish in all the world ungratified; you knew yourself to be pardoned, you felt yourself to be an heir of heaven, Christ was precious to you; you knew that you walked in the light of your Father's countenance; you had cast all your worldly care on him, for he cared for you. You felt at that hour that if death could smite away your dearest friends, or if calamity should remove the most valuable part of your possessions on earth, yet you could say, "The Lord gave, and the Lord hath taken away, blessed be the name of the Lord." Your spirit floated along the stream of grace without a struggle; you were not as the swimmer, who breasts the billows and tugs and toils for life. Your soul was made to lie down in green pastures, beside the still waters. You were passive in God's hands; you knew no will but his. Oh! that sweet day!

> That heavenly calm within the breast,
> Was the sure pledge of glorious rest,

Which for the church of God remains,
The end of cares, the end of pains.

No, it was more than a pledge; it was a part of the rest itself. It was a morsel taken from the loaf of delights; it was a sip out of the wine vats of immortal joy; it was silver spray from the waves of glory. So, then, whenever we are quiet and at peace—"For we which have believed do enter into rest," and have ceased from our own works, as God did from his—when we can say, "O God, my heart is fixed, my heart is fixed; I will sing and give praise"—when our spirit is full of love within us, and our peace is like a river, and our righteousness like the wave of the sea—then we already know, in some degree, what heaven is. We have but to make that peace deeper, and yet more profound, lasting, and more continual; we have but to multiply it eternally, and we have obtained a noble idea of the rest which remains for the people of God.

But, second, there is a passage in the book of Revelation which may sometimes puzzle the uninstructed reader, where it is said concerning the angels that "they rest not day and night," and as we are to be as the angels of God, it must undoubtedly be true in heaven, that in a certain sense, they rest not day nor night. They always rest, so far as ease and freedom from care is concerned; they never rest, in the sense of indolence or inactivity. In heaven, spirits are always on the wing; their lips are always singing the eternal *hallelu-jahs* unto the great *Jehovah* that sits upon the throne; their fingers are never divorced from the strings of their golden harps; their feet never cease to run in obedience to the eternal will; they rest, but they rest on the wing; as the poet pictured the angel as he flew—not needing to move his wings, but resting, and yet darting swiftly through the ether, as though he were a flash shot from the eye of God.

So shall it be with the people of God eternally, ever singing—never hoarse with music; ever serving—never wearied with their service. "They rest not day and night." Have there never been times with you, when you have had both the pledge and the earnest of this kind of heaven? Yes, when we have preached once, and again and again and again, in one day, and some have said, "But the constitution will be destroyed, the mind will be weakened, such toil as this will bring the man low." But we have been able to reply, "We do not feel it; for the more toil has been cast upon us, the more strength has been given." Have you ever known what it is to have the pastor's work in revival times, when he has to sit hour after hour, seeing convert after convert—when the time for one meal is past, and he has forgotten it, and the time for another meal has come and gone, and he has forgotten that, for he has been so busy and so happy with his feast of ingatherings, that he has been like his Master, and has forgotten to eat bread, and positively did not hunger and did not thirst, because the joy of the service had taken away all fatigue?

Just at this hour, our missionaries are engaged throughout Jamaica, in a sweltering sun, preaching the Word. Perhaps there has never been a more glorious revival than that which God has sent to that island—an island which has often been blessed, but which now seems to have received a sevenfold portion. One missionary, in writing home, says that he had not been in bed one night for a week, and he had been preaching all day and all night long; and I do not doubt but his testimony to you would be, that, at least during the first part of the labor, it seemed not to be labor. He could sleep on the wing; he could rest while he worked; the joy of success took away from him the feeling of lassitude; the blessed prospect of seeing so many added to the church of God had made him forget even to eat bread. Well, then, at such a time as that, he had a foretaste of the rest, and the service too, which remains for the people of God. Oh, do not doubt, if you find comfort in serving God—and such comfort that you grow not weary in his service—do not doubt, I say, but that you shall soon join that hallowed throng, who "day without night circle his throne rejoicing," who rest not, but serve him day and night in his temple! These feelings are foretastes, and they are pledges too. They give some inklings of what heaven must be, and they make your title to heaven clear.

But let us pass on. Heaven is a place of *communion* with all the people of God. I am sure that in heaven they know each other. I could not perhaps just now prove it in so many words, but I feel that a heaven of people who did not know each other, and had no fellowship, could not be heaven because God has so constituted the human heart that it loves society, and especially the renewed heart is so made that it cannot help communing with all the people of God. I always say to my Strict Baptist brethren who think it a dreadful thing for baptized believers to commune with the unbaptized, "But you cannot help it. If you are the people of God, you must commune with all saints, baptized or not. You may deny them the outward and visible sign, but you cannot keep from them the inward and spiritual grace." If a man be a child of God, I do not care what I may think about him—if I be a child of God, I *do* commune with him, and I must, for we are all parts of the same body, all knit to Christ, and it is not possible that one part of Christ's body should ever be in any state but that of communion with all the rest of the body. Well, in glory I feel I may say we know we shall converse with each other. We shall talk of our trials on the way there—talk most of all of him who by his faithful love and his potent arm has brought us safely through. We shall not sing solos, but in chorus shall we praise our King. We shall not look upon our fellows there like men in the iron mask, whose name and character we do not know; for there we shall know even as we are known. You shall talk with the prophets, you shall have conversation with the martyrs, you shall sit again at the feet of the great reformers and all your brethren in faith who have fallen before you, or who have rather entered into rest before; these shall be your companions on the other side the grave. How sweet must that be! How blessed—that holy converse, that happy union, that general assembly and church of the Firstborn whose names are written in heaven!

Have we anything on earth like this? Yes, that we have, in miniature. We have the pledge of this; for if we love the people of God, we may know that we shall surely be with them in heaven. We have the *earnest* of it; for how often has it been our privilege to hold the highest and sweetest fellowship with our fellow Christians? Why, you and I have often said, "Did not our hearts burn within us, while we talked together by the way, and Christ was with us both?" When we have been together and the doors have been shut, has not the Master said, "Peace be unto you"? When love has gone from heart to heart, and we have all felt knit together as one man, when party names were all forgotten, when all jealousies and bickerings were driven out of doors, and we felt that we were one family, and all did bear the same one name, having "one Lord, one faith, and one baptism," then it was that we had the earnest, the foretaste, the first drinking of that well of Bethlehem which is on the other side the pearly gate of the Celestial City.

I have to be brief on each of these points, for there are so many to mention. Part of the bliss of heaven will consist *in joy over sinners saved*. The angels look down from the battlements of the city which has foundations, and when they see prodigals return they sing. Jesus calls together his friends and his neighbors, and he says unto them, "Rejoice with me, for I have found the sheep which was lost." The angels begin the theme; the sacred fire runs through the host, and all the saints above take up the strain. Hark, how they sing before the throne, for it has just been whispered there of some Saul, "Behold, he prays!" Hark how their songs get a new inspiration—how their eternal Sabbath seems to be sabbatized afresh, and "the rest" becomes more joyous far, while they sing of newborn sons added to the family, and new names written in the register of the church below!

Part of the joy of heaven, and no mean part of it, will be to watch the fight on earth, to see the conqueror as he marches on, and to behold the trophies of his grace, and the spoils which his hands shall win. Is there anything like this on earth? Yes, that there is, when the Spirit of God gives to *us joy* over sinners saved. The other evening, when some of us sat in church meeting, what joy was there, when one after another, those who had been plucked from the deepest hell of sin made avowal of their faith in Christ! Some of us look back upon those church meetings as the gladdest nights we ever spent; when first one and then another has said, "*I* have been plucked as a brand from the burning," and the tale of grace has been told; and a third has stood up and said, "And I, too, was once a strange wandering far from God, and Jesus sought me." Why, we have some of us gone home and felt that it was heaven below to have been there. We have felt more joy over the conversion of others, we have sometimes thought, than even over our own. It has been such bliss while we have taken the hand of the convert, and the tear has been in both eyes, when the word of gratitude has been spoken, and Jesus Christ has been magnified by lips that once blasphemed him.

My brothers and sisters, though the whole world should censure me, I cannot help it; I must tell it, to the praise of God's free grace and boundless love. There are hundreds here that are the most wonderful trophies of grace that ever lived on earth. My heart has been gladdened, and your hearts have been gladdened too. I must not keep it back; I *will* not. It was my Master's work, it is to his honor, it is to his praise. We will tell *that* on earth which we will sing in heaven. They *have* washed their robes and made them white in the blood of the Lamb; and I do believe that the joy we felt when sinners have been converted has been an earnest and a pledge that we shall be partakers of the like joy in heaven.

But to proceed. Here is another earnest of heaven, which is rather a personal matter than one which is drawn from others. Did you ever get a knotty passage in Scripture which repeated itself in your mind so many times that you could not get rid of it? You borrowed some commentaries; you opened them, and you found that you might inquire within, but get no information whatever upon the particular subject you wished most to be informed about. Commentaries generally are books which are written to explain those parts of Scripture which everybody understands, and to make these that are dark more mysterious than they were before. At any rate, if that was the aim of the different authors, they have most of them admirably succeeded. I do not believe in great commentaries upon the whole Bible; no one man can write such a book so that all of it shall be valuable. When a man gives his whole lifetime to some one book, that one is worth reading. When a man has taken up, as some have done, the Epistle to the Romans, or the book of Genesis, and gone on year after year toiling through it, then such a book has been a monument of labor, and has been valuable to the Christian student, but, generally, large commentaries give little information where most it is needed. Well, disappointed, you have gone back to your Bible, and have said, "I must not meddle with this text, it is above me." But it has repeated itself in your ears; you could not make it out; it has followed you—dogged your steps—it would not go away from you. At last you thought, "There was a message from God in that text to you." You prayed over it; while you were praying, some one word in the text seemed to lift itself right out of the connection and shone upon you like a star, and in the light of that one word you could see the meaning of all the words that preceded and followed, and you rose up from your knees, feeling that you knew the mind of the Spirit there, and had got a step forward in scriptural knowledge.

You remember the day, some of you, when you first learned the doctrines of grace. When we were first converted, we did not know much about them. We did not know whether God had converted us, or we had converted ourselves, but we heard a discourse one day in which some sentences were used, which gave us the clue to the whole system, and we began at once to see how God the Father planned, and God the Son carried out, and God the Holy Spirit applied, and we found ourselves on a sudden brought into the midst of a system of truths, which we might perhaps have believed before, but which we could not have clearly stated and did not understand. Well, the joy of that advance in knowledge was exceedingly great. I know it was to me. I can remember well the day and hour when first I received those truths in my own soul—when they were burned into me, as John Bunyan says—burned as with a hot iron into my soul; and I can recollect how I felt I had grown on a sudden from a babe into a man—that I had made progress in scriptural knowledge, from having got a hold once for all of the clue to the truth of God. Well, now, in that moment when God the Holy Spirit increased your knowledge and opened the eyes off your understanding, you had the earnest that you shall one day see, not through a glass darkly, but face to face, and by and by you shall know the whole truth, even as you are known.

But further than this—to put two or three thoughts into one, for brevity's sake: whenever, Christian, you have achieved a victory over your lusts—whenever after hard struggling you have laid a temptation dead at your feet—you have had in that day and hour a foretaste of the joy that awaits you, when the Lord shall shortly tread Satan under your feet. That victory in the first skirmish is the pledge and the earnest of the triumph in the last decisive battle. If you have overcome *one* foe, you shall overthrow them all. If the walls of Jericho

have been dismantled, so shall every fort be carried, and you shall go up a conqueror over the ruins thereof; and when, believer, you have known your security in Christ—when you have been able to say, "I *know* that my Redeemer
lives, and I am persuaded that he is able to keep that which I have committed
to him"—when you felt sure that earth and heaven might reel, but *his* love
could never pass away—when you have sung out the strong lines of Toplady,

> *My name from the palms of his hands*
> *Eternity will not erase;*
> *Impress'd on his heart it remains*
> *In marks of indelible grace;*

when you could put your foot upon a rock and feel that you stood securely,
knowing that you were safe in him, and because he lived, you must live also,
in that hour you had the pledge and the foretaste of that glorious security
which should be yours, when you are beyond gunshot of the infernal fiend,
beyond even the howling of the infernal dog. O Christian, there are many windows to heaven, through which God looks down on you; and there are some
windows through which you may look up to him. Let these *past* enjoyments
be guarantees of your future bliss, let them be to you as the grapes of Eshcol
were to the Jews in the wilderness; they were the fruit of the land, and when
they tasted them, they said, "It *is* a land that flows with milk and honey."
These enjoyments are the products of Canaan; they are handfuls of heavenly
flowers thrown over the wall; they are bunches of heaven's spices, brought to
times by angel hands across the stream. Heaven is full of joys like these. You
have but a few of them; heaven is shown with them. There your golden joys
are but as stones, and your most precious jewels are as common as the pebbles
of the brook. *Now* you drink drops and they are so sweet that your palate does
not soon forget them; but there you shall put your lips to the cup and drink
but never drain it dry; there you shall sit at the wellhead and drink as much as
you can draw and draw as much as you can desire. Now you see the glim-
merings of heaven as a star twinkling from leagues of distance. Follow that
glimmering and you shall see heaven no more as a star, but as the sun which
shines in its strength.

Permit me to remark yet once more, there is one foretaste of heaven
which the Spirit gives, which it were very wrong for us to omit. And now, I
shall seem, I dare say, to those who understand not spiritual mysteries, to be
as one that dreams. There are moments when the child of God has real fellowship with the Lord Jesus Christ. You know what fellowship between man
and man means. There is as real a fellowship between the Christian and

Christ. Our eyes can look on *him*. I say not that these human optics can behold the very flesh of Christ, but I say that the eyes of the soul can here on earth more truly see Christ, after a spiritual sort, than ever eyes of man saw him when he was in the flesh on earth. Today, your head may lean upon the Savior's bosom; today, he may be your sweet companion, and with the spouse you may say, "Let him kiss me with the kisses of his mouth, for his love is better than wine." I pray you, think not that I rave now. I speak what I do know, and testify what I have seen, and what many of you have seen and known too. There are moments with the believer, when, whether in the body or out of the body, he cannot tell—God knows—but this he knows, that Christ's left hand is under his head, and his right hand does embrace him. Christ has shown to him his hands and his side. He could say, with Thomas, "My Lord and my God," but he could not say much more. The world recedes, it disappears. The things of time are covered with a pall of darkness; Christ only stands out before the believer's view. I have known that some believers, when they have been in this state, could say with the spouse, "Stay me with apples, comfort me with flagons, for I am sick of love." Their love of Christ and Christ's love to them had overcome them. Their soul was something in the state of John, whom we described last Lord's Day morning: "When I saw *him*, I fell at his feet as dead." A sacred faintness overcomes my soul, I die—I die to prove the fullness of redeeming love, the love of Christ to me. Oh, these seasons! Talk not of feasts, you sons of mirth; tell us not of music, you who delight in melodious sound; tell us not of wealth and rank and honor and the joys of victory. One hour with Christ is worth an eternity of all earth's joys. May I but see *him*, may I but see *his* face, but behold *his* beauties—come winds, blow away all earthly joys I have—this joy shall well content my soul. Let the hot sun of tribulation dry up all the water brooks; but this fresh spring shall fill my cup full to the brim—yes, it shall make a river of delight, wherein my soul shall bathe. To be with Christ on earth is the best, the surest, the most ecstatic foretaste and earnest of the joys of heaven. Forget not this, Christian! If you have ever known Christ, heaven is yours; and when you have enjoyed Christ, you have learned a little of what the bliss of futurity shall be.

I do not doubt, also, that on dying beds men get foretastes of heaven which they never had in health. When death begins to pull down the old clay house he knocks away much of the plaster, and then the light shines through the chinks. When he comes to deal with our rough garment of clay, he pulls it to rags first; and then it is we begin to get a better view of the robes of righteousness, the fair white linen of the saints, with which we are always covered though we know it not. The nearer to death, the nearer to heaven, with the believer; the more sick, the nearer he is to health. The darkest part of his night is indeed the dawning of the day; just when he shall think he dies, he shall begin to live; and when his flesh drops from him, then is he prepared to be clothed upon with his house which is from heaven. Children of God in dying have said wonderful things which it were scarcely lawful for us to utter here. It needs the stillness of the room; the solemn silence of the last hour; the failing eye, the chinked utterance, the pale thin hand, to put a soul into their utterances. I remember when a Christian brother, who had often preached with me the gospel, was sorely sick and dying, he was suddenly smitten with blindness, which was a first monition of the approach of death, and he said to me—

> And when ye see my eye-strings break,
> How sweet my moments roll;
> A mortal paleness on my cheek,
> But glory in my soul.

And said it with such emphasis, as a man who, but two or three minutes after, stood before his God, that I can never read those lines without feeling how well the poet must have foreseen a death like his. Yes, there are mystic syllables that have dropped from the lips of dying men that have been priceless as the richest pearls. There have been sights of heaven seen in the midst of Jordan which these eyes cannot see, until this breast shall be chilled in the dread and cold stream. All these things that we have mentioned are the fruits of "that Holy Spirit of promise, which is the earnest of our inheritance until the redemption of the purchased possession."

2. A few minutes only—and, O God, do help us!—with all solemnity, I utter a few sentences upon *the black reverse of the joyous picture I have presented to you.*

There is another world for the wicked, as well as for the righteous. They who believe not in Christ are no more annihilated than those who do believe in him. Immortality awaits us all. We die, but we die not; we live *forever*; and if we fear not God, that immortality is the most frightful curse that ever fell on creature—

> To linger in eternal death,
> Yet death forever fly.

Can we tell what that world of woe is? In vain do we talk to you about the pit that is bottomless, and the fire that never can be quenched, and the worm that dies not. These are but images, and images which are used so often that we fear they are almost threadbare in your estimation, and you will scarcely give an ear to them. Listen, then. If you be this day without God and without Christ in the world, you have in yourself a few sparks of that eternal fire; you have already been singed by the vehement heat of that furnace which to some men has been so hot that even when they have passed it on earth, like Nebuchadnezzar's mighty men, they have fallen down, smitten by the heat thereof, before they came within its flames. Ungodly, unconverted men have an uneasiness of spirit; they are never contented, They want something; if they have that, they will want something more. They do not feel happy; they see through the amusements which the world presents to them; they are wise enough to see that they are hollow; they understand that the fair cheek is painted; they know that its beauty is but mere pretense; they are not befooled, God has awakened them. They are sensible enough to know that this world cannot fill a man's heart; they know that an immortal spirit is never to be satisfied with mortal joys. They are uneasy; they wish to kill time; it hangs heavy on their hands. They wish they could sleep three and twenty hours out of the four and twenty, or drink half the day. They try if they cannot find some pleasure that may wake up their energies—some new device, some novelty, even though it were novelty of sin, which might give a little excitement to a palate that has lost all power to be pleased. Now when a man gets into that uneasy state, he may make a guess of what hell will be. It will be that uneasiness intensified, magnified to the extreme: to wander through dry places, seeking rest and finding none, always thirsting, but never having a drop of water to cool that thirst; hungering, but feeding upon wind and hungering still; longing, yearning, groaning, sighing, conscious of misery, sensible of emptiness, feeling poverty, but never getting anything whereby that poverty may be made rich, or that hunger may be stayed. Ah! you uneasy ones, may your uneasiness bring you to Christ!

But unconverted men without Christ have another curse, which is a sure foretaste to them of hell. They are uneasy about death. I have my mind now upon a person who trembles like an aspen leaf during a thunderstorm, and I know another man who could bear a storm very well, but if there be the slightest thing the matter with him, if he has a cough, he fears his lungs are affected—if he feels a little hoarse, he is sure he will have bronchitis and die, and that thought of dying, he cannot bear. He will hear you talk about it, and crack a joke over it, merely for the sake of covering up his own dismay. He fancies you cannot see through him; but you can plainly discover that he is as afraid of dying as ever he can be. I know at this moment a family where the governess was instructed, when she took the situation, never to mention the subject of death to the children, or else she would be instantly discharged. That fear of dying which haunts some men! Not when their blood boils and they are excited—then they could rush to the cannon's mouth, but when they are cool and steady and look at it—when it is not the sword's point and glory, but dying, mere dying, then they shiver. Oh, how these strong men start and how they quail! Full many an infidel has recanted his infidelity then—given it all up when he has come to deal with the awful mysteries of death. But those already of death are but the foreshadows of that darker gloom which must gather round your spirit, except you believe in Christ. With some men it has even gone further than this. When a man has long resisted the invitations of the gospel, long gone from bad to worse, from sin to sin, a horror, an unspeakable horror, will seize hold upon him at times, especially if he be a man who is given to intoxication. Then a delirium will come upon him, mingled with a remorse, which will make his life intolerable. It has been my unhappy lot to see one or two such cases of persons who have been ill, and have been vexed with fears, fears of a most hideous caste, which you could not remove. You speak to them about Christ, they say, "What have I to do with him? I have cursed him hundreds of times." You speak to them about faith in Christ. "Faith in Christ," they say, "what is the use of that to me? I am past hope, I am given up, and I do not care about it either." And then they collapse—go back again into that dull despair which is the sure advance guard of damnation itself. With these men one may pray; they bid you pray for them, and then they say, "Get up, sir, it is of no use; God will never hear you for me." They will ask you to go home and pray, but assure you that it will be useless to do so. You read the Bible to them. "Don't read the Scriptures," say they; "every text cuts me to the quick, for I have neglected the Word of God, and all my time now is past." You tell them that

> While the lamp holds out to burn,
> The vilest sinner may return.

No, no, *they* cannot. You may tell them that there is hope—that Jesus Christ calls many at the eleventh hour; you picture to them the thief on the cross. No, no, they put far from them all hope, and choose their own delusions and perish. Now, such men give the gravest picture of what hell must be, in these forebodings of the wrath to come. I saw one man, now in eternity, and where he is, God knows. I could not describe to you what I saw that day of him. He said he would not die and walked up and down as long as there was life in him, under the notion, as he said, that if he could walk about he knew he should not die. He would not die, he said, he would live, he *must* live. "I cannot die," said he, "for I must be damned if I die; I feel I must," and that poor wretch, sometimes giving ear to your admonitions, then cursing you to your face, bidding you pray, and then blaspheming—dying with hell commenced, with all the horrors of perdition just beginning—a sort of infant perdition strangling to be born within him! Oh! may God deliver you from ever knowing this vilest premonition of destruction! And how shall you be delivered, but by this? "Believe in the Lord Jesus Christ, and you shall be saved; for he that believeth and is baptized shall be saved"—so says the Scripture— "he that believeth not shall be damned." Trust Christ and you are saved, be you who you may. Come to the foot of the cross, and cast yourself where his blood is dropping, and you are saved. Give your heart to him, believe in him, repose your confidence in him. May the Spirit of God enable you to do this! May he help you to repent of sin, and having repented, may he bring you to Christ, as the sin propitiator! And may you go away this day, saying, "I do believe in Christ; my soul rests in him!" And if you can say that, the joy and peace in believing, which must follow a simple faith in Christ, shall be to you the work of "the Holy Spirit of promise and the earnest of our inheritance, until the redemption of the purchased possession."

Foretastes of the Heavenly Life

Intended for Reading on Lord's Day, January 29, 1899 (C. H. Spurgeon Memorial Sabbath); delivered early in the year 1857, at New Park Street Chapel, Southwark. No. 2607.

> *And they took of the fruit of the land in their hands, and brought it down unto us, and brought us word again, and said, "It is a good land which the LORD our God doth give us."* —DEUTERONOMY 1:25

You remember the occasion concerning which these words were written. The children of Israel sent twelve men as spies into the land of Canaan, and they brought back with them the fruit of the land, among the rest a bunch of grapes from Eshcol too heavy to be borne by one man, and which, therefore. two of them carried on a staff between them. I shall not say much, at this time, concerning the Israelites; but I want to show you that, as they learned something of what Canaan was like by the fruit of the land brought to them by the spies, so you and I, even while we are on earth, if we are the Lord's chosen people, may learn something of what heaven is—the state to which we are to attain hereafter—by certain blessings which are brought to us even while we are here.

The Israelites were sure that Canaan was a fertile land when they saw the fruit of it which was brought by their brethren, and when they ate thereof. Perhaps there was but little for so many, and yet those who did eat were made at once to understand that it must have been a goodly soil that produced such fruit. In like manner, beloved, we who love the Lord Jesus Christ have had clusters of the grapes of a bettor Eshcol; we have had some of the fruits of heaven even while we have been on earth, and by them we are able to judge of the richness of the soil of paradise which brings forth such rare and choice delights.

I shall, therefore, present to you a series of views of heaven in order to give you some idea how it is that the Christian on earth enjoys a foretaste of the blessings that are yet to be revealed. Possibly, there are scarcely two Christians who have exactly the same ideas concerning heaven; though they all expect the same heaven, yet the most prominent feature in it is different to each mind according to its constitution.

1. Now, I will confess to you what is to me the most prominent feature of heaven, judging at the present moment. At another time, I may love heaven better for another thing; but, just lately, I have learned to love heaven as *a place of security.*

We have been greatly saddened as we have seen some professors dishonoring their profession—yes, and worse still, some of the Lord's own beloved committing grievous faults and slips, which have brought disgrace upon their character and injury to their souls; and we have learned to look up to heaven as a place where we shall never, never sin—where our feet shall be fixed firmly upon the rock—where there is neither tripping nor slipping—where faults shall be unknown—where we shall have no need to keep watch against an indefatigable enemy, because there is no foe that shall annoy us—where we shall not be on our guard day and night watching against the incursion of foes, for "there the wicked cease from troubling; and there the weary are at rest." We have looked upon heaven as the land of complete security, where the garment shall be always white, where the face shall be always anointed with fresh oil, where there is no fear of our turning away from our Lord, for there we shall stand fast forever. And I ask you, if that be a true view of heaven—and I am sure it is one feature of it—do not the saints, even on earth, in this sense enjoy some fruits of paradise? Do we not, even in these huts and villages below, sometimes taste the joys of blissful security? The doctrine of God's Word is that all who are in union with the Lamb are safe, that all believers must hold on their way, that those who have committed their souls to the keeping of Christ shall find him a faithful and immutable keeper. Believing this doctrine, we enjoy security even on earth; not that high and glorious security which renders us free from every slip and trip; but, nevertheless, a security well-nigh as great, because it secures us against ultimate ruin and renders us certain that we shall attain to eternal felicity.

And, beloved, have you never sat down and reflected on the doctrine of the perseverance of the saints? I am sure you have, and God has brought home to you a sense of your security in the person of Christ; he has told you that your name is graven on his hand; he has whispered in your ear the promise, "Fear thou not, for I am with thee." You have been led to look upon the great surety of the covenant as faithful and true, and, therefore, bound and engaged to present you, the weakest of the family, with all the chosen race, before the throne of God; and in such a sweet contemplation I am sure you have been drinking some of the juice of his spiced pomegranates, you have had some of the choice fruits of paradise, you have had some of the enjoyments which the perfect saints above have in a sense of your complete and eternal security in Christ Jesus. Oh, how I love that doctrine of the perseverance of the saints! I shall at once renounce the pulpit when I cannot preach it, for any other form of teaching seems to me to be a blank desert and a howling wilderness, as unworthy of God as it would be beneath even my acceptance, frail worm as I am. I could never either believe or preach a gospel which saves me today and rejects me tomorrow—a gospel which puts me in Christ's family one hour, and makes me a child of the devil the next—a gospel which first justifies and then condemns me—a gospel which pardons me, and afterward casts me down to hell. Such a gospel is abhorrent to reason itself, much more is it contrary to the mind of the God whom we delight to serve. Every true believer in Jesus can sing, with Toplady—

> *My name from the palms of his hands*
> *Eternity will not erase;*
> *Impressed on his heart it remains*
> *In marks of indelible grace:*
> *Yes, I to the end shall endure,*
> *As sure as the earnest is given;*
> *More happy, but not more secure,*
> *The glorified spirits in heaven.*

Yes, beloved, we do enjoy a sense of perfect security even as we dwell in this land of wars and fightings. As the spies brought to their brethren in the wilderness bunches of the grapes of Canaan, so, in the security we enjoy, we have a foretaste and earnest of the bliss of paradise.

2. In the next place, most probably the greater part of you love to think of heaven under another aspect, as *a place of perfect rest*.

Son of toil, you love the sanctuary because it is there you sit to hear God's Word and rest your wearied limbs. When you have wiped the hot sweat from your burning brow, you have often thought of heaven as the place where your labors shall be over, and you have sung, with sweet emphasis—

> *There shall I bathe my weary soul*
> *In seas of heavenly rest,*
> *And not a wave of trouble roll*
> *Across my peaceful breast.*

Rest, rest, rest, this is what you want, and to me also this idea of heaven is exceedingly beautiful. Rest I know I never shall have beneath this sky while

Christ's servants continue to be so unreasonable as they are. I have served them to the utmost of my power, yet I am well-nigh hounded to my grave by Christian ministers perpetually wanting me to do impossibilities that they know no mortal strength can accomplish. Willing am I to labor till I drop, but I cannot do more than I am doing; yet I am perpetually assailed on this side and the other, till, go where I may, there seems no rest for me till I slumber in my grave; and I do look forward to heaven, with great happiness, because there I shall rest from labors constant and arduous, though much loved.

And you, too, dear Christian friend, who have been toiling long to gain an object you have eagerly sought, you will be glad when you get to heaven. You have said that if you could attain your desire, you would gladly lie down and rest. You have longed to lay up a certain amount of riches. You have said that, if you could once gain a competence, you would then make yourself at ease; or, you have been laboring long to secure a certain position, and you have said that if you could only reach it, you would rest. Yes, but you have not reached it yet; and you love to think of heaven because it is the goal to the racer, the target of the arrow of existence; the couch of repose for time's tired toilers; yes, an eternal rest for the poor weary struggler upon earth. You love it because it is a place of rest; and do we never enjoy a foretaste of heaven upon earth in that sense? Oh yes, beloved! Blessed be God, "we which have believed do enter into rest." Our peace is like a river and our righteousness like the waves of the sea. God does give rest to his people even here: "there remaineth therefore a rest to the people of God." We have stormy trials and bitter troubles in the world, but we have learned to say, "Return unto your rest, O my soul; for the Lord has dealt bountifully with you." Did you never, in times of great distress, climb up to your closet and there on your knees pour out your heart before God? Did you never feel, after you had so done, that you had, as it were, bathed yourself in rest, so that—

> Let cares like a wild deluge come,
> And storms of sorrow fall,

you cared not one whit for them? Though wars and tumults were raging around you, you were kept in perfect peace, for you had found a great protecting shield in Christ; you were able to remain restful and calm, for you had looked upon the face of God's Anointed. Ah Christian! that rest, so placid and serene, without a billow of disturbance, which in your deepest troubles you have been enabled to enjoy upon the bosom of Christ, is to you like a bunch from the vintage of heaven, one grape of the heavenly cluster of which you shall soon partake in the land of the hereafter. Thus, again, you see, we can have a foretaste of heaven, and realize what it is even while we are here upon earth.

That idea of heaven as a place of rest will just suit some indolent professors, so I will turn the subject round, and show you that the very opposite idea is also true, and may be more useful to certain people. I do believe that one of the worst sins of which a man can be guilty is to be idle; I could almost forgive a drunkard, rather than a lazy man; he who is idle has as good reason to be penitent before God as David had when he was an adulterer; indeed, David's adultery probably resulted from his idleness. It is an abominable thing to let the grass grow up to your knees and do nothing toward making it into hay. God never sent a man into the world to be idle; and there are some who make a profession of being Christians who do nothing to serve the Lord from one year's end to the other.

3. A true idea of heaven is, that it is *a place of uninterrupted service.*

It is a land where they serve God day and night in his temple, and never know weariness and never require to slumber. Do you know, dear friends, the deliciousness of work? Although I must complain when people expect impossibilities of me, it is the highest enjoyment of my life to be busily engaged for Christ. Tell me the day when I do not preach, I will tell you the day in which I am not happy; but the day in which it is my privilege to preach the gospel, and labor for God, is generally the day of my peaceful and quiet enjoyment after all. Service is delight. Praising God is pleasure. Laboring for him is the highest bliss a mortal can know. Oh, how sweet it must be to sing his praises and never feel that the throat is dry! Oh, how blessed to flap the wing forever and never feel it flag! Oh, what sweet enjoyment to fly upon his errands evermore, to circle round the throne of God in heaven while eternity shall last, and never once lay the head on the pillow, never once feel the throbbing of fatigue, never once the pangs that admonish us that we need to cease, but to keep on forever like eternity's own self—a broad river rolling on with perpetual floods of labor! Oh, that must be enjoyment! That must be heaven, to serve God day and night in his temple! Many of you have served God on earth and have had foretastes of that bliss.

I wish some of you knew more of the sweets of labor, for although labor breeds sweat, it breeds sweets too—more especially labor for Christ. There is a satisfaction before the work; there is a satisfaction in the work; there is a satisfaction after the work; and there is a satisfaction in looking for the fruits of the work; and a great satisfaction when we get the fruits. Labor for Christ is, indeed, the robing room of heaven; if it be not heaven itself, it is one of the most blissful foretastes of it. Thank God, Christian, if you can do anything for your Master. Thank him if it is your privilege to do the least thing for him; but remember, in so doing, he is giving you a taste of the grapes of Eshcol. But you indolent people do not get the grapes of Eshcol because you are too lazy to carry that big bunch. You would like them to come into your mouths without the trouble of gathering them. You do not care to go forth and serve God. You sit still and look after yourselves, but what do you do for other people? You go to your place of worship; you talk about your Sunday school and sick visitation society, yet you never teach in the Sunday school, and you never visit a sick person; you take a great deal of credit to yourself while you do nothing at all. You cannot expect to know much of the enjoyments of heavenly glory until you have experienced a little of the delight of working in the kingdom of heaven on earth.

4. Another view of heaven is, that it is *a place of complete victory and glorious triumph.*

This is the battlefield; there is the triumphal procession. This is the land of the sword and the spear; that is the land of the wreath and the crown. This is the land of the garment rolled in blood and of the dust of the fight; that is the land of the trumpet's joyful sound, that is the place of the white robe and of the shout of conquest. Oh, what a thrill of joy shall shoot through the hearts of all the blessed when their conquests shall be complete in heaven, when death itself, the last of foes, shall be slain, when Satan shall be dragged captive at the chariot wheels of Christ, when Jesus shall have overthrown sin and trampled corruption as the mire of the streets, when the great song of universal victory shall rise from the hearts of all the redeemed! What a moment of pleasure shall that be! But, dear brethren, you and I have foretastes of even that joy. We know what conflicts, what soul battles we have even here; did you never struggle against unbelief and at last overcome it? Oh, with what joy did you lift your eyes to heaven, the tears flowing down your cheeks, and say, "Lord, I bless you that I have been able to vanquish that sin." Did you ever meet a strong temptation and wrestle hard with it, and know what it was to sing with great joy, "My feet well-nigh slipped; but thy mercy held me up"? Have you, like Bunyan's Christian, fought with old Apollyon, and have you seen him flap his dragon wings and fly away? There you had a foretaste of heaven; you had just a hint of what the ultimate victory will be. In the death of that one Philistine, you saw the destruction of the whole army; that Goliath who fell through your sling and stone was but one out of the multitude who must yield their bodies to the fowls of heaven. God gives you partial triumphs that they may be the earnest of ultimate and complete victory. Go on and conquer, and let each conquest, though a harder one and more strenuously contested, be to you as a grape of Eshcol, a foretaste of the joys of heaven!

5. Furthermore, without doubt, one of the best views we can ever give of heaven is, that it is *a state of complete acceptance with God,* recognized and felt in the conscience.

I suppose that a great part of the joy of the blessed saints consists in a knowledge that there is nothing in them to which God is hostile; that their peace with God has not anything to mar it; that they are so completely in union with the principles and thoughts of the most High, that his love is set on them, that their love is set on him, and they are one with him in every respect. Well, beloved, and have we not enjoyed a sense of acceptance here below? Blotted and blurred by many doubts and fears, yet there have been moments when we have known ourselves as truly accepted as we shall know ourselves to be even when we stand before the throne. There have been bright days with some of us, when we could set to our seal that God was true; and when, afterward, feeling that "the Lord knows them that are his," we could say, "And we know that we are his, too." Then have we known the meaning of Dr. Watts when he sang—

> *When I can say, "My God is mine,"*
> *When I can feel thy glories shine,*
> *I tread the world beneath my feet,*
> *And all that earth calls good or great.*
>
> *While such a scene of sacred joys*
> *Our raptured eyes and souls employ,*
> *Here we could sit and gaze away*
> *A long, an everlasting day.*

We had such a clear view of the perfection of Christ's righteousness that we felt that God had accepted us, and we could not be otherwise than happy; we had such a sense of the efficacy of the blood of Christ that we felt sure our sins were all pardoned and could never be mentioned against us forever. And, beloved, though I have spoken of other joys, let me say, this is the cream of all of them, to know ourselves accepted in God's sight. Oh, to feel that I, a guilty worm, am now at rest in my Father's bosom; that I, a lost prodigal, am now feasting at his table with delight; that I, who once heard the voice of his anger, now listen to the notes of his love! This is a joy that is worth more than all worlds. What more can they know up there than that? And were it not that our sense of it is so imperfect, we might bring heaven down to earth, and might at least dwell in the suburbs of the Celestial City, if we could not be privileged to go within the gates, So you see, again, we can have, in that sense, bunches of the grapes of Eshcol. Seeing that heaven is a state of acceptance, we, too, can know and feel that acceptance, and rejoice in it.

6. And again, heaven is *a state of great and glorious manifestations*.

As you look forward to your experience in heaven, you sing—

> *Then shall I see, and hear, and know*
> *All I desired or wished below;*
> *And every power find sweet employ*
> *In that eternal world of joy.*

You are now looking at it darkly, through a glass; but there you shall see face to face. Christ looks down on the Bible, and the Bible is his looking glass. You look into it and see the face of Christ as in a mirror, darkly; but soon you shall look upon him face to face. You expect heaven to be a place of peculiar manifestations; you believe that there Jesus will unveil his face to you; that—

> *Millions of years your wondering eyes*
> *Shall o'er your Savior's beauties rove.*

You are expecting to see his face and never, never sin. You are longing to know the secrets of his heart. You believe that, in that day, you shall see him as he is, and shall be like him in the world of spirits. Well, beloved, though Christ does not manifest himself to us as he does to the bright ones there, have we not had blessed manifestations even while we have been in this vale of tears? Speak, believer; let your heart speak; have you not had visions of Calvary? Has not your Master sometimes touched your eyes with eye salve and let you see him on his cross? Have you not said—

> *"Sweet the moments, rich in blessing,*
> *Which before the cross I spend,*
> *Life, and health, and peace possessing,*
> *From the sinner's dying friend.*
>
> *Here I'll sit forever viewing*
> *Mercy's streams, in streams of blood;*

> Precious drops! my soul bedewing,
> Plead and claim my peace with God."?

Have you not wept both for joy and for grief when you beheld him nailed to the tree for your sakes and saw him bleeding out his life for you? Oh yes! I know you have had such manifestations of him. And have you not seen him in his risen glories? Have you not beheld him there exalted on his throne? Have you not, by faith, beheld him as the Judge of the quick and the dead, and as the Prince of the kings of the earth? Have you not looked through the dim future and seen him with the crown of all kingdoms on his head, with the diadems of all monarchs beneath his feet, and the scepters of all thrones in his hand? Have you not anticipated the moment of his most glorious triumphs, when—

> "He shall reign from pole to pole,
> With illimitable sway."?

Yes, you have, and therein you have had foretastes of heaven. When Christ has thus revealed himself to you, you have looked within the veil, and, therefore, you have seen what is there; you have had some glimpses of Jesus while here: those glimpses of Jesus are but the beginning of what shall never end. Those joyous melodies of praise and thanksgiving are but the preludes of the songs of paradise.

7. Last, the highest idea of heaven is, that it is *a place of most hallowed and blissful communion.*

I have not given you even half that I might have told you of the various characteristics of heaven, as described in God's Word, but communion is the best. Communion! That word so little spoken of, so seldom understood. Blessed word, "communion"! Dearly beloved, you hear us say, "And the communion of the Holy Ghost be with you all"; but there are many of you who do not know the meaning of that sweet heaven in a word—communion! It is the flower of language; it is the honeycomb of words—communion! You like best to talk of corruption, do you not? Well, if you like that ugly word, you are very willing to meditate upon it. I do so when I am forced to do it; but communion seems to me to be a far sweeter word than that. You like to talk a great deal about affliction, do you not? Well, if you love that black word, you may have reason to love it; and if you care to be happy about it, you may do so; but give me for my constant text and for my constant joy, communion, and

I will not choose which kind of communion it shall be. Sweet Master, if you give me communion with you in your sufferings, if I have to bear reproach and shame for your name's sake, I will thank you; if I may have fellowship with you in it, and if you will give me to suffer for your sake, I will call it an honor, that so I can be a partaker of your sufferings; and if you give me sweet enjoyments, if you do raise me up, and make me to sit with you in heavenly places in Christ, I will bless you. I will bless God for ascension communion—communion with Christ in his glories. Do you not say the same? And for communion with Christ in death; have you died unto the world, as Christ did die unto it himself? Then, have you had communion with him in resurrection? Have you been raised to newness of life, even as he was raised from the grave? And have you had communion with him in his ascension, so that you know yourself to be an heir to a throne in glory? If so, you have had the best earnest you can receive of the joys of paradise. To be in heaven is to lean one's head upon the breast of Jesus; have you not done that on earth? Then you know what heaven is. To be in heaven is to talk to Jesus, to sit at his feet, to let our heart beat against his heart. If you have had that bliss on earth, you have already tasted some of the grapes of heaven.

Cherish, then, these foretastes of whatever kind they may have been in your individual case. Differently constituted, you will all look at heaven in a different light. Keep your foretaste just as God gave it to you. He has given each of you a separate experience of it which is most suitable to your own condition. Treasure it up; think much of it; but think more of your Master, for, remember, it is, "Christ in you, the hope of glory," that is your best foretaste of heaven; and the more you realize that blessed truth, the more fully prepared shall you be for the bliss of the joyous ones in the land of the happy.

Heaven Above and Heaven Below

⋘⟨⟩⟩⋙

Delivered on Lord's Day morning, February 2, 1890, at the Metropolitan Tabernacle, Newington. No. 2128.

They shall hunger no more, neither thirst any more, neither shall the sun light on them, nor any heat. For the Lamb which is in the midst of the throne shall feed them, and shall lead them unto living fountains of waters.
—REVELATION 7:16–17

They shall not hunger nor thirst; neither shall the heat nor sun smite them for he that hath mercy on them shall lead them, even by the springs of water shall he guide them. —ISAIAH 49:10

Jordan is a very narrow stream. It made a sort of boundary for Canaan; but it hardly sufficed to divide it from the rest of the world, since a part of the possessions of Israel was on the eastern side of it. Those who saw the Red Sea divided, and all Israel marching through its depths, must have thought it a small thing for the Jordan to be dried up and for the people to pass through it to Canaan. The greatest barrier between believers and heaven has been safely passed. In the day when we believed in the Lord Jesus Christ, we passed through our Red Sea, and the Egyptians of our sins were drowned. Great was the marvel of mercy! To enter fully into our eternal inheritance, we have only to cross the narrow stream of death; and scarcely that, for the kingdom of heaven [is on this side of the] river as well as on the other. I start by reminding you of this, because we are very apt to imagine that we must endure a kind of purgatory while we are on earth, and then, if we are believers, we may break loose into heaven after we have shuffled off this mortal coil. But it is not so. Heaven must be in us before we can be in heaven; and while we are yet in the wilderness, we may spy out the land, and may eat of the clusters of Eshcol. There is no such gulf between earth and heaven as gloomy thoughts suggest. Our dreams should not be of an abyss, but of a ladder whose foot is on the earth, but whose top is in glory. There would not be one hundredth part so much difference between earth and heaven if we did not live so far below our privileges. We live on the ground, when we might rise as on the wings of eagles. We are all too conscious of this body. Oh, that we were oftener where Paul was when he said, "Whether in the body or out of the body, I cannot tell: God knows"! If not caught up into paradise, yet may our daily life be as the garden of the Lord.

Listen a while, you children of God; for I speak to you and not to others. To unbelievers, what can I say? They know nothing of spiritual things and will not believe them, though a man should show them unto them. They are spiritually blind and dead: the Lord quicken and enlighten them! But to you that are begotten again unto a lively hope by the resurrection of Jesus Christ from the dead, I speak with joy. Think of what you are by grace, and remember that what you will be in glory is already outlined and foreshadowed in your life in Christ. Being born from above, you are the same men that will be in heaven. You have within you the divine life—the same life which is to enjoy eternal immortality. "He that believeth on the Son hath everlasting life": it is your possession now. As the quickened ones of the Holy Spirit, the life which is to last on forever has begun in you. At this moment you are already, in many respects, the same as you ever will be. I might almost repeat this passage in Revelation concerning some of you at this very hour: "What are these? and whence came they? These are they that came out of great tribulation, and have washed their robes and made them white in the blood of the Lamb." I might even go on to say, "Therefore are they before the throne of God"—for you abide in close communion with the King—"and serve him day and night in his temple: and he that sitteth on the throne shall dwell among them." I am straining no point when I thus speak of the sanctified.

Beloved, you are now "elect according to the foreknowledge of God," and you are "the called according to his purpose." Already you are as much forgiven as you will be when you stand without fault before the throne of God. The Lord Jesus has washed you whiter than snow, and none can lay anything to your charge. You are as completely justified by the righteousness of Christ as you ever can be; you are covered with his righteousness, and heaven itself cannot provide a robe more spotless. "Beloved, now are we the sons of God." "He hath made us accepted in the beloved." Today we have the spirit of adoption, and enjoy access to the throne of the heavenly grace; yes, and today by faith we are raised up in Christ, and made to sit in the heavenlies in him. We are now united to Christ, now indwelt by the Holy Ghost: are not these great things, and heavenly things? The Lord has brought us out of darkness into his marvelous light. Although we may, from one point of view, lament the dimness of the day, yet, as compared with our former darkness, the light is marvelous; and, best of all, it is the same light which is to brighten from dawn into midday. What is grace but the morning twilight of glory?

Look you, beloved: the inheritance that is to be yours tomorrow is, in very truth, yours today; for in Christ Jesus you have received the inheritance, and you have the earnest of it in the present possession of the Holy Spirit, who dwells in you. It has been well said, that all the streets of the New Jerusalem begin here. See, here is the High Street of Peace, which leads to the central palace of God; and now we set our foot on it. "Being justified by faith, we have peace with God." The heavenly street of Victory, where are the palms and the harps, surely we are at the lower end of it here; for "this is the victory that overcomes the world, even our faith." Everything that is to be ours in the home country is, in measure, ours at this moment. As sleeps the oak within the acorn, so slumbers heaven within the first cry of "Abba, Father!" Yes, and the hallelujahs of eternity lie hidden within the groans of penitence. "God be merciful to me a sinner" has in its bowels the endless "We praise you, O Lord." O saints, little do you know how much you have in what you have!

If I could bring believers consciously nearer to the state of glory by their more complete enjoyment of the privileges of the state of grace, I should be exceedingly glad. Beloved, you will never have a better God: and "this God is our God forever and ever." Delight yourselves in him this day. The richest saint in glory has no greater possession than his God: and even I also can say, in the words of the psalm, "Yea, mine own God is he."

Despite your tribulation, take full delight in God, your exceeding joy this morning, and be happy in him. They in heaven are shepherded by the Lamb of God, and so are you: he still carries the lambs in his bosom, and does gently lead those that are with young. Even here he makes us to lie down in green pastures: what would we have more? With such a God, and such a Savior, all you can want is that indwelling Spirit, who shall help you to realize your God, and to rejoice in your Savior; and you have this also; for the Spirit of God dwells with you and is in you: "know you not that you are the temple of God?" God the Holy Ghost is not far away, neither have we to entreat his influence as though it were rays from a far-off star; for he abides in his people evermore.

I will not say that heavenly perfection is not far superior to the highest state that we ever reach on earth; but the difference lies more in our own failure than in the nature of things. Grace, if realized to its full, would brighten off into glory. When the Holy Spirit fully possesses our being, and we yield ourselves to his power, our weakness is strength, and our infirmity is to be gloried in. Then is it true, that on earth God is with us; and there is but a step between us and heaven, where we are with God.

Thus I have conducted you to my two texts, which I have put together as an illustration of what I would teach. In the New Testament text we have the heavenly state above; and in the Old Testament text we have the state of the Lord's flock while on the way to their eternal rest. Very singular, to my mind, is the sameness of the description of the flock in the fold, and the flock feeding in the ways. The verses are almost word for word the same. When John would describe the white-robed host, he can say no more of them than Isaiah said of the pilgrim band, led by the God of mercy.

1. First, *let us consider the heavenly state above.* The beloved John tells us what he heard and saw.

The first part of the description assures us of *the supply of every need.* "They shall hunger no more, neither thirst anymore." In heaven no need is unsatisfied, and no desire ungratified. They can have no want as to their bodies, for they are as the angels of God. Children of poverty, your straitness of bread will soon be ended, and your care shall end in plenty. The worst hunger is that of the heart; and this will be unknown above. There is a ravenous hunger, fierce as a wolf, which possesses some men: all the world cannot satisfy their greed. A thousand worlds would be scarce a mouthful for their lust. Now, in heaven there are no sinful and selfish desires. The ravening of covetousness or of ambition enters not the sacred gate. In glory there are no desires which should not be, and those desires which should be are all so tempered or so fulfilled that they can never become the cause of sorrow or pain; for "they shall hunger no more." Even the saints need love, fellowship, rest: they have all these in union to God, in the communion of saints, and in the rest of Jesus. The unrenewed man is always thirsting; but Christ can stay this even now, for he says, "He that drinketh of the water that I shall give him shall never thirst." Be you sure, then, that from the golden cup of glory we shall drink that which will quench all thirst forever. There is not, in all the golden streets of heaven, a single person who is desiring what he may not have, or wanting what he cannot obtain, or even wishing for that which he has not to his hand. Oh, happy state! Their mouth is satisfied with good things; they are filled with all the fullness of God.

And as there is in heaven a supply for every need, so is there *the removal of every ill.* Thus says the Spirit, "Neither shall the sun light on them, nor any heat." We are such poor creatures that excess of good soon becomes evil to us. I love the sun: if you have ever seen it shining in the clear blue heavens, you would not wonder that I speak with emphasis. Life, joy, and health stream from it in lands where it is enough of pleasure to bask in its beams. But too much of the sun overpowers us; his warmth makes men faint, his stroke destroys them. Too great a blessing may prove too heavy a cargo for the ship of life. Hence we need guarding from dangers which, at the first sight, look as if they were not perilous. In the beatific state, if these bodies of flesh and blood were still our dwelling place, we could not live under the celestial conditions. Even here, too much of spiritual joy may prostrate a man and cast him into a swoon. I would like to die of the disease; but still, a sickness comes upon one to whom heavenly things are revealed in great measure and enjoyed with special vividness. One of the saints cried out in an agony of delight, "Hold, Lord, hold! Remember I am but an earthen vessel and can contain no more!" The Lord has to limit his revelations because we cannot bear them now. I have heard of one who looked upon the sun imprudently and was blinded by the light. The very sunlight of divine revelation, favor, and fellowship could readily prove too much for our feeble vision, heart, and brain. Therefore, in the glorious state, flesh and blood shall be removed, and the raised body shall be strengthened to endure that fierce light which beats about the throne of Deity. As for us, as we now are, we might well cry, "Who among us shall dwell with the devouring fire?" But when the redemption of the body has come about, and the soul has been strengthened with all might, we shall be able to be at home with our God, who is a consuming fire. "Neither shall the sun light on them, nor any heat." May God grant us to enjoy the anticipation of that happy period when we shall behold his face, when his secret shall be with us, and we shall know even as we are known! Oh, for that day when we shall enter into the holiest and shall stand before the presence of his glory; and yet, so far from being afraid, shall be filled with exceeding joy!

But, further, the description of the heavenly life has this conspicuous feature—*the leading of the Lamb*. "The Lamb which is in the midst of the throne shall feed them, and shall lead them." It is heaven to be personally shepherded by him who is the great sacrifice. In this present state, we have earthly shepherds; and when God graciously feeds us by men after his own heart, whom he himself instructs, we prize them much. Those whom the Lord ordains to feed his flock we love, and their faith we follow, for the Lord makes them of great service to us; but still, they are only underlings, and we do not forget their imperfections, and their dependence upon their Lord. But in the glory land, "that great shepherd of the sheep" will himself personally minister to us. Those dear lips that are as lilies, dropping sweet-smelling myrrh, shall speak directly to each one of our hearts. We shall hear his voice; we shall behold his face; we shall be fed by his hand; we shall follow at his heel. How gloriously will he "stand and feed"! How restfully shall we lie down in green pastures!

He shall feed us in his dearest character. As the Lamb he revealed his greatest love, and as the Lamb will he lead and feed us forever. The Revised Version wisely renders the passage, "The Lamb in the midst of the throne shall be their shepherd." We are never fed so sweetly by our Lord himself as when he reveals to us most clearly his character as the sacrifice for sin. The atoning sacrifice is the center of the sun of infinite love, the light of light. There is no truth like it for the revelation of God. Christ in his wounds and bloody sweat is Christ indeed. "He his own self bore our sins in his own body on the tree." With this truth before us, his flesh is meat indeed, and his blood is drink indeed. In heaven we shall know him far better than we do now as the Lamb slain from before the foundation of the world, the Lamb of God's Passover, "the Lamb of God, which taketh away the sin of the world." That deep peace, that eternally unbroken rest which we shall derive from a sight of the great sacrifice, will be a chief ingredient in the bliss of heaven. "The Lamb shall feed them."

But though we shall see our Lord as a lamb, it will not be in a state of humiliation, but in a condition of power and honor. "The Lamb which is in the midst of the throne shall feed them." Heaven will largely consist of expanded views of King Jesus and nearer beholdings of the glory which follows upon his sacrificial grief. Ah brethren, how little do we know his glory! We scarce know who he is that has befriended us. We hold the doctrine of his deity tenaciously; but in heaven we shall perceive his Godhead in its truth so far as the finite can apprehend the infinite. We have known his friendship to us, but when we shall behold the King in his beauty in his own halls, and our eyes shall look into his royal countenance, and his face, which outshines the sun, shall beam ineffable affection upon each one of us, then shall we find our heaven in his glory. We ask no thrones; his throne is ours. The enthroned Lamb himself is all the heaven we desire.

Then the last point of the description is full of meaning. *The drinking at the fountain* is the secret of the ineffable bliss. "The Lamb which is in the midst of the throne shall feed them, and lead them unto living fountains of waters." We are compelled to thirst at times, like the poor flock of slaughter which we see driven through our London streets; and, alas, we stop at the very puddles by the way, and would refresh ourselves at them if we could. This will never happen to us when we reach the land where flows the river of the water of life. There the sheep drink of no stagnant waters or bitter wells, but they are satisfied from living fountains of waters. Comfort is measurably to be found in the streams of providential mercies, and therefore they are to be received with gratitude; but yet common blessings are unfilling things to souls quickened by grace. Corn can fill the barn, but not the heart. Of the wells of earth we may say, "Whosoever drinketh of this water shall thirst again"; but when we go beyond temporal supplies, and live upon God himself, then the soul receives a draft of far truer and more enduring refreshment; even as our Lord Jesus said to the woman at the well, "He that drinketh of the water that I shall give him shall never thirst; but the water that I shall give him shall be in him a well of water springing up into everlasting life." In heaven the happy ones live not on bread, which is the staff of life, but on God, who is life itself. The second cause is passed over, and the first cause alone is seen.

In the home country souls have no need of the means of grace, for they have reached the God of grace. The means of grace are like conduit pipes which bring down the living water to us: but we have found them fail us; and at times we have used them in so faulty a way that the water has lost its freshness, or has even been made to taste of the pipe through which it flowed. Fruit is best when gathered fresh from the garden: the fingering of the market destroys the bloom. We have too much of this in our ministries. Brethren, we shall soon drink living water at the wellhead, and gather the golden fruit from him who is "as the apple tree among the trees of the wood." We shall have no need of baptisms and breakings of bread, nor of churches and pastors. We shall not need the golden chalices or the earthen vessels which now serve our turn so well, but we shall come to the river's source, and drink our fill. "He shall lead them unto living fountains of water."

At times, alas, we know what it is to come to the pits and find no water; and then we try to live on happy memories. We sing and sigh; or sigh and sing—

> *What peaceful hours I once enjoyed,*
> *How sweet their memory still!*
> *But they have left an aching void*
> *The world can never fill.*

A cake made of memories will do for a bite now and then, but it makes poor daily bread. We want the present enjoyment of God. We need still to go to the fountain for new supplies; for water which stands long in the pitcher loses its cool and refreshing excellence. Happy is the man that is not living upon the memories of what he used to enjoy, but is even now in the banqueting house! The present and perpetual renewal of first love and first delight in God is heaven.

Heaven is to know the substance and the secret of the divine life, not to hold a cup, but to drink of the living water. The doctrine is precious, but it is far better to know the thing about which the doctrine speaks. The doctrine is the salver of silver, but the blessing itself is the apple of gold. Blessed are they that are always fed on the substance of the truth, the verity of verities, the essence of essential things.

"He shall lead them unto fountains." There the eternal source is unveiled: they not only receive the mercy, but they see how it comes, and whence it flows: they not only drink, but they drink with their eye upon the glorious well-head. Did you ever see a boy on a hot day lie down, when he has been thirsty, and put his mouth down to the top of the water at the brim of the well? How he draws up the cool refreshment! Drink away, poor child! He has no fear that he will drink the well dry, nor have we. How pleasant it is to take from the inexhaustible! That which we drink is all the sweeter because of the measureless remainder. Enough is not enough: but when we have God for our all in all, then are we content. When I am near to God and dwell in the overflowing of his love, I feel like the cattle on a burning summer's day when they take to the brook which ripples around them up to their knees, and there they stand, filled, cooled, and sweetly refreshed. O my God, in you I feel that I have not only all that I can contain, but all that contains me. In you I live and move with perfect content. Such is heaven! We shall have bliss within and bliss around us; we ourselves drinking at the source, and dwelling by the well forever. The fact is, that heaven is God fully enjoyed. The evil that God hates will be wholly cast out; the capacity which God gives will be enlarged and prepared for full fruition, and our whole being will be taken up with God, the ever blessed, from whom we came, and to whom it will be heaven to return. Who knows God knows heaven. The source of all things is our fountain of living waters.

Thus I could occupy all the morning with my first head; but I must not tarry, or I shall miss my aim, which is to show you that, even here, we may outline glory and in the wilderness we may have the pattern of things in the heavens. This you will see by carefully referring to the second text.

2. Let us consider the heavenly state below.

I think I have heard you saying, "Ah! this is all about heaven; but we have not yet come to it. We are still wrestling here below." Well, well, if we cannot go to heaven at once, heaven can come to us. The words which I will now read refer to the days of earth, the times when the sheep feed in the ways, and come from the north and from the south at the call of the Shepherd. *"They shall not hunger nor thirst; neither shall the heat nor sun smite them: for he that hath mercy on them shall lead them, even by the springs of water shall he guide them."*

Look at the former passage and at this. The whole description is the same. When I noticed this parallel, I stood amazed. John, you are a great artist; I entreat you, paint me a picture of heaven! Isaiah, you also have a great soul; draw me a picture of the life of the saintly ones on earth when their Lord is with them! I have both pictures. They are masterpieces. I look at them, and they are so much alike that I wonder if there be not some mistake. Surely they are depicting the same thing. The forms, the lights and shades, the touches and the tones are not only alike, but identical. Amazed, I cry, "Which is heaven, and which is the heavenly life on earth?" The artists know their own work, and by their instruction I will be led. Isaiah painted our Lord's sheep in his presence on the way to heaven, and John drew the same flock in the glory with the Lamb; and the fact that the pictures are so much alike is full of suggestive teaching. Here are the same ideas in the same words. Brethren, may you and I as fully believe and enjoy the second passage as we hope to realize and enjoy the first Scripture when we get home to heaven.

First, here is a promise that *every want shall be supplied*. "They shall not hunger nor thirst." If we are the Lord's people and are trusting in him, this shall be true in every possible sense. Literally, "your bread shall be given you, your water shall be sure." You shall have no anxious thought concerning what you shall eat, and what you shall drink. But, mark you, if you should know the trials of poverty, and should be greatly tried, and brought very low in temporal things, yet the Lord's presence and sensible consolations shall so sustain you that spiritually and inwardly you shall know neither hunger nor thirst. Many saints have found riches in poverty, ease in labor, rest in pain, and delight in affliction. Our Lord can so adapt our minds to our circumstances that the bitter is sweet and the burden is light. Paul speaks of the saints "as sorrowful, yet always rejoicing." Note well that the sorrow has an "as" connected with it; but the rejoicing is a fact. "They shall not hunger nor thirst." If you live in God, you shall have no ungratified desire. "Delight thyself also in the Lord, and he shall give thee the desires of thine heart." There may be many things that you would like to have, and you may never have them; but then you will prefer to be without them, saying, "Nevertheless, not as I will, but as you will." If Christ be with you, you will be so happy in him that wanton, wandering wishes will be like the birds which may fly over your head but dare not make their nests in your hair. You will be without a peevish craving or a pining ambition or a carking care. "Oh," says a believer, "I wish I could reach that state." You may reach it: you are on the way to it. Only love Christ more, and be more like him, and you shall be satisfied with favor, and sing, "All my springs are in you"; "My soul, wait only upon God; for my expectation is from him."

I do not mean that the saints find a full content in this world's goods, but that they find such content in God, that with them or without them they live in wealth. A man's life consists not in the abundance of that which he possesses; and many a man who has had next to nothing that could be seen with eyes or handled with hands, has been a very millionaire for true wealth in possessing the kingdom of the most High. The Lord has brought some of us into that state in which we have all things in him; and it is true to us, "They shall not hunger nor thirst."

Then, next, there is such a thing as having *every evil removed* from you while yet in this wilderness. "Neither shall the heat nor sun smite them." Suppose God favors you with prosperity; if you live near to God you will not be rendered proud or worldly minded by your prosperity. Suppose you should become popular because of your usefulness; you will not be puffed up if Christ Jesus is your continual leader and Shepherd. If you live near to him, you will be lowly. If your days are spent in sunlight, and you go from joy to joy, yet still no sunstroke shall smite you. If still you dwell in God, and your heart is full of Christ, and you are led as a sheep by him, no measure of heat shall overpower you. It is a mistake to think that our safety or our danger is according to our circumstances; our safety or our danger is according to our nearness to God or our distance from him. A man who is near to God can stand on the pinnacle of the temple, and the devil may tempt him to throw himself down, and yet he will be firm as the temple itself. A man that is without God may be in the safest part of the road, and traverse a level way, and yet he will stumble. It is not the road, but the Lord that keeps the pilgrim's foot. O heir of heaven, commit your way unto God, and make him your all in all, and rise above the creature into the Creator, and then shall you hunger no more, neither thirst anymore, neither shall the heat nor the sun smite you.

Further, it is said, that on earth we may enjoy *the leading of the Lord.* See how it is put: "For he that hath mercy on them shall lead them." Here we have not quite the same words as in Revelation, for there we read, "The Lamb that is in the midst of the throne shall lead them." Yet the sense is but another shade of the same meaning. Oh, but that is a sweet, sweet name, is it not? "He that hath mercy on them." He has saved them, and so has had mercy on them. Yes, that is very precious, but the word is sweeter still—"he that hath mercy on them," he that is always having mercy on them, he that follows them with mercy all the days of their lives, he that continually pardons, upholds, supplies, strengthens, and thus daily loads them with benefits: "He that hath mercy on them shall lead them."

Do you know, beloved friends, what it is to be led of the Lord? Many are led by their own tastes and fancies. They will go wrong. Others are led by their own judgments. But these are not infallible, and they may go wrong. More are led by other people; these may go right, but it is far from likely that they will. He that is led of God, he is the happy man, he shall not err. He shall be conducted providentially in a right way to the city of habitations. Commit your way unto the Lord: trust also in him, and he will bring it to pass. It may be a rough way, but it must be a right way if we follow the track of the Lord's feet. The true believer shall be led by the Spirit of God in sacred matters: "He will guide you into all truth." He that has mercy on us in other things will have mercy on us by teaching us to profit. We shall each one sing, "He leadeth me in the paths of righteousness for his name's sake." We shall be led into duty and through struggles; we shall be led to happy attainments and gracious enjoyments; we shall go from strength to strength.

In the case of the gracious soul, earth becomes like heaven because he walks with God. He that has mercy on him visits him, communes with him, and manifests himself to him. A shepherd goes before his flock, and the true sheep follow him. Blessed are they who follow the Lamb whithersoever he goes. They have a love to their Lord, and therefore they only want to know which way he would have them go, and they feel drawn along it by the cords of love and the bands of a man. If they can get a glance from their Lord's eye, it suffices them: as it is written, "I will guide thee with mine eye." Every day they stand anxiously attentive to do the King's commandment, be it what it may. They yield themselves and their members to him to be instruments of righteousness, vessels fit for the Master's use. Beloved, this is heaven below. If you have ever tried it, you know it is so. If you have never fully tried it, try it now, and you will find a new joy in it. Jesus says to you, "Take my yoke upon you, and learn of me, and ye shall find rest unto your souls."

I do not know anything more delightful than to be such a fool, as the world will call you, as to yield your intellect to the teaching of the Lord; and to be so weak that you cannot judge but accept his will; and so incapable that even to will and to do must be worked in you of the Lord. Oh, to be so unselfed as to take anything from Christ far more gladly than you would choose of your own accord! If your Lord puts his hand into the bitter box, you will think the potion sweet; and if he scourge, you will thank him for being so kind as to think of you at all. When you get to that point, that you are as a sheep to whom God himself is the Shepherd, it is well with you. Then you will realize, even in the pastures of the wilderness, how the rain from heaven drops upon the inheritance of the Lord and refreshes it when it is weary. "The peace of God, which passeth all understanding, shall keep your hearts and minds through Christ Jesus." God give you to know it, dear friends! I can speak experimentally of it: it is not only the antepast of heaven, but a part of the banquet itself.

But now the last touch is *the drinking at the springhead*. We were not surprised to find, in our description of heaven, that the Lamb led them to the fountains of waters; but we are delighted to find that, here below, "even by the springs of water shall he guide them." Beloved, covet earnestly this drinking at the springs. It is not all who profess to be Christians who will know what I am talking about this morning: they will think I have got into the way of the mystics, and am dreaming of things unpractical. I will not argue with them; let me speak to those who understand me.

Beloved in the Lord, you can even now live upon God himself, and there is no living comparable to it. You can get beyond all the cisterns and come to the river of the water of life, even as they do in heaven. To live by second causes is a very secondary life: to live on the First Cause is the first of living. I exhort you to do this with regard to the inspired Word. This is a day of man's opinions, views, judgments, criticisms. Leave them all, good, bad, and indifferent, and come to this Book, which is the pure fount of inspiration undefiled. When you study the Word of God, live upon it as his Word. I am not going to defend it; it needs no defense. I am not going to argue about its inspiration; if you know the Lord aright, his Word is inspired to you, if to no one else. You know not only that it was inspired when it was written, but that it is inspired still; and, moreover, its inspiration affects you in a way in which no other writings can ever touch you. It breathes upon you; it breathes *life* into you and makes you to speak words *for* God which prove to be words *from* God to other souls. Oh, it is wonderful, if you read the Word of God in a little company, morning by morning—simply read it and pray over it, what an effect it may have upon all who listen! I speak what I do know. If you read the inspired words themselves, and look up to him who spoke them, their spiritual effect will be the witness of their inspiration. This is a miracle-working Book: it may be opposed, but never conquered; it may be buried under unbelief, but it must rise again. Blessed are they to whom the Word is meat and drink. They quit the cistern of man for the fountain of God; and they do well. "By the springs of water shall he guide them."

Yet I would exhort you not even to tarry at the letter of God's Word, but believingly and humbly advance to drink from the Holy Ghost himself. He will not teach you anything which is not in the Bible, but he will take of the things of Christ and will show them unto you. A truth may be like a jewel in the Word of God, and yet we may not see its brilliance until the Holy Spirit holds it up in the light and bids us mark its luster. The Spirit of God brings up the pearl from the deeps of revelation, and sets it where its radiance is perceived by the believing eye. We are such poor scholars that we learn little from the Book till "the Interpreter, one of a thousand," opens our heart to the Word, and opens the Word to our heart. The Holy Ghost who revealed truth in the Book must also personally reveal it to the individual. If ever you get a hold of truth in that way, you will never give it up. A man who has learned truth from one minister may unlearn it from another minister; but he that has been taught it of the Holy Ghost has a treasure which no man takes from him.

Beloved, we would exhort you to drink of the springs of living water while you are here. Be often going back to fundamental doctrines. Especially get back to the consideration of covenant engagements. Whence come all the deeds of mercy from God our Father, and from our Lord Jesus Christ? Come they not from eternal purposes and from that covenant, "ordered in all things, and sure," made ere the earth was, between the Father and the ever-blessed Son? Get you often to the well of the covenant. I know of nothing that can make you so happy as to know in your very soul how the Father pledged himself by oath to the Son, and the Son pledged himself to the eternal Father concerning the great mystery of our redemption. Eternal love and covenant faithfulness: these are ancient wells. Do not hesitate to drink deep at the fountain of electing love. The Lord himself chose you, having loved you with an everlasting love. Everything comes to the saints "according as he hath chosen us in him before the foundation of the world." The Philistines have stopped this well full many a time, but they cannot prevent its waters bubbling up from among the stones which they have cast into it. There it stands. "I have loved thee with an everlasting love: therefore with loving-kindness have I drawn thee." Get you back to the love that had no cause but the First Cause, to the love that knows no change, to the love that knows no limit, no hesitancy, no diminution, the love that stands, like the Godhead itself, eternal and immovable. Drink from eternal springs; and if you do so, your life will be more and more "as the days of heaven upon the earth." God grant us to get away from the deceitful brooks to "the deep which lieth under," and with joy may we draw water.

Christ's presence and fountain drinking—give me these two things, and I ask no more. The Lamb to feed me and the fountain to supply me; these are enough. Lord, whom have I in heaven but thee? Come poverty, come sickness, come shame, come casting out by brethren; yes, come death itself, nothing can I want, and nothing can harm me if the Lamb be my Shepherd and the Lord my fountain.

Before another Sunday some of us may be in heaven. Before this month has finished, some of us may know infinitely more about the eternal world than the whole assembly of divines could tell us. Others of us may have to linger here a while. Yet are we not in banishment. Here we dwell with the King for his work. We will endeavor to keep close to our Master, and if we may serve him and see his face, we will not grudge the glorified their fuller joys.

You that know nothing about these things, God grant you spiritual sense to know that you do not know, and then give you further grace to pray to him, "Lord, lead me to the living fountains." There is an inner life; there is a heavenly secret; there is a surpassing joy—some of us know it—we wish that you, also, had it. Cry for it. Jesus can give it to you at once. Believe in the Lord Jesus Christ, and you shall live forever. The new birth goes with faith in Christ. May he give it to you this morning, and may you begin to be heavenly here, that you may be fit for heaven hereafter. The Lord bless you, dear friends, for Jesus' sake! Amen.

Saints in Heaven and Earth, One Family

⬧✣⬧

Delivered on Lord's Day morning, August 8, 1875, at the Metropolitan Tabernacle, Newington. No. 1249.

The whole family in heaven and earth. —EPHESIANS 3:15

Bereavements are among the sorest griefs of this mortal life. We are permitted by God to love those whom he gives to us, and our heart eagerly casts its tendrils around them, and therefore when suddenly the beloved objects are withdrawn by death, our tenderest feelings are wounded. It is not sinful for us to lament the departure of friends, for Jesus wept; it would be unnatural and inhuman if we did not mourn for the departed—we should be less feeling than the beasts of the field. The Stoic is not a Christian and his spirit is far removed from that of the tenderhearted Jesus.

The better the friend, the greater our regret at his loss, although there also lie within that fact more abundant sources of consolation. The mourning for Josiah was very sore because he was so good a prince. Because Stephen was so full of the Holy Ghost, and so bold for the faith, devout men carried him to his burial and made great lamentation over him. Dorcas was wept for and bewailed because of her practical care for the poor. Had they not been true saints, the mourning had not been so great; and yet, had they been wicked, there had been graver cause for woe. Brethren, we cannot but sorrow this day, for the Lord has taken away a sister, a true servant of the church, a consecrated woman who'll be honored above many, and to whom he gave many crowns of rejoicing; and we cannot but sorrow all the more, because so loving a mother in Israel has fallen asleep, so useful a life has come to a close, and so earnest a voice is hushed in silence. I have this day lost from my side one of the most faithful, fervent, and efficient of my helpers, and the church has lost one of her most useful members.

Beloved, we need comfort. Let us seek it where it may be found. I pray that we may view this source of grief, not with our natural, but with our spiritual eyes. The things external are for the natural eye, and from that eye they force full many a tear, for in his natural life man is the heir of sorrow; but there is an inward and spiritual life which God has given to believers, and this life has an inner eye, and to this inner eye there are other scenes presented than the senses can perceive. Let that spiritual vision indulge itself now. Close your eyes as much as your tears will permit you to the things which are seen, for they are temporal and shadowy and look to the eternal, secret, underlying truths, for these are realities. Take a steady look into the invisible, and the text, I think, sets before us something to gaze upon which may minister comfort to us. The saints in heaven, though apparently sundered from us, are in reality one with us; though death seems to have made breaches in the church of God, it is in fact perfect and entire; though the inhabitants of heaven and believers on earth might seem to be two orders of beings, yet in truth they are "one family."

> Let all the saints terrestrial sing,
> With those to glory gone;
> For all the servants of our King
> In earth and heaven, are one.

So sings the poet. The text tells us that there is a "whole family"; it speaks not of a broken family, nor of two families, but of "the whole family in heaven and earth." It is one undivided household still, notwithstanding all the graves which crowd the cemetery. To this thought I shall call your attention, hoping that thereby you may enter into that "one communion," in which saints above are bound up with saints below. I invite you to consider the ties which bind us to those who have gone before, and the indissoluble kinship in Christ which holds us as much as ever in one sacred unity.

1. First, let us think of *the points of this great family union.*

In what respects are the people of our God in heaven and earth our family? We answer, in very many; for their family relationship is so ancient, so certain, and so paramount, that it may be seen in a vast variety of ways.

Let us note, first, concerning those in heaven and earth whom the Lord loves that their names are all *written in our family register.* That mystical roll which eye has not seen contains all the names of his chosen. They are born by degrees, but they are chosen at once; by one decree set apart from the rest of mankind, by one declaration, "They shall be mine," separated forever as hallowed things unto the most High. "Blessed be the God and Father of our Lord Jesus Christ, who hath blessed us with all spiritual blessings in heavenly places in Christ: according as he hath chosen us in him before the foundation of the world, that we should be holy and without blame before him in love: having predestinated us unto the adoption of children by Jesus Christ to himself, according to the good pleasure of his will, to the praise of the glory of his grace, wherein he hath made us accepted in the beloved." We like to keep our own family registers; we are pleased to look back to the place where our parents recorded our names with those of our brothers and sisters. Let us gaze by faith upon that great book of life where all the names of the redeemed stand indelibly written by the hand of everlasting love, and as we read those beloved names let us remember that they make but one record. The faithful of modern times are on the same page with the saints of the Old Testament, and the names of the feeblest among us are written by the same hand which inscribed the apostles and the martyrs. We confidently believe that Mrs. Bartlett's name is found in the same roll which contains yours, my sister, though you may be the most obscure of the Lord's daughters. "Even as ye are called in one hope of your calling," so were you all comprehended in one election of grace.

The saints above and below are also *one family in the covenant*, "ordered in all things and sure," made with them in the person of their one great federal Head, the Lord Jesus Christ. Sadly one are all the members of the human race in our first father, Adam, for in Adam we all fell. We realize that we are one family by the common sweat of the face, the common tendency to sin, the common liability to death: but there is a second Adam, and all whom he represented are most surely one family beneath his blessed headship. What the Lord Jesus has accomplished was achieved for all his people; his righteousness is theirs, his life is theirs, his resurrection is the pledge of their resurrection, his eternal life is the source and guarantee of their immortal glory.

> With him, their Head, they stand or fall—
> Their life, their surety, and their all.

Let us think how close we are together then, for we are in very truth nearer to the saints in heaven than we are to the ungodly with whom we dwell. We are in one covenant headship with just men made perfect, but not with the unregenerate. We are fellow citizens with the glorified, but we are strangers and foreigners among worldlings. Christ Jesus represented us even as he represented the glorified ones in the old eternity, when the covenant was signed, and in that hour when the covenant stipulations were fulfilled upon the bloody tree, and he represents us with the glorified ones still as he takes possession of the inheritance in the names of all his elect and dwells in the glory which he is preparing for his one church.

It is sweet to remember that all the saints in heaven and earth have *the covenant promises secured to them by the selfsame seal.* You know the seal of the covenant; your eyes delight to dwell upon it; it is the sacrifice of the bleeding Lamb. And what, my brethren, is the ground of the security of the saints above, but the covenant of divine grace, sealed and ratified by the blood of the Son of God? We are rejoiced to see that, in the Epistle to the Hebrews, in connection with the spirits of just men made perfect, the Holy Spirit mentions Jesus the mediator of the new covenant, and the blood of sprinkling, which speaks better things than that of Abel. The promise and the oath of God, those two immutable things, in which it is impossible for God to lie, are given to all the heirs of promise whether they be militant or triumphant, and to them all has the Lord said, "I will be to them a God, and they shall be to me a people." Glory be to his name, the blood which is the ground of our hope of heaven guarantees to the perfected that they shall abide in their bliss. They are there as the "redeemed from among men," which we also are this day. That same blood which has made white their robes has also cleansed us from all sin.

The family in heaven and earth, again, will be plainly seen to be one if you remember that they are *all born of the same Father*, each one in process of time. Every soul in heaven has received the new birth, for that which is born of the flesh cannot inherit a spiritual kingdom, and therefore even babes snatched away from the womb and before yet they had fallen into actual sin, have entered heaven by regeneration. All there, whether they lived to old age or died in childhood, have been begotten again into a lively hope by the resurrection of Jesus Christ from the dead, and are born as to their heavenly state, not of blood, nor of the will of the flesh, nor of the will of man, but of God.

The nature of all regenerate persons is the same, for in all it is the living and incorruptible seed which lives and abides forever. The same nature is in the saints above as in the saints below. They are called the sons of God and so are we; they delight in holiness and so also do we; they are of the church of the firstborn and so are we; their life is the life of God and so is ours; immortality pulses through our spirits as well as through theirs. Not yet, I grant, is the body made immortal, but as to our real life we know who has said, "Whosoever liveth and believeth in me shall never die." Is it not written, "Ye are made partakers of the divine nature, having escaped the corruption which is in the world through lust"? I know there is no higher nature than the divine, and this is said to have been bestowed upon the saints below. The new life in heaven is more developed and mature; it has also shaken off its dust, and has put on its beautiful garments, yet it is the same. In the sinner born to God but yesterday there is a spark of the same fire which burns in the breasts of the glorified above. Christ is in the perfected and the same Christ is in us, for we are "all of one" and he calls us all brethren. Of the same Father begotten, into the same nature born, with the same life quickening us, are we not one family? Oh, it needs but little alteration in the true saint below to make him a saint above. So slight the change that in an instant it is accomplished. "Absent from the body and present with the Lord." The work has proceeded so far that it only remains for the Master to give the last touch to it, and we shall be meet for glory and shall enter into the heavenly rest with capacities of joy as suitable for heaven as the capacities of those who have been there these thousand years.

We are one yet further brethren, because all saints, whether in heaven or earth, are *partakers in the same divine love.* "The Lord knoweth them that are his," not merely those in heaven but those below. The poor struggling child of God in poverty is as well known by God as you bright songster who walks the golden streets. "The eyes of the Lord are upon the righteous, and his ears are open to their cry." I tell you, timid, trembling woman, humbly resting on your Savior, that you are as truly beloved of God as Abraham, Isaac, and Jacob, who sit down at his table in glory. The love of God toward his children is not affected by their position, so that he loves those in heaven better and those on earth less. God forbid. You, being evil, are not so partial as to bestow all your love upon a son who has prospered in the world, and give none of it to another who is bearing the burden of poverty. Our great Father loves the world of his elect with love surpassing thought and has given himself to each one of them to be the portion of each individual forever. What more can he do for those in heaven? What less has he done for us? Jesus has engraved the names of all the redeemed upon his hands and heart, and loves them all unto perfection. If then they all dwell in the bosom of God as the dearly beloved of his soul, are they not indeed one family?

As they all receive the same love so are they all *heirs of the same promises* and the same blessed inheritance. I am bold to say that as a believer in Christ, heaven is as much mine as it is Paul's or Peter's; they are there to enjoy it, and I am waiting to obtain it, but I hold the same title deeds as they do, and as an heir of God, and joint heir with Jesus Christ, my heritage is as broad and as sure as theirs. Their only right to heaven lay in the grace of God which brought them to believe in Jesus; and if we also have been brought by grace to believe in Jesus, our title to eternal glory is the same as theirs. O child of God, do not think that the Lord has set apart some very choice and special blessings for a few of his people—all things are yours. The land is before you, even the land which flows with milk and honey, and the whole of it is yours, though you may be less than the least of all saints. The promise is sure to all the seed, and all the seed have an interest in it. Remember that blessed passage. "If children, then heirs, heirs of God, joint heirs with Jesus Christ"—not if full-grown children, not if well-developed children, not if strong, muscular children, but "if children," and that is all; regeneration proves you to be heirs, and alike heirs, for there can be no difference in the heirship if they are all heirs of God and joint heirs with Jesus Christ. Will you think of this, you who are little in Israel? You who rank with the Benjamites, will you sit down and think of this? You are one of the same family as those bright spirits who shine as the stars forever and ever, and their inheritance is also yours, though as yet you have not come of age, and like a minor must wait till you have been trained under tutors and governors and educated for heaven. You are a prince, though as yet an infant; one of the Redeemer's kings and priests, as yet uncrowned; waiting, waiting, but still secure of the inheritance; tarrying till the day breaks and the shadows flee away, but sure in the morning the crown of life so long reserved will be brought forth, and you also shall sit with Jesus on his throne.

So might I continue showing the points in which the saints above and the saints below are akin, but this last must suffice.

They are all members of one body, and are necessary to the completion of one another. In the Epistle to the Hebrews we are told concerning the saints above that "they without us cannot be made perfect." We are the lower limbs as it were of the body, but the body must have its inferior as well as its superior members. It cannot be a perfect body should the least part of it be destroyed. Hence it is declared that in the dispensation of the fullness of time, he will gather together in one all things in Christ, both which are in heaven and which are on earth. The saints above with all their bliss must wait for their resurrection until we also shall have come out of great tribulation; like ourselves they are waiting for the adoption, to wit, the redemption of the body. Until all who were predestinated to be conformed to the image of the First-born shall have been so conformed, the church cannot be complete. We are linked to the glorified by bonds of indispensable necessity. We think that we cannot do without them, and that is true; but they also cannot do without us. "As the body is one and has many members, and all the members of that one body, being many are one body, so also is Christ." How closely this brings us together. Those for whom we sorrow cannot be far away, since we are all "the body of Christ and members in particular." If it be dark, my hand knows that the head cannot be far off, nor can the foot be far removed: eye, ear, foot, hand, head, are all comprised within the limits of one body; and so if I cannot see my beloved friend, if I shall not again hear her pathetic voice on earth, nor see her pleading tears, yet am I sure she is not far away, and that the bond between us is by no means snapped, for we are members of our Lord's body, of which it is written, "not a bone of him shall be broken." Thus have I according to my ability set forth some of the points of this family union; may the Holy Spirit give us to know them for ourselves.

2. Let us now speak upon *the inseparableness of this union.*

"The whole family in heaven and earth," not the two families nor the divided family, but the whole family in heaven and earth. It appears at first sight as if we were very effectually divided by the hand of death. Can it be that we are one family when some of us labor on and others sleep beneath the greensward? There was a great truth in the sentence which Wordsworth put into the mouth of the little child when she said, "O master, we are seven."

> *"But they are dead: those two are dead!*
> *Their spirits are in heaven!"*
> *'Twas throwing words away, for still*
> *The little maid would have her will,*
> *And said "Nay, we are seven."*

Should we not thus speak of the divine family, for death assuredly has no separating power in the household of God. Like the apostle, we are persuaded that death cannot separate us from the love of God. The breach caused by the grave is only apparent; it is not real, the family is still united: for if you think of it, when there is a loss in a family, the father is bereaved, but you cannot conceive of our heavenly Father's being bereaved. Our Father which are in heaven, you have lost none of your children. We wept and went to the grave, but you did not, for your child is not dead; rather had your child come closer unto your bosom to receive a sweeter caress, and to know more fully the infinity of your love! When a child is lost from a family, the elder brother is a mourner, for he has lost one of his brethren. But our Elder Brother is not bereaved; Jesus has lost none of his; no, has he not rather brought home to himself his own redeemed? Has he not rejoiced exceedingly to see his good work perfected in one whom he loved? There is no break toward the Father, and no break toward the Elder Brother, and therefore it must be our mistake to fancy that there is any break at all. It cannot be that death divides our Israel; were not the tribes of Reuben and Gad and Manasseh one with the rest of Israel, though the Jordan rolled between? It is a *whole* family, that redeemed household in heaven and in earth.

How little death prevents actual intercourse it is impossible for us to tell. Some attractive, but worthless, books have been written pretending to unfold to us the connection between departed spirits and ourselves, but I trust you will not be led into such idle speculations. God has not revealed these things to us, and it is not for us to go dreaming about them, for we may dream ourselves into grievous errors if we once indulge our fancies. We know nothing about the commerce of the glorified with earth, but we do know that all departed saints are supremely blessed, and that they are with Christ; and if they be with Christ, and we are with Christ, we cannot be far from each other. We meet all the saints of every age whenever we meet with God in Christ Jesus. In fellowship with Jesus you are come unto the city of the living God, the heavenly Jerusalem, and to an innumerable company of angels, to the general assembly and church of the Firstborn, whose names are written in heaven, and to the spirits of just men made perfect. It is impossible to restrict our communion with the people of God by the bounds of sect, race, country, or time, for we are vitally one with them all. Come, brethren, let us join our hands with those who have gone before, and let us with equal love join hands with those below, who before long will be numbered with the selfsame company. Death has removed part of the family to an upper room, but we are one family still: there may be two brigades, but we are one army; we may feed in two pastures, but we are only one flock; we may dwell awhile in separate habitations, but one homestead will before long receive us all.

As a matter which grows out of death, it may be well to say that *space* makes no inroads into the wholeness of the Lord's family. So far as spirits are limited to place, there must be a vast distance between the saint in heaven and the saint on earth; but we ought to remember that space, which seems vast to us, is not vast relatively, either as to God or to spiritual beings. Space is but the house of God; no, God comprehends all space, and space, therefore, is but the bosom of the Eternal. Space also is scarcely to be reckoned when dealing with spiritual beings. We can love and commune with those who are across the Atlantic with as much ease as we can have fellowship with those in the next house. Our friends in Australia, though on the other side of the world, are by no means too distant for our spiritual embrace. Thought flies more swiftly than electricity; spirits defy space and annihilate distance; and we, in spirit, still meet with the departed in our songs of praise, rejoicing with them in our Lord Jesus Christ. Space does not divide: there are many mansions, but they are all in our Father's house.

And, dear brethren, it is such a great mercy that sin, that greatest of all separators, does not now divide us; for we are made near by the blood of Christ. When we think of those bright spirits before the throne, they seem to be of a superior race to us, and we are half tempted to bow at their feet; but this feeling is rebuked in us, as it was in John, by the voice which said, "See thou do it not; I am of thy fellow servants, the prophets: worship God." They are one with us, after all; for they have washed their robes and made them white in the blood of the Lamb, and that is exactly what we have done. Beloved in Christ, we are already justified and accepted in the beloved as much as the glorified. The veil is rent for us as well as for them, the dividing mountains of sin are overturned for us as well as for them. Sinners as we are, we have access to God by the blood of Jesus, and with joy we draw near the throne. They have attained to perfectness, and we are following after: they see the Lord face to face, but we also who are pure in heart have grace given us to see God. The atoning blood has removed the middle wall, and we are one in Christ Jesus.

Neither do *errors* and failures of understanding divide the family of God; if, indeed, they did, who among us could be of the same family as those who know even as they are known? The little child makes a thousand mistakes, and his elder brethren smile sometimes, but they do not deny that he is their brother because he is so ignorant and childish. Even so, dear brothers and sisters, we know very little now; like the apostle we may each one say, "I spoke as a child, I understood as a child, I thought as a child." For now we see through a glass darkly, and only know in part, but this does not disprove our kinship with those who see "face to face." We are of the same school, though on a lower form, and it is written, "All thy children shall be taught of the Lord." What they know they learned at those same feet at which we also sit.

Neither can *sorrow* separate us. Ah, they know no tears, their griefs are ended and their toils, but we must abide awhile in the stern realities of life's battle, to wrestle, and to suffer; but it is evident that we are not divided from them, for we are all spoken of in one sentence, as "These are they that are coming out of great tribulation," for so the translation may run. Those who are already arrived and those who are on the way are described as one company. The sick child is of the same family as his brother in perfect health; soldiers who are enduring the brunt of the battle are of the same army as those who have gained their laurels. To deny that your warring soldier is a part of the host would be a great mistake; to say that he is not of the army because he is in the midst of the conflict would be cruel and false. The saints militant are of the same host as the triumphant; those who are suffering are of the same company as the beatified. None of these things part us—we are still one family in Christ Jesus. Who shall separate us?

3. A topic of deep interest now comes before us—*the present display of the union.*

We have been speaking of our being one family, but perhaps it appears to you to be only a pleasing theory, and therefore we will notice certain points in which our unity practically appears.

I like to think, first, that the *service* of those who have departed blends with ours. I do not mean that they can descend to earth to preach and teach and labor, but I do mean this, that they being dead, yet speak; their service projects itself beyond this life. A good man is not dead as to his influential life and real service for God as soon as the breath leaves his body; his work has a momentum in it which makes it roll on: his influence abides. "Even in their ashes live their wonted fires." A very large part of the power which the Holy Spirit gives to the church is found in the form of influence derived from the testimonies and examples of departed saints. Today the church of God feels the influence of Paul and Peter; at this very moment the work of the apostles is telling upon the nations. Is it not certain that the energetic souls of Luther and Calvin have left vital forces behind them which throb and pulsate still? Perhaps the Reformers are doing as much today as they did when they were alive. So each man, according to his talent and grace, leaves behind him not merely his arrow and his bow, his sword and his shield, for other hands to use; but the arrows which he shot before he died are still flying through the air, and the javelin which he hurled before his hand was paralyzed in death is yet piercing through the bucklers of the foe. The influence of my dear sister, Mrs. Bartlett, will operate upon some of you as long as you live; and you will transmit it to your successors. You Christians will be the more intense because of her glowing example; and you sinners will find it the harder to live in sin when you remember her tearful warnings. Some of you, I do not doubt, will be her posthumous children, born unto her after she has entered into her rest. Do not let the living think that they are the sole champions in this holy war, for, to all intents and purposes, the spirits of the just made perfect stand side by side with them; and the battle is being carried on, in no small measure, by cannon which they cast and weapons which they forged. Though the builders be absent in body, yet the gold, silver, and precious stones which they built their Lord will establish forever.

Then again, we are one family in heaven and earth, and that very visibly, because the influence of *the prayers* of those in heaven still abides with us. Do not mistake me, I am no believer in the intercession of the saints above. I believe that they pray, but I believe it to be a damnable error to urge anyone to seek their intercession. What I mean is very different. I mean that prayers offered while they were here, and unanswered in their lifetime, still remain in the church's treasury of prayer. Many a mother dies with her children unsaved, but the prayers she continually offered for them will prevail after her death. Many a minister, and many a private member, pleads with God for blessing on the church, and perhaps does not see it; but prayer must be answered, and fifty years afterward it is possible that the church will reap the result of those supplications. Is not Scotland today the better and the holier for the prayers of John Knox? Is not England the brighter for the prayers of Latimer and Ridley? The august company of the glorified have ceased to kneel with us in person, but in effect they do so. They have gone to other work, but the incense which they kindled when they were below still perfumes the chambers of the church of God.

Further, the unity of the church will be seen in this, that their *testimony* from above blends with ours. The church is ordained to be a witness. My brethren, we try to witness as God helps us to the truth as it is in Jesus, even as those who are above once witnessed with us here in life and in death. What a sweet witness dying Christians often bear when they cannot speak, in the gleam of the eye, in the perfect rest of soul, which others may well envy, enjoyed just in the moment when pain was most severe, and the flesh was failing. But now that these spirits have entered within the veil, do they cease their testimony? No. Hear them. They bear witness to the Lamb, saying, "for thou wast slain and hast redeemed us to God by thy blood." They make known to angels and principalities and powers in heavenly places the manifold wisdom of God, according to the eternal purpose which he purposed in Christ Jesus our Lord. We are engaged with them in revealing the abundant mercy and all-sufficiency of the Lord. You are comrades with us, you shining ones; you are fellow witnesses for Jesus, and therefore you are one with us. The main employment of saints above is *praise*. Beloved, what is ours but praise too? Is it not well put by our poet?

> They sing the Lamb in hymns above,
> And we in songs below.

Their music is sweeter than ours, freer from discord, and from all that is cold or wandering, but still the theme is the same, and the song springs from the same motive and was wrought in the heart by the same grace. I think I shall never praise my Lord in heaven more sincerely than I often praise him now, when my mouth cannot speak for the overfloodings of my soul's delight and joy in my God, who has taken me up out of the horrible pit and out of the miry clay, and set my feet upon a rock, and established my goings, and put a new song into my mouth. The deep obligations of every day overwhelm me with indebtedness; I cannot but praise my God, when I think of dire necessities perpetually supplied, multiplied sin continually pardoned, wretched infirmity graciously helped. Yes, we are one family, because when holy worship goes up into the ear of the Eternal, our praise blends with the praise of those who are glorified above, and we are one.

Brethren, I believe we are one in some other points as well. Do you not rejoice over sinners? Is it not one of our holidays on earth when the prodigal returns? "Verily I say unto you, there is joy in the presence of the angels of God over one sinner that repenteth." Do you ever cry out against sin and groan because of the power of error in the land? Know you not that the souls under the altar also cry with the selfsame indignation, "O Lord, how long! Wilt thou not judge and avenge thine own elect?" Do you not expect each day the coming of your Lord, and look for it with rapture? They also do the same. They say there is no hope in heaven, but who told them so? The saints, like ourselves, are looking for the blessed hope, the glorious appearing of our Lord and Savior Jesus Christ. Your joy, your desire, your hope, are not these the same as theirs before the throne?

Towering over all is the fact that *the Well Beloved [One] is the common joy of saints in heaven and on earth*. What makes *their* heaven? Who is the object of all their worship? Who is the subject of all their songs? In whom do they delight themselves all the day long? Who leads them to living fountains of waters and wipes all tears from their eyes? Beloved, he is as much all in all to us as he is to them. Jesus, *we* know you, and *they* know you; Jesus, we love you, and they love you; Jesus, we embrace you, and they embrace you; Jesus, we are oftentimes lost in you, and they are lost in you—you Sun of our soul, you Life of our life, you Light of our delight, you are that to us which you are to them, and herein we are all one.

4. Last of all, there is to come, before long, *a future manifestation of this family union*, much brighter than anything we have as yet seen.

We are one family, and we shall meet again. If they cannot come to us, we shall go to them by and by. It does not often happen that we carry to the grave one who is known to all this congregation, but seldom does a week pass but what one or other of our number, and frequently two or three, are taken home. I have to look upon you and upon myself as so many shadows, and when I meet you, how often does the question occur to me, "Who will go next?" Naturally, I think of some of you who have grown gray in your Master's service, and have passed your threescore years and ten. You must go soon, my brethren and my sisters; and I know you are not grieved at the prospect. Yet the young as well as the old are taken home, and men in middle life, with the marrow moist in their bones, are removed, even as those who lean upon their staff for very age.

Who knows but what I may leave you soon? My brother, who knows but that you may be called away? Well, in that blessed day when we leave the earth, we shall perceive that as we were free of the church below, we are citizens of the church above. Whenever some of us enter an assembly of believers, they recognize and welcome us: the like reception awaits us above! We shall be quite at home in heaven, when we get there. Some of you have more friends in heaven than on earth. How few are left of your former friends, compared with the many who have gone above. In the day when you enter into heaven, you will perceive that the church is one family, for they will welcome you heartily and recognize in you a brother, and a friend, and so, together with them, you shall adore your Lord.

Remember there is coming another day in which the family union of the church will be seen, and that is when the trumpet shall sound and the dead shall be raised. It may be that we shall all be of the company of those who sleep, and if so, when the trumpet sounds, the dead in Christ shall rise first, and we shall have our share in the first resurrection. Or, if our Lord should come before we die, we shall be "alive and remain"; but we shall undergo a change at the same moment as the dead are raised, so that this corruptible shall put on incorruption. What a family we shall be when we all rise together, and all the changed ones stand with us, all of one race, all regenerate, all clothed in the white robe of Jesus' righteousness! What a family! What a meeting it will be!

> How loud shall our glad voices sing,
> When Christ his risen saints shall bring
> From beds of dust, and silent clay,
> To realms of everlasting day.

Beloved, I cannot dwell upon what glory will follow on earth, but if our Lord shall live and reign on earth a thousand years, and if there shall be set up a great empire, which shall outshine all other monarchies as much as the sun outshines the stars, we shall all share in it, for he will make us all kings and priests unto God, and we shall reign with him upon the earth. Then, when comes the end, and he shall deliver up the kingdom to God, even the Father, and God shall be all in all, we shall forever be with the Lord. My soul anticipates that grandest of all family meetings, when all the chosen shall assemble around the throne of God. It is but a little while and it shall come; it is but the twinkling of an eye and it shall all be matter of fact. We talk of time as though it were a far-reaching thing; I appeal to you gray heads who know what seventy years mean; are they not gone as a watch in the night? Well, let the waiting be prolonged for ten thousand years, if the Lord pleases; the ten thousand years will end, and then forever and forever we shall be as one family where Jesus is. This hope should cheer us. Death, where is your sting? Grave, where is your victory? Cheered by the prospect of an everlasting reunion, we defy you to sadden us! Encouraged by the glory which God has decreed, we laugh at your vain attempts to make breaches in the ranks of the one and indivisible family of the living God!

The practical point is—*do we belong to that family?* I will leave that naked question to work in every heart. Do I belong to that family? Am I born of God? Am I a believer in Jesus? If not, I am an heir of wrath and not in the family of God.

If we do belong to the family, *let us show our relationship* by loving all the members of it. I should not like a brother to be gone to heaven and to reflect that I was unkind to him; I should not like to think that I might have smoothed his pathway, and I did not; or I might have cheered him and refused. Dear brethren, we shall live together in heaven forever; let us love each other now with a pure heart fervently. Help your poor brethren, cheer your desponding sisters; let no man look only on his own things, but every man also on the things of others. Brother, be brotherly; sister, be a true sister. Let us not love in word only, but in deed and in truth, for we shall soon be at home together in our Father's house on high.

Heavenly Rest

Delivered on Sabbath morning, May 24, 1857, at the Music Hall, Royal Surrey Gardens. No. 133.

There remaineth therefore a rest to the people of God. —HEBREWS 4:9

The apostle proved, in the former part of this and the latter part of the preceding chapter, that there was a rest promised in Scripture called the rest of God. He proved that Israel did not attain that rest; for God swore in his wrath, saying, "They shall not enter into my rest." He proved that this did not merely refer to the rest of the land of Canaan; for he says that after they were in Canaan, David himself speaks again in after ages concerning the rest of God, as a thing which was yet to come. Again he proves, that "seeing those to whom it was promised did not enter in, because of unbelief, and it remaineth that some must enter in, therefore," says he, "there remaineth a rest to the people of God."

"*My* rest," says God: the rest of God! Something more wonderful than any other kind of rest. In my text it is (in the original) called the *Sabbatism*—not the Sabbath, but the rest of the Sabbath—not the outward ritual of the Sabbath, which was binding upon the Jew, but the inward spirit of the Sabbath, which is the joy and delight of the Christian. "There remaineth therefore"—because others have not had it, because some are to have it—"there remaineth therefore a rest to the people of God."

Now, this rest, I believe, is partly enjoyed on earth. "We that have believed do enter into rest," for we have ceased from our own works, as God did from his. But the full fruition and rich enjoyment of it remains in the future and eternal state of the beatified on the other side the stream of death. Of that it shall be our delightful work to talk a little this morning. And oh! if God should help me to raise but one of his feeble saints on the wings of love to look within the veil and see the joys of the future, I shall be well contented to have made the joy bells ring in one heart at least, to have set one eye flashing with joy, and to have made one spirit light with gladness. The rest of heaven! I shall try first to *exhibit it* and then to *extol it*.

1. First, I shall try to *exhibit* the rest of heaven; and in doing so I shall exhibit it, first by way of contrast, and then by way of comparison.

To begin then, I shall try to exhibit heaven *by way of contrast*. The rest of the righteous in glory is now to be contrasted with certain other things.

We will contrast it, first, *with the best estate of the worldling and the sinner*. The worldling has frequently a good estate. Sometimes his vats overflow, his barns are crammed, his heart is full of joy and gladness, there are periods with him when he flourishes like a green bay tree, when field is added to field, and house to house, when he pulls down his barns and builds greater, when the river of his joy is full, and the ocean of his life is at its flood with joy and blessedness. But ah! beloved, the state of the righteous up there is not for a moment to be compared with the joy of the sinner; it is so infinitely superior, so far surpassing it, that it seems impossible that I should even try to set it in contrast. The worldling, when his corn and his wine are increased, has a glad eye and a joyous heart; but even then he has the direful thought that *he may soon leave his wealth*. He remembers that death may cut him down, that he must then leave all his fair riches behind him, and sleep like the meanest of the land in a narrow coffin, six feet of earth his only heritage. Not so the righteous man: he has obtained an inheritance which is "undefiled, and that fadeth not away." He knows that there is no possibility of his losing his joys—

> *He is securely blessed,*
> *Has done with sin, and care, and woe,*
> *And doth with Jesus rest.*

He has no dread of dissolution, no fear of the coffin or the shroud, and so far the life of heaven is not worthy to be put in comparison with the life of the sinner. But the worldling, with all his joys, always has *a worm at the root* of them. You votaries of pleasure! The blush upon your cheek is frequently but a painted deception. Ah! you sons and daughters of gaiety! The light foot of your dance is not in keeping with the heavy woe of your miserable spirits. Do you not confess that if by the excitement of company you for a while forget the emptiness of your heart, yet silence, and the hour of midnight, and the waking watches of your bed, bid you sometimes think that there must be something more blessed than the mere wanderings of gaiety in which you now are found? You are trying the world, some of you; speak then! Do you not find it empty? Might it not be said of the world, as an old philosopher said of it when he represented a man with it in his hands smiting it and listening to its ringing? Touch it, touch it! Make it ring again; it is empty. So it is with the world. You know it is so; and if you know it not as yet, the day is coming when after you have plucked the sweets, you shall be pricked with the thorn, and when you shall find that all is unsatisfactory that does not begin and end with God.

Not so the Christian in heaven. For him there are no nights; and if there be times of solitude and rest, he is ever filled with ecstatic joy. His river flows ever full of bliss, without one pebble of sorrow over which it ripples; he has no aching conscience, no "aching void the world can never fill." He is supremely blessed, satisfied with favor, and full with the goodness of the Lord.

And you know, you worldlings, that your best estates often bring you great anxiety, *lest they should depart from you.* You are not so foolish yet as to conceive that riches endure forever. You men of business are frequently led to see that riches take to themselves wings and fly away. You have accumulated a fortune; but you find it is harder to retain than it is to get. You are seeking after a competence; but you find that you grasp at shadows that flit away—that the everlasting vicissitudes of business and the constant changes of mankind are causes of prudent alarm to you, for you fear that you shall lose your gods, and that your gourd shall be eaten by the worm, and fall down, and your shadow shall be taken away.

Not so the Christian. He lives in a house that can never hasten to decay; he wears a crown, the glister of which shall never be dim; he has a garment which shall never wax old; he has bliss that never can depart from him, nor he from it. He is now firmly set, like a pillar of marble in the temple of God. The world may rock, the tempest may sway it like the cradle of a child; but there, above the world, above the perpetual revolution of the stars, the Christian stands secure and immovable; his rest infinitely surpasses yours. Ah, if you shall go to all the fabled luxuries of eastern monarchs, and see their dainty couches and their luscious wines—behold the riches of their pleasantry! How charming is the music that lulls them to their sleep! How gently moves the fan that wafts them to their slumber! But ah!

> I would not change my blessed estate
> For all the world calls good or great;
> And whilst my faith can keep her hold
> I envy not the sinner's gold.

I reckon that the richest, highest, noblest condition of a worldly man is not worthy to be compared with the joy that is to be revealed hereafter in the breasts of those who are sanctified. O you spendthrift mortals, that for one merry dance and a giddy life will lose a world of joys! O fools that catch at bubbles and lose realities! O ten thousand times mad men, that grasp at shadows and lose the substance! What! Sirs, do you think a little round of pleasure, a few years of gaiety and merriment, just a little time of the tossing about, to and fro, of worldly business, is a compensation for eternal ages of unfading bliss? Oh! how foolish will you conceive yourselves to be, when you are in the next state, when cast away from heaven you will see the saints blessed! I think I hear your mournful soliloquy, "Oh! how cheaply did I sell my soul! What a poor price did I get for all I have now lost! I have lost the palace and the crown, and the joy and bliss forever, and am shut up in hell! And for what did I lose it? I lost it for the lascivious wanton kiss. I lost it for the merry drunken song; I lost it for just a few short years of pleasures, which, after all, were only painted pleasures!" Oh! I think I see you in your lost estates, cursing yourselves, rending your hair, that you should have sold heaven for counters [mere change] and have traded away eternal life for pitiful farthings, which were spent quickly and which burned your hand in the spending of them! Oh! that you were wise, that you would weigh those things, and reckon that a life of the greatest happiness here is nothing compared with the glorious hereafter: "There remaineth a rest to the people of God."

Now let me put it in *more pleasing contrast*. I shall contrast the rest of the believer above with the miserable estate of the believer sometimes here below. Christians have their sorrows. Suns have their spots, skies have their clouds, and Christians have their sorrows too. But oh! how different will the state of the righteous be up there, from the state of the believer here! Here the Christian has to suffer anxiety. He is anxious to serve his Master, to do his best in his day and generation. His constant cry is—"Help me to serve you, O my God," and he looks out, day after day, with a strong desire for opportunities of doing good. Ah! if he be an active Christian, he will have much labor, much toil, in endeavoring to serve his Master; and there will be times when he will say, "My soul is in haste to be gone; I am not wearied of the labor; I am wearied in it. To toil thus in the sun, though for a good Master, is not the thing that just now I desire." Ah! Christian, the day shall soon be over, and you shall no longer have to toil; the sun is nearing the horizon; it shall rise again with a brighter day than you have ever seen before. There, up in heaven, Luther has no more to face a thundering Vatican; Paul has no more to run from city to city, and continent to continent; there Baxter has no more to toil in his pulpit, to preach with a broken heart to hard-hearted sinners; there no longer has Knox to "cry aloud and spare not" against the immoralities of the false church; there no more shall be the strained lung and the tired throat and the aching eye; no more shall the Sunday school teacher feel that his Sabbath is a day of joyful weariness; no more shall the tract distributor meet with rebuffs. No, there, those who have served their country and their God, those who have toiled for man's welfare, with all their might, shall enter into everlasting rest. Sheathed is the sword; the banner is furled; the fight is over; the victory won; and they rest from their labors.

Here, too, the Christian is always *sailing onward*; he is always in motion; he feels that he has not yet attained. Like Paul he can say, "Forgetting the things that are behind, I press forward to that which is before." But there his weary head shall be crowned with unfading light. There the ship that has been speeding onward shall furl its sails in the port of eternal bliss. There he who like an arrow has sped his way shall be fixed forever in the target. There we who like fleeting clouds were driven by every wind shall gently distill in one perennial shower of everlasting joy. There is no progress, no motion there; they are at rest; they have attained the summit of the mountain; they have ascended to their God and our God. Higher they cannot go; they have reached the *Ultima Thule*; there are no fortunate islands beyond; this is life's utmost end of happiness; and they furl their sails, rest from their labors, and enjoy themselves forever. There is a difference between the progress of earth and the perfect fixity of the rest of heaven.

Here, too, the believer is often the subject of *doubt and fear.* "Am I his or am I not?" is often the cry. He trembles lest he should be deceived; at times he almost despairs and is inclined not to put his name down as one of the children of God. Dark insinuations are whispered into his ears; he thinks that God's mercy is clean gone forever, and that he will not be mindful of him any more. Again, his sins sometimes upbraid him, and he thinks God will not have mercy on him. He has a poor fainting heart; he is like Ready-to-Halt—he has to go all his way on crutches; he has a poor feeble mind, always tumbling down over a straw and fearing one day he shall be drowned in a cart rut. Though the lions are chained he is as much afraid of them as if they were loose. Hill Difficulty often frightens him, going down into the Valley of Humiliation is often troublesome work to him. But there, there are no hills to climb, no dragons to fight, no foes to conquer, no dangers to dread. Ready-to-Halt, when he dies, will bury his crutches, and Feeble-Mind will leave his feebleness behind him; Fearing will never fear again; poor Doubting-Heart will learn confidently to believe. Oh, joy above all joys! The day is coming when I shall "know as I am known," when I shall not want to ask whether I am his or not, for in his arms encircled, there shall be no room for doubt. O Christian, you think there are slips between your lips and that cup of joy, but when you grasp the handle of that cup with your hand and are drinking drafts of ineffable delight, then you will have no doubt or fear.

> There you shall see his face,
> And never, never sin.
> There from the rivers of his grace,
> Drink endless pleasures in.

Here, too, on earth, the Christian has to suffer; here he has the aching head and the pained body; his limbs may be bruised or broken, disease may rack him with torture; he may be an afflicted one from his birth, he may have lost an eye or an ear or he may have lost many of his powers; or if not, being of a weakly constitution, he may have to spend the most of his days and nights upon the bed of weariness.

Or if his body be sound, yet what suffering he has in his mind! Conflicts between depravity and gross temptations from the evil one, assaults of hell, perpetual attacks of diverse kinds, from the world, the flesh, and the devil. But there, no aching head, no weary heart; there, no palsied arm, no brow plowed with the furrows of old age; there, the lost limb shall be recovered, and old age shall find itself endowed with perpetual youth; there, the infirmities of the flesh shall be left behind, given to the worm and devoured by corruption. There, they shall flit, as on the wings of angels, from pole to pole, and from place to place, without weariness or anguish; there, they shall never need to lie upon the bed of rest, or the bed of suffering, for day without night, with joy unflagging, they shall circle God's throne rejoicing, and ever praise him who has said, "The inhabitants there shall never be sick."

There, too, they shall be free from persecution. Here Sicilian Vespers and St. Bartholomew and Smithfield are well-known words; but there, shall be none to taunt them with a cruel word or touch them with a cruel hand. There, emperors and kings are not known, and those who had power to torture them cease to be. They are in the society of saints; they shall be free from all the idle converse of the wicked, and from their cruel jeers set free forever. Set free from persecution! You army of martyrs, you were slain; you were torn asunder; you were cast to wild beasts; you wandered about in sheepskins and goatskins, destitute, afflicted, and tormented. I see you now, a mighty host. The habiliments [clothes] you wear are torn with thorns; your faces are scarred

with sufferings; I see you at your stakes, and on your crosses; I hear your
words of submission on your racks; I see you in your prisons; I behold you
in your pillories, but—

> Now ye are arrayed in white,
> Brighter than the noonday sun,
> Fairest of the sons of light,
> Nearest the eternal throne.

These are they, who "for their Master died, who love the cross and
crown"; they waded through seas of blood in order to obtain the inheritance;
and there they are, with the bloodred crown of martyrdom about their heads,
that ruby brightness, far excelling every other. Yes, there is no persecution
there. "There remaineth a rest for the people of God." Alas! In this mortal
state, the child of God is also subject to sin; even he fails in his duty and wan-
ders from his God; even he does not walk in all the law of his God blameless,
though he desires to do it. Sin now troubles him constantly; but there, sin is
dead; there, they have no temptation to sin, from without or from within, but
they are perfectly free to serve their Master. Here, the child of God has sometimes to weep repentingly of his backslidings; but there, they never shed tears
of penitence, for they have never cause to do so.

And last of all, here, the child of God has to wet the cold ashes of his rel-
atives with *tears*; here, he has to bid adieu to all that is lovely and fair of mortal race; here it is he hears, "earth to earth, and dust to dust, and ashes to
ashes," while the solemn music of the dust upon the coffin lid beats doleful
time to those words. Here, is the mother buried, the child snatched away, the
husband rent from the bosom of a loving wife, the brother parted from the
sister. The plate upon the coffin, the last coat of arms of earth, earth's last
emblems are here ever before our eyes. But there, never once shall be heard
the toll of the funeral bell; no hearse with plumes has ever darkened the
streets of gold; no emblems of sorrow have ever intruded into the homes of
the immortal; they are strangers to the meaning of death; they cannot die—
they live forever, having no power to decay, and no possibility of corruption.
O rest of the righteous, how blessed are you, where families shall again be
bound up in one bundle, where parted friends shall again meet to part no
more, and where the whole church of Christ united in one mighty circle, shall
together praise God and the Lamb throughout eternal ages.

Brethren, I have tried thus to set the rest of the righteous in the way of
contrast; I feel I have failed. Poor are the words I can utter to tell you of
immortal things. Even holy Baxter himself, when he wrote of the *Saints' [Ever-*

lasting] Rest, paused, and said, "But these are only tinklings compared with the full thunders of heaven." I cannot tell you, dear friends, nor can mortal tell, what God has prepared for them that love him.

And now I shall try very briefly to exhibit this contrast *in the way of comparison.* The Christian has some rest here, but nothing compared with the rest which is to come.

There is the *rest of the church.* When the believer joins the church of God, and becomes united with them, he may expect to rest. The good old writer of *The Pilgrim's Progress* says, that when the weary pilgrims were once admitted to the house Beautiful, they were shown to sleep in a chamber called "peace," or "rest." The church member at the Lord's table has a sweet enjoyment of rest in fellowship with the saints; but ah! up there the rest of church fellowship far surpasses anything that is known here; for there are no divisions there, no angry words at the church meetings, no harsh thoughts of one another, no bickerings about doctrine, no fightings about practice. There, Baptist and Presbyterian and Independent and Wesleyan and Episcopalian, serving the same Lord, and having been washed in the same blood, sing the same song and are all joined in one. There pastors and deacons never look coolly on each other; no haughty prelates there, no lofty-minded ministers there, but all meek and lowly, all knit together in brotherhood; they have a rest which surpasses all the rest of the church on earth.

There is, again, a rest of *faith* which a Christian enjoys; a sweet rest. Many of us have known it. We have known what it is, when the billows of trouble have run high, to hide ourselves in the breast of Christ and feel secure. We have cast our anchor deep into the rocks of God's promise; we have gone to sleep in our chamber and have not feared the tempest; we have looked at tribulation and have smiled at it; we have looked at death himself and have laughed him to scorn; we have had much trust by Christian faith that, dauntless and fearless, nothing could move us. Yes, in the midst of calumny, reproach, slander, and contempt, we have said, "I shall not be moved, for God is on my side." But the rest up there is better still—more unruffled, more sweet, more perfectly calm, more enduring, and more lasting than even the rest of faith.

And, again, the Christian sometimes has the blessed rest of *communion.* There are happy moments when he puts his head on the Savior's breast— when, like John, he feels that he is close to the Savior's heart, and there he sleeps. "God giveth his beloved sleep"; not the sleep of unconsciousness, but the sleep of joy. Happy, happy, happy are the dreams we have had on the couch of communion; blessed have been the times, when, like the spouse in

Solomon's song, we could say of Christ, "His left hand was under my head, and with his right hand did he embrace me."

> But sweeter still the fountainhead,
> Though sweet may be the stream.

When we shall have plunged into a very bath of joy, we shall have found the delights even of communion on earth to have been but the dipping of the finger in the cup, but the dipping of the bread in the dish, whereas heaven itself shall be the participation of the whole of the joy, and not the mere antepast of it. Here, we sometimes enter into the portico of happiness; there, we shall go into the presence chamber of the King; here, we look over the hedge and see the flowers in heaven's garden; there, we shall walk between the beds of bliss and pluck fresh flowers at each step; here, we just look and see the sunlight of heaven in the distance, like the lamps of the thousand-gated cities shining afar off, but there, we shall see them in all their blaze of splendor; here, we listen to the whisperings of heaven's melody, borne by winds from afar; but there, entranced, amid the grand oratorio of the blessed, we shall join in the everlasting hallelujah to the great Messiah, the God, the I AM. Oh! again I say, do we not wish to mount aloft and fly away, to enter into the rest which remains to the people of God?

2. And now, yet more briefly, and then we shall have done. I am to endeavor to *extol* this rest, as I have tried to *exhibit* it.

I would extol this rest for many reasons; and oh! that I were eloquent, that I might extol it as it deserves! Oh! for the lip of angel and the burning tongue of cherub, to talk now of the bliss of the sanctified and of the rest of God's people!

It is, first, a *perfect* rest. They are wholly at rest in heaven. Here, rest is but partial. I hope in a little time to cease from everyday labors for a season, but then the head will think, and the mind may be looking forward to prospective labor, and while the body is still, the brain will yet be in motion. Here, on Sabbath days a vast multitude of you sit in God's house, but many of you are obliged to stand and rest but little except in your mind, and even when the mind is at rest, the body is wearied with the toil of standing. You have a weary mile, perhaps many miles, to go to your homes on the Sabbath day. And let the Sabbatarian say what he will, you may work on the Sabbath day, if you work for God; and this Sabbath day's work of going to the house of God is work for God, and God accepts it. For yourselves you may not labor; God commands you to rest, but if you have to toil these three, these four, these five, these six miles, as many of you have done, I will not and I must not blame you. "The priests in the sanctuary profane the Sabbath, and are blameless." It is toil and labor, it is true, but it is for a good cause—for your Master. But there, my friends, the rest is perfect; the body there rests perpetually, the mind too always rests; though the inhabitants are always busy, always serving God, yet they are never weary, never toilworn, never exhausted; they never fling themselves upon their couches at the end of the day, and cry, "Oh! when shall I be away from this land of toil?" They never stand up in the burning sunlight and wipe the hot sweat from their brow; they never rise from their bed in the morning, half refreshed, to go to laborious study. No, they are perfectly at rest, stretched on the couch of eternal joy. They know not the semblance of a tear; they have done with sin, and care, and woe, and with their Savior rest.

Again, it is a *seasonable* rest. How seasonable it will be for some of you! You sons of wealth, you know not the toils of the poor; the callous-handed laborer, perhaps, you have not seen, and you know not how he has to tug and to toil. Among my congregation I have many of a class upon whom I have always looked with pity, poor women who must rise tomorrow morning with the sun and begin that everlasting "stitch, stitch" that works their finger to the bone. And from Monday morning till Saturday night, many of you, my members, and multitudes of you, my hearers, will not be able to lay aside your needle and your thread, except when, tired and weary, you fall back on your chair and are lulled to sleep by your thoughts of labor! Oh! how seasonable will heaven's rest be to you! Oh! how glad will you be, when you get there, to find that there are no Monday mornings, no more toil for you, but rest, eternal rest! Others of you have hard manual labor to perform; you have reason to thank God that you are strong enough to do it, and you are not ashamed of your work; for labor is an honor to a man. But still there are times when you say, "I wish I were not so dragged to death by the business of London life." We have but little rest in this huge city; our day is longer, and our work is harder than our friends in the country. You have sometimes sighed to go into the green fields for a breath of fresh air; you have longed to hear the song of the sweet birds that used to wake you when you were lads; you have regretted the bright blue sky, the beauteous flowers, and the thousand charms of a country life. And perhaps you will never get beyond this smoky city, but remember, when you get up there, "sweet fields arrayed in living green" and "rivers of delight" shall be the place where you shall rest; you shall have all the joys you can conceive of in that home of happiness. And though worn and weary, you come to your grave, tottering on your staff; having journeyed through the wilderness of life like a weary camel, which has only stopped on the Sabbath to sip its little water at the well, or to be baited at the oasis, there you will arrive at your journey's end, laden with gold and spices, and enter into the grand caravansary of heaven, and enjoy forever the things you have wearily carried with you here.

And I must say, that to others of us who have not to toil with our hands, heaven will be a seasonable rest. Those of us who have to tire our brain day after day will find it no slight boon to have an everlasting rest above. I will not boast of what I may do; there may be many who do more; there may be many who are perpetually and daily striving to serve God and are using their mind's best energies in so doing. But this much I may say, that almost every week I have the pleasure of preaching twelve times, and often in my sleep do I think of what I shall say next time. Not having the advantage of laying out my seven shillings and sixpence in buying manuscripts, it costs me hard diligent labor to find even something to say. And I sometimes have a difficulty to keep the hopper full in the mill; I feel that if I had not now and then a rest I should have no wheat for God's children. Still it is on, on, on, and on we must go; we hear the chariot wheels of God behind us, and we dare not stop; we think that eternity is drawing nigh, and we must go on. Rest to us now is more than labor; we want to be at work; but oh! how seasonable it shall be, when to the minister it shall be said—

> Servant of God, well done!
> Rest from thy loved employ;
> The battle fought, the victory won,
> Enter thy Master's joy.

It will be seasonable rest. You that are weary with state cares, and have to learn the ingratitude of men; you that have sought honors, and have got them to your cost, you seek to do your best, but your very independence of spirit is called servility, while your servility would have been praised! You who seek to honor God, and not to honor men, who will not bind yourselves to parties, but seek in your own independent and honest judgment to serve your country and your God; you, I say, when God shall see fit to call you to himself, will find it no small joy to have done with parliaments, to have done with states and kingdoms, and to have laid aside your honors, to receive honors more lasting among those who dwell forever before the throne of the most High.

One thing, and then once more, and then farewell. This rest, my brethren, ought to be extolled, because it is *eternal*. Here, my best joys bear "mortal" on their brow; here, my fair flowers fade; here, my sweet cups have dregs and are soon empty; here, my sweetest birds must die, and their melody must soon be hushed; here, my most pleasant days must have their nights; here, the flowings of my bliss must have their ebbs; everything does pass away, but there, everything shall be immortal; the harp shall be unrusted, the crown unwithered, the eye undimmed, the voice unfaltering, the heart unwavering, and the being wholly consolidated unto eternity. Happy day, happy day, when mortality shall be swallowed up of life, and the mortal shall have put on immortality!

And then, last, this glorious rest is to be best of all commended for its *certainty*. "There remaineth a rest to the people of God." Doubting one, you have often said, "I fear I shall never enter heaven." Fear not, all the people of God shall enter there; there is no fear about it. I love the quaint saying of a dying man, who, in his country brogue, exclaimed, "I have no fear of going home; I have sent all before me. God's finger is on the latch of my door, and I am ready for him to enter." "But," said one, "are you not afraid lest you should miss your inheritance?" "No," said he, "no, there is one crown in heaven that the angel Gabriel could not wear; it will fit no head but mine. There is one throne in heaven that Paul the apostle could not fill; it was made for me, and I shall have it. There is one dish at the banquet that I must eat, or else it will be untasted, for God has set it apart for me." O Christian, what a joyous thought! Your portion is secure! "There remaineth a rest." "But cannot I forfeit it?" No, it is entailed. If I be a child of God, I shall not lose it. It is mine as securely as if I were there.

> Come, Christian, mount to Pisgah's top,
> And view the landscape o'er.

See you that little river of death, glistening in the sunlight, and across it do you see the pinnacles of the eternal city? Do you mark the pleasant suburbs and all the joyous inhabitants? Turn your eye to that spot. Do you see where that ray of light is glancing now? There is a little spot there; do you see it? That is your patrimony; that is yours. Oh, if you could fly across, you would see written upon it: "This remains for such a one, preserved for him only. He shall be caught up and dwell forever with God." Poor doubting one, see your inheritance; it is yours. If you believe in the Lord Jesus, you are one of the Lord's people; if you have repented of sin, you are one of the Lord's people; if you have been renewed in heart, you are one of the Lord's people, and there is a place for you, a crown for you, a harp for you. No one else shall have it but yourself, and you shall have it before long. Just pardon me one moment if I beg of you to conceive of yourselves as being in heaven. Is it not a strange thing to think of—a poor clown in heaven? Think, how will you feel with your crown on your head? Weary matron, many years have rolled over you. How changed will be the scene when you are young again. Ah, toilworn laborer, only think when you shall rest forever. Can you conceive it? Could you but think for a moment of yourself as being in heaven now, what a strange surprise would seize you. You would not so as much say, "What! Are these streets of gold? What! Are these walls of jasper?" "What, am I here? In white? Am I here, with a crown on my brow? Am I here singing, that was always groaning? What! I praise God that once cursed him? What! I lift up my voice in his honor? Oh, precious blood that washed me clean! Oh, precious faith that set me free! Oh, precious Spirit that made me repent, else I had been cast away and been in hell! But oh! what wonders! Angels! I am surprised. I am enraptured! Wonder of wonders! Oh! gates of pearls, I long since heard of you! Oh! joys that never fade, I long since heard tell of you! But I am like the Queen of Sheba, the half has not yet been told me. Profusion, oh profusion of bliss! Wonder of wonders! Miracle of miracles! What a world I am in! And oh! that I am here, this is the topmost miracle of all!" And yet 'tis true, 'tis true; and that is the glory of it. It is true. Come, worm, and prove it; come, pall; come shroud; come, and prove it. Then come, wings of faith, come, leap like a seraph; come, eternal ages, come, and you shall prove that there are joys that the eye has not seen, which the ear has not heard, and which only God can reveal to us by his Spirit. Oh! my earnest prayer is that none of you may come short of this rest, but that you may enter into it, and enjoy it forever and ever. God give you his great blessing, for Jesus' sake! Amen.

The Good Man's Life and Death

Delivered on Sabbath morning, August 16, 1857, at the Music Hall, Royal Surrey Gardens. No. 146.

For to me to live is Christ, and to die is gain. —PHILIPPIANS 1:21

How ominously these words follow each other in the text—"live," "die." There is but a comma between them, and surely as it is in the words so is it in reality. How brief the distance between life and death! In fact there is none. Life is but death's vestibule, and our pilgrimage on earth is but a journey to the grave. The pulse that preserves our being beats our death march, and the blood which circulates our life is floating it onward to the deeps of death. Today we see our friends in health; tomorrow we hear of their decease. We clasped the hand of the strong man, but yesterday and today we close his eyes. We rode in the chariot of comfort but an hour ago, and in a few more hours the last black chariot must convey us to the home of all living.

Oh, how closely allied is death to life! The lamb that sports in the field must soon feel the knife. The ox that lows in the pasture is fattening for the slaughter. Trees do but grow that they may be felled. Yes, and greater things than these feel death. Empires rise and flourish; they flourish but to decay, they rise to fall. How often do we take up the volume of history and read of the rise and fall of empires. We hear of the coronation and the death of kings. Death is the black servant who rides behind the chariot of life. See life! And death is close behind it. Death reaches far throughout this world and has stamped all terrestrial things with the broad arrow of the grave. Stars die perhaps; it is said that conflagrations have been seen far off in the distant ether, and astronomers have marked the funerals of worlds, the decay of those mighty orbs that we had imagined set forever in sockets of silver to glisten as the lamps of eternity. But blessed be God; there is one place where death is not life's brother, where life reigns alone; "to live," is not the first syllable which is to be followed by the next, "to die." There is a land where death knells are never tolled, where winding sheets are never woven, where graves are never dug. Blessed land beyond the skies! To reach it we must die. But if after death we obtain a glorious immortality, our text is indeed true: "to die is gain."

If you would get a fair estimate of the happiness of any man, you must judge him in these two closely connected things, his life and his death. The heathen Solon said, "Call no man happy until he is dead; for you know not what changes may pass upon him in life." We add to that—Call no man happy until he is dead; because the life that is to come, if that be miserable, shall far outweigh the highest life of happiness that has been enjoyed on earth. To estimate a man's condition we must take it in all its length. We must not measure that one thread which reaches from the cradle to the coffin. We must go further; we must go from the coffin to the resurrection, and from the resurrection on throughout eternity. To know whether acts are profitable, I must not estimate their effects on me for the hour in which I live, but for the eternity in which I am to exist. I must not weigh matters in the scales of time; I must not calculate by the hours, minutes, and seconds of the clock, but I must count and value things by the ages of eternity.

Come, then, beloved; we have before us the picture of a man, the two sides of whose existence will both of them bear inspection; we have his life, we have his death: we have it said of his life, *"to live is Christ,"* of his death, *"to die is gain"*; and if the same shall be said of any of you, oh! you may rejoice! You are among that thrice-happy number whom the Lord has loved, and whom he delights to honor.

We shall now divide our text very simply into these two points, *the good man's life* and *the good man's death*.

1. As to *his life,* we have that briefly described thus: "For me to live is Christ."

The believer did not always live to Christ. When he was first born into this world, he was a slave of sin and an heir of wrath, even as others. Though he may have afterward become the greatest of saints, yet until divine grace has entered his heart, he is "in the gall of bitterness and in the bonds of iniquity." He only begins to live to Christ when God the Holy Spirit convinces him of his sin and of his desperate evil nature, and when by grace he is brought to see the dying Savior making a propitiation for his guilt. From that moment when by faith he sees the slaughtered victim of Calvary, and casts his whole life on him, to be saved, to be redeemed, to be preserved, and to be blessed by the virtue of his atonement and the greatness of his grace, from that moment the man begins to live to Christ.

And now shall we tell you as briefly as we can what living to Christ means. It means, first, that *the life of a Christian derives its parentage from Christ.* "For me to live is Christ." The righteous man has two lives. He has one which he inherited from his parents; he looks back to an ancestral race of which he is the branch, and he traces his life to the parent stock; but he has a second life, a life spiritual, a life which is as much above mere mental life, as mental life is above the life of the animal or the plant; and for the source of this spiritual life he looks not to father or mother, nor to priest nor man, nor to himself, but he looks to Christ. He says, "O Lord Jesus, the everlasting Father, the Prince of peace, you are my spiritual parent; unless your Spirit had breathed into my nostrils the breath of a new, holy, and spiritual life, I had been to this day 'dead in trespasses and sins.' I owe my third principle, my spirit, to the implantation of your grace. I had a body and a soul by my parents; I have received the third principle, the spirit from you, and in you I live, and move, and have my being. My new, my best, my highest, my most heavenly life, is wholly derived from you. To you I ascribe it. My life is hid with Christ in God. It is no longer I that live, but Christ that lives in me."

And so the Christian says, "For me to live is Christ," because for me to live is to live a life whose parentage is not of human origin, but of divine, even of Christ himself. Again he intended to say, that *Christ was the sustenance of his life*, the food his newborn spirit fed upon. The believer has three parts to be sustained. The body, which must have its proper nutriment; the soul, which must have knowledge and thought to supply it; and the spirit which must feed on Christ. Without bread I become attenuated to a skeleton, and at last I die; without thought my mind becomes dwarfed and dwindles itself until I become the idiot, with a soul that has just life, but little more. And without Christ my newborn spirit must become a vague shadowy emptiness. It cannot live unless it feeds on that heavenly manna which came down from heaven. Now the Christian can say, "The life that I live is Christ," because Christ is the food on which he feeds and the sustenance of his newborn Spirit.

The apostle also meant that *the fashion of his life was Christ*. I suppose that every man living has a model by which he endeavors to shape his life. When we start in life, we generally select some person, or persons, whose combined virtues shall be to us the mirror of perfection. "Now," says Paul, "if you ask me after what fashion I mold my life, and what is the model by which I would sculpture my being, I tell you, it is Christ. I have no fashion, no form, no model by which to shape my being, except the Lord Jesus Christ. Now, the true Christian, if he be an upright man, can say the same. Understand, however, what I mean by the word *"upright."* An upright man means a straight-up man—a man that does not cringe and bow and fawn to other men's feet; a man that does not lean for help on other men, but just stands with his head heavenward, in all the dignity of his independence, leaning nowhere except on the arm of the Omnipotent. Such a man will take Christ alone to be his model and pattern.

This is the very age of conventionalities. People dare not now do a thing unless everybody else does the same. You do not often say, "Is a thing right?" The most you say is, "Does So-and-So do it?" You have some great personage or other in your family connection who is looked upon as being the very standard of all propriety; and if he do it, then you think you may safely do it. And oh! what an outcry there is against a man who dares to be singular, who just believes that some of your conventionalities are trammels and chains, and kicks them all to pieces and says, "I am free!" The world is at him in a minute; all the bandogs of malice and slander are at him, because he says, "I will not follow your model! I will vindicate the honor of my Master and not take your great masters to be forever my pattern."

Oh! I would to God that every statesman, that every minister, that every Christian were free to hold that his only form, and his only fashion for imitation, must be the character of Christ. I would that we could scorn all superstitious attachments to the ancient errors of our ancestors; and while some would be forever looking upon age and upon hoary antiquity with veneration, I would we had the courage to look upon a thing, not according to its age, but according to its rightness, and so weigh everything, not by its novelty, or by its antiquity, but by its conformity to Christ Jesus and his holy gospel; rejecting that which is not, though it be hoary with years, and believing that which is, even though it be but the creature of the day, and saying with earnestness, "For me to live is not to imitate this man or the other, but 'for me to live is Christ.'"

I think, however, that the very center of Paul's idea would be this: *the end of his life is Christ.* You think you see Paul land upon the shores of Philippi. There, by the riverside, were ships gathered and many merchant men. There you would see the merchant busy with his ledger and overlooking his cargo, and he paused and put his hand upon his brow, and said as he gripped his money bag, "For me to live is gold." And there you see his humbler clerk, employed in some plainer work, toiling for his master, and he, perspiring with work, mutters between his teeth, "For me to live is to gain a bare subsistence." And there stands for a moment to listen to him, one with a studious face and a sallow countenance, and with a roll full of the mysterious characters of wisdom. "Young man," he says, "for me to live is learning." "Aha, aha!" says another, who stands by, clothed in mail, with a helmet on his head, "I scorn your modes of life; for me to live is glory." But there walks one, a humble tentmaker, called Paul; you see the lineaments of the Jew upon his face, and he steps into the middle of them all and says, "For me to live is Christ." Oh! how they smile with contempt upon him, and how they scoff at him, for having chosen such an object! "For me to live is Christ." And what did he mean? The learned man stopped and said, "Christ! Who is he? Is he that foolish, mad fellow, of whom I have heard, who was executed upon Calvary for sedition?" The meek reply is, "It is he who died, Jesus of Nazareth, the King of the Jews." "What?" says the Roman soldier, "and do you live for a man who died a slave's death? What glory will you get by fighting his battles?" "What profit is there in your preaching?" chimes in the trader. Ah! and even the merchant's clerk thought Paul mad, for he said, "How can he feed his family? How will he supply his wants if all he lives for is to honor Christ?" Yes, but Paul knew what he was at. He was the wisest man of them all. He knew which way was right for heaven, and which would end the best. But, right or wrong, his soul was wholly possessed with the idea — "For me to live is Christ."

Brethren and sisters, can you say, as professing Christians, that you live up to the idea of the apostle Paul? Can you honestly say that for you to live is Christ? I will tell you my opinion of many of you. You join our churches; you are highly respectable men; you are accepted among us as true and real Christians; but in all honesty and truth, I do not believe that for you to live is Christ. I see many of you whose whole thoughts are engrossed with the things of earth; the mere getting of money, the amassing of wealth, seems to be your only object. I do not deny that you are liberal; I will not dare to say that you are not generous, and that your checkbook does not often bear the mark of some subscription for holy purposes, but I dare to say, after all, that you cannot in honesty say that you live wholly for Christ. You know that when you go to your shop or your warehouse, you do not think, in doing business, that you are doing it for Christ; you dare not be such a hypocrite as to say so. You must say that you do it for self-aggrandizement and for family advantage. "Well!" says one, "and is that a mean reason?" By no means; not for you, if you are mean enough to ask that question, but for the Christian it is. He professes to live for Christ; then how is it he dares to profess to live for his Master, and yet does not do so, but lives for mere worldly gain?

Let me speak to many a lady here. You would be shocked if I should deny your Christianity. You move in the highest circles of life, and you would be astonished if I should presume to touch your piety, after your many generous donations to religious objects; but I dare to do so. You — what do you do? You rise late enough in the day: you have your carriage out, and call to see your

friends or leave your card by way of proxy. You go to a party in the evening;
you talk nonsense, and come home and go to bed. And that is your life from
the beginning of the year to the end. It is just one regular round. There comes
the dinner or the ball, and the conclusion of the day; and then, amen, so be it,
forever. Now you don't live for Christ. I know you go to church regularly, or
attend at some dissenting chapel; all well and good. I shall not deny your piety,
according to the common usage of the term, but I deny that you have got to
anything like the place where Paul stood when he said, "For me to live is
Christ."

I, my brethren, know that with much earnest seeking I have failed to realize the fullness of entire devotion to the Lord Jesus. Every minister must
sometimes chasten himself and say, "Am I not sometimes a little warped in my
utterances? Did I not in some sermon aim to bring out a grand thought
instead of stating a home truth? Have I not kept back some warning that I
ought to have uttered because I feared the face of man?" Have we not all good
need to chasten ourselves because we must say that we have not lived for
Christ as we should have done? And yet there are, I trust, a noble few, the elite
of God's elect, a few chosen men and women on whose heads there is the
crown and diadem of dedication, who can truly say, "I have nothing in this
world I cannot give to Christ—I have said it, and mean what I have said—

'Take my soul and body's powers,
All my goods and all my hours,
All I have and all I am.'

Take me, Lord, and take me forever." These are the men who make our missionaries; these are the women to make our nurses for the sick; these are they
that would dare death for Christ; these are they who would give of their substance to his cause; these are they who would spend and be spent, who would
bear ignominy and scorn and shame if they could but advance their Master's
interest. How many of this sort have I here this morning? Might I not count
many of these benches before I could find a score? Many there are who do in
a measure carry out this principle; but who among us is there (I am sure he
stands not here in this pulpit) that can dare to say he has lived wholly for
Christ, as the apostle did? And yet, till there be more Pauls and more men ded-
icated to Christ, we shall never see God's kingdom come, nor shall we hope
to see his will done on earth, even as it is in heaven.

Now this is the true life of a Christian, its source, its sustenance, its fashion, and its end, all gathered up in two words, Christ Jesus; and, I must add, its
happiness, and its glory, is all in Christ. But I must detain you no longer.

2. I must go to the second point, *the death of the Christian.*

Alas, alas, that the good should die; alas, that the righteous should fall! Death, why do you not hew the deadly upas [tropical Asian tree]? Why do you not mow the hemlock? Why do you touch the tree beneath whose spreading branches weariness has rest? Why do you touch the flower whose perfume has made glad the earth? Death, why do you snatch away the excellent of the earth, in whom is all our delight? If you would use your ax, use it upon the cumber-grounds, the trees that draw nourishment but afford no fruit; you might be thanked then. But why will you cut down the cedars, why will you fell the goodly trees of Lebanon? O death, why do you not spare the church? Why must the pulpit be hung in black; why must the missionary station be filled with weeping? Why must the pious family lose its priest and the house its head? O death, what are you at? Touch not earth's holy things; your hands are not fit to pollute the Israel of God. Why do you put your hand upon the hearts of the elect? Oh, stay you, stay you; spare the righteous, death, and take the bad!

But no, it must not be; death comes and smites the goodliest of us all; the most generous, the most prayerful, the most holy, the most devoted must die. Weep, weep, weep, O church, for you have lost your martyrs; weep, O church, for you have lost your confessors, your holy men are fallen. Howl, fir tree, for the cedar has fallen, the godly fail, and the righteous are cut off. But stay awhile; I hear another voice. Say you thus unto the daughter of Judah, Spare your weeping. Say you thus unto the Lord's flock, Cease, cease your sorrow; your martyrs are dead, but they are glorified; your ministers are gone, but they have ascended up to your Father and to their Father; your brethren are buried in the grave, but the archangel's trumpet shall awake them, and their spirits are ever now with God.

Hear you the words of the text, by way of consolation, "to die is gain." Not such gain as you wish for, you son of the miser; not such gain as you are hunting for, you man of covetousness and self-love; a higher and a better gain is that which death brings to a Christian.

My dear friends, when I discoursed upon the former part of the verse, it was all plain. No proof was needed; you believed it, for you saw it clearly. "To live is Christ" has no paradox in it. But "to die is gain" is one of the gospel riddles which only the Christian can truly understand. To die is not gain if I look upon the merely visible; to die is loss, it is not gain. Has not the dead man lost his wealth? Though he had piles of riches, can he take anything with him? Has it not been said, "Naked came I out of my mother's womb, and naked shall I

return there"? "Dust you are, and unto dust shall you return." And which of
all your goods can you take with you? The man had a fair estate and a goodly
mansion; he has lost that. He can no more tread those painted halls nor walk
those verdant lawns. He had abundance of fame and honor; he has lost that,
so far as his own sense of it is concerned, though still the harp string trembles
at his name. He has lost his wealth, and buried though he may be in a costly
tomb, yet is he as poor as the beggar who looked upon him in the street in
envy. That is not gain; it is loss, and he has lost his friends: he has left behind
him a sorrowing wife and children, fatherless, without his guardian care; he
has lost the friend of his bosom, the companion of his youth. Friends are there
to weep over him, but they cannot cross the river with him; they drop a few
tears into his tomb, but with him they must not and cannot go. And has he not
lost all his learning, though he has toiled ever so much to fill his brain with
knowledge? What is he now above the servile slave, though he has acquired all
knowledge of earthly things? Is it not said,

> "Their memory and their love are lost
> Alike unknowing and unknown"?

Surely death is loss. Has he not lost the songs of the sanctuary and the
prayers of the righteous? Has he not lost the solemn assembly and the great
gathering of the people? No more shall the promise enchant his ear, no more
shall the glad tidings of the gospel wake his soul to melody. He sleeps in the
dust, the Sabbath bell tolls not for him, the sacramental emblems are spread
upon the table, but not for him. He has gone to his grave; he knows not that
which shall be after him. There is neither work nor device in the grave, where
we all are hastening. Surely death is loss. When I look upon you, you clay-cold
corpse, and see you just preparing to be the palace of corruption and the car-
nival for worms, I cannot think that you have gained. When I see that your eye
has lost light, and your lip has lost its speech, and your ears have lost hearing,
and your feet have lost motion, and your heart has lost its joy, and they that
look out of the windows are darkened, the grinders have failed, and no sounds
of tambourine and of harp wake up your joys, O clay-cold corpse, then have
you lost, lost immeasurably. And yet my text tells me it is not so. It says, "to
die is gain." It looks as if it could not be thus, and certainly it is not, so far as
I can see. But put to your eye the telescope of faith—take that magic glass
which pierces through the veil that parts us from the unseen. Anoint your eyes
with eye salve, and make them so bright that they can pierce the ether and see
the unknown worlds. Come, bathe yourself in this sea of light, and live in holy
revelation and belief, and then look, and oh, how changed the scene! Here is

the corpse, but there the spirit; here is the clay, but there the soul; here is the carcass, but there the seraph. He is supremely blessed; his death is gain.

Come now, what did he lose? I will show that in everything he lost, he gained far more. He lost his friends, did he? His wife, and his children, his brethren in church fellowship, are all left to weep his loss. Yes, he lost them, but, my brethren, what did he gain? He gained more friends than ever he lost. He had lost many in his lifetime, but he meets them all again. Parents, brethren and sisters who had died in youth or age, and passed the stream before him, all salute him on the further brink. There the mother meets her infant, there the father meets his children, there the venerable patriarch greets his family to the third and fourth generation, there brother clasps brother to his arms, and husband meets with wife, no more to be married or given in marriage, but to live together, like the angels of God.

Some of us have more friends in heaven than in earth. We have more dear relations in glory than we have here. It is not so with all of us, but with some it is so; more have crossed the stream than are left behind. But if it be not so, yet what friends we have to meet us there! Oh, I reckon on the day of death it were much gain if it were for the mere hope of seeing the bright spirits that are now before the throne; to clasp the hand of Abraham and Isaac and Jacob, to look into the face of Paul the apostle, and grasp the hand of Peter; to sit in flowery fields with Moses and David, to bask in the sunlight of bliss with John and Magdalene. Oh, how blessed! The company of poor imperfect saints on earth is good; but how much better the society of the redeemed. Death is no loss to us by way of friends. We leave a few, a little band below, and say to them, "Fear not, little flock," and we ascend and meet the armies of the living God, the hosts of his redeemed. "To die is gain." Poor corpse! You have lost your friends on earth; no, bright spirit, you have received a hundredfold in heaven.

What else did we say he lost? We said he lost all his estate, all his substance and his wealth. Yes, but he has gained infinitely more. Though he were rich as Croesus, yet he might well give up his wealth for that which he has attained. Were his fingers bright with pearls, and has he lost their brilliancy? The pearly gates of heaven glisten brighter far. Had he gold in his storehouse? Mark you, the streets of heaven are paved with gold, and he is richer far. The mansions of the redeemed are far brighter dwelling places than the mansions of the richest here below. But it is not so with many of you. You are not rich; you are poor. What can you lose by death? You are poor here; you shall be rich there. Here you suffer toil; there you shall rest forever. Here you earn your bread by the sweat of your brow; but there, no toil. Here wearily you cast yourself upon your bed at the week's end, and sigh for the Sabbath; but there Sabbaths have no end. Here you go to the house of God, but you are distracted with worldly cares and thoughts of suffering; but there, there are no groans to mingle with the songs that warble from immortal tongues. Death will be gain to you in point of riches and substance.

And as for the *means of grace* which we leave behind, what are they when compared with what we shall have hereafter? Oh, might I die at this hour, I think I would say something like this, "Farewell, Sabbaths; I am going to the eternal Sabbath of the redeemed. Farewell, minister; I shall need no candle, neither light of the sun, when the Lord God shall give me light and be my life forever and ever. Farewell, you songs and sonnets of the blessed; farewell, I shall not need your melodious burst; I shall hear the eternal and unceasing hallelujahs of the beatified. Farewell, you prayers of God's people; my spirit shall hear forever the intercessions of my Lord and join with the noble army of martyrs in crying, 'O Lord, how long?' Farewell, O Zion! Farewell, house of my love, home of my life! Farewell, you temples where God's people sing and pray; farewell, you tents of Jacob, where they daily burn their offering! I am going to a better Zion than you, to a brighter Jerusalem, to a temple that has foundations, whose builder and maker is God!" O my dear friends, in the thought of these things, do we not, some of us, feel as if we could die!

> E'en now by faith we join our hands
> With those that went before,
> And greet the blood-besprinkled bands
> Upon th' eternal shore.
>
> One army of the living God,
> At his command we bow,
> Part of the host have crossed the flood,
> And part are crossing now.

We have not come to the margin yet, but we shall be there soon: we soon expect to die.

And again, one more thought. We said that when men died, they lost their knowledge; we correct ourselves. Oh no, when the righteous die, they know infinitely more than they could have known on earth.

> There shall I see and hear and know
> All I desired or wished below;
> And every power find sweet employ,
> In that eternal world of joy.

"Here we see through a glass darkly, but there face to face." There, what "eye hath not seen nor ear heard" shall be fully manifest to us. There, riddles shall be unraveled, mysteries made plain, dark texts enlightened, hard providences made to appear wise. The meanest soul in heaven knows more of God than the greatest saint on earth. The greatest saint on earth may have it said of him, "Nevertheless he that is least in the kingdom of heaven is greater than he." Not our mightiest divines understand so much of theology as the lambs of the flock of glory. Not the greatest masterminds of earth understand the millionth part of the mighty meanings which have been discovered by souls emancipated from clay. Yes, brethren, "to die is gain." Take away, take away that hearse, remove that shroud; come, put white plumes upon the horses' heads and let gilded trappings hang around them. There, take away that fife, that shrill sounding music of the death march. Lend me the trumpet and the drum. O hallelujah, hallelujah, hallelujah; why weep we the saints to heaven; why need we lament? They are not dead, they are gone before. Stop, stop that mourning, refrain your tears, clap your hands, clap your hands.

> They are supremely blessed,
> Have done with care and sin and woe;
> And with their Savior rest.

What! Weep, weep for heads that are crowned with coronals of heaven? Weep, weep for hands that grasp the harps of gold? What, weep for eyes that see the Redeemer? What, weep for hearts that are washed from sin and are throbbing with eternal bliss? What, weep for men that are in the Savior's bosom? No, weep for yourselves, that you are here. Weep that the mandate has not come which bids *you* to die. Weep that you must tarry. But weep not for them. I see them turning back on you with loving wonder, and they exclaim, "Why weepest thou?" What, weep for poverty that it is clothed in riches? What, weep for sickness that it has inherited eternal health? What, weep for shame that it is glorified; and weep for sinful mortality that it has become immaculate? Oh, weep not, but rejoice. "If ye knew what it was that I have said unto you, and whither I have gone, ye would rejoice with a joy that no man should take from you." "To die is gain." Ah, this makes the Christian long to die—makes him say,

> Oh, that the word were given!
> O Lord of hosts, the wave divide,
> And land us all in heaven!

And now, friends, does this belong to you all? Can you claim an interest in it? Are you living to Christ? Does Christ live in you? For if not, your death will not be gain. Are you a believer in the Savior? Has your heart been renewed, and your conscience washed in the blood of Jesus? If not, my hearer, I weep for you. I will save my tears for lost friends; there, with this handkerchief I'd stanch my eyes forever for my best beloved that shall die, if those tears could save you. Oh, when you die, what a day! If the world were hung in sackcloth, it could not express the grief that you would feel. You *die*. O death! O death! How hideous are you to men that are not in Christ! And yet, my hearer, you shall soon die. Save me your bed of shrieks, your look of gall, your words of bitterness! Oh, that you could be saved the dread hereafter! Oh! the wrath to come! the wrath to come! the wrath to come! who is he that can preach of it? Horrors strike the guilty soul! It quivers upon the verge of death; no, on the verge of hell. It looks over, clutching hard to life, and it hears there the sullen groans, the hollow moans, and shrieks of tortured ghosts, which come up from the pit that is bottomless, and it clutches firmly to life, clasps the physician, and bids him hold, lest he should fall into the pit that burns. And the spirit looks down and sees all the fiends of everlasting punishments, and back it recoils. But die it must. It would barter all it has to gain an hour; but no, the fiend has got its grip, and down it must plunge. And who can tell the hideous shriek of a lost soul? It cannot reach heaven; but if it could, it might well be dreamed that it would suspend the melodies of angels, might make even God's redeemed weep, if they could hear the wailings of a damned soul. Ah! you men and women, you have wept; but if you die unregenerate, there will be no weeping like that, there will be no shriek like that, no wail like that. May God spare us from ever hearing it or uttering it ourselves! Oh, how the grim caverns of Hades startle, and how the darkness of night is frightened, when the wail of a lost soul comes up from the ascending flames, while it is descending in the pit.

"Turn ye, turn ye; why will ye die, O house of Israel?" Christ is preached to you. "This is a faithful saying, and worthy of all acceptation, that Christ Jesus came into the world to save sinners." Believe on him and live, you guilty, vile, perishing; believe and live. But this know—if you reject my message, and despise my Master, in that day when he shall judge the world in righteousness by that man, Jesus Christ, I must be a swift witness against you. I have told you—at your soul's peril reject it. Receive my message, and you are saved; reject it—take the responsibility on your own head. Behold, my skirts are clear of your blood. If you be damned, it is not for want of warning. O God grant you may not perish.

The Unbeliever's Unhappy Condition

❧

Delivered on Lord's Day morning, September 24, 1871, at the Metropolitan
Tabernacle, Newington. No. 1012.

*He that believeth not the Son shall not see life; but the wrath of God abideth
on him.* —JOHN 3:36

This is a part of a discourse by John the Baptist. We have not many sermons by that mighty preacher, but we have just sufficient to prove that he
knew how to lay the ax at the root of the tree by preaching the law of God
most unflinchingly; and also that he knew how to declare the gospel, for no
one could have uttered sentences which more clearly contain the way of salvation than those in the text before us. Indeed, this third chapter of the Gospel
according to the evangelist John is notable among clear and plain Scriptures—
notable for being yet clearer and plainer than almost any other. John the Baptist was evidently a preacher who knew how to discriminate—a point in
which so many fail—he separated between the precious and the vile, and
therefore he was as God's mouth to the people. He does not address them as
all lost nor as all saved, but he shows the two classes; he keeps up the line of
demarcation between him that fears God and him that fears him not.

He plainly declares the privileges of the believer; he says he has even now
eternal life; and with equal decision he testifies to the sad state of the unbeliever—"he shall not see life; but the wrath of God abideth on him." John the
Baptist might usefully instruct many professedly Christian preachers.
Although he that is least in the kingdom of heaven is greater than John the
Baptist, and ought, therefore, more clearly to bear witness to the truth, yet
there are many who muddle the gospel, who teach philosophy, who preach a
mingle-mangle which is neither law nor gospel; and these might well go to
school to this rough preacher of the wilderness and learn from him how to
cry, "Behold the Lamb of God which taketh away the sin of the world."

I desire this morning to take a leaf out of the Baptist's lesson book; I
would preach as he did the gospel of the Lord Jesus, "whose shoes I am not
worthy to bear." It is my earnest desire to enjoy the delight of expounding to

you the deep things of God; I feel a profound pleasure in opening up the blessings of the covenant of grace and bringing forth out of its treasury things new and old. I should be happy to dwell upon the types of the Old Testament, and even to touch upon the prophecies of the New; but, while so many yet remain unsaved, my heart is never content except when I am preaching simply the gospel of Jesus Christ. My dear unconverted hearers, when I see you brought to Christ, I will then advance beyond the rudiments of the gospel; but, meanwhile, while hell is gaping wide, and many of you will certainly help to fill it, I cannot turn aside from warning you. I dare not resist the sacred impulse which constrains me to preach over and over again to you the glad tidings of salvation. I shall, like John, continue laying the ax at the root of the trees and shall not go beyond crying, "Repent ye, for the kingdom of heaven is at hand." As he did, we shall now declare the sad estate of him who believes not the Son of God.

This morning, with the burden of the Lord upon us, we shall speak upon the words of the text. Our first point shall be a discovery of *the guilty one*, "he that believeth not the Son." Next, we shall consider *his offense*; it lies in "not believing the Son"; third, we shall lay bare the *sinful causes which create this unbelief*; and, fourth, we shall show the terrible result of not believing in the Son: "he shall not see life; but the wrath of God abideth on him." May the Spirit help us in all.

1. To begin, then, who is *the guilty one*?

Who is the unhappy man here spoken of? Is he a person to be met with only once in a century? Must we search the crowds through and through to find out an individual in this miserable plight? Ah no! the persons who are here spoken of are common; they abound even in our holy assemblies; they are to be met with by thousands in our streets. Alas, alas! They form the vast majority of the world's population. Jesus has come unto his own, and his own have not received him, the Jewish race remain unbelieving; while the Gentiles, to whom he was to be a light, prefer to sit in darkness and reject his brightness. We shall not be talking this morning upon a recondite theme with only a remote relation to ourselves, but there are many here of whom we shall be speaking, and we devoutly pray that the word of God may come with power to their souls.

The persons here spoken of are those who believe not the Son of God. Jesus Christ, out of infinite mercy, has come into the world, has taken upon himself our nature, and in that nature has suffered the just for the unjust, to bring us to God. By reason of his sufferings, the gospel message is now proclaimed to all men, and they are honestly assured that "whosoever believeth in him shall not perish, but have everlasting life." The unhappy persons in this text will not believe in Jesus Christ—they reject God's way of mercy; they hear the gospel but refuse obedience to its command. Let it not be imagined that these individuals are necessarily avowed skeptics, for many of them believe much of revealed truth. They believe the Bible to be the Word of God; they believe there is a God; they believe that Jesus Christ is come into the world as a Savior; they believe most of the doctrines which cluster around the cross.

Alas! They may do this, but yet the wrath of God abides on them if they believe not the Son of God. It may surprise you to learn that many of these persons are very much interested in orthodoxy. They believe that they have discovered the truth, and they exceedingly value those discoveries, so that they frequently grow very warm in temper with those who differ from them. They have read much, and they are matters of argument in the defense of what they consider to be sound doctrine. They cannot endure heresy, and yet sad is the fact, that believing what they do, and knowing so much, they have not believed the Son of God. They believe the doctrine of election, but they have not the faith of God's elect: they swear by final perseverance, but persevere in unbelief. They confess all the five points of Calvinism, but they have not come to the one most needful point of looking unto Jesus, that they may be saved. They accept in creed the truths that are assuredly believed among us, but they have not received that faithful saying, worthy of all acceptance, that Christ Jesus came into the world to save sinners; at any rate, they have not received it personally and practically for their souls' salvation.

It must be admitted that not a few of these persons are blameless as to their morals. You could not, with the closest observation, find either dishonesty, falsehood, uncleanness, or malice in their outward life; they are not only free from these blots, but they manifest positive excellences. Much of their character is commendable. They frequently are courteous and compassionate, generous and gentle minded. Oftentimes they are so amiable and admirable that, while looking upon them, we understand how our Lord, in a similar case, loved the young man who asked, "What lack I yet?" The one thing needful they are destitute of—they have not believed in Christ Jesus, and loath as the Savior was to see them perish, yet it cannot be helped. One doom is common to all who believe not. They shall not see life, but the wrath of God abides on them.

In many cases these persons are, in addition to their morality, religious persons after a fashion. They would not absent themselves from the usual service of the place of worship. They are most careful to respect the Sabbath;

they venerate the Book of God; they use a form of prayer; they join in the songs of the sanctuary; they sit as God's people sit, and stand as God's people stand, but, alas, there is a worm in the center of that fair fruit; they have missed the one essential thing which, being omitted, brings certain ruin; they have not believed on the Son of God. Ah, how far a man may go, and yet, for lack of this one thing, the wrath of God may still abide upon him. Beloved of parents who are hopeful of the conversion of their boy, esteemed by Christians who cannot but admire his outward conversation, yet for all that, the young man may be under the frown of God, for "God is angry with the wicked every day." The wrath of God abides on the man, whoever he may be, that has not believed in Jesus.

Now, if our text showed that the wrath of God was resting on the culprits in our jails, most persons would assent to the statement, and none would wonder at it. If our text declared that the wrath of God abides upon persons who live in habitual unchastity and constant violation of all the laws of order and respectability, most men would say, "Amen"; but the text is aimed at another character. It is true that God's wrath does rest upon open sinners; but, O sirs, this too is true—the wrath of God abides upon those who boast of their virtues but have not believed in Jesus his Son. They may dwell in palaces; but, if they are not believers, the wrath of God abides on them. They may sit in the senate house and enjoy the acclamations of the nation; but, if they believe not on the Son, the wrath of God abides on them. Their names may be enrolled in the peerage and they may possess countless wealth, but the wrath of God abides on them. They may be habitual in their charities and abundant in external acts of devotion; but, if they have not accepted the appointed Savior, the Word of God bears witness that "the wrath of God abideth on them."

2. Now let us, with our hearts awakened by God's Spirit, try to think upon *their offense.*

What is this peculiar sin which entails the wrath of God upon these people? It is that they have not believed the Son of God. What does that amount to? It amounts to this, first of all, that they refuse to accept the mercy of God. God made a law, and his creatures were bound to respect and obey it. We rejected it and turned aside from it. It was a great display of the heart's hatred, but it was not in some respects so thoroughly and intensely wicked a manifestation of enmity to God as when we reject the gospel of grace. God has now presented not the law but the gospel to us, and he has said: "My creatures, you have broken my law, you have acted very vilely toward me. I must punish for sin, else I were not God, and I cannot lay aside my justice; but I have devised a way by which, without any injury to any of my attributes, I can have mercy upon you. I am ready to forgive the past and to restore you to more than your lost position, so that you shall be my sons and my daughters. My only command to you is, believe in my Son. If this command be obeyed, all the blessings of my new covenant shall be yours. Trust him and follow him; for, behold, I give him as a leader and commander to the people. Accept him as making atonement by his substitution, and obey him."

Now, to reject the law of God shows an evil heart of unbelief; but who shall say what a depth of rebellion must dwell in that heart which refuses not only the yoke of God but even the gift of God. The provision of a Savior for lost men is the free gift of God. By it all our wants are supplied, all our evils are removed, peace on earth is secured to us, and glory forever with God: the rejection of this gift cannot be a small sin. The all-seeing One, when he beholds men spurning the supreme gift of his love, cannot but regard such rejection as the worst proof of the hatred of their hearts against himself. When the Holy Spirit comes to convince men of sin, the special sin which he brings to light is thus described: "of sin, because they believe not on me." Not because the heathen were licentious in their habits, barbarians in their ways, and bloodthirsty in their spirit. No: "of sin, because they believe not on me." Condemnation has come upon men, but what is the condemnation? "That light is come into the world, and men love darkness rather than light, because their deeds are evil." Remember, also, that expressive text: "He that believeth not is condemned already"; and what is he condemned for? "Because he hath not believed in the name of the only begotten Son of God."

Let me remark, further, that in the rejection of divine mercy as presented in Christ, the unbeliever has displayed an intense venom against God, for observe how it is. He must either receive the mercy of God in Christ, or he must be condemned—there is no other alternative. He must trust Christ whom God has set forth to be the propitiation for sin, or else he must be driven from the presence of God into eternal punishment. The unbeliever in effect says, "I had sooner be damned than I would accept God's mercy in Christ." Can we conceive a grosser insult to the infinite compassion of the great Father? Suppose a man has injured another, grossly insulted him, and that repeatedly, and yet the injured person, finding the man at last brought into a wretched and miserable state, goes to him and, simply out of kindness to him, says, "I freely forgive you all the wrong you ever did me, and I am ready to relieve your poverty, and to succor you in your distress." Suppose the other replies, "No, I would sooner rot than take anything from you"; would not you have in such a resolve a clear proof of the intense enmity that existed in his heart? And so when a man says, and everyone of you unbelievers do practically say so, "I would sooner lie forever in hell than honor Christ by trusting him," this is a very plain proof of his hatred of God and his Christ.

Unbelievers hate God. Let me ask, for what do you hate him? He keeps the breath within your nostrils; he it is that gives you food and raiment and sends fruitful seasons. For which of these good things do you hate him? You hate him because he is good. Ah, then, it must be because you yourself are evil, and your heart very far removed from righteousness. May God grant that this great and crying sin may be clearly set before your eyes by the light of the eternal Spirit, and may you repent of it and turn from your unbelief and live this day.

But yet further, the unbeliever touches God in a very tender place by his unbelief. No doubt it was to the great Maker a joyous thing to fashion this world, but there are no expressions of joy concerning it at all equal to the joy of God in the matter of human redemption. We would be guarded when we speak of him; but, as far as we can tell, the gift of his dear Son to men, and the whole scheme of redemption, is the master work even of God himself. He is infinite in power and wisdom and love; his ways are as high above our ways as the heavens are above the earth; but Scripture, I think, will warrant me in saying—

> That in the grace which rescued man
> His brightest form of glory shines;
> Here on the cross 'tis fairest writ,
> In precious blood and crimson lines.

Now, the man who says, "There is no God," is a fool, but he who denies God the glory of redemption, in addition to his folly, has robbed the Lord of the choicest jewel of his regalia and aimed a deadly blow at the divine honor. I may say of him who despises the great salvation, that, in despising Christ, he touches the apple of God's eye. "This is my beloved Son," says God, "hear ye him." Out of heaven he says it, and yet men stop their ears and say, "We will not have him." No, they wax wrath against the cross and turn away from God's salvation. Do you think that God will always bear this? The times of your ignorance he has winked at, but "now commands all men everywhere to repent." Will you stand out against his love? His love that has been so inventive in ingenious plans by which to bless the sons of men? Shall his choicest work be utterly contemned by you? If so, it is little wonder that it is written, "The wrath of God abides on him."

I must, still further, unveil this matter by saying that the unbeliever perpetrates an offense against every person of the blessed Trinity. He may think that his not believing is a very small business, but, indeed, it is a barbed shaft

shot against the Deity. Take the Persons of the blessed Trinity, beginning with
the Son of God who comes to us most nearly. It is to me the most surprising
thing I ever heard of, that "the Word was made flesh and dwelt among us." I
do not wonder that in Hindustan the missionaries are often met with this
remark: "It is too good to be true that God ever took upon himself the nature
of such a thing as man!" Yet, more wonderful does it seem to be, that, when
Christ became man, he took all the sorrows and infirmity of man, and, in
addition, was made to bear the sin of many. The most extraordinary of all
facts is this: that the infinitely Holy should be "numbered with the transgressors," and, in the words of Isaiah, should "bear their iniquities." The Lord has
made him, who knew no sin, to be made sin for us. Wonder of wonders! It is
beyond all degree amazing that he who distributes crowns and thrones should
hang on a tree and die, the just for the unjust, bearing the punishment due to
sinners for guilt. Now, knowing this, as most of you do, and yet refusing to
believe, you do, in effect, say, "I do not believe that the incarnate God can
save." "Oh no," you reply, "we sincerely believe that he can save." Then, it
must be that you feel, "I believe he can, but I will not have him to save me."
Wherein I excuse you in the first place, I must bring the accusation more heavily in the second. You answer that "you do not say you will not believe him."
Why do you then remain in unbelief? The fact is, you do not trust him; you
do not obey him. I pray you account for the fact. "May I believe him?" says
one. Have we not told you ten thousand times over that whosoever will, may
take the water of life freely. If there be any barrier, it is not with God; it is not
with Christ; it is with your own sinful heart. You are welcome to the Savior
now, and if you trust him now, he is yours forever. But oh, unbeliever, it
appears to be nothing to you that Christ has died. His wounds attract you not.
His groans for his enemies have no music in them to you. You turn your back
upon the incarnate God who bleeds for men, and in so doing you shut yourselves out of hope, judging yourselves unworthy of eternal life.

Furthermore, the willful rejection of Christ is also an insult to God the
Father. "He that believeth not hath made God a liar, because he hath not
believed the record that God gave of his Son." God has himself often borne testimony to his dear Son. "Him hath God the Father set forth to be a propitiation
for our sins." In rejecting Christ, you reject God's testimony and God's gift. It
is a direct assault upon the truthfulness and loving-kindness of the gracious
Father, when you trample on or cast aside his priceless, peerless gift of love.

And, as for the blessed Spirit, it is his office here below to bear witness to
Christ. In the Christian ministry, the Holy Spirit daily cries to the sons of men
to come to Jesus. He has striven in the hearts of many of you, given you a

measure of conviction of sin, and a degree of knowledge of the glory of Christ, but you have repressed it, you have labored to your utmost to do despite to the Spirit of God. Believe me, this is no slight sin. An unbeliever is an enemy to God the Father, to God the Son, and God the Holy Ghost. Against the blessed Trinity in unity, O unbeliever, your sin is a standing insult: you are now to God's face insulting him by continuing an unbeliever.

And, I must add, that there is also in unbelief an insult against every attribute of God. The unbeliever in effect declares, "If the justice of God is seen in laying the punishment of sin upon Christ, I do not care for his justice; I will bear my own punishment." The sinner seems to say, "God is merciful in the gift of Christ to suffer in our stead; I do not want his mercy; I can do without it." Others may be guilty, and they may trust in the Redeemer, but I do not feel such guilt, and I will not sue for pardon." Unbelievers attack the wisdom of God, for, whereas the wisdom of God is in its fullness revealed in the gift of Jesus, they say, "It is a dogma, unphilosophical, and worn out." They count the wisdom of God to be foolishness, and thus cast a slight upon another of the divine attributes. I might in detail mention every one of the attributes and prerogatives of God, and prove that your nonacceptance of the Savior is an insult to every one of them, and to God himself: but the theme is too sad for us to continue upon it, and, therefore, let us pass to another phase of the subject, though I fear it will be equally grievous.

3. Third, let us consider *the causes of this unbelief.*

In a great many, unbelief may be ascribed to a careless *ignorance* of the way of salvation. Now, I should not wonder if many of you imagine that, if you do not understand the gospel, you are therefore quite excused for not believing it. But, sirs, it is not so. You are placed in this world, not as heathens in the center of Africa, but in England, where you live in the full blaze of gospel day. There are places of worship all around you, which you can without difficulty attend. The Book of God is very cheap; you have it in your houses; you can all read it or hear it read. Is it so, then, that the King has been pleased to reveal himself to you and tell you the way to salvation, and yet you, at the age of twenty, thirty, or forty, do not know the way of salvation? What do you mean, sir? What can you mean? Has God been pleased to reveal himself in Scripture and tell you how to escape from hell and fly to heaven, and yet have you been too idle to inquire into that way? Dare you say to God, "I do not think it worth my while to learn what you have revealed, neither do I care to know of the gift which you have bestowed on men." How can you think that such ignorance is an excuse for your sin? What could be a more gross aggravation of it? If you do not know, you ought to know; if you have not learned the gospel message, you might have learned it, for there are some of us whose language it is not difficult for even the most illiterate to understand, and who would, if we caught ourselves using a hard word, retract it and put it into little syllables, so that not even a child's intellect need be perplexed by our language. Salvation's way is plain in the Book; those words, "Believe and live," are in this Christian England almost as legible and as universally to be seen as though they were printed on the sky. That trust in the Lord Jesus saves the soul is well-known news. But if you still say you have not known all this, then I reply, "Dear sir, do try to know it. Go to the Scriptures, study them, see what is there. Hear, also, the gospel, for it is written, "Incline your ear to come unto me; hear, and your soul shall live." "Faith comes by hearing, and hearing by the word of God." For your soul's sake I charge you, be no longer ignorant of that which you must know, or else must perish.

In some others, the cause is *indifference*. They do not think the matter to be of any very great consequence. They are aware that they are not quite right, but they have a notion that somehow or other they will get right at last; and, meanwhile, it does not trouble them. O man, I pray you, as your fellow creature let me speak with you a word of expostulation. God declares that his wrath abides upon you as an unbeliever, and do you call that nothing? God says, "I am angry with you," and you say to him, "I do not care; it is of very small importance to me. The rise or fall of the consols [funded government securities in Great Britain] is of much more consequence than whether God is angry with me or not. My dinner being done to a turn concerns me a great deal more than whether the infinite God loves me or hates me." That is the English of your conduct, and I put it to you whether there can be a higher impertinence against your Creator, or a direr form of arrogant revolt against the eternal ruler. If it does not trouble you that God is angry with you, it ought to trouble you; and it troubles *me* that it does not trouble *you*. We have heard of persons guilty of murder, whose behavior during the trial has been cool and self-possessed. The coolness with which they pleaded "not guilty" has been all of a piece with the hardness of tears which led them to the bloody deed. He who is capable of great crime is also incapable of shame concerning it. A man who is able to take pleasure and be at ease while God is angry with him shows that his heart is harder than steel.

In certain cases, the root of this unbelief lies in another direction. It is fed by pride. The person who is guilty of it does not believe that he needs a Savior. His notion is that he will do his very best, attend the church or the meetinghouse very regularly, subscribe occasionally or frequently, and go to heaven partly by what he does, and partly by the merits of Christ. So that not believing in Christ is not a matter of any great consequence with him because he is not naked and poor and miserable; but he is rich and increased in goods [though not] in spiritual things. To be saved by faith is a religion for harlots and drunkards and thieves; but for respectable persons such as he is, who have kept the law from their youth up, he does not see any particular need of laying hold upon Christ. Such conduct reminds me of the words of Cowper—

> Perish the virtue, as it ought, abhorr'd,
> And the fool with it that insults his Lord.

God believed it needful, in order to save man, that the Redeemer should die; yet you self-righteous ones evidently think that death a superfluity: for if a man could save himself, why did the Lord descend and die to save him? If there be a way to heaven by respectability and morality without Christ, what is the good of Christ? It is utterly useless to have an expiator and a mediator, if men are so good that they do not require them. You tell God to his face that he lies unto you, that you are not so sinful as he would persuade you, that you do not need a substitute and sacrifice as he says you do. O sirs, this pride of yours is an arrogant rebellion against God. Look at your fine actions, you that are so good—your motives are base, your pride over what you have done has defiled, with black fingers, all your acts. Inasmuch as you prefer your way to God's way, and prefer your righteousness to God's righteousness, the wrath of God abides on you.

Perhaps I have not hit the reason of your unbelief, therefore let me speak once more. In many, *love of sin* rather than any boasted self-righteousness keeps them from the Savior. They do not believe in Jesus, not because they have any doubt about the truths of Christianity, but because they have an enslaving love for their favorite sin. "Why," says one, "if I were to believe in Christ, of course, I must obey him; to trust and to obey go together. Then I could not be the drunkard I am; I could not trade as I do; I could not practice secret licentiousness; I could not frequent the haunts of the ungodly, where laughter is occasioned by sin, and mirth by blasphemy. I cannot give up these my darling sins." Perhaps, this sinner hopes that one day, when he cannot any longer enjoy his sin, he will meanly sneak out of it and try to cheat the devil of his soul; but, meanwhile, he prefers the pleasures of sin to obedience to God, and unbelief to acceptance of his salvation. O sweet sin! O bitter sin! How you are murdering the souls of men! As certain serpents before they strike their prey fix their eyes upon it and fascinate it, and then at last devour it, so does sin fascinate the foolish sons of Adam; they are charmed with it, and perish for it. It yields but a momentary joy, and the wage thereof is eternal misery, yet are men enamored of it. The ways of the strange woman, and the paths of uncleanness lead most plainly to the chambers of death, yet are men attracted thereto as moths by the blaze of the candle, and so are they destroyed. Alas! that men wantonly dash against the rocks of dangerous lusts and perish willfully beneath the enchantment of sin. Sad pity it is to prefer a harlot to the eternal God, to prefer a few pence made by dishonesty to heaven itself, to prefer the gratification of the belly to the love of the Creator and the joy of being reconciled and saved. It was a dire insult to God when Israel set up a golden calf, and said, "These be thy gods, O Israel." Shall the image of an ox that eats grass supplant the living God? He that had strewn the earth with manna, had made Sinai to smoke with his presence, and the whole wilderness to tremble beneath his marchings, is he to be thrust aside by the image of a bullock that has horns and hoofs? Will men prefer molten metal to the infinitely holy and glorious Jehovah? But, surely, the preference of a lust to God is a greater insult still: to obey our passions rather than his will, and to prefer sin to his mercy; this is the crime of crimes. May God deliver us from it, for his mercy's sake.

4. We have heavy tidings in the last head of my discourse, *the terrible result* of unbelief.

"He shall not see life, but the wrath of God abideth on him." "The wrath of God!" No words can ever fully explain this expression. Holy Whitefield, when he was preaching, would often hold up his hands, and, with tears streaming down his eyes, would exclaim, "Oh, the wrath to come! the wrath to come!" Then would he pause because his emotions checked his utterance. The wrath of God! I confess I feel uneasy if anybody is angry with me, and yet one can bear the anger of foolish, hot-tempered persons with some equanimity. But the wrath of God is the anger of One who is never angry without a cause, One who is very patient and longsuffering. It takes much to bring the choler into Jehovah's face, yet is he wroth with unbelievers. He is never angry with anything because it is feeble and little, but only because it is wrong. His anger is only his holiness set on fire. He cannot bear sin; who would wish that he should?

What right-minded man would desire God to be pleased with evil? That were to make a devil of God. Because he is God, he must be angry with sin wherever it is. This makes the sting of it, that his wrath is just and holy anger. It is the anger, remember, of an omnipotent Being who can crush us as easily as a moth. It is the anger of an infinite Being, and therefore infinite anger, the heights and depths and breadths and lengths of which no man can measure. Only the incarnate God ever fully knew the power of God's anger. It is beyond all conception, yet the anger rests on you, my hearer. Alas, for you, if you are an unbeliever, for this is your state before God. It is no fiction of mine, but the word of inspired truth: "the wrath of God abideth on him."

Then notice the next word, it "*abides*." This is to say, it is upon you now. He is angry with you at this moment, and always. You go to sleep with an angry God gazing into your face; you wake in the morning, and if your eye were not dim, you would perceive his frowning countenance. He is angry with you, even when you are singing his praises, for you mock him with solemn sounds upon a thoughtless tongue; angry with you on your knees, for you only pretend to pray—you utter words without heart. As long as you are not a believer, he must be angry with you every moment. "God is angry with the wicked every day."

That the text says it abides, and the present tense takes a long sweep, for it always will abide on you. But may you not, perhaps, escape from it, by ceasing to exist? The test precludes such an idea. Although it says that you "shall not see life," it teaches that God's wrath is upon you, so that the absence of life is not annihilation. Spiritual life belongs only to believers; you are now without that life, yet you exist, and wrath abides on you, and so it ever must be. While you shall not see life, you shall exist in eternal death, for the wrath of God cannot abide on a nonexistent creature. You shall not see life, but you shall feel wrath to the uttermost. It is horror enough that wrath should be on you now; it is horror upon horrors, and hell upon hell, that it shall be upon you forever.

And notice that it must be so, because you reject the only thing that can heal you. As George Herbert says, "Whom oils and balsams kill, what salve can cure?" If Christ himself has become a savor of death unto death unto you, because you reject him, how can you be saved? There is but one door, and if you close it by your unbelief, how can you enter heaven? There is one healing medicine, and if you refuse to take it, what remains but death? There is one water of life, but you refuse to drink it; then must you thirst forever. You put from you, voluntarily, the one only Redeemer; how then shall you be ransomed? Shall Christ die again, and in another state be offered to you once more? O sirs, you would reject him then as you reject him now. But there remains no more sacrifice for sin. On the cross God's mercy to the sons of men was fully revealed, and will you reject God's ultimatum of grace, his last appeal to you? If so, it is at your own peril: Christ being raised from the dead dies no more; he shall come again, but without a sin offering unto the salvation of his people.

Remember, sirs, that the wrath of God will produce no saving or softening effect. It has been suggested that a sinner, after suffering God's wrath awhile, may repent and so escape from it. But our observation and experience prove that the wrath of God never softened anybody's heart yet, and we believe it never will: those who are suffering divine wrath will go on to harden and harden and harden; the more they suffer, the more they will hate: the more they are punished, the more will they sin. The wrath of God abiding on you will produce no good results to you, but rather you shall go from evil to evil, further and further from the presence of God.

The reason why the wrath of God abides on an unbeliever is partly because all his other sins remain on him. There is no sin that shall damn the man who believes, and nothing can save the man who will not believe. God removes all sin the moment we believe; but while we believe not, fresh cords fasten upon us our transgressions. The sin of Judah is written as with an iron pen, and graven with a point of a diamond. Nothing can release you from guilt while your heart remains at enmity with Jesus Christ your Lord. Remember that God has never taken an oath, that I know of, against any class of persons, except unbelievers. "To whom sware he that they should not enter into his rest, but to them that believed not?" Continued unbelief God never will forgive, because his word binds him not to do so. Does he swear an oath, and shall he go back from it? It cannot be. Oh, that you might have grace to relinquish your unbelief, and close in with the gospel and be saved.

Now, I hear someone object, "You tell us that certain people are under the wrath of God, but they are very prosperous." I reply, that yonder bullock will be slaughtered. Yet it is being fattened. And your prosperity, O ungodly man, is but a fattening of you for the slaughter of justice. Yes, but you say, "They are very merry, and some of those who are forgiven are very sad." Mercy lets them be merry while they may. We have heard of men who, when driven to Tyburn in a cart, could drink and laugh as they went to the gallows. It only proved what bad men they were. And so, whereas the guilty can yet take comfort, it only proves their guiltiness.

Let me ask: what ought to be your thoughts concerning these solemn truths which I have delivered to you? I know what my thoughts were; they made me go to my bed unhappy. They made me very grateful because I hope I have believed in Jesus Christ; yet they made me start in the night, and wake this morning with a load upon me. I come here to say to you, must it be so that you will always remain unbelievers and abide under the wrath of God? If it must be so, and the dread conclusion seems forced upon me, at any rate, do look it in the face, do consider it. If you are resolved to be damned, know what you are at. Take advice and consider. O sirs, it cannot need an argument to convince you that it is a most wretched thing to be now under the wrath of God. You cannot want any argument to show that it must be a blessed thing to be forgiven—you must see that. It is not your reason that wants convincing, it is your heart that wants renewing.

The whole gospel lies in this nutshell. Come, you guilty one, just as you are, and rest yourself upon the finished work of the Savior, and take him to be yours forever. Trust Jesus now. In your present position it may be done. God's Holy Spirit blessing your mind, you may at this moment say, "Lord, I believe, help thou mine unbelief." You may now confide in Jesus, and some who came in here unforgiven may make the angels sing because they go down yonder steps saved souls, whose transgressions are forgiven, and whose sins are covered. God knows one thing, that if I knew by what study and what art I could learn to preach the gospel so as to affect your hearts, I would spare no cost or pains. For the present, I have aimed simply to warn you, not with adornment of speech, lest the power should be the power of man; and now I leave my message and commit it to him who shall judge the quick and the dead. But this know, if you receive not the Son, I shall be a swift witness against you. God grant it be not so, for his mercy's sake. Amen.

Noah's Flood

Delivered on Thursday evening, March 5, 1868, at the Metropolitan Tabernacle, Newington. No. 823.

The flood came, and took them all away. —MATTHEW 24:39

We commonly say that "there is no rule without an exception," and certainly the rule that there is no rule without an exception has an exception to itself, for the rules of God are without exception. The rule that God will punish the ungodly is without an exception; the rule that all who are out of Christ shall perish is a rule without an exception; and the rule that all who are in Christ shall be saved is also without an exception.

1. I shall have to call your attention tonight to three rules that are without exception, and the first is the one before us—*"the flood came, and took them all away."*

The destruction caused by the deluge was universal. It did not merely sweep away some who were out of the ark, but it swept them all away. There were, doubtless, distinctions in those days, as there are now, for never has there been one dead level of equality among the sons of Adam since men multiplied on the face of the earth. Many in that time were wealthy. They had accumulated stores of gold and silver. They were rich in merchandise, invention, or plunder. They were rich in the produce of the field. They owned broad acres of land. They had multiplied to themselves the conveniences and the luxuries of life, but the flood came and swept them all away. Not one rich man could escape with all his hoards, neither could he purchase life if he had given all his wealth, for the flood came and swept them all away. There were no rafts of costly cedar, or towers of expensive masonry which could out-top the devouring deluge: death laughed at miser and merchant, millionaire and monarch; all, all were swallowed up in the angry flood.

There were some in those days who were extremely poor. They worked hard to gain enough to keep body and soul together, and they were scarcely able to do that; they had to suffer every day—

> *The oppressor's wrongs,*
> *the proud man's contumely;*

but I do not find that as a reward for their sufferings they were spared. No; when the flood came it swept them all away. The pauper out of the ark perished as well as the prince. The poor and miserable peasant died, washed away from the filth of his mud hovel as monarchs were from their palaces. The beggar without a shoe to his foot died; the flood had no pity on his rags. He who swept the street crossing and stood waiting for a casual alms was taken away with the aristocrats who had pitied him. The flood came and swept them all away; the unrelenting billows meted out an equal fate to all who were outside the one ark of safety.

And so will it be at the last. As the great man will not purchase an escape by all that which he has stored up, so neither will the man be delivered because of his poverty. There was a rich man in hell, we read: poor men have been there, and are there now. As riches cannot save from hell, so neither can poverty raise to heaven. The grace and justice of God are independent of society and rank and state and condition. What matters it to the Lord how much or how little of yellow metal you have about you! He measures no man by his purse, but by his soul; and he whose soul is unpardoned is lost, be he rolling in plenty or pining in want. You must be born again; you must believe in Jesus; you must, in one word, get into the ark, or when the flood comes it will sweep you all away, be you rich as Dives or poor as Lazarus.

There were in those days *learned* men in the world—men who searched the stars at night; who had deciphered the constellations, who had pried into the secrets of matter; men who had ransacked science, and, so far as men had gone (and we do not know but what they went a very long way then), had pierced into the innermost recesses of knowledge; but when the flood came it swept them all away. There goes the philosopher; you can hear his dying gurgle. There, floating on the stream, is the head of an antediluvian Solomon. The flood has swept away masters of arts, doctors of law, and rabbis in divinity. No man was able to escape the deluge by all that he had ever learned. Knowledge is no life buoy, logic is no swimming belt, rhetoric no lifeboat. Down, down they go, and all their science with them, beneath the shoreless waves.

And as for *the illiterate,* who were, no doubt, numerous then as now, who could only count as many as the number of their fingers, who knew none of the niceties of learning or of eloquence, when the flood came it swept them all away. So that knowledge, except it be of one particular kind, namely, the heart knowledge of Christ Jesus, will not deliver us from the final destruction; and, on the other hand, although ignorance, if it be not willful, is some palliation for sin, yet is it never such an excuse for it as to suffer sin to go unpunished. There is a hell for those who knew their Master's will and did it not; and there is also a hell for those who would not know, but who lived and died willfully ignorant of the things of God. The flood came and swept them all away. You men who are orthodox in doctrine, you who can talk about theology, and claim to be masters in Israel, if you do not belong to Christ, the flood shall sweep you all away. And you who say, "What does it matter? Creeds, what are they but handles of old rubbish? We do not study our Bibles, and do not want to know the doctrines taught therein." I tell you, sirs, except you know Christ, and are found in him, your ignorance shall be no sufficient excuse for you, for when the flood of fire shall come, it shall sweep you all away.

I doubt not that among those who perished in Noah's flood, *there were many who were very zealous in the cause of religion;* perhaps some who had officiated as priests in the midst of their families, and possibly even at God's altar. They were not a godless race in those days, so far as the form and profession went; they had a religion; even those sons of Cain had a religion; and indeed, generally when men are worst at heart, they prate most about outward religion. We may suppose it was so in Noah's day. But when the flood came, these men being out of the ark, whether priests or not, did not escape; it swept them all away. And there were others, no doubt, who were *profane,* who lived in disregard of God, or who hectored out infidel expressions concerning him. But the flood made no distinction between the hypocritical priest and the direct blasphemer; when it came, it swept them all away. O you sons of Levi, you who wear the robes of priesthood and profess to be sent of God to teach others, with all your boasted magical powers, if you do not believe in Jesus as poor guilty sinners and look up to the cross alone for your salvation, when the flood comes, it will sweep you all away. You will drown, Sir Priest, despite your baptismal regeneration and your sacramental efficacy! You will sink with a lying absolution on your lips down to the nethermost hell!

And, O you who rail against religion and boast that you are no hypocrites, you doubtless think yourselves honest, but do not imagine that your impudent "honesty," as you choose to call it, will exonerate you at the last tremendous day, for in that day of wrath the fiery deluge shall sweep you also all away. Short work will God make with doubters then. They shall behold him and wonder and perish, for a short and sharp work will he make in the earth. Quick work will he make with the hypocrites in that day; for though they call, he will not answer them; and when they begin to cry to him, he will mock at their calamity and laugh when their fear comes. The flood shall sweep all at last—whether religious or profane—away, for they have not fled to the ark and so have rejected the one only shelter.

Let me solemnly remind you in this congregation tonight, that in that day of destruction *some of the oldest men that have lived perished*—older men than you, though your head be gray or bald; older women than you, though you have nourished and brought up children and dandled your grandchildren and your great-grandchildren upon your knee: they went down the stream with others, perishing as though they had never seen the light. And the young died too. That one dreadful destruction took away the little child in his beauty, and the young man in his strength, and the maiden in her bloom. The flood took them all away; and so with all of us who have attained to adult years and have arrived at knowledge so as to judge between good and evil; if we be found not in Christ, the flood shall take us all away. We know not at how young an age we may be responsible. Let the child never presume upon its youth. We have heard of fools of twenty pleading "infancy" in our courts of law, and of all pieces of roguery sanctioned by the law, I have thought that the plea of "infancy" from young men of nineteen and twenty years of age, who have purchased jewelry and I know not what, to spend upon their lusts—of all pieces of villany, I say, that seems to me to be the most intolerable. But there shall be no such plea of infancy for you boys and girls and young people, at the last great day. If you know right from wrong, and if you can understand the gospel of Jesus Christ, at your peril do you reject it, at your peril do you neglect it! No, neither shall the young nor the old escape except by coming to Christ. "Ye must be born again" is of universal application to you who are young and to you who are gray headed. No youth can excuse, no experience can exempt, but alike will the flood of divine wrath overwhelm every human soul unless we find refuge in the ark of the covenant of grace, even the work and person of Jesus, the bleeding Lamb of God.

This universality I shall have to illustrate in yet another way. I can suppose that when Noah built the ark—a most absurd thing to do upon all the principles of common reason apart from his faith in God—*there were a great many persons who heard of this and wondered*. It was a very huge ship—the greatest that ever had been built, a conception in navigation which altogether staggered the minds of men in his day. When Noah built this vessel and built it on the dry land, far removed from any river or sea, it must have been a very great wonder and have caused abundance of talk through all the neighboring nations. I should not wonder but what the tidings spread far and wide, and there were some who, as soon as they heard of it, said, "A madman! I wonder his friends do not confine him; what a lunatic he must be!" Having made that remark, they cracked a joke or two about it and fell into the habit of sneering at a thing so very absurd, so that it passed into a proverb, and when a man did a silly thing, they said, "Why, he is as foolish as old Noah!" Ribald jests were all that Noah could get from them; they despised, ridiculed, and contemned him utterly, but the flood came and took *them* all away, and there was an end to their jests, their sarcasms, their jeers.

The flood had silenced *them* most effectually. So will it be with any of you who have ridiculed the gospel of Christ; you will find in the great and terrible day of the Lord, that your laughter shall have no power over death and win you no reprieve from the agonies of hell. There will be no room for infidelity in that tremendous day. God will be all too real to you when he tears you in pieces, and there is none to deliver; and the judgment will be all too real when the thunderclaps shall wake the dead and the books shall be opened and read by the blaze of lightning, and the sentence shall be pronounced, "Depart, you cursed!" Beware, you despisers, and wonder, and perish. Beware, now, while yet there is a day of grace to light you to heaven, for remember it will not last forever. May eternal love save any of us from perishing in devouring fire as Noah's despisers did in the devouring flood.

There were other people, no doubt, who, when they heard about Noah, *criticized his building.* I can imagine some of the shipbuilders of the time looking on and telling him that the keel was not arranged quite rightly; and that ingenious plan of pitching the great ship within and without would be sure to be very closely criticized, for it seems to have been a great novelty, not an invention of man, but a revelation from God. Then there was the making of only one window—why, we who read about it now do not know what it means, and all the plans that have ever been drawn of Noah's ark do not seem to realize the description given of it. Why, said the wise shipwright, "that thing will never float on the top of the flood, if it should chance to come; and besides, it has been so long in building that it will be sure to get the dry rot." What wise things were said about it! If they had been able to print them in those days, how many critical treatises would have been published against "that old wooden box of Noah's," as they very likely would have called it! All these critics could have built it a great deal better, I have no doubt, but they did not build at all; and though they found fault, and could do it so much better than Noah did, yet, somehow or other, they were drowned, and he was saved.

So in this world now, we constantly find men who eat up the sins of God's people as they eat bread. "Oh! yes," they can say, "there is something in religion, no doubt, but then look at your imperfections and your faults!" And, brethren, they need not look long to find them out. They can soon find ten thousand points in which we might be a little improved, and sometimes I have no doubt that our critics are in some respects better than we are. Many a worldly man has a better temper than a genuine Christian. I am sorry to say it, but I have known unconverted people much more generous than some who are converted. They do excel in some qualities, but still, still, still, there is the solemn truth that the sharpest and most philosophical critic of other people, if he be out of Christ, will be swept away, while the men whom he criticized and condemned, if they be found humbly believing in Jesus, shall be saved through faith in him. It all hinges on this one matter, inside or outside the ark: inside the ark a thousand imperfections, but all saved; outside the ark a thousand excellencies, but all drowned without a single exception at last!

Now there may have been, on the other hand, among those who came to see father Noah and his big ship, *some who took his part.* I never knew a man so big a fool but what some sided with him. So, perhaps, there were some who said, "Well, after all, do not be too hard upon him, he is a respectable patriarch; he is a man who follows up his convictions: his convictions are very absurd, no doubt, but still it is a fine thing in these days to see a man really practically sincere; we do like to see the man so infatuated, but though we cannot help wishing that he was a sane man, yet still it is almost better to see a man insane and carry out his convictions, than to see him trifling as so many are childishly trifling with their principles." Many a gentleman who looked at the ark when he said that went home with wonderful ease of conscience, and thought, "Now I have said a very good thing; I have put a spoke in the wheel of some of those cavilers; I have stood up for the good old man, for a very good old man, I have no doubt he is, though very much deceived." Ah! but when the flood came, it swept all these people away as well. They were very kind in their remarks, and very patronizing in their air, but the flood swept them all away.

And do you not know such people now? Why, there are some of them here tonight. Listen to their gentlemanly talk, how generously they speak: "Well, yes; I like to see these Christian people so earnest; I daresay they do a great deal of good; you know, I like to hear a preacher speaking out so plainly; I like to see these people very zealous—in these days it is very refreshing to see people zealous about anything, for there is so much latitudinarianism and policy and so on, that we like to find people decided, even though we should think them a little too dogmatic and bigoted." O sirs, we thank you for your good opinion of us, but except you repent you shall likewise perish. Your excellent remarks will not save you, and your very lenient and gentlemanly and broad-church views of religion will not assist you. You may hold all those views which are so tolerant and so excellent, and we are glad you do hold them, and yet you may have no share in Christ's salvation. You are a sensible man for holding such charitable views, but, sensible as you are, except you come to Christ, you will have to perish, even as the most bigoted persecutors.

Besides these, there were some other people *who liked Noah better still;* they not only excused and defended him, but they sometimes grew very warm about it. They said, "Father Noah is right; we see his life, we mark his manners and conversation, and he is a better man than they are who ridicule and despise him; we are convinced by his preaching that his testimony is true, and we will help him and stand up for him; we do not like to hear the jeers and uncivil remarks that are made about him; they cut us to the quick." Then I suppose you are going into the ark, are you not? "Well, we do not know ourselves about that yet. Perhaps we may, by and by; we are thinking of it; we have taken the matter into very serious consideration, and we think it to be a very proper thing to do, a very right thing to do, but at the same time, it is hardly convenient yet; we will wait a little longer." "Why," says one, "I am not married yet." And another says, "There is a banquet to be held on such-and-such a day; I must go to that; you know men must eat and drink, and therefore I am not going into the ark just yet." Well, now, these well-meaning, procrastinating people, who were postponing and putting off, what became of them? Did one of them escape? Alas! no; when the flood came, it took them all away. What, not save one of them, those who would be right if they had a little longer time? Not spare those who have good resolutions in their throats, who are almost persuaded to be Christians? No, not one of them; they all went down in the common wreck and perished in the universal destruction, for good resolutions save no man unless they are put into practice. Almost persuaded to be a Christian is like the man who was almost pardoned, but he was hanged; like the man who was almost rescued, but he was burned in the house. As old Henry Smith says, "A door that is almost shut is open; a man that is almost honest is a thief; a man that is almost saved is damned." Oh, take heed of that, you halters between two opinions, you awakened but not decided, you aroused but not converted! Noah's friends perished, his very dearest friends who were not in the ark. When the flood came, it swept them all away; and so must you, our sons and daughters, if you give not your hearts to the Lord.

So, to close this recapitulation, you have often been told that *the very workmen who worked for Noah,* and who were, no doubt, paid their wages, or they would not have worked, perished also. They helped to saw the wood, to lay the keel, to drive the bolts, to put in the oakum, to use the pitch, to strengthen the timbers, but after all that they had done, not one of them escaped. And so the chapel keeper, the pew opener, the elder, the deacon, the minister, the bishop, the archbishop, all those who have had a function in the church, who have had something to do with the good staunch vessel of Christ's gospel, except they, themselves, be in Christ by a living faith, they must perish as much as the despisers and the outcasts. Here, then, is the solemn truth: all out of Christ lost, all in Christ saved; all unbelievers perishing, all believers preserved in him. Here is a rule without an exception.

Very briefly we shall now have to speak upon a second subject.

2. It appears that when the flood came, it found them all eating and drinking, marrying, and giving in marriage, and, according to the text, *this also* was a rule without an exception.

Is it not a very solemn thing that it is so now, that without any exception the mass of mankind are still neglectful of their souls, still busy about their fleeting interests, and negligent of eternal realities? There are no exceptions to this rule among natural men. Gracious men care for these things, but all natural men are like these men in the days of Noah. While I was musing this afternoon, I felt surprised at it. I said to myself, "What, not one man in Noah's day that was anxious to be saved in the ark—not one?" Why, the population of the globe is supposed by some to have been greater at that time than it is now. Owing to the extreme length of years to which men then lived, the deaths were fewer, and the population increased more rapidly, and yet out of them all was there not one that sought after God naturally—not one? It was an extraordinary thing that there was not one who would believe in the reiterated prophecies of Noah and find a shelter in the ark. But is it not more strange still, only it is strangely true, that out of all the unregenerate, until they are quickened by divine grace, there is not one who cares to flee to Christ? "Ye will not come unto me that ye might have life" is a rule of universal application. Men will not come to Christ, but had rather perish in their sins than come and put their trust in him.

I suppose the reason lies in three things. First, there is men's *universal indifference* about their souls—a wanton carelessness about their noblest part, their truest selves. But that is a strange thing! A man is always earnest about his life—"Skin for skin; yea, all that a man hath will he give for his life." If a man thinks he is likely to perish by burning, what cries he will raise! What exertions he will make to get out of the room! If he is near to drowning, how he kicks and struggles! If he be sick, how quickly he sends for the doctor, and how anxious he is to get the best advice within his reach, so that his life may be preserved! And yet the preservation of his highest life seems to be to him a matter of no consequence at all! Every thinking man must feel that his true self is his spirit, his soul, that his body is not he himself, but simply a sort of garment that himself wears, a house in which himself lives; and yet men spend their time from morning till night in finding clothes and food for this outside house, but the tenant that dwells within is—poor creature!—quite forgotten. That is odd, is it not? Does it not seem to prove that man is degraded into something less than a reasonable creature by his sin, so that he acts like a beast?

When a man has to live but a little time in this world, he wishes to be happy in it. If a man only stops for an hour in an inn, what a noise he makes if the chimney smokes, if the tablecloth is not clean, if chops are not done to a turn; and while he knows that his better self must live forever in another world, he does not concern himself about that world, or whether he shall be happy in it or not! Strange! 'Tis strange; 'tis passing strange; 'tis wonderful.

It is a miracle of madness that men should be so indifferent to the interest of their souls, their immortal souls, that they should go to sleep, not knowing whether they will wake up with the never-dying worm or arise to enjoy with Jesus the surpassing splendors of eternity. Yet this indifference is universal. O brethren, you and I have need to pray that God would stir this dead sea, that he would speak with his quickening voice, and make men alive to these spiritual things, or else in the graves of their indifference they will rot forever.

The second reason for this indifference lay, no doubt, in universal unbelief. Is it not a strange thing that they did not one of them believe Noah? Noah was an honest man; some of them had known him for many years, yes, for hundreds of years they had known him, for they lived so long then. He spoke like an honest man. He preached with vehemence and power, but not one believed him, not one soul believed him so as to escape from the wrath to come, not one! Now that is odd, for as I have said before, no lie that was ever told was so incredible but what somebody or other was found to believe it, much more should some be found to receive the truth. Yet here was a truth that looked so probable, on account of the sin of man, and yet nobody was found to believe it, but they universally rejected it. Even so it is with the gospel of Christ. We come and tell our fellowmen that the Son of God was made flesh to redeem men, that whosoever trusts in him shall be saved. But they will not believe it, though we have proved it, hundreds of us, thousands of us, and we tell them as solemnly and as earnestly as we can, that we have tasted and handled of these things, that they are not cunningly devised fables, but are in very truth most precious and proven realities; and yet, without the grace of God, there is not a single one, high or low, rich or poor, that will so believe as to try for himself; but they shake their heads and go on their way, and universally live and die in unbelief, unless sovereign grace steps in. A strange thing, a marvelous thing! "Jesus marveled because of their unbelief," and well may we marvel because of the universality of this sin.

Then a third cause for this general indifference was, *that they were always and altogether given to worldliness.* The text seems to hint that they did not think of preparing for the coming flood because they were so busy in the base enjoyment of mere eating. Some of them were gluttons, and others who did not eat so much, yet ate right well when they did eat, and daintily. They were worshiping that god that Paul speaks of—the belly. Alas! good feeding ruins many, and men dig their way to hell with their teeth. Like brutes, they care only to be filled. Others were drunkards. Ah! how merry were they in their cups! How they judged a glass of wine and told its age to a year! They were bent upon swallowing hogsheads of dainty liquor. They were drowned, like Duke Clarence, in their butts [casks] of wine. No doubt they had, in their way, their lord mayors' feasts, and their aldermen's and companies' dinners, and I know not what besides, and they were all so occupied with these things, these crying necessities of the life of swine, that they did not and could not think of anything superior to that. They were married and given in marriage; this was a serious business, and must be attended to—how could they forsake their wedding feasts and their newly married brides? These things engrossed all their thoughts. And yet, friends, and yet, what was the use of eating and drinking, when they were to be drowned the next day? And what was the use of being married, when they were to be drowned on the morrow? If they had looked at these things in the light of faith, they would have despised them; but they only used the blear eye of sense, and thus they set great store upon these present things of mirth.

Yes, and so it is with the wicked man nowadays. He gets rich, but what is the use of being wealthy if you must be damned? Fool that he is, if he buys a gold coffin, how would that help him? Suppose he is laid out with a bag of gold in each hand, and a pile of it between his legs, how will that help him? Others seek to get learning, but what is the good of learning if you sink to perdition with it? Take up the learned man's skull, and what is the difference between that and the skull of the merest pauper that scarcely knew his letters? Brown unpalpable powder, they both crumble down into the same elements. To die in a respectable position, what is the use of it? What are a few more plumes on the hearse, or a longer line of mourning coaches? Will these ease the miseries of Tophet? Ah! friends, you have to die. Why not make ready for the inevitable? Oh! if men were wise, they would see that all earth's joys are just like the bubbles which our children blow with soap; they glitter and they shine, and then they are gone, and there is not even a wreck left behind. Oh, that they were wise to enter the ark, to look to Christ, so that when the floods arise they might be found safe in him.

Here, then, comes this general rule, never to be too much lamented, and which ought to make every Christian's heart break with heaviness, that universally and everywhere, in the very presence of the coming judgment, and between the very jaws of death and hell, the whole human race remains indifferent, unbelieving, worldly, and still will so remain until the flood of fire comes and sweeps them all away. Thus will they all sport until they perish, unless eternal love prevent.

3. The last consideration shall be but very briefly handled, but it is a very comforting one, namely, that *all who were in the ark were safe*.

Nobody fell out of that divinely appointed refuge; nobody was dragged out; nobody died in it; nobody was left to perish in it. All who went in came out unharmed. They were all preserved in it; they were all safely brought through the dread catastrophe. The ark preserved them all, and so will Jesus Christ preserve all in him. Whoever may come to him shall be secure. None of them shall perish, neither shall any pluck them out of his hand. Think what strange creatures they were that were preserved! Why, there went into that ark unclean animals two and two. May God bring some of you who have been like unclean animals unto Christ; great swine of sin, you have wandered furthest in iniquity and defiled yourselves—yet when the swine were in the ark they were safe, and so shall you be. You ravens, you black ravens of sin, if you fly to Christ he will not cast you out, but you shall be secure. If electing love shall pick you out, and effectual grace shall draw you to the door of that ark, it shall be shut upon you and you shall be saved. Within that ark there was the timid hare, but its timidity did not destroy it; there was the weak coney, but despite its weakness, in the ark it was all safe. There were to be found such slow-moving creatures as the snail; some darkness-loving creatures like the bat, but they were all safe; and the mouse was as safe as the ox, and the snail was as safe as the greyhound, and the squirrel was as secure as the elephant, and the timid hare was as safe as the courageous lion—not safe because of what they were, but safe because of where they were, namely, in the ark.

Oh! what a medley the Lord's people are! What strange beings! Some few of them fathers, but not many; the great mass of them little children, who, though they should have grown are still very carnal, and only babes in Christ instead of full-grown men. Yet all safe; all alike in security, however much they may differ; varying temperament, but unvarying security; differing in experience, but the same in oneness to Christ, and all in him. "Wherefore, being justified by faith, we have peace with God, through our Lord Jesus Christ"; and so we have, whether we be great or small.

> To us the covenant stands secure,
> Tho' earth's old columns bow;
> The strong, the feeble, and the weak,
> Are one in Jesus now.

When the storm beat upon the ark, it might have destroyed the lion quite as soon as the mouse, but it destroyed neither, because the sides of the ark could bear the tempest; and when the floods came, the vessel could mount higher and higher and nearer toward heaven, the deeper the waters were. So with us: let storms and furious tempests come and our sins assail us, and our sorrows too, yet we who are weakest are quite as secure as the strongest, because we are in Christ, and Christ shall outlive the storm, and bear us upward, nearer and nearer to the heaven of God.

May God grant us grace to be found of him in peace in the day of the Lord's appearing, when the elements shall melt and the skies be rolled up like a scroll. As I have already said, it all hangs upon that question, "Do you believe in Christ?" If your heart trusts Christ, you are safe, come what may; but if your heart rests not in him, you are lost, come what will. God save you, for Jesus' sake. Amen.

> Come to the ark, come to the ark;
> To Jesus come away:
> The pestilence walks forth by night,
> The arrow flies by day.
>
> Come to the ark: the waters rise,
> The seas their billows rear

While darkness gathers o'er the skies,
Behold a refuge near.

Come to the ark, all, all that weep
Beneath the sense of sin!
Without, deep calleth unto deep
But all is peace within.

Come to the ark, ere yet the flood
Your lingering steps oppose!
Come, for the door which open stood
Is now about to close.

The Scales of Judgment

Delivered on Sabbath morning, June 12, 1859, at the Music Hall, Royal Surrey Gardens. No. 257.

TEKEL; Thou art weighed in the balances, and art found wanting.
—DANIEL 5:27

There is a weighing time for kings and emperors, and all the monarchs of earth, albeit some of them have exalted themselves to a position in which they appear to be irresponsible to man. Though they escape the scales on earth, they must surely be tried at the bar of God. For nations there is a weighing time. National sins demand national punishments. The whole history of God's dealings with mankind proves that though a nation may go on in wickedness, it may multiply its oppressions; it may abound in bloodshed, tyranny, and war, but an hour of retribution draws nigh. When it shall have filled up its measure of iniquity, then shall the angel of vengeance execute its doom. There cannot be an eternal damnation for nations as nations; the destruction of men at last will be that of individuals, and at the bar of God each man must be tried for himself. The punishment, therefore, of nations, is national. The guilt they incur must receive its awful recompense in this present time state.

It was so with the great nation of the Chaldeans. They had been guilty of blood. The monuments which still remain, and which we have lately explored, prove them to have been a cruel and ferocious race. A people of a strange language they were, and stranger than their language were their deeds. God allowed that nation for a certain period to grow and thrive, till it became God's hammer, breaking in pieces many nations. It was the ax of the Almighty—his battle ax, and his weapon of war. By it he smote the loins of kings, yes, and slew mighty kings. But its time came at last. She sat alone as a queen, and said, "I shall see no sorrow," nevertheless, the Lord brought her low, and made her grind in the dust of captivity, and gave her riches to the spoiler, and her pomp to the destroyer.

Even so must it be with every nation of the earth that is guilty of oppression. Humbling itself before God, when his wrath is kindled but a little, it may for a while arrest its fate; but if it still continue in its bold unrighteousness, it shall certainly reap the harvest of its own sowing. So likewise shall it be with the nations that now abide on the face of the earth. There is no God in heaven if the iniquity of slavery go unpunished. There is no God existing in heaven above if the cry of the Negro do not bring down a red hail of blood upon the nation that still holds the black man in slavery. Nor is there a God anywhere if the nations of Europe that still oppress each other and are oppressed by tyrants do not find out to their dismay that he executes vengeance. The Lord God is the avenger of everyone that is oppressed, and the executor of everyone that oppresses. I see, this very moment, glancing at the page of the world's present history, a marvelous proof that God will take vengeance. Piedmont, the land which is at this time sodden with blood, is only at this hour suffering the vengeance that has long been hanging over it. The snows of its mountains were once red with the blood of martyrs. It is not yet forgotten how there the children of God were hunted like partridges on the mountains; and so has God directed it, that the nations that performed that frightful act upon his children shall there meet, rend, and devour each other in the slaughter, and both sides shall be almost equal, and nothing shall be seen but that God will punish those who lift their hands against his anointed.

There has never been a deed of persecution—there has never been a drop of martyr's blood shed yet, but shall be avenged, and every land guilty of it shall yet drink the cup of the wine of the wrath of God. And especially certain is there gathering an awful storm over the head of the empire of Rome— that spiritual despotism of the firstborn of hell. All the clouds of God's vengeance are gathering into one—the firmament is big with thunder, God's right arm is lifted up even now, and before long the nations of the earth shall eat her flesh and burn her with fire. They that have been made drunk with the wine of her fornication, shall soon also have to drink with her of the wine of the fierceness of his wrath; and they shall reel to and fro, their loins shall be loose, their knees shall smite together, when God fulfills the old handwriting on the rock of Patmos.

Our duty at this time is to take heed to ourselves as a nation that we purge ourselves of our great sins. Although God has given so much light, and kindly favored us with the dew of his Spirit, yet England is a hoary sinner. Favorably with mercy does God regard her, so much the rather then let each Christian try to shake off the sins of his nation from his own skirt, and let each one to the utmost of his ability labor and strive to purify this land of blood and oppression, and of everything evil that still clings to her. So may God preserve this land; and may its monarchy endure till he shall come, before whom both kings and princes shall lose their power right cheerfully even as the stars fade when the king of light—the sun—lifts up his golden head.

With this brief preface, I will leave nations and kings all to themselves, and consider the text principally as it has relation to each one of us; and may God grant that when we go out of this hall most of us may be able to say, "I thank God I have a good hope that when weighed in the scales at last I shall not be found wanting." Or, if that is too much to expect, may I yet trust some will go away convinced of sin, crying in their own spirits, "I am wanting now, but if God in his mercy meet with me, I shall not be wanting long."

I shall notice, first, that there are certain preliminary weighings which God would have us put ourselves to in this world, and which indeed he has set up as kind of tests whereby we may be able to discover what shall be the result of the last decisive weighing. After I have mentioned these, I shall then come to speak of the last tremendous weighing of the judgment day.

1. Let us judge ourselves that we that we may not be judged.

It is for us now to put ourselves through the various tests by which we may be able to discover whether we are, at this present time, short weight or not.

The first test I would suggest is that of *human opinion.* Now understand me. I do believe that the opinion of man is utterly valueless when that opinion is based upon false premises, and therefore draws wrong conclusions. I would not trust the world to judge God's servants, and it is a mercy to know that the world shall not have the judging of the church, but rather, the saints shall judge the world. There is a sense in which I would say with the apostle, "With me it is a very small thing that I should be judged of you, or of man's judgment: yea, I judge not myself." Human opinion is not to be put in competition with divine revelation. But I speak now of judging ourselves, and I do not think it safe, when weighing our own character, to prefer our own and exclude our neighbor's judgment. The esteem or contempt of honest men, which is instinctively shown without reference to party or prejudice, is not by any means to be despised. When a man knows that he is right, he may snap his fingers in the face of all men, but when a man's conscience tells him that he is wrong—if at the judgment bar of men he is found guilty, he must not despise it; he must rather look on the judgment of men as being the first intimation of what shall be the judgment of God.

Are you, my hearer, at this time in the estimation of all your fellow creatures condemned as one who should be avoided? Do you clearly perceive that the righteous shun you because your example would contaminate them? Have you discovered that your character is not held to be estimable among honest and respectable men? Let me assure you that you have good reason to be afraid, for if you cannot stand the trial of an honest fellow creature—if the law of your country condemn you, if the very laws of society exclude you—if the imperfect judgments of earth pronounce you too vile for its association, how fearful must be your condemnation when you are put into the far more rigid scale of God's justice, and terrible must be your fate when the perfect community of the Firstborn in heaven shall rise as one man and demand that you shall never behold their society? When a man is so bad that his fellow creatures themselves, imperfect though they be, are able to see in him, not the mere seeds, but the very flower, the full bloom of iniquity, he should tremble. If you cannot pass that test, if human opinion condemn, if your own conscience declare that opinion to be just, you have good need to tremble indeed, for you are put into the balances and are found wanting.

I have thought it right to mention this balance. There may be some present to whom it may be pertinent, but at the same time, there are far better tests for men, tests which are not so easily to be misunderstood. And I would go through some of these. One of the scales into which I would have every man put himself, at least once in his life—I say at least once, because, if not, heaven is to him a place, the gates of which are shut forever—I would have every man put himself into the scales of the *divine law.* There stands the law of God. This law is a balance which will turn, even were there but a grain of sand in it. It is true to a hair. It moves upon the diamond of God's eternal immutable truth. I put but one weight into the scale; it is this: "Thou shalt love the Lord thy God with all thy heart, with all thy mind, with all thy soul, and with all thy strength," and I invite any man who thinks himself to be of the right stamp, and flatters himself that he has no need of mercy, no need of washing in the blood of Jesus Christ, no need of any atonement—I invite him to put himself into the scales and see whether he be full weight, when there be but so much as this one commandment in the other scale. O my friends, if we did but try ourselves by the very first commandment of the law, we must acknowledge that we are guilty. But when we drop in weight after weight, till the whole sacred ten are there, there is not a man under the cope [covering] of heaven who has one grain of wit left, but must confess that he is short of the mark, that he falls below the standard which the law of God requires. Mrs. Too-Good has often declared that she herself has done all her duty, and perhaps a little more; that she has been even more kind to the poor than there was any occasion for; that she has gone to church more frequently than even her religion requires; that she has been more attentive to the sacraments than the best of her neighbors, and if *she* does not enter heaven, she does not know who will. "If I have not a portion among the saints, who can possibly hope to see God's face in light?" No, madam, but I am sorry for you; you are light as a feather when you go into the scales. In these wooden balances of your own ceremonies you may, perhaps, be found right enough, but in those eternal scales, with those tremendous weights—the Ten Commandments of the law—the declaration is suspended over your poor foolish head. "Thou art weighed in the balances, and art found wanting."

There may, perhaps, in congregations like this, be some extremely respectable body who has from his youth up, as he imagines, kept God's law; his country, family, or associates can bring no charge against him, and so he wraps himself up and considers that really he is the man, and that when he appears at the gate of heaven, he will be received as a rightful owner and proprietor of the reward of the righteous. Ah, my friend, if you would take the trouble just to sit down and weigh yourself in the scales of the law—if you would take but one command, the one in which you think yourself least guilty, the one that you imagine you have kept best, and really look at its intent, and spirit, and view it in all its length and breadth, in truth I know you would keep out of the scale and say, "Alas, when I hoped to have gone down with a sound of congratulation, I find myself hurled up, light as the dust of the balance, while the tremendous law of God comes sounding down and shakes the house." Let each man do this, and every one of us must retire from this place saying, "I am weighed in the balances, and I am found wanting."

And now the true believer comes forward, and he claimed to be weighed in another balance, for, says he, according to this balance, if I be what I profess to be, I am not found wanting, for I can bring with me the perfect righteousness of Jesus Christ, and that is full weight, even though the Ten Commandments of the law be weighed against it. I bring with me the full atonement, the perfect satisfaction of Jesus' blood, and the perfect righteousness of a divine being, the spotless righteousness of Jesus the Son of God. I can be weighed against the law, and yet sit securely, knowing that now and forever, I am equal to the law. It has nothing against me since Christ is mine. Its terrors have no power to frighten me, and as for its demands, they can exact nothing of me for they are fulfilled to the utmost in Christ.

Well, I propose now to take professors and put them into the scales and try them. Let each one of us put ourselves into the scale of *conscience*. Many make a profession of religion in this age. It is the time of shams. There were never so many liars in the world since the days of Adam, as there are now. The father of lies has been more prolific of children at this than at any other period. There is such an abundance of newspapers and of talkers and of readers: and consequently flying reports, wrong news, and evil tales, are far more numerous than ever. So, too, there is a great deal of vain show with religion. I sometimes fear we have not a grain more religion in England now than we had in the time of the Puritans. Then, though the stream in which it ran was narrow, it did run very deep indeed; now, the banks have been burst; a great extent of country is covered with religious profession; but I tremble lest we should find at last that the flood was not deep enough to float our souls to heaven.

Will each one now in this congregation put himself into the scale of *conscience,* sit down and ask, "Is my profession true? Do I feel that before God I am an heir of the promises? When I sit at my Savior's table, have I any right to be a guest? Can I truly say that when I profess to be converted, I only profess what I have actually proved? When I talk experimentally about the things of the kingdom of God, is that experience a borrowed tale, or have I felt what I say in my own breast? When I stand up to preach, do I preach that which I have really tasted and handled, or do I only repeat that which I have learned to utter with the lip, though it has never been fused in the crucible of my own heart?" Conscience is not very readily cheated. There are some men whose consciences are not a safe balance; they have by degrees become so hardened in sin that conscience refuses to work; but still I will hope that most of us may abide by the test of our own conscience, if we let it freely work. Dear friends, I would that you would often retire to your chambers alone; shut the door and shut out all the world, and then sit and review your past life; scan carefully your present character and your present position; and do, I beseech you, try to get an honest answer from your own conscience. Bring up everything that you can think of that might lead you to doubt. You need be under no difficulty here; for are there not enough sins committed by us every day to warrant our suspicions that we are not God's children? Well, let all these black accusers for death, let them all have their say. Do not cloak your sins. Read your diary through, let all your iniquities come up before you (this is the pith of confession); and then ask conscience whether you can truly say, "I have repented of all these. God is my witness, I hate these things with a perfect hatred. God also hears me witness that my trust is fixed alone in him who is the Savior of sinners, for salvation and justification. If I be not awfully deceived, I am a partaker of divine grace, having been regenerated and begotten again unto a lively hope." Oh, that conscience may help each of us to say, "I am not a mere painted image of life, but I trust I have the life of Jesus made manifest in my body." My profession is not the pompous pageantry with which dead souls are carried respectably to perdition; but it is the joy, the hope, the confidence of one who is being borne along in the chariot of mercy, to his Father's home above.

"Ah! how many people are really afraid to look their religion in the face! They know it to be so bad, they dare not examine it. They are like bankrupts that keep no books. They would be very glad for a fire to consume their books, if they ever kept any, for they know the balance is all on the wrong side. They are losing, breaking up, and they would not wish to keep an account of their losses or villainies. A man who is afraid to examine himself may rest assured that his ship is rotten, and that it will not be long before it founders in the sea, to his eternal shipwreck. Call up conscience; put yourself in the scale, and God help you, that the verdict may not be against you—that it may not be said of you, "You are weighed in the balances, and are found wanting."

I would have every man also weigh himself in the scales of *God's Word*— not merely in that part of it which we call legal, and which has respect to us in our fallen state; but let us weigh ourselves in the scale of the gospel. You will find it sometimes a holy exercise, to read some psalm of David, when his soul was most full of grace; and if you were to put questions as you read each verse, saying to yourself, "Can I say this? Have I felt as David felt? Have my bones ever been broken with sin as his were when he penned his penitential psalms? Has my soul ever been full of true confidence in the hour of difficulty, as his was when he sang of God's mercies in the cave of Adullam or the holds of Engedi? Can I take the cup of salvation and call upon the name of the Lord? Can I pay my vows now unto the Lord, in the courts of his house, in the presence of all his people?" I am afraid that the book of Psalms itself would be enough to convince some of you that your religion is but superficial, that it is but a vain show and not a vital reality. God help you often to try yourselves in that scale.

Then read over the life of Christ, and as you read, ask yourselves whether you are conformed to him, such as he describes a true disciple. Endeavor to see whether you have any of the meekness, any of the humility, any of the lovely spirit which he constantly inculcated and displayed. Try yourselves by the Sermon on the Mount—you will find it a good scale in which to weigh your spirits. Take then the epistles and see whether you can go with the apostle in what he said of his experience. Have you ever cried out like him: "O wretched man that I am! who shall deliver me from the body of this death?"? Have you ever felt like him, that "this is a faithful saying, and worthy of all acceptation, that Christ Jesus came into the world to save sinners"? Have you ever known his self-abasement? Could you say that you seemed to yourself the chief of sinners and always accounted yourself less than the least of all saints? And have you known anything of his devotion? Could you join with him and say, "For me to live is Christ, and to die is gain"? O brethren! The best of us—

if we put the Bible into the scales for the proof of our state, if we read God's Word as a test of our spiritual condition—the very best of us has cause to tremble. Before almighty God, on our bended knees, with our Bible before us, we have good reason to stop many a time and say, "Lord, I feel I have never yet been here, oh, bring me here! Give me true penitence, such as this I read of. Give me real faith. Oh, let me not have a counterfeit religion! Give me that which is the current coin of the realm of heaven—your own sterling grace, which shall pass in the great day, when the gates of heaven shall be opened, and, alas! the gates of hell wide open too." Try yourselves by God's Word, and I fear there are some who will love to rise from it, and say, "I am weighed in the balances and found wanting."

Yet again, God has been pleased to set another means of trial before us. When God puts us into the scales I am about to mention, namely, the scales of providence, it behooves us very carefully to watch ourselves and see whether or not we be found wanting. Some men are tried in the scales of adversity. Some of you, my dear friends, may have come here very sorrowful. Your business fails, your earthly prospects are growing dark; it is midnight with you in this world; you have sickness in the house; the wife of your bosom languishes before your weeping eyes; your children perhaps, by their ingratitude, have wounded your spirits. But you are a professor of religion; you know what God is doing with you now; he is testing and trying you. He knows you, and he would have you know that a summertime religion is not sufficient; he would have you see whether your faith can stand the test of trial and trouble. Remember Job; what a scale was that in which he was put! What weights of affliction were those cast in one after another, very mountains of sore trouble; and yet he could bear them all, and he came out of the scales proof against all the weight that even satanic strength could hurl into the scale.

And is it so with you? Can you now say, "The Lord gave, and the Lord hath taken away, blessed be the name of the Lord"? Can you submit to his will without murmuring? Or if you cannot master such a phase of religion as this, are you able still to feel that you cannot complain against God? Do you still say, "Though he slay me, yet will I trust in him"? O my friends, remember that if your religion will not stand the day of adversity, if it afford you no comfort in the time of storms, you would be better in that case without it than with it; for with it you are deceived, but without it you might discover your true condition and seek the Lord as a penitent sinner. If you are now broken in pieces by a little adversity, what will become of you in the day when all the tempests of God shall be let loose on your soul? If you have run with the footmen, and they have wearied you, what will you do in the swellings of Jordan? If you cannot endure the open grave, how can you endure the trump of the archangel and the terrific thunders of the last great day? If your burning house is too much for you, what will you do in a burning world? If thunder and lightning alarm you, what will you do when the world is in a blaze, and when all the thunders of God leave their hiding place and rush pealing through the world? If mere trial distress you and grieve you, oh, what will you do when all the hurricanes of divine vengeance shall sweep across the earth and shake its very pillars till they reel and reel again? Yes, friends, I would have you, as often as you are tried and troubled, see how you bear it—whether your faith then stands and whether you could see God's right hand, even when it is wrapped in clouds, whether you can discover the silver lining to the black clouds of tribulation. God help you to come out of the scales, for many are weighed in them and have been found wanting.

Another set of scales there is, too, of an opposite color. Those I have described are painted black; these are of golden hue. They are the scales of *prosperity*. Many a man has endured the chills of poverty who could not endure sunny weather. Some men's religion is very much like the palace of the queen of Russia, which had been built out of solid slabs of ice. It could stand the frost; the roughest breeze could not destroy it; the sharp touch of winter could not devour it; they but strengthened and made it more lasting. But summer melted it all away, and where once were the halls of revelry, nothing remained but the black rolling river. How many have been destroyed by prosperity? The fumes of popularity have turned the brains of many a man. The adulation of multitudes has laid thousands low. Popular applause has its foot in the sand, even when it has its head among the stars. Many have I known who in a cottage seemed to fear God but in a mansion have forgotten him. When their daily bread was earned with the sweat of their brow, then it was they served the Lord and went up to his house with gladness. But their seeming religion all departed when their flocks and herds increased, and their gold and silver was multiplied.

It is no easy thing to stand the trial of prosperity. You know the old fable; I will just put it in a Christian light. When the winds of affliction blow on a Christian's head, he just pulls around him the cloak of heavenly consolation and girds his religion about him all the tighter for the fury of the storm. But when the sun of prosperity shines on him, the traveler grows warm and full of delight and pleasure; he ungirds his cloak and lays it aside, so that what the storms of affliction never could accomplish, the soft hand and the witchery of prosperity has been able to perform. It has loosed the loins of many a mighty man. It has been the Delilah that has shorn the locks and taken away the strength of many a Samson. This rock has witnessed the most fatal wrecks.

> More the treacherous calm I dread,
> Than tempests rolling over head.

But shall we be able to say after passing through prosperity, "This is not my rest, this is not my God. Let him give me what he may, I will thank him for it, yet will I rejoice in the giver rather than the gift; I will say unto the Lord, you only are my rest"? It is well if you can come out of these scales enabled honestly to hope that you are not found wanting.

There are again the scales of *temptation*. Many and many a man seems for a time to run well; but it is temptation that tries the Christian. In your business you are now honest and upright, but suppose a speculation cross your path which involve but a very slight departure from the high standard of Christianity, and indeed would not involve any departure from the low standard which your fellow tradesmen follow. Do you think you would be able to say, "How can I do this great wickedness and sin against God?"? Could you say, "Should such a man as I do this? Shall I haste to be rich, for if I do, I shall not be innocent?"? How has it been with you? You have had your trial time. There has been an opportunity of making a little: have you taken it? Has God enabled you to endure when tempted, whether to unlawful gain or to lustful pleasure or to pride and vanity? Have you been enabled to stand proof against all these, and to say, "Get thee behind me, Satan, for thou savorest not the things which be of God, but those which be of man and of sin"? How have you stood the test of temptation?

If you have never been tempted, you know nothing about this. How can we tell the worthiness of the ship till she has been at sea in the storm? You cannot know what you are till you have been through the practical test of everyday life. How then has it been with you? Have you been weighed in the balance, and have you been enabled to say, "I know through grace I have been kept in the hour of temptation, and with the temptation the Lord has always sent a way of escape. And here I am glorying in his grace; I cannot rest in myself, but still I can say, 'I am truly his.' The work within me is not of man, neither by man: it is the work of the Spirit. I have found succor and support when my heart and my flesh have failed me"?

It is probable, my hearers, that most of you are professors of religion; let me ask you again very earnestly to test and try yourselves, whether your religion be real or not. If there be many false prophets in the world, and those prophets have followers, must there not be many false men who are fatally deceived? Do not suppose, I beseech you, because you are a deacon—or have been baptized, or are a member of the church, or are professors—you are therefore safe. The bleaching bones of the skeletons of self-deceived ones should warn you. On the rock of presumption, thousands have been split that once sailed merrily enough. Take care, O mariner! though your bark may be gaily trimmed and may be brightly painted, yet it is none the surer after all. Take heed, lest the rocks be seen beneath the keel, lest they pierce you through, and lest the waters of destruction overwhelm you. Oh! do not, I entreat you, say, "Why make this stir? I daresay I shall be all right at last." Do not let your eternal state be a matter of suspicion or doubt. Decide now, I beseech you, decide now in your conscience whether you are Christ's or not. Of all the most miserable men in the world, and the most hopeless, I think those are most to be pitied who are indifferent and careless about religion. There are some men whose feelings never run deeper than their skin; they either have no heart, or else it is so set round with fatness that you can never touch them. I like to see a man either desponding or rejoicing; either anxious about his eternal state or else confident about it. But you who never will question yourselves—you are just like the bullock going to the slaughter or like the sheep that will enter the very slaughterhouse and lick the knife that is about to take its blood. I wish I could speak this morning somewhat more earnestly. Oh, that some sparks from the divine fire could now light up my soul, I think I could speak to you like some of the prophets of old, when they stood in the midst of a professing generation, to warn them. Oh, that the very voice of God would speak to each heart this morning! While God is thundering on high, may he thunder below in your souls! Be warned, my hearers, against self-deception. Be true to yourselves. If God be God, serve him, and do it truly; if the devil be God, serve him, and serve him honestly, and serve him faithfully. But do not pretend to be serving God while you are really indifferent and careless about it.

2. I must now close by endeavoring to speak of *the last great balance*; and here would I speak very solemnly, and may the Spirit of God be with us.

Time shall soon be over; eternity must soon begin; death is hurrying onward; the pale horse at his utmost speed is coming to every inhabitant of this earth. The arrow of death is fitted to the string, and soon shall it be sent home. Man's heart is the target. Then, after death, comes the judgment; the dread assize shall soon commence. The trump of the archangel shall awake the sleeping myriads, and, standing on their feet, they shall confront the God against whom they have sinned. I think I see the scales hanging in heaven, so massive that none but the hand of Deity can uphold them. Let me cast my eye upward and consider that hour when I must myself enter those scales and be weighed once for all.

Come, let me speak for each man present. Those scales yonder are exact; I may deceive my fellows here, but deceive God I cannot then. I may be weighed in the balances of earth, which shall give but a partial verdict, and so commit myself to a false idea that I am what I am not, that I am hopeful when I am hopeless. But *those* scales are true. There is no means whatever of flattering them into a false declaration; they will cry aloud and spare not. When I get there, the voice of flattery shall be changed into the voice of honesty. Here I may go daily on crying, "Peace, peace, when there is no peace"; but there the naked truth shall startle me, and not a single word of consolation shall be given me that is not true. Let me therefore ponder the fact, that those scales are exactly true and cannot be deceived. Let me remember also, that whether I will or not, into those scales I must go. God will not take me on my profession. I may bring my witnesses with me; I may bring my minister and the deacons of the church to give me a character, which might be thought all-sufficient among men, but God will tolerate no subterfuge. Into the scales he will put me, do what I may, whatever the opinion of others may be of me and whatever my own profession. And let me remember, too, that I must be altogether weighed in the scales. I cannot hope that God will weigh my head and pass over my heart—that because I have correct notions of doctrine, therefore he will forget that my heart is impure or my hands guilty of iniquity. My all must be cast into the scales. Come, let me stretch my imagination and picture myself about to be put into those scales. Shall I be able to walk boldly up and enter them, knowing whom I have believed, and being persuaded that the blood of Christ and his perfect righteousness shall bear me harmless through it all; or shall I be dragged with terror and dismay? Shall the angel come and say, "You must enter"? Shall I bend my knee and cry, "Oh, it is all right," or shall I seek to escape? Now, thrust into the scale, do I see myself waiting for one solemn moment. My feet have touched the bottom of the scales, and there stand those everlasting weights and now which way are they turned? Which way shall it be? Do I descend in the scale with joy and delight, being found through Jesus' righteousness to be full weight, and so accepted; or must I rise, light, frivolous, unsound in all my fancied hopes, and kick the beam? Oh, shall it be, that I must go where the rough hand of vengeance shall seize and drag me downward, into fell despair? Can you picture the moments of suspense? I can see a poor man standing on the drop with the rope round his neck, and oh, what an instant of apprehension must that be; what thoughts of horror must float through his soul! How must a world of misery be compressed into a second! But, O my hearers, there is a far more terrible moment still for you that are godless, Christless, careless: that have made a profession of religion, and yet have it not in your hearts. I see you in the scales, but what shall we say? The wailings of hell seem not sufficient to express your misery, in the scales without Christ! Not long before you shall be in the jaws of hell, without pity and without compassion.

O my dear hearers! if you could hope to get to heaven without being weighed—if God would believe what you say without testing you, I would not care about asking you this morning to ascertain the state of your own hearts. But if God will try you, try yourselves; if he will judge you, judge your own hearts. Don't say that because you profess to be religious therefore you are right—that because others imagine you to be safe that therefore you are so. Weigh yourselves; put your hearts into the balance. Do not be deceived. Pull the bandage from your eyes, that your blindness may be removed, and that you may pass a just opinion upon yourselves as to what you are. I would have you not only see yourselves as others see you, but I would have you see yourselves as God sees you; for that, after all, is your real state; his eye is not to be mistaken; he is the God of truth, and just and right is he.

How fearful a thing will it be, if any of us who are members of Christ's church shall be cast into hell at last. The higher we ascend, the greater will be our fall, like Icarus in the old parable, who flew aloft with waxen wings, till the sun did melt them and he fell. And some of you are flying like that: you are flying up with waxen wings. What if the terrible heat of the judgment day should melt them! I sometimes try to picture, how terrible the reverse to me if found to be rejected at last. Let what I shall say for myself suit for all. No, and must it be, if I live in this world and think I am a Christian and am not— must it be that I must go from the songs of the sanctuary to the cursings of the synagogue of Satan? Must I go from the cup of the Eucharist to the cup of devils? Must I go from the table of the Lord to the feast of fiends? Shall these lips that now proclaim the word of Jesus one day utter the wailings of perdition? Shall this tongue that has sung the praises of the Redeemer be moved with blasphemy? Shall it be that this body which has been the receptacle of so many a mercy—shall it become the very house and home of every misery that vengeance can invent? Shall these eyes that now look on God's people one day behold the frightful sights of spirits destroyed in that all-consuming fire? And must it be that the ears that have heard the hallelujahs of this morning shall one day hear the shrieks and groans and howls of the lost and damned spirits? It must be so if we be not Christ's. Oh, how frightful will it be! I think I see some grave professor at last condemned to hell. There are multitudes of sinners, lying in their irons and tossing on their beds of flame; lifting themselves upon their elbows for a moment, they seem to forget their tortures as they see the professor come in, and they cry, "Are you become like one of us? Is the preacher himself damned? What! is the deacon of the church below come to sit with drunkards and with swearers? Ah," they cry, "aha, aha, are you bound up in the same bundle with us after all?" Surely the mockery of hell must be itself a most fearful torture; professing sinners mocked by those who never professed religion. But mortal fire can never describe the miseries of a disappointed, blasted hope, when that hope is lost—it involves the loss of mercy, the loss of Christ, the loss of life—and it involves, moreover, the terrible destruction and the awful vengeance of almighty God.

Let us one and all go home this day, when yet God's sky is heavy, and let us bend ourselves at his altar and cry for mercy. Every man apart—husband apart from wife. Apart, let us seek our chambers of praying again and again, "Lord renew me; Lord forgive me; Lord accept me." And while, perhaps, the tempest which is now lowering over the sky, and before another tempest direr still, shall fall on us with its fearful terrors, may you find peace. May we not then find ourselves lost, lost forever, where hope can never come! It shall be my duty to search myself. I hope I shall be enabled to put myself into the scale; promise me, my hearers, that each of you will do the same. I was told one day this week by someone, that having preached for several Sabbaths lately upon the comforting doctrines of God's Word, he was afraid that some of you would begin to console yourselves with the idea that you were God's elect when perhaps you were not. Well, at least, such a thing shall not happen if I have done what I hoped to do this morning. God bless you, for Jesus' sake.

"I Would; but Ye Would Not"

Intended for reading on Lord's Day, October 7, 1894; delivered on Lord's Day evening, July 22, 1888, at the Metropolitan Tabernacle, Newington. No. 2381.

> O Jerusalem, Jerusalem, thou that killest the prophets, and stonest them which are sent onto thee, how often would I have gathered thy children together, even as a hen gathereth her chickens under her wings, and ye would not!
> —MATTHEW 23:37

This is not and could not be the language of a mere man. It would be utterly absurd for any man to say that he would have gathered the inhabitants of a city together, "even as a hen gathereth her chickens under her wings." Besides, the language implies that, for many centuries, by the sending of the prophets, and by many other warnings, God would often have gathered the children of Jerusalem together as a hen gathers her chickens under her wings. Now, Christ could not have said that throughout those ages, he would have gathered those people, if he had been only a man. If his life began at Bethlehem, this would be an absurd statement; but, as the Son of God, ever loving the sons of men, ever desirous of the good of Israel, he could say that, in sending the prophets, even though they were stoned and killed, he had again and again shown his desire to bless his people till he could truly say, "How often would I have gathered your children together!"

Some who have found difficulties in this lament have said that it was the language of Christ as man. I beg to put in a very decided negative to that; it is, and it must be, the utterance of the Son of man, the Son of God, the Christ in his complex person as human and divine. I am not going into any of the difficulties just now; but you could not fully understand this passage, from any point of view, unless you believed it to be the language of one who was both God and man.

This verse shows also that the ruin of men lies with themselves. Christ puts it very plainly, "I would; but ye would not." "How often would I have gathered thy children together, and ye would not!" That is a truth, about which, I hope, we have never had any question; we hold tenaciously that salvation is all of grace, but we also believe with equal firmness that the ruin of man is entirely the result of his own sin. It is the will of God that saves; it is the will of man that damns. Jerusalem stands and is preserved by the grace and favor of the most High; but Jerusalem is burned, and her stones are cast down, through the transgression and iniquity of men, which provoked the justice of God.

There are great deeps about these two points; but I have not been accustomed to lead you into any deeps, and I am not going to do so at this time. The practical part of theology is that which it is most important for us to understand. Any man may get himself into a terrible labyrinth who thinks continually of the sovereignty of God alone, and he may equally get into deeps that are likely to drown him if he meditates only on the free will of man. The best thing is to take what God reveals to you and to believe that. If God's Word leads me to the right, I go there; if it leads me to the left, I go there; if it makes me stand still, I stand still. If you so act, you will be safe; but if you try to be wise above that which is written, and to understand that which even angels do not comprehend, you will certainly befog yourself. I desire ever to bring before you practical rather than mysterious subjects, and our present theme is one that concerns us all. The great destroyer of man is the will of man. I do not believe that man's free will has ever saved a soul; but man's free will has been the ruin of multitudes. "Ye would not" is still the solemn accusation of Christ against guilty men. Did he not say, at another time, "Ye will not come unto me, that ye might have life"? The human will is desperately set against God, and is the great devourer and destroyer of thousands of good intentions and emotions which never come to anything permanent because the will is acting in opposition to that which is right and true.

That, I think, is the very marrow of the text, and I am going to handle it in this fashion.

1. First, consider from the very condescending emblem used by our Lord, *what God is to those who come to him.*

He gathers them, "as a hen gathereth her chickens under her wings." Let us dwell upon that thought for a few minutes. It is a very marvelous thing that God should condescend to be compared to a hen, that the Christ, the Son of the Highest, the Savior of men, should stoop to so homely a piece of imagery as to liken himself to a hen. There must be something very instructive in this metaphor, or our Lord would not have used it in such a connection.

Those of you who have been gathered unto Christ know, first, that *by this wonderful gatherer, you have been gathered into happy association.* The chickens, beneath the wings of the hen, look very happy all crowded together. What a sweet little family party they are! How they hide themselves away in great

contentment and chirp their little note of joy! You, dear friends, who have
never been converted, find very noisy fellowship, I am afraid, in this world;
you do not get much companionship that helps you, blesses you, gives you
rest of mind; but if you had been gathered to the Lord's Christ, you would
have found that there are many sweetnesses in this life in being beneath the
wings of the most High. He who comes to Christ finds father and mother and
sister and brother; he finds many dear and kind friends who are themselves
connected with Christ, and who therefore love those who are joined to him.
Among the greatest happinesses of my life, certainly, I put down Christian fellowship; and I think that many who have come from the country to London,
have, for a long time, missed much of this fellowship till, at last, they have
fallen in with Christian people, and they have found themselves happy again.
O lonely sinner, you who come in and out of this place, and say, "Nobody
seems to care about me," if you will come to Christ, and join with the church
which is gathered beneath his wings, you will soon find happy fellowship! I
remember that, in the times of persecution, one of the saints said that he had
lost his father and his mother by being driven away from his native country,
but he said, "I have found a hundred fathers, and a hundred mothers, for into
whatsoever Christian house I have gone, I have been looked upon with so
much kindness by those who have received me as an exile from my native
land, that everyone has seemed to be a father and a mother to me." If you
come to Christ, I feel persuaded that he will introduce you to many people
who will give you happy fellowship.

But that is merely the beginning. A hen is to her little chicks, next, a cover
of safety. There is a hawk in the sky; the mother bird can see it, though the
chickens cannot; she gives her peculiar cluck of warning, and quickly they
come and hide beneath her wings. The hawk will not hurt them now; beneath
her wings they are secure. This is what God is to those who come to him by
Jesus Christ—he is the giver of safety. "He shall cover thee with his feathers, and
under his wings shalt thou trust: his truth shall be thy shield and buckler."
Even the attraction of your old sins, or the danger of future temptations—
you shall be preserved from all these perils when you come to Christ, and thus
hide away under him.

The figure our Lord used is full of meaning, for, in the next place, the hen
is to her chicks the source of comfort. It is a cold night, and they would be frozen
if they remained outside; but she calls them in, and when they are under her
wings, they derive warmth from their mother's breast. It is wonderful, the
care of a hen for her little ones; she will sit so carefully and keep her wings so
widely spread, that they may all be housed. What a cabin, what a palace, it is

for the young chicks to get there under the mother's wings! The snow may fall, or the rain may come pelting down, but the wings of the hen protect the chicks; and you, dear friend, if you come to Christ, shall not only have safety, but comfort. I speak what I have experienced. There is a deep, sweet comfort about hiding yourself away in God, for when troubles come, wave upon wave, blessed is the man who has a God to give him mercy upon mercy. When affliction comes, or bereavement comes, when loss of property comes, when sickness comes, in your own body, there is nothing wanted but your God. Ten thousand things, apart from him, cannot satisfy you, or give you comfort. There, let them all go; but if God be yours, and you hide away under his wings, you are as happy in him as the chickens are beneath the hen.

Then the hen is also to her chicks *the fountain of love*. She loves them; did you ever see a hen fight for her chickens? She is a timid enough creature at any other time; but there is no timidity when her chicks are in danger. What an affection she has for them; not for all chicks, for I have known her kill the chickens of another brood; but for her own what love she has! Her heart is all devoted to them. But, oh, if you want to know the true fountain of love, you must come to Christ! You will never have to say, "Nobody loves me; I am pining, with an aching heart, for a love that can fill and satisfy it." The love of Jesus fills to overflowing the heart of man and makes him well content under all circumstances. I would that God had gathered you all, my dear hearers. I know that he has gathered many of you, blessed be his name; but still there are some here, chicks without a hen, sinners without a Savior, men and women and children who have never been reconciled to God.

The hen is also to her chicks *the cherisher of growth*. They would not develop if they were not taken care of; in their weakness they need to be cherished, that they may come to the fullness of their perfection. And when the child of God lives near to Christ, and hides beneath his wings, how fast he grows! There is no advancing from grace to grace, from feeble faith to strong faith, and from little fervency to great fervency, except by getting near to God.

The emblem used by our Lord is a far more instructive figure than I have time to explain. When the Lord gathers sinners to himself, then it is that they find in him all that the chicks find in the hen, and infinitely more.

2. Now notice, secondly, *what God does to gather men.*

They are straying, and wandering about, but he gathers them. According to the text, Jesus says, "How often would I have gathered thy children together!" How did God gather those of us who have come to him?

He gathers us, first, *by making himself known to us*. When we come to understand who he is and what he is, and know something of his love and tenderness and greatness, then we come to him. Ignorance keeps us away from him; but to know God, and his Son, Jesus Christ, is eternal life. Hence I urge you diligently to study the Scriptures, and to be as often as you can hearing a faithful preacher of the gospel, that, knowing the Lord, you may by that knowledge be drawn toward him. These are the cords of love with which the Spirit of God draws men to Christ. He makes Christ known to us. He shows us Christ in the grandeur of his divine and human nature, Christ in the humiliation of his sufferings, Christ in the glory of his resurrection, Christ in the love of his heart, in the power of his arm, in the efficacy of his plea, in the virtue of his blood; and, as we learn these sacred lessons, we say, "That is the Christ for me, that is the God for me"; and thus we are gathered unto him.

But God gathers many to himself *by the call of his servants*. You see that, of old, he sent his prophets; now, he sends his ministers. If God does not send us to you, brethren, we shall never gather you; if we come to you in our own name, we shall come in vain; but if the Lord has sent us, then he will bless us, and our message will be made to you by means of gathering you to Christ. I would much rather cease to preach than be allowed to go on preaching but never to gather souls to God. I can truly say that I have no wish to say a pretty thing or turn a period or utter a nice figure of speech; I want to win your souls, to slay your sin, to do practical work for God, with each man, each woman, each child, who shall come into this tabernacle; and I ask the prayers of God's people that it may be so. It is thus that God gathers men to himself, by the message which he gives to them through his servants.

The Lord has also *many other ways of calling men to himself*. You saw, this morning, that Peter was called to repentance by the crowing of a cock; and the Lord can use a great many means of bringing sinners to himself! Omnipotence has servants everywhere; and God can use every kind of agent, even though it appears most unsuitable, to gather together his own chosen ones. He has called some of you; he has called some of you who have not yet come to him. The text says, "How often!" It does not tell us how often; but it puts it as a matter of wonder, "How often!," with a note of exclamation.

Let me ask you, how often has God called some of you? Conscience has whispered its message to the most of you. When you come to see men dying, if you talk seriously with them, they will sometimes tell you that they are unprepared, but that they have often had tremblings and suspicions; they have long suffered from unrest, and sometimes they have been "almost persuaded." I should not think that there is a person in this place who has not been sometimes made to shake and tremble at the thought of the world to come. How often has it been so with you? "How often," says God, "would I have gathered you?"!

The Lord sometimes speaks to us, not so much by conscience, as by providence. That death in the family, what a voice it was to us! When your mother died, when your poor father passed away, what a gathering time it seemed to be then! You soon forgot all about it; but you did feel it then. Ah, my dear woman, when your babe was taken from your bosom, and the little coffin left the house, you remember how you felt; and you, father, when your prattling boy sang the Sunday school hymn to you on his dying bed and well-nigh broke your heart, then was the Lord going forth in his providence to gather you. You were being gathered, but you would not come; according to our text, you "would not."

It has not always been by death that the Lord has spoken to you; for you have had other calls. When you have been brought low or have been out of a situation [employment], when, sometimes, a Christian friend has spoken to you, when you have read something in a tract or paper which has compelled you to pull up and made you stand aghast for a while, has not all that had a reference to this text, "How often, how often, how often would I have gathered thee?"? God knocks many times at some men's doors. I know that there is a call of his which is effectual; oh, that you might hear it! But there are many other calls which come to men, of whom Christ says, "Many are called, but few are chosen." How often has he called *you*? I wish you would try and reckon up how often the almighty God has come to you and spread out his warm wide wings, and yet this has been true, "I would have gathered you, but you would not."

One more way in which God gathers men is *by continuing still to have patience with them, and sending the same message to them.* I am always afraid that you, who hear me constantly, will get to feel, "We have heard him so long and so often that he cannot say anything fresh." Why, did I not use to shake you, when first you heard me, and compel you to shed many tears in the early days of your coming to this house? And now—well, you can hear it all without a tremor; you are like the blacksmith's dog, that goes to sleep while the sparks are flying from the anvil. Down in Southwark, at the place where they make the big boilers, a man has to get inside to hold the hammer while they are riveting. There is an awful noise—the first time that a man goes in he feels that he cannot stand it, and that he will die. He loses his hearing, it is such a terrible din. But they tell me that, after a while, some have been known even to go to sleep while the men have been hammering. So it is in hearing the gospel; men grow hardened, and that which was, at one time, a very powerful call, seems to be, at the last, no call at all. Yet still, here you are, and your hair is getting gray; here you are, you have long passed the prime of life; here you are, you were in a shipwreck once, or you had an accident, or you caught the fever, but you did not die, and here you are. God still speaks to you, not saying, "Go," but "Come, come." Christ has not yet said to you, "Depart, you cursed," but he still cries, "Come unto me, all ye that labor and are heavy laden, and I will give you rest." This is how God calls, and how he gathers men by the pertinacity of his infinite compassion, in still inviting them to come unto him that they may obtain eternal life.

3. Well, now, a third point, and a very important one is this, *what men need to make them come to God.*

According to the text, God does gather men; but what is wanted on their part? Our Savior said of those that rejected him, "Ye would not."

What is wanted is, first, *the real will to come to God.* You have heard a great deal, I daresay, about the wonderful faculty of free will. I have already told you my opinion of free will; but it also happens that that is the very thing that is wanted, a will toward that which is good. There is where the sinner fails; what he needs is a real will. "Oh yes!" men say, "We are willing, we are willing." But you are not willing. If we can get the real truth, you are not willing; there is no true willingness in your hearts, for a true willingness is *a practical willingness.* The man who is willing to come to Christ says, "I must away with my sins, I must away with my self-righteousness, and I must seek him who alone can save me."

Men talk about being willing to be saved, and dispute about free will; but when it comes to actual practice, they are not willing. They have no heart to repent; they will to keep on with their sin; they will to continue in their self-righteousness; but they do not will, with any practical resolve, to come to Christ. There is need of *an immediate will.* Every unconverted person here is willing to come to Christ before he dies; I never met with a person yet who was not; but are you willing to come to Christ now? That is the point. "Today, if you will hear his voice, harden not your hearts." But you answer, "Our hearts are not hardened, we only ask for a little more time." A little more time for what? A little more time in which to go on rebelling against God? A little more time in which to run the awful risk of eternal destruction? So, you see, it is a real will and an immediate will that is needed.

With some, it is *a settled will* that is wanted. Oh yes, they are ready! They feel as soon as the preacher begins to speak; they are impressed during the singing of the first hymn. There is a revival service, and after the meeting they begin telling you what they have felt. Look at those people on Wednesday. They have got over Monday and Tuesday with some little "rumblings of heart"; but what about Wednesday? They are as cold as a cucumber; every feeling that they had on Sunday is gone from them; they have no memory of it whatever. Their goodness is as the morning cloud, and as the early dew it passes away. How some people do deceive us with their good resolves, in which there is nothing at all, for there is no settled will!

With others, what is lacking is *a submissive will*. Yes, they are willing to be saved; but then they do not want to be saved by grace; they are not willing to give themselves up altogether to the Savior; they will not renounce their own righteousness and submit themselves to the righteousness of Christ. Well, that practically means that there is not any willingness at all, for unless you accept God's way of salvation, it is no use for you to talk about your will. Here is the great evil that is destroying you, and that will destroy you before long, and land you in hell: "You would not, you would not." Oh, that God's grace might come upon you, subduing and renewing your will, and making you willing in the day of his power!

4. My last point is a very solemn one. I shall not weary you with it. *What will become of men who are not gathered to Christ?*

What will become of men of whom it continues to be said, "You would not"?

The text suggests to us two ways of answering the question. What becomes of chicks that do not come to the shelter of the hen's wings? What becomes of chicks that are not gathered to the hen? Well, the hawk devours some, and the cold nips others; they miss the warmth and comfort that they might have had. That is something. If there were no hereafter, I should like to be a Christian. If I had to die like a dog, the joy I find in Christ would make me wish to be his follower. You are losers in this world if you love not God; you are losers of peace and comfort and strength and hope, even now; but what will be your loss hereafter, with no wing to cover you when the destroying angel is abroad, no feathers beneath which you may hide when the dread thunderbolts of justice shall be launched, one after another, from God's right hand? You have no shelter and consequently no safety.

> He that hath made his refuge God,
> Shall find a most secure abode.

But he who has not that refuge shall be among the great multitude who will call to the rocks and the mountains to fall upon them, to hide them from the face of him that sits upon the throne, and from the wrath of the Lamb. O sirs, I pray you, run not the awful risk of attempting to live without the shelter of God in Christ Jesus!

But the text suggests a second question, *What became of Jerusalem in the end?* "O Jerusalem, Jerusalem, how often would I have gathered thy children together, but you would not!" Well, what happened to Jerusalem, after all? I invite you, who are without God and without Christ, to read Josephus, with the hope that he may be of service to you. What became of the inhabitants of that guilty city of Jerusalem? Well, they crucified the Lord of glory, and they hunted out his disciples, and yet they said to themselves, "We live in the city of God, no harm can come to us; we have the temple within our walls, and God will guard his own holy place." But very soon they tried to throw off the Roman yoke, and there were different sets of zealots who determined to fight against the Romans, and they murmured and complained, and began to fight among themselves.

Before the Romans attacked Jerusalem, the inhabitants had begun to kill one another. The city was divided by the various factions, three parties took possession of different portions of the place, and they fought against one another, night and day. This is what happens to ungodly men; manhood breaks loose against itself, and when there are inward contentions, one part of man's soul fighting against another part, there is an internal war of the most horrible kind. What is the poor wretch to do who is at enmity with himself, one part of his nature saying, "Go," another part crying, "Go back," and yet a third part shouting, "Stop where you are"?

Are there not many of you who are just like battlefields trampled with the hoofs of horses, torn up with the ruts made by the cannon wheels, and stained with blood? Many a man's heart is just like that. "Rest?" says he. "That has gone from me long ago." Look at him in the morning after a drinking bout; look at him after he has been quarrelling with everybody; look at the man who has been unfaithful to his wife, or that other man who has been dishonest to his employer, or that other who is gambling away all that he has. Why, how does he sleep, poor wretch? He does not rest; he dreams, he starts, he is always in terror. I would not change places with him, no, not for five minutes. The depths of poverty, and an honest conscience, are immeasurably superior to the greatest luxury in the midst of sin. The man who is evidently without God begins to quarrel with himself.

By and by, one morning, they who looked over the battlements of Jerusalem cried, "The Romans are coming, in very deed they are marching up toward the city." Vespasian came with an army of sixty thousand men, and, after a while, Titus had thrown up mounds round about the city, so that no one could come in or go out of it. He had surrounded it so completely that they were all shut in. It was, as you remember, at the time of the Passover, when the people had come from every part of the land, a million and more of them; and he shut them all up in that little city. So a time comes, with guilty men, when they are shut up; this sometimes happens before they die; they are shut up; they cannot have any pleasure in sin as they used to have, and they have no hope. They seem cooped up altogether; they have not been gathered by God's love, but now, at last, they are gathered by an avenging conscience, they are shut up in God's justice.

I shall never forget being sent for, in my early days, to see a man who was dying. As I entered the room, he greeted me with an oath; I was only a youth, a pastor about seventeen and a half years of age, and he somewhat staggered me. He would not lie down on his bed; he defied God; he said he would not die. "Shall I pray for you?," I asked. I knelt down, and I had not uttered many sentences before he cursed me in such dreadful language that I started to my feet, and then again he cried and begged me to pray with him again, though it was not any good. He said, "It is no use. Your prayer will never be heard for me; I am damned already"; and the poor wretch spoke as though he really were so and were realizing it in his own soul. I tried to persuade him to lie down upon his bed. It was of no avail; he tramped up and down the room as fast as he could go; he knew that he should die, but he could not die while he could keep on walking, and so he kept on. Then again I must pray with him, and then would come another awful burst of blasphemy, because it was not possible that the prayer should be heard. It does not often happen that one sees a person quite as bad as that; but there is a condition of heart that is not so visible, but which is quite as sad, and which comes to men dying without Christ. They are shut up; the Roman soldiers are, as it were, marching all round the city, and there is no escape, and they begin to feel it, and so they die in despair. But then, when the Roman soldiers did come, the woes of Jerusalem did not end. There was a famine in the city, a famine so dreadful that what Moses said was fulfilled, and the tender and delicate woman ate the fruit of her own body. They came to search the houses, because they thought there was food there; and a woman brought out half of her own babe, and said, "Well, eat that, if you can," and throughout the city they fed upon one another; and oh, when there is no God in the heart, what a famine it makes in a man's soul! How he longs for a something which he cannot find, and that all the world cannot give him, even a mouthful to stay the ravenousness of his spirit's hunger!

And this doom will be worse still in the next world. You know that Jerusalem was utterly destroyed—not one stone was left upon another—and this is what is to happen to you if you refuse your Savior. You will be destroyed, you will be an eternal ruin, no temple of God, but an everlasting ruin. Destroyed—that is the punishment for you; destroyed from the presence of the Lord and the glory of his power, and so abiding forever, with no indwelling God, no hope, no comfort. How terrible will be your doom unless you repent!

> Ye sinners, seek his grace
> Whose wrath ye cannot bear;
> Fly to the shelter of his cross,
> And find salvation there.

I pray you, do so, for the Lord Jesus Christ's sake! Amen.

Sermons on the Last Days

The text of this book is set in Dante 11/14 and Delphin IA,
with Poetica® Ornaments.

Typeset in QuarkXPress.

These sermons by Charles Spurgeon have been
gently edited and updated for the modern reader.

Interior design and typesetting by Rose Yancik,
Y Designs, Colorado Springs, CO.